Behavioral Interventions in Cognitive Behavior Therapy

Behavioral Interventions in Cognitive Behavior Therapy

PRACTICAL GUIDANCE FOR PUTTING THEORY INTO ACTION

Richard F. Farmer
Alexander L. Chapman

AMERICAN PSYCHOLOGICAL ASSOCIATION

WASHINGTON, DC

Published by
American Psychological Association
750 First Street, NE
Washington, DC 20002
www.apa.org

To order
APA Order Department
P.O. Box 92984
Washington, DC 20090-2984
Tel: (800) 374-2721; Direct: (202) 336-5510
Fax: (202) 336-5502; TDD/TTY: (202) 336-6123
Online: www.apa.org/books/
E-mail: order@apa.org

In the U.K., Europe, Africa, and the Middle East, copies may be ordered from
American Psychological Association
3 Henrietta Street
Covent Garden, London
WC2E 8LU England

Typeset in Goudy by Stephen McDougal, Mechanicsville, MD

Printer: Maple-Vail Book Manufacturing, Binghamton, NY
Cover Designer: Berg Design, Albany, NY
Technical/Production Editor: Tiffany L. Klaff

The opinions and statements published are the responsibility of the authors, and such opinions and statements do not necessarily represent the policies of the American Psychological Association.

Library of Congress Cataloging-in-Publication Data

Farmer, Richard F., PhD.
    Behavioral interventions in cognitive behavior therapy : practical guidance for putting theory into action / Richard F. Farmer and Alexander L. Chapman. — 1st ed.
        p. cm.
    Includes bibliographical references.
    ISBN-13: 978-1-4338-0241-6
    ISBN-10: 1-4338-0241-4
    1. Cognitive therapy—Methodology. I. Chapman, Alexander L. (Alexander Lawrence) II. American Psychological Association. III. Title.
    [DNLM: 1. Cognitive Therapy—methods. 2. Mental Disorders—therapy. WM 425.5.C6 F234b 2008]

    RC489.C63F37 2008
    616.89'142—dc22   2007027272

British Library Cataloguing-in-Publication Data
A CIP record is available from the British Library.

Printed in the United States of America
First Edition

To Janice Howard
and
Katherine Chapman
for their support and encouragement.

CONTENTS

FOREWORD: REINTRODUCING THE BEHAVIORAL FOUNDATIONS OF COGNITIVE BEHAVIOR THERAPY

G. ALAN MARLATT

In their preface to this book, Richard F. Farmer and Alexander L. Chapman note that they were inspired by a book published over 3 decades ago, *Clinical Behavior Therapy*, written by Marvin Goldfried and Gerald Davison (1976). As a new faculty member in a clinical psychology doctoral training program when that book was published, I was impressed with the scope and breadth of the text and with its emphasis on translating behavioral theory into guidelines for clinical practice in the growing field of behavior therapy. This text was soon to become a classic. Now that cognitive behavior therapy (CBT) has become the standard practice in conducting evidence-based therapy for a wide range of clinical problems, it is timely to reintroduce the behavioral foundations of this approach. Farmer and Chapman have continued in the footsteps of Goldfried and Davison by putting together what seems to be another classic text in the field of behavioral interventions. In short, they have put the B back into CBT.

This book is a useful clinical guide that provides a global road map of "practical guidance for putting theory into action" as outlined in the book's subtitle. The first four chapters provide an overview of the general territory to be covered in setting up a therapeutic plan for individual clients, including the initial assessment session, developing a behavioral case formulation, and coming up with a treatment plan. The first chapter emphasizes the role of behavioral assessment and intervention in the clinical process and discusses how behavioral and cognitive factors might be involved in both conceptualizing clinical cases and developing an effective treatment plan.

The remaining seven chapters provide specific action plans that have evolved from the behavioral perspective. These chapters include traditional behavioral interventions such as environmental change (e.g., contingency management and modification of behavioral antecedents), behavioral skills training, and exposure-based interventions (e.g., cue exposure and response prevention). The authors also include more recently developed clinical methods such as behavioral activation in the treatment of depression. As for the domain of cognitive processes, behavioral theorists often described the thinking process and thoughts as the "behavior of the mind." Two chapters focus on cognitive activities. The first applies a functional analytic perspective on thinking as a covert behavior that can be modified by changing both antecedents and consequences. The second covers the newly emerging area of acceptance- and mindfulness-based interventions, recently described as the "new wave" of CBT by proponents of this approach. The final chapter is devoted to the topic of bringing therapy to a close and establishing aftercare treatment, including considerations regarding relapse prevention. In my own recent work, I have developed a new treatment program that combines mindfulness training and relapse prevention, so including both of these topics in this book is timely for this reader!

I highly recommend this book to a variety of readers, including students, therapists, clinical researchers, and those who provide academic training and supervision. The authors present their material in a clear and comprehensive style, complete with citations of recently published articles and reviews for easy access to the relevant literature. Farmer and Chapman present clinical intervention procedures in a practical and useful manner and describe case studies to illustrate various clinical intervention techniques. Overall, I think the authors are to be commended for their successful attempt to provide readers with an updated classic—one that follows so well the tradition established years ago by Goldfried and Davison in their original *Clinical Behavior Therapy* book.

FOREWORD: A FRESH LOOK AT BEHAVIORAL PRINCIPLES AND COGNITIVE BEHAVIOR THERAPY

KEITH S. DOBSON

Cognitive behavior therapy (CBT) has attained a dominant position in the range of existing psychotherapies. An important part of that dominance is the efficacy literature related to this approach. *Behavioral Interventions in Cognitive Behavior Therapy* nicely serves to remind those practicing in the field that another important part of the strength of CBT lies in its strong conceptual bases and the interventions that derive from those bases. In particular, this volume discusses the importance of behavioral conceptions of change and the importance of the techniques of behavioral therapy that have now been fully incorporated into contemporary CBT.

As noted by Farmer and Chapman, behavioral principles and practices permeate CBT in several ways. In some instances, the clinical focus of change relates to behaviors themselves; thus behavioral models and interventions are highly appropriate. In other cases, cognitive interventions effect behavioral change and more adaptive functioning. In these cases, the clinician may emphasize the intrapsychic processes of choice, motivation, effort, conflict avoidance, and others related to the individual's ability to make desired change. But often, the environment has a major role in the development and maintenance of dysfunctional behavior. In such cases, clinicians need to conceptualize factors external to the client as part of the problem and explicitly incorporate them into the treatment plan. This volume excels in the way that it consistently reminds people in the field of CBT of the importance of the environment in the genesis and change of desired outcomes.

One real strength of this volume is its reliance on both available evidence related to the principles and practices that are discussed as well as well-defined and articulated clinical considerations and practical issues. This work is a living example of the integration of science and practice into CBT. It draws on contemporary, and sometimes provocative, findings from science to suggest how clinicians can maximally benefit their clients. For example, the authors cite recent studies that suggest that exposure is perhaps the single most effective strategy for overcoming anxiety disorders, and behavioral activation may be as effective as an integrated cognitive and behavior therapy for depression. These findings run somewhat counter to the field at present, but if valid, represent important truths for those in the field to grapple with.

This volume is not only scholarly but also presents sound clinical advice. The outline of the book is logical, and the authors proceed through the various stages of behavioral assessment, case formulation, and treatment planning, leading to the definition of specific behavioral interventions. The authors supplement these definitions with descriptions of how to implement key behavioral interventions, considerations about when to use them, and explanations of how to evaluate clinical outcomes. The description of these interventions includes indications for their application, specific steps associated with their implementation, and markers of resultant therapeutic change. The considerable clinical intelligence in these chapters will be of value to beginning and seasoned clinicians alike.

An innovative part of the book is the chapter related to acceptance-based interventions. Behavior therapies, and the use of behavioral techniques in CBT, are almost always in the service of clinically meaningful change. Some aspects of the acceptance-based methods involve skills, such as developing mindfulness and awareness of momentary states, but are not behavioral in the traditional sense of the term. Certainly, some aspects of acceptance involve a change in attitude more than a change in action, and as such are not only behavioral but also cognitive interventions. It will be of interest to see if these methods—some of which are quite novel—gain acceptance in the behavioral community.

Overall, *Behavioral Interventions in Cognitive Behavior Therapy* is an excellent and welcome addition to the growing set of books in CBT. It is artfully written, with well-chosen clinical examples that help concretize the principles and models that it presents. I strongly recommend this book to clinicians in the field for its scientific bases, clinical wisdom, and practical strategies.

PREFACE

In the preface to their classic work *Clinical Behavior Therapy* published in 1976, Marvin Goldfried and Gerald Davison commented on the "distance between written descriptions of behavior therapy and what occurs in practice" (p. *vii*). In response, they filled a large void with their detailed presentation of behavior techniques and applications commonly used in clinical practice. Generations of students, practitioners, and clinical researchers have been influenced by their landmark work, which has since been republished and remains popular to this day. Despite frequent misunderstandings or mischaracterizations, behavioral approaches to therapy have endured, developed, and matured, accumulating along the way an impressive body of empirical support for their effectiveness. Behavior therapy and behavioral interventions have a prominent role in almost all well-established treatments for specific clinical problems.

With this book, we attempt to follow in the same path carved out by Goldfried and Davison over 30 years ago by providing a contemporary and practical description of behavioral interventions in cognitive behavior therapy. Our overarching goal is to faithfully reflect the application of behavioral interventions in clinical practice. While keeping theoretical principles and technical jargon to a minimum, we attempt to bridge theory and practice by revealing how behaviorally oriented practitioners think about a wide range of clinical problems and how they conceptualize and implement behavioral interventions based on their case formulations.

The first four chapters of this book provide the theoretical and conceptual foundation of the practice of behavior therapy. Within these chapters, we discuss the initial stages of assessment, case conceptualization, and treatment planning. The chapters that follow describe techniques and methods for facilitating positive behavior change, even with clients who have long-standing, multiple, and severe problem areas. Within this presentation, we also include chapters that focus on areas that have, until relatively recently, received little emphasis within behavior therapy. Some of these areas include behavioral approaches to conceptualizing and treating issues related to cognition and mindfulness and acceptance-oriented approaches to reduce human suffering.

Our hope is that this book will be useful to a variety of readers who are learning and applying behavioral interventions in clinical practice. We have written about a wide range of topics and hope that readers will come away with some practical knowledge of how to derive behavioral case formulations and implement many types of behavioral interventions. We hope, too, that this book will be interesting and useful to beginning students who are learning about behavior therapy as well as seasoned therapists who already have significant training and experience in behavioral interventions.

We extend our sincere appreciation to several people for helping us think through and improve this book. We thank Tiffany Klaff, Anne Gasque, Ron Teeter, and Susan Reynolds in the American Psychological Association Books department for their wonderful editorial support and assistance. We are also most grateful to Michael Addis, Janice Howard, and Carl Lejuez for their insightful comments on earlier drafts and their recommendations for enhancing the quality and sophistication of our work.

Behavioral Interventions in Cognitive Behavior Therapy

1

OVERVIEW

Cognitive behavior therapy (CBT) has emerged as a widely used and efficacious treatment approach for a variety of psychological conditions (Dobson & Khatri, 2000), including depression, anxiety disorders, personality disorders, substance abuse disorders, eating disorders, and couple's distress. Since the early 1970s when the term *cognitive–behavioral* began to take hold and gain momentum, CBT interventions have undergone considerable scientific evaluation and refinement. For these reasons, it is perhaps not surprising that CBT interventions dominate the American Psychological Association's list of empirically supported therapies (Chambless et al., 1996).

CBT is a broad concept and represents a variety of therapeutic approaches that emphasize, to varying degrees, cognitive, behavioral, and environmental factors in relation to psychological disorders. There are at least 10 different schools that can be identified under the umbrella of CBT (David & Szentagotai, 2006). One such school is represented by the influential cognitive approach to understanding and treating psychological disorders advanced by Aaron T. Beck (1963, 1976; A. T. Beck, Freeman, & Associates, 1990) and Judith S. Beck (1995, 2005). A primary assumption of their model is that distorted and dysfunctional thinking influences mood and behavior and that inaccurate and biased forms of thinking are common to all psychological disorders. Each individual disorder, however, is characterized by a unique set of thought distortions and underlying core beliefs specific to that condition. An implication of this cognitive model is that therapeutic activities should be geared toward the promotion of realistic, accurate, and balanced thinking, whereby the modification of thinking will, in turn, produce changes in mood and behavior. An additional assumption of this model is that the modification of underlying beliefs, or *schemas*, is required to bring about lasting therapeutic change (J. S. Beck, 1995).

Cognitive perspectives that have informed developments in CBT vary in the degree to which the environment is viewed as a determinant of thinking, emotion, and action. Some cognitive theories, for example, emphasize a cognitively constructed environment over the physical environment as the primary determinant of emotion and behavior (e.g., Mahoney, 1991). Other models highlight the role of concepts such as schemas, which are regarded as cognitive structures central to the evaluation and interpretation of experiences that, in some instances, also predispose persons to emotional and behavioral disorders (e.g., Young, Weinberger, & Beck, 2001). Other cognitive-oriented theories place the environment on equal footing with perceptions of the self or environment as determinants of behavior and emotion (e.g., Bandura, 1986).

In contrast to models that emphasize the predisposing or causal properties of cognitive constructs, behavior theory and therapy generally avoid ascribing mental concepts a causal role in behavior and instead place primary emphasis on the physical environment (Baum, 1994; Farmer & Nelson-Gray, 2005). From a behavioral perspective, thinking and emotional responding are examples of behavior and are subject to many of the same influences as more observable behaviors. Later in this chapter we highlight several primary determinants of behavior from a behavioral perspective (which are further elaborated in detail in chap. 2) as well as the different origins of cognitive and behavior therapies. Perhaps because of their different origins and frequently conflicting theories regarding the determinants of behavior, there has occasionally been an uneasy marriage between these two psychotherapy traditions. Indeed, the term *cognitive behavior therapy* incorporates several points of view that can, at times, be contradictory or even incompatible.

There are many excellent resources that describe cognitive-oriented therapeutic interventions geared toward the modification of evaluations, attitudes, underlying beliefs, and schemas (e.g., A. T. Beck, Rush, Shaw, & Emery, 1979; J. S. Beck, 1995; Burns, 1980; Dobson, 2001; Leahy, 2003; Young, 1994; Young et al., 2001). Although we touch on cognitive therapy and cognitive change techniques throughout this book, we primarily highlight and emphasize the theory, rationale, and application of behavioral interventions within CBT. Even though cognitive and behavioral interventions can occasionally be at odds in relation to therapeutic assumptions and goals, we also strive to highlight areas of compatibility and instances in which integration is possible.

BEHAVIORAL INTERVENTIONS IN CBT: UNDERLYING ASSUMPTIONS, COMMON FEATURES, AND INDICATORS OF EFFECTIVENESS

In this section, we provide an overview of behavioral perspectives on abnormality and psychological disorders and briefly review several of the core underlying assumptions associated with behavior therapy and behavioral interventions. We then discuss some of the primary features that differentiate behavior therapies from other approaches and conclude with a brief review of the effectiveness of behavioral interventions within CBT.

Behavioral Views on Abnormality

Within psychology and psychiatry, "deviant" or "defect" models of abnormality predominate (Farmer & Nelson-Gray, 2005; Martell, Addis, & Jacobson, 2001). That is, individuals who have psychological disorders or who display problematic behaviors are often regarded as deviant or abnormal, principally on the basis of what he or she presumably has. Within cognitive therapy, for example, those with psychological disorders are often regarded as having maladaptive schemas that serve as psychological nuclei of behavioral and emotional disorders (A. T. Beck et al., 1990; Young, 1994). Within medical model approaches, underlying diseases or biological processes such as neurochemical imbalances are often presumed to underlie psychological syndromes (Markovitz, 2001). Within psychodynamic models, the quality, integration, and differentiation of internalized self- and other mental representations and the relative maturity of inner defensive coping mechanisms are viewed as etiologically relevant for psychological disorders (Kernberg, Selzer, Koenigsberg, Carr, & Appelbaum, 1989). In each instance, the presumed internal defect that the person has (e.g., maladaptive schemas, abnormal neurochemistry, internalized self and object relations) is targeted for therapy; it is assumed that this internal anomaly must be changed, removed, or altered in some way if the person is to no longer be disordered.

Behavior theory and therapy have a different view. Within these traditions, the search for internal causes of behavior is largely avoided. Although it is acknowledged that genetic endowments might predispose individuals to respond in certain ways when relevant situational features are present (Skinner, 1971, 1989), the behavioral tradition is primarily concerned about what one does and the contexts within which behavior occurs (Nelson & Hayes, 1986b; Nelson-Gray & Farmer, 1999). Furthermore, from the behavioral perspective, notions of what constitutes normality and abnormality are found in cultural norms, values, and practices. Culture provides the context for referencing which behaviors are acceptable or valued and which are deviant (Farmer & Nelson-Gray, 2005). Notions of what are normal or abnormal behaviors occasionally shift as cultural values and practices shift over time.

In the mid-1800s in the United States, for example, the Louisiana Medical Association produced a report that proposed a mental disease unique to Black slaves called *drapetomania*, or a mania to seek freedom, which caused slaves to run away from their masters (Zimbardo & Gerrig, 1996). Similarly, both the American Psychiatric Association and the American Psychological Association prior to the mid-1970s regarded homosexuality as a form of mental disorder (Morin & Rothblum, 1991). Cultural influences on the definition and determination of abnormality would also predict that cultures vary as to which behavioral patterns are regarded as normal or deviant, and mounting evidence suggests that this is, in fact, the case (Alarcon, Foulks, & Vakkur, 1998).

From a behavioral perspective, the determinants of what might be regarded as abnormal behavior are no different from the determinants that shape and maintain normal behavior. For this reason, the behavioral perspective assumes that there is nothing inherently defective or deviant about persons who report emotional or behavioral problems.

Behavioral Interventions Within CBT: Description and Application

Some people have unpleasant reactions to terms such as *behavior therapy*, *behavior modification*, or *behaviorism*. As noted by Martell et al. (2001), such terms tend "to call up associations with rats, mazes, M&Ms, and an obsession with predicting and controlling people's actions" (p. *xxv*). Although sometimes it is easy to understand how these reactions might have come about, it is also true that these reactions are often the result of a profound misunderstanding of behavior theory and behavioral approaches to therapy (Todd & Morris, 1983). Just like Martell et al. (2001), we ask that if you have any preconceptions about behavior theory and therapy, you suspend these for the time being, as contemporary behavior theory and therapy might not be what you think it is.

A Focus on Behavior and Its Context

Behavioral perspectives are associated with a number of assumptions about the individual, the context within which he or she lives, and the factors that influence his or her behavior. As suggested earlier, psychological disorders from a behavioral perspective are defined by behavior, occurring both within the individual (sometimes called *covert behavior*) and as overt actions that can be observed by others (or *overt behavior*). Behavioral perspectives on psychological disorders are further concerned with the functional relationships that exist between the behavior of a person and the environment that establishes the context for such behavior. Within some forms of behavior theory, the *three-term contingency* represents the basic unit of analysis (Skinner, 1969). When applied to behavior therapy, the three-term contingency concept refers to the interaction of the person with his or her environment and includes three elements: the occasion within which behavior occurs, the behavior itself, and the consequences that follow behavior. When behavior therapists attempt to develop hypotheses about behavior, this framework is often used.

The first of these three elements, the *antecedents of behavior*, includes antecedent conditions or antecedent stimuli that set the occasion for behavior to occur. Antecedent conditions or stimuli can include specific persons, places, objects, or events. Among the factors that influence whether a person will engage in a particular form of behavior in a given setting is the person's learning history for such behavior under similar conditions. That is, if a certain form of behavior was enacted in similar situations before, and if such behavior resulted in reinforcing outcomes, then the behavior is more likely to occur in similar current and future environments.

The second of these three elements, *behavior*, refers to anything a person does. This includes not only behavior that other people can potentially observe another person do, such as speak or perform some other physical movement, but also covert behaviors. Covert behaviors are those behaviors that occur "within the skin" or on the inside and are at least observable or noticeable by the person within which they occur. Such covert behaviors would include thoughts, emotions, and physical sensations.

The last element of the three-term contingency, *consequences*, refers to the effect that behavior produces. Technically speaking, behavior is reinforced if the consequences that follow behavior increase the likelihood of that behavior again occurring on future occasions. However, a behavior is punished if the consequences that follow decrease the likelihood of that behavior again occurring in similar future situations.

A Focus on Why People Act the Way They Do

When behaviorally oriented clinicians talk about the function of behavior, they are basically talking about why people behave the way they do. *Functionalism* is based on Darwinian evolutionary principles (Farmer & Nelson-Gray, 2005; Rachlin, 1976). In Darwinian evolutionary theory, the physical structure of a particular species is determined by its associated function. Natural selection involves the selection of the most adaptive physical structures on the basis of functional properties associated with that structure, namely those associated with the enhancement of gene fitness. When the concept of functionalism is applied in behavior theory and therapy, behavior of an individual that is functional in particular environmental contexts (i.e., produces reinforcing consequences) is selected or made more likely, whereas behavior that is not functional (i.e., does not produce reinforcing consequences) is not selected or becomes extinguished.

Within functional or selectionist accounts of human behavior, behavior is largely, if not exclusively, determined (Hull, Langman, & Glenn, 2001). For selection to occur there must be variation along some dimension, as the absence of variation precludes the possibility of differential selection. In behavior theory, forms of behavior produced by an individual vary, and some units of behavior are selected because they prove more successful than others (Baum, 1994). Similarly, the selection of cultural replicators (e.g., customs, rules, values) involves the process of selection acting on variations and the transfer to selected practices from one member of a group to another through behavior transfer processes such as imitation, modeling, reinforcement for rule following, and arrangement of social contingencies (Baum, 1994). Those cultural practices that prove to be the most beneficial or enhance fitness tend to be retained by a culture over time. *Environmental determinism* is the overarching process associated with selection of variations in an individual's behavior during his or her lifetime and in cultural practices over successive generations (Skinner, 1981).

Behavioral accounts are also typically associated with the concept of *contextualism*. Contextual approaches to the study of behavior found in many behavioral theories are concerned with how events and behavior are organized and linked together in meaningful ways (i.e., "the act in context"). Contextualism, then, is concerned with the context within which behavior takes place, or the *contextual flow* in which behavior occurs (Hayes, Hayes, Reese, & Sarbin, 1993).

Common Features Among Behavioral Assessments and Interventions

The focus of psychological therapies varies in accordance with underlying theory and presumed mechanisms of behavior change. Interpersonal therapies, for example, tend to focus on social behavior and relations with others. Cognitive therapies focus on automatic thoughts, underlying assumptions, and schemas. Humanistic therapies tend to emphasize immediate experiences, emotions, and the provision of validation by the therapist for these experiences and emotions. Psychodynamic therapies emphasize historical material, mental representations of self and other, and the use of particular defense mechanisms. Biological therapies tend to emphasize neurochemical functions. Each therapy targets what is understood through associated theory to be the most central determinant or cause of problematic behavior. Consequently, the types of interventions used and the means by which they are delivered vary considerably across these general classes of therapies.

In the assessment of clients, contemporary behavior therapies are concerned about the contexts within which problematic behavior occurs. This is because behavior therapists often place primary emphasis on potentially modifiable internal and external antecedents and consequences associated with the maintenance of problematic behavior (Follette, Naugle, & Linnerooth, 2000). Behavior therapists are also concerned about the client's behavioral repertoire based on the idea that some clients display problematic behaviors because they have not yet learned alternative and more adaptive forms of action. In the case of behavioral deficits, for example, a behaviorally oriented therapist might seek to teach new behaviors that can replace or substitute for problematic behaviors. Behavior therapists also assess a client's motivation for change. Generally, a behavior therapist thinks about the concept of motivation a bit differently than therapists from other orientations. Rather than viewing motivation as an inner drive or some other inner force that causes people to act, behavior therapists are more inclined to view motivation as a state or condition resulting from environmental events (an idea we develop more fully in the next chapter when describing establishing operations and rules). When viewed in this way, motivation is modifiable, something that can be increased or decreased as a result of environmental manipulations.

In the behavioral assessment of clients, several features associated with the functional context of behavior are assessed and evaluated (Farmer & Nelson-Gray, 2005; Hayes, Strosahl, Bunting, Twohig, & Wilson, 2004). Among these are the following areas:

- *The antecedents of problematic behavior.* Are there situations in which problematic behaviors frequently occur? Are there common internal antecedents that immediately precede problematic behavior? What environmental cues have been previously associated with reinforcement for behavior, and consequently occasion behavior when present in current situations? Are there verbal rules that govern problematic behavior (e.g., "If I make myself vomit afterwards, I can eat this ice cream and not gain any weight.")? Are there establishing operations that increase the reinforcing value of certain behaviors (e.g., engagement in overly restrictive dieting practices as an establishing operation for subsequent binge-eating episodes)?
- *The consequences of problematic behavior.* What are the consequences that follow problematic behavior? Are the short-term consequences similar to or different from the long-term consequences of such behavior? Are positive reinforcing (rewarding) consequences instrumental in the maintenance of behavior, or are negative reinforcing (relieving) consequences more likely influencing behavior?
- *The client's learning history as it relates to current problematic behaviors.* What factors in the client's past might have shaped and established the behaviors that the client seeks to change? Are these factors of any influence today?
- *The client's current behavioral repertoire.* A comprehensive assessment of the client's behavioral repertoire would cover four different response domains: overt or motor behaviors, thoughts (including mental images), emotions, and physiological sensations.

- *Overt behaviors.* What forms do the client's problem behaviors take? Are there skill deficits? Does the client display adequate coping, social, and problem-solving skills? Is the person's behavioral repertoire sufficiently large so as to allow for the possibility of responding flexibly in common situations? Do avoidance coping repertoires predominate? Are there behavioral excesses that are problematic (e.g., substance abuse, gambling, risky sexual behavior)?
- *Thoughts.* Is the person plagued by negative evaluations of self, world, or future? Does the person confuse evaluations of events and objects with the actual events and objects ("I am a bad person," versus "I am having the evaluation that I am a bad person, but thinking this doesn't necessarily make it so.")? Are experiences such as emotions and thoughts and the evaluations of those experiences confused (e.g., "Anxiety is bad and must be avoided.")? Is the client preoccupied with the past or anticipated future possibilities? Is the client able to be fully in the present moment and respond as effectively as possible to what is occurring currently?
- *Emotions.* Does the client excessively experience negative emotions? Are the client's expressed emotional experiences appropriate in situations in which they are displayed (e.g., are they restricted, exaggerated, intense, or excessive)? Is the client overly emotionally reactive, or flat in his or her emotional responsiveness?
- *Physiological sensations or responses.* Do certain physiological responses define part of a larger response pattern (e.g., flushing or sweating while also experiencing anxiety-related emotions)? Does the client associate normal physiological activity with catastrophic outcomes (e.g., an increased heart rate is associated with an impending heart attack, shortness of breath is associated with smothering, feelings of fullness after a meal are associated with becoming fat)?
- *The client's motivation for change.* Does the client indicate a willingness or motivation to change his or her behavior? Can the client articulate personal values or goals? Is the client's current behavior consistent with his or her values or goals? Does the client see a discrepancy between current actions and valued outcomes or goals? Is the client aware of likely outcomes associated with unhealthy patterns of behavior and, if so, does this affect the client's behavior?

Decisions as to which behavioral interventions are appropriate are decided individually for each client given the outcomes associated with these assessments. That is, behavior theory and therapy suggest that the factors that influence behavior vary across individuals. Even though two people may have similar problematic behavior patterns, it is recognized that factors that account for these behavior problems likely differ. Several typologies of alcoholism, for example, suggest two distinct subtypes. One type is characterized by persons who display anxious–dependent traits, binge drinking versus continuous episodes, and avoidant coping styles, and the other type is typified by an early age of onset, continuous versus episodic binge drinking, and engagement in aggressive or criminal behavior when intoxicated (Wulfert, Greenway, & Dougher, 1996). Whereas the form of problematic behavior might appear to be the same among members of both groups (e.g., excessive drinking), the maintaining factors associated with each subtype, namely negative reinforcement processes in the former and positive reinforcement processes in the latter, suggest different functional properties associated with the same behavior across individuals.

In chapters 5 through 10 we discuss in greater detail specific behavioral interventions. There are a number of general characteristics of behavioral interventions (Farmer & Nelson-Gray, 2005; O'Leary & Wilson, 1987; Spiegler, 1983; Spiegler & Guevremont, 2003), some of which are shared by other schools of therapy, including the following:

- *An empirical orientation*, as reflected in its grounding in the basic behavioral sciences; use of empirically supported intervention strategies; and use of ongoing assessments of the client's behaviors targeted for therapeutic change.
- *Therapist–client collaboration*, whereby the client is an active participant in the therapeutic process and the client and therapist work together to develop a formulation of the client's problem areas and a plan for therapy based on this formulation.
- *An active orientation*, whereby clients are actively encouraged to do something about their problem areas rather than only talk about them.
- *A flexible approach*, whereby hypotheses concerning the client's problem areas undergo continuous evaluation and testing, with the overall client formulation and corresponding therapeutic activities modified and adjusted as warranted by new information or observations.
- *An emphasis on environment–behavior relations*, with clients described in terms of what they do; that is, the actions they perform and the thoughts, emotions, and physical sensations they experience. These actions are further conceptualized with reference to the situational contexts within which they occur.
- *A time-limited and present focus*, whereby the time allotted for therapy varies in accordance with the nature and severity of

the problem areas addressed in therapy, with emphasis placed on one's current situation rather than the past.

- A *problem- and learning focus*, whereby solutions to problematic behaviors are sought, with these solutions generally geared toward the teaching of new adaptive behaviors; changing aspects of malignant environments; or providing information relevant to behaviors of interest.
- An *emphasis on both change and acceptance processes*, whereby interventions that promote therapeutic change are undertaken in a context that conveys valuation of the client and encourages the development of client self-validation and the adoption of a nonjudgmental approach to the experience of thoughts, feelings, and bodily sensations as they occur.

Do Behavioral Interventions Within CBT Work?

Studies have been performed to identify the components of CBT that are most strongly associated with positive treatment effects. In all likelihood, the active ingredients of CBT vary in relation to which disorder is targeted in therapy (Dobson & Khatri, 2000). In the case of depressive and anxiety disorders, however, there is an emerging view that cognitive and behavioral elements within CBT are equally effective and that cognitive interventions do not necessarily add to the effectiveness of behavioral interventions (Longmore & Worrell, 2007).

In the case of CBT for major depressive disorder, for example, the cognitive components of CBT appear to add little in the way of therapeutic benefit beyond behavioral interventions, both at posttreatment (Jacobson et al., 1996) and up to 2 years following therapy completion (Gortner, Gollan, Dobson, & Jacobson, 1997). Additionally, in a large randomized trial of therapies for major depression in adults (Dimidjian et al., 2006), a behavioral intervention commonly embedded within many CBT therapies for depression (e.g., behavioral activation) was as effective as antidepressant medication in reducing depressed mood among severely depressed persons, and both of these treatments were more effective than cognitive therapy.

As with depressive disorders, there is also accumulating evidence that suggests behavioral interventions within CBT for anxiety disorders are most strongly associated with overall treatment effects. Exposure techniques, in which clients confront anxiety-evoking material either directly or in imagination, appear to be most consistently associated with reductions in anxiety-related symptoms. This appears to be true for the treatment of posttraumatic stress disorder (Foa et al., 2005) and many types of phobia (Barlow, Esler, & Vitali, 1998; T. E. Davis & Ollendick, 2005), including social phobia (Feske & Chambless, 1995). In the treatment of obsessive-compulsive disorder, the combination of exposure and response prevention is frequently regarded as the treatment of choice (Franklin & Foa, 1998; Steketee, 1993). For panic disorder with agoraphobia, data on the effectiveness of behavioral versus cognitive components within a CBT treatment package are more equivocal (Craske & Barlow, 2001), with some studies suggesting that cognitive and behavioral interventions vary in effectiveness depending on whether the outcome variable is based on agoraphobic or panic symptoms (van den Hout, Arntz, & Hoekstra, 1994).

Findings such as these have widespread implications not only for isolating the active ingredients of CBT but also for informing theories of disorder maintenance and future therapy refinements. They also indicate that behavioral interventions within CBT are important and potent agents of therapeutic change.

PUTTING BEHAVIORAL AND COGNITIVE THERAPIES INTO THEIR CONTEXT: A BRIEF OVERVIEW OF THE HISTORY OF BEHAVIOR THERAPY AND BEHAVIORAL INTERVENTIONS WITHIN CBT

A sense of the history of the behavior therapy movement is a good starting point for understanding the role of behavioral interventions in CBT. The next sections offer a brief overview of the history of the movement. More detailed accounts are provided elsewhere (Dobson & Dozois, 2001; Farmer & Nelson-Gray, 2005; Hayes, 2004b; Kazdin, 1978; O'Donohue, 1998).

Basic Theories of Learning

The theoretical roots of contemporary behavioral interventions are found in the foundations of modern learning theories. In the late 1800s and early 1900s, Russian physiologists such as Ivan Sechenov, Vladimir Bechterev, and Ivan Pavlov investigated reflexive and conditioning processes. This body of research eventuated into the learning paradigm referred to as *classical* or *respondent* conditioning. The basic idea behind classical conditioning is that some environmental stimuli, when presented in a particular way, yield a reflexive, innate (or unlearned) response. For example, when a rubber hammer is struck right below the kneecap (*unconditional stimulus*, or UCS), a reflexive knee-jerk response follows (which in this case would be an *unconditional response*, or UCR). The knee-jerk is an unlearned, innate response to the type of stimulation that a rubber hammer strike against the knee produces.

In the case of classical conditioning, Pavlov and colleagues (Pavlov, 1927) demonstrated that a neutral stimulus object or event, when repeatedly paired or associated with the UCS, will come to acquire certain stimulus properties over time (i.e., this previously neutral stimulus will become a *con-*

ditional stimulus, or CS). This CS, in turn, will come to elicit a response (i.e., a *conditional response*, or CR) under some circumstances that appears quite similar to the UCR produced by the UCS. Pavlov and colleagues further demonstrated that CRs often occurred in the presence of stimuli that resembled or were similar to the CS in some way, a process called *generalization*. Additionally, Pavlov and colleagues found that if the CS were repeatedly presented without the UCS, the CR would eventually disappear. This process was referred to as *extinction*.

In clinical contexts, classical conditioning processes are perhaps most evident in the conditioned emotional responses that some clients have acquired to stimulus events that, on the surface, seem quite neutral. This is perhaps most strikingly apparent in the case of emotional reactions to trauma-related stimulus cues. What becomes a traumatic event for an individual can often be thought of as a UCS that, at the time of the original trauma, elicits a number of reflexive or unlearned responses (UCR), such as fear. By definition, persons with posttraumatic stress disorder have strong emotional reactions, or CRs, to events or objects (CSs) that are in some way similar to those that were present at the time the original traumatic event occurred. Even though these CSs, or trauma-related cues, are no longer directly associated with the original UCS, they nonetheless continue to elicit CRs that look and feel very much like the original UCRs. Classical conditioning processes have also been suggested in the acquisition of some phobias (Merckelbach, Arntz, & deJong, 1991).

During the late 1800s and early 1900s in the United States, experimental investigations into learning processes were also beginning to take place, beginning with Edward Thorndike's (1898) doctoral research. In his research with hungry cats, Thorndike demonstrated that the time latencies for displaying escape behaviors that allow access to food (e.g., pulling on a wire loop to open a door) decreased gradually and steadily over successive trials. In accounting for his observations, Thorndike proposed that it was the consequences associated with the cats' actions that determined whether such actions would be strengthened. If a response typically resulted in reward, in this case access to food, then it would be strengthened. Those actions, however, that did not result in reward would, over time, become weakened. In Thorndike's theory, referred to as *the law of effect*, the learning process and associated behaviors are influenced by the consequences that follow behavior.

B. F. Skinner further developed and refined Thorndike's theory of instrumental behavior, which resulted in an operant theory of behavior. An *operant* was defined by Skinner (1938) as a unit of behavior that operates on the environment by producing consequences. Whereas in classical conditioning a stimulus (S) event elicits a response (R), or S → R, in operant conditioning the concept of selection by consequence (C) was emphasized, or R → C. That is, Skinner suggested that much of the behavior that people display is selected and shaped over the course of a lifetime by the consequences that such behavior produces. Skinner regarded selection by consequence as a form of ontogenetic selection. In addition to ontogenetic selection processes, Skinner (1981) proposed that human behavior is also the result of phylogenetic selection processes (or Darwinian or natural selection) and cultural selection processes (or the selection of cultural practices based on their associated consequences). A common core element associated with each form of selection (phylogenetic, ontogenetic, and cultural) is evolutionary theory. As suggested by Skinner (1981), human behavior is

> the joint product of (i) the contingencies of survival responsible for the natural selection of the species and (ii) the contingencies of reinforcement responsible for the repertoires acquired by its members, including (iii) the special contingencies maintained by an evolved social environment. (Ultimately, of course, it is all a matter of natural selection, since operant conditioning is an evolved process, of which cultural practices are special applications). (p. 213)

When applied to accounts of human behavior, the theory of selection by consequences suggests that the effects produced by behavior directly influence future behavior (see also Biglan, 2003). Several of the behavioral interventions described in this book are based on this basic principle.

Early Applications of Learning Theories to Behavior Change

Although the first empirical observations that eventuated into modern learning theory go back to the late 1800s and early 1900s, it was not until the early 1960s that therapeutic interventions based on behavioral principles began to have widespread influence. There were, however, some early efforts to apply learning theory to behavior change. Examples include the work of Mary Cover Jones (1924a), who demonstrated that a child's fear of an animal could be decreased through counterconditioning methods, whereby the feared stimulus (in this case a rabbit) is paired with a positive stimulus (which in this instance was the child's favorite food). The bell and pad method for treating enuresis developed by Mowrer and Mowrer (1938) is another example, as is Andrew Salter's (1949) book-length treatise on therapy methods grounded in Pavlovian conditioning. These early efforts to translate behavioral principles and modern learning theory into behavior change techniques, however, did not result in an immediate impact on clinical research and practice.

The Emergence of Behavior Therapy

More than 50 years elapsed between the first experimental studies on basic learning processes and the formal beginnings of the behavior therapy movement. In the late 1950s, important simultaneous developments took place in three countries, the aggregate of which heralded the beginnings of behavior therapy (Kazdin, 1978). In 1958, Joseph Wolpe, a psychiatrist working in South Africa, published the first manualized treatment protocol. The treatment was based on the behavior-change principle that he termed *reciprocal inhibition* that, in turn, was grounded in Pavlovian and Hullian behavior theory. Wolpe suggested that anxiety or neurotic states could be reduced or eliminated by pairing the experience of anxiety with an incompatible feeling state, such as relaxation. The publication of the treatment procedure allowed clinicians and researchers worldwide to evaluate the efficacy of this approach and its associated underlying theory.

Hans Eysenck (1959), a psychologist in England, published a paper that introduced the term *behavior therapy* to a broad audience. (Although Lindsley, Skinner, & Solomon [1953] as well as Lazarus [1958] published works prior to Eysenck that used the term *behavior therapy*, the dissemination of these works was more restricted.) This was followed in 1960 with the publication of an edited book that described a number of treatment methods such as desensitization, negative practice, and aversion therapy (Eysenck, 1960). Evident among these treatment techniques was the influence of Pavlovian learning theory, most notably notions of classical conditioning and extinction. This book was the first to bring together diverse treatment applications under the name of behavior therapy. In 1963, Eysenck established the journal *Behaviour Research and Therapy*, the first professional journal of its type.

In the late 1950s and early 1960s in the United States, behavioral techniques based on Skinnerian principles of operant conditioning were being developed and evaluated. Operant learning principles and methods were applied to the behavior of children (Bijou & Baer, 1966), persons with developmental disabilities (Lovaas, Freitag, Gold, & Kassorla, 1965), and individuals with psychosis (Ayllon & Michael, 1959). By the mid-1960s, the term *behavior modification* became widely applied to the practice of applying learning principles to producing behavior change (e.g., Krasner & Ullmann, 1965; Ullmann & Krasner, 1965). The 1970s also witnessed an emergence of behavioral assessment technologies to complement behavior modification approaches (Ciminero, Calhoun, & Adams, 1977; Goldfried & Kent, 1972; Nelson, 1977).

The Emergence of Cognitive Behavior Therapy

Although early manifestations of cognitive therapy can be found in the work of George Kelly (1955), Albert Ellis (1957, 1962) and Aaron T. Beck (1963), it was not until the 1970s and 1980s that contemporary cognitive behavior therapy became firmly established and gained considerable momentum. Bandura's (1977) *social learning theory*, later termed *social cognitive theory* (Bandura, 1986), elevated symbolic cognitive processes to determinants of behavior. In his theory of reciprocal determinism, for example, behavior, cognitive factors, and environmental influences reciprocally and continuously interact and influence one another. For his concept of self-efficacy, Bandura proposed that an individual's beliefs about his or her personal efficacy, or ability to successfully perform coping behavior, were determinants of whether such behavior will be demonstrated. The social learning theory movement was influenced not only by fundamental learning principles but also by principles derived from basic research in experimental and social psychology (O'Donohue, 1998). At this time, the "cognitive revolution" was well underway within academic psychology, and clinicians and researchers sought to incorporate cognitive mediators of learning into their models of abnormal behavior. In so doing, greater use was made of unobservable, hypothetical constructs to explain behavior. Although this was already a feature of some learning theories (e.g., Wolpe, Eysenck), the use of nonobservable or nonmanipulable constructs or processes to explain behavior was generally avoided by those from an operant learning perspective (e.g., Skinner).

Beginning around the late 1970s, interest in behavior therapies began to wane. One factor that contributed to this was the cognitive revolution, now firmly established and highly influential within academic psychology. Another was the publication of several groundbreaking scholarly works that described new and innovative therapies largely consisting of cognitive restructuring interventions (see Dobson & Dozois, 2001, for a review), including A. T. Beck and colleagues' (1979) treatment manual entitled *Cognitive Therapy of Depression*. Similarly, around this time a number of influential books on cognitive behavior therapy were beginning to be published (e.g., Mahoney, 1974; Meichenbaum, 1977).

A defining feature of cognitive therapies, both historically and currently, is the strong emphasis on the cognitive mediation of behavior—specifically, how individuals interpret their world, view themselves, or think about the future (A. T. Beck et al., 1979). Central cognitive concepts such as automatic thoughts, processing biases, core beliefs, and schemas are often used to explain variations in emotion and behavior and are central treatment targets in many cognitive therapy interventions. From a cognitive therapy perspective, primary therapeutic tasks involve assisting the client in identifying his or her idiosyncratic way of thinking and modifying thought processes through rational examination and logic (e.g., examining the evidence for or against a thought, evaluating the meaning one associates to a particular thought, hypothesis testing the validity of certain thoughts, replacing illogical or biased thoughts with more accurate ways of thinking).

Toward the Next Generation of Cognitive and Behavior Therapies

The past decade has witnessed the emergence of a new generation of cognitive and behavior therapies (Hayes, 2004a). This latest generation represents a marked theoretical evolution over previous generations and has been applied to phenomena that received comparatively little emphasis in previous iterations of cognitive behavior therapy. For instance, many new-generation approaches such as acceptance and commitment therapy (ACT; Hayes, Strosahl, & Wilson, 1999) and dialectical behavior therapy (DBT; Linehan, 1993a) emphasize factors such as emotion and language. ACT, DBT and other recent cognitive behavior therapies also incorporate mindfulness and acceptance principles, techniques, and practices into the framework of therapy (Hayes, Follette, & Linehan, 2004; Segal, Williams, & Teasdale, 2002). Emphasis on values identification and clarification in ACT (Hayes, Strosahl, et al., 1999) and on interpersonal relations in DBT, functional analytic psychotherapy (Kohlenberg & Tsai, 1991), and integrative behavioral couples therapy (Jacobson & Christensen, 1996b) also represent new additions to the traditional CBT frameworks.

Similarly, behaviorally oriented researchers and clinicians have incorporated into their models the important symbolic function of language. Among other functions, language provides persons with emotional experiences without exposure to actual physical events or objects represented by words (Forsyth & Eifert, 1998). For example, the phrase "big, hairy tarantula" is often enough to produce a moderate emotional reaction in a person with severe spider phobia. Feelings in humans are closely tied to language (Forsyth & Eifert, 1998), as exemplified by the frequent pairing of the emotional experience (anxiety) with the evaluation of that experience ("it's bad"), such that the two become functionally equivalent ("anxiety is bad"). New behaviorally oriented theories of cognition and language have emerged in recent years (e.g., Hayes, Barnes-Holmes, & Roche, 2001), as have therapies tied to this emerging perspective (Hayes, Strosahl, et al., 1999).

Another key feature that distinguishes this most recent generation of approaches from previous generations is their collective focus on the context, broadly defined, in which behavior occurs (e.g., Biglan & Hayes, 1996; Martell et al., 2001). That is, comparatively less emphasis is placed on the modification of the physical environment to alter behavior or on the modification of the content of particular behaviors, thoughts, and feelings to promote therapeutic change. Rather, in these newer cognitive behavior therapies, a greater emphasis is placed on the modification of contexts in which these responses are experienced. For instance, mindfulness-based approaches encourage clients to experience their thoughts from a context within which thoughts are regarded simply as thoughts, not literal truths or unqualified representations of reality. Similarly, acceptance-based interventions are geared toward altering the context from one whereby unwanted thoughts and emotions must be changed or eliminated to one in which such experiences are accepted, valued, and used adaptively. Taken together, this latest generation of cognitive behavior therapies more broadly deals with the range of human experience and, in so doing, delves into areas and change principles not previously acknowledged or systematically addressed in more traditional behavioral and cognitive therapies.

LOOKING AHEAD

This book is intended to serve as a general reference, and our primary goal is to offer an informative and easy-to-understand presentation on the basic theory and essential applications of behavioral interventions within the CBT framework. In the course of our presentation, we provide a description of the theory and practice of behavior therapy for adults that we hope is both useful and accessible to students and clinicians with varying degrees of behavioral training. We aim to provide some insight into how therapists with a behavioral perspective think about a client, his or her problem areas, and about the therapeutic process. Finally, our hope is that readers will find the behavioral interventions described in this book to be useful additions to their therapeutic armamentarium.

Chapters 2 through 4 deal with behavioral assessment, case formulation, and treatment planning. In chapter 2, we outline the principles, goals, and structure of the initial assessment sessions. In so doing, we delineate the objectives, processes, and applications of behavioral assessment approaches used in the development of a case formulation and explain how data from these assessments inform treatment selection and the evaluation of therapy outcome. We also emphasize the importance of a solid, collaborative, and respectful working therapist–client relationship in CBT.

In chapter 3, we summarize the primary elements of a behavioral case formulation of the client's problem area and outline the procedures and considerations associated with developing and exploring the formulation with the client. Chapter 4 extends the discussion further by providing guidelines for translating the case formulation into a plan for therapy. We also address related issues such as deciding on an appropriate framework for therapy, engaging in the collaborative exploration of the therapy plan with the client, establishing or enhancing client motivation and commitment for therapy, and identifying and sharing potential obstacles to therapy.

Chapters 5 through 10 detail specific behavioral interventions including indications for their application, steps associated with their implementation, and markers of resultant therapeutic change. Chapter 5, for example, describes several strategies used in behavior therapy to increase or decrease clinically relevant behaviors by changing the environment. Procedures discussed in this chapter primarily involve the altering of the antecedents or consequences that occasion clinically relevant behaviors.

In chapter 6, we describe examples of behavioral intervention strategies for altering the functional aspects of thinking patterns. The approach taken here is somewhat novel, as we emphasize the functional properties of detrimental modes of thinking rather than the modification of distorted or inaccurate thought content. Chapter 7 describes a set of interventions designed to help clients learn how to engage in particular behaviors in an effective and flexible manner to attain goals or enhance quality of life. The emphasis here is on changing behaviors by building skills. Several contemporary CBT-oriented treatments include skills training as a key component of the overall treatment approach given that skills-based interventions have demonstrated effectiveness for a variety of clinical problems.

In chapter 8, we describe a behavioral approach to the therapy of depression that is gaining broad empirical support as an effective therapy, *behavioral activation*. In this chapter, we not only describe behavioral activation as a therapeutic technique but also use this as an opportunity to illustrate several behavioral perspectives on psychological disorders. Chapter 9 describes an intervention framework for reducing unjustified and maladaptive emotional responding and corresponding behavioral tendencies. *Exposure-based interventions* involve exposing the client to stimuli that elicit an emotional response and the blocking of action tendencies that are consistent with the unwanted or undesirable emotional response. Although exposure interventions are most commonly used and perhaps most effective for clinical problems related to anxiety and fear, they are also increasingly applied to other clinical problems and emotional experiences.

Along with the behavior-change methods described in this book, *acceptance* and *mindfulness-oriented interventions* have great potential to help clients achieve their goals, reduce suffering, and enhance the quality of their lives. In chapter 10, we describe these interventions, which have found a place in several contemporary forms of CBT. In addition, we describe considerations related to achieving an optimal balance of acceptance versus change-oriented methods in therapy work with clients as a means to enhance the overall effectiveness of therapy.

In chapter 11, we discuss considerations and approaches for bringing therapy to a close. Within the chapter, we discuss the importance of addressing termination issues periodically throughout therapy and as early as the treatment planning stage. We also describe the potential benefits of adding a continuation phase and booster sessions following the conclusion of the acute phase of therapy as means for reducing the likelihood of relapse and problem recurrence, respectively. In the course of this discussion, we also describe several relapse prevention intervention strategies.

2

PRINCIPLES, GOALS, AND STRUCTURE OF INITIAL ASSESSMENT SESSIONS

Behavioral assessment is an approach for assessing persons, what they do, and the circumstances under which they are most likely to engage in behaviors of clinical interest (Nelson & Hayes, 1986a). When viewed from this perspective, behavioral assessment is not defined by a set of techniques. Rather, the behavioral assessment approach is primarily guided by the theoretical principles on which it is based. One key principle is that behavior varies in relation to the antecedent conditions that occasion behavior and the consequences that behavior produces. Together, these constitute the context of behavior. A primary goal associated with behavioral assessments is the identification of potentially modifiable contextual features associated with maintenance of problematic behavior (Follette, Naugle, & Linnerooth, 2000). Knowledge of the common contexts for behavior can suggest hypotheses about why a person does what he or she does. This knowledge, in turn, can be used in the selection of intervention approaches that specifically alter the contextual landscape within which problematic behavior occurs, thus affecting the frequency or intensity of those behaviors over time.

In this chapter, we provide an overview of the principles, structure, and goals of the initial assessment sessions. We begin with a description of the central distinguishing features of behavioral assessments. We then discuss the importance of therapist–client relationship factors in recognition that these are important features of all therapies, including cognitive behavior therapy (CBT). Much of the remainder of the chapter focuses on the goals, processes, and applications of behavioral assessment approaches used in the development of a case formulation that, in turn, informs treatment selection and the evaluation of treatment outcome. Included within these sections are descriptions of techniques that can aid in the identification of the client's primary problem areas, methods for evaluating both the form and function of potential target behaviors, and strategies for evaluating impairments in functioning and coping resources. We conclude this chapter by describing some considerations associated with bringing initial assessment sessions to closure.

CORE FEATURES OF BEHAVIORAL ASSESSMENTS

A therapist who works within a CBT framework and approaches the assessment of a client's problem areas from a behavioral perspective recognizes the uniqueness of the individual and his or her context. Behavioral assessments are *idiographic*, or person centered, which is often in contrast to other approaches that are largely centered on the assessment of variables or constructs. One of the more common variable-centered approaches is the medical model approach, whereby the goal is to evaluate the presence of behavioral and physiological markers indicative of a disease, and make a positive diagnosis when enough key markers are evident. This practice is most apparent in the use of psychiatric diagnoses in categorizing individuals. In the *Diagnostic and Statistical Manual of Mental Disorders* (4th ed., text rev.; *DSM–IV–TR*; American Psychiatric Association, 2000), syndrome or disorder markers are largely defined by emotional experiences, certain behavioral acts, and idiosyncratic ways of thinking. If a person displays a threshold number of markers or symptoms, a positive diagnosis is made and a treatment is selected on the basis of the diagnosis. The focus of treatment, then, is on the diagnosis, specifically the symptoms that define the diagnostic concept, and not the whole person in interaction with his or her environment.

Behavioral approaches to assessment are distinguished from medical model and other approaches by a unique set of goals and features. These distinguishing aspects of behavioral assessment are delineated in the following section.

Goals of Behavioral Assessments

In clinical behavioral assessment the primary emphasis is on the person; the clinically relevant behaviors he or she displays; and the environmental variables that select, influence, and maintain those behaviors (Dougher

& Hayes, 2000; Sturmey, 1996). Given this emphasis, there are at least five general goals associated with behavioral assessment (Nelson & Hayes, 1986b; Spiegler & Guevremont, 2003). These include

- a clarification of the nature of the client's problems, and identification of associated target behaviors;
- an evaluation of the extent to which the client's problems impair his or her functioning (e.g., in the areas of family life, social and occupational functioning, personal distress);
- the identification of factors that support and maintain problem areas;
- the collaborative development of a formulation of the client's problems, and development of a therapeutic intervention plan based on this formulation; and
- an ongoing evaluation of the effectiveness of the treatment strategy.

In this chapter, we are primarily concerned with the first three goals; in chapters 3 and 4 we will discuss the two remaining goals.

Distinguishing Features of Behavioral Assessments and Therapy

Several specific features distinguish behavioral assessment approaches from more traditional approaches (Hawkins, 1986; Nelson & Hayes, 1986b). Among the more important are the following:

- The level of analysis in behavioral assessment is the act in context, or the whole person in interaction with the environment.
- There is recognition that each person lives in a unique context and has a unique learning history and genetic endowment, with behavioral assessment and treatment approaches tailored to the client's uniqueness and individual needs.
- There is recognition that behavior is often situation specific rather than cross-situationally general, which highlights the importance of external influences on behavior.
- Limited inference is used in behavioral assessment; construct labels are generally avoided as explanations for behavior, and behavior itself is the focus of therapy.
- The client's problem areas are clearly defined in behavioral terms.
- The overall emphasis in therapy is on the development of effective behavior and competencies.

These features, and how they are manifested within behavioral assessment and treatment approaches, are elaborated in the next section and in several of the chapters that follow.

CLIENT–THERAPIST RELATIONSHIP FACTORS

Initial contacts with the client are perhaps among the most important, as several studies suggest that the likelihood of dropping out of therapy is high within the first few sessions (e.g., Fiester & Rudestam, 1975). Clients often come to therapy with a good deal of ambivalence and fear, and perhaps some degree of guilt or shame associated with their behavior. They may also have somewhat unrealistic expectations about what therapy can offer and disappointed to learn that there is no "magic bullet" that can resolve long-standing problems within a session or two. For these and other reasons, an important therapeutic goal within the first few sessions is to establish a warm and collaborative therapeutic relationship and clarify for the client what he or she can expect as the therapeutic process unfolds. This would include orienting the client as to what will happen at each stage and providing a realistic therapy timeline. In so doing, the therapist must be aware that correcting misunderstandings about what therapy can accomplish might contribute to client disappointment and hopelessness. When providing clients with reasonable and realistic expectations for therapy, it is important that therapists instill hope and confidence concerning its potential effectiveness.

Establishing Rapport With the Client

A number of perspectives converge on the idea that the therapy process is enhanced when the therapist demonstrates genuineness, respect, warmth, acceptance, validation, and accurate empathy (Morganstern & Tevlin, 1981). These characteristics help the therapist establish rapport with the client and set the foundation for the development of a trusting relationship. Other important therapist behaviors include appropriate demeanor (e.g., relaxed, interested, sympathetic, engaged); facial expressions (e.g., smiles, nods); and eye contact (not too much or too little), along with a body posture that conveys interest and attentiveness and a style of communicating that is easily understandable and relatively free of technical language (Livesley, 2001; Morrison, 1995).

Ideally, the therapist and client work together to develop and maintain a therapeutic context whereby relationship issues can be constructively addressed as they emerge (Linehan, 1993a; Livesely, 2001). This includes an understanding between both parties that behaviors displayed by either the client or therapist that interfere with therapy (e.g., lateness, verbally or physically expressed hostility, failures to keep agreements, noncompletion of between-session activities) are open for constructive discussion (Linehan, 1993a).

A therapist might keep in mind, too, that the therapeutic relationship is itself a context that can facilitate behavior change. Clients, for example, who have weak social skills can benefit from a therapeutic relationship that strengthens appropriate social behavior through natural social reinforcement (Kohlenberg & Tsai, 1991). Similarly, a therapist can discourage problematic interpersonal behaviors when a client displays them and suggest more adaptive alternatives. If, for example, a client's problem area includes excessive demands on others, a therapist might elect not to reinforce demands when the client states them. A therapist might instead attempt to evoke other behaviors inconsistent with excessive demandingness or dependency, but which have similar functions (e.g., the assertive expression of needs, the making of appropriate requests). A therapist might alternatively try to facilitate behaviors that are the opposite of problematic ones. In the case of excessive dependency, for example, the therapist might elect to naturally reinforce occasions when the client demonstrates autonomous action.

Developing a Collaborative Therapist–Client Relationship

CBT is an action-oriented approach to therapy; therefore, it is important for the client to be an active participant in the therapeutic process and to share responsibility in carrying out the therapy. To this end, the client might be encouraged to be actively involved in all aspects of therapy, including the development of a formulation of his or her problem areas and any decisions concerning how to best approach these areas therapeutically. Stylistically, the therapist can facilitate the development of a collaborative relationship by frequently checking in with the client with questions such as "Do you have anything you would like to add?" or "Is it alright if we now turn attention to your drinking habits?" Other stylistic approaches for enhancing the therapeutic relationship include taking the client's agenda seriously, assessing and highlighting the importance of the client's goals and values, using "we" statements, and conveying that the therapist and client are a "team" working together toward the same goals.

CONDUCTING INITIAL ASSESSMENTS: CLARIFYING THE CLIENT'S PROBLEMS AND IDENTIFYING TARGET BEHAVIORS

How a therapist conducts initial sessions will often vary in accordance with his or her theoretical orientation (Sundberg, Taplin, & Tyler, 1983). This is particularly evident in the types of information a therapist attends to during initial meetings with the client, and in the selection of areas or concepts to assess that have relevance for the subsequent development of a *case formulation*. As defined by Eells (1997), a case formulation is "a hypothesis about the causes, precipitants, and maintaining influences of a person's psychological, interpersonal, and behavioral problems" (p. 1). Therapists working from various perspectives will frequently generate case formulations that emphasize hypothesized causes of behavior suggested by their theoretical frame of reference. Their therapeutic activities, in turn, will often be directed at influencing theoretically prescribed determinants of behavior to bring about positive therapeutic change. In this section we highlight both general procedures for identifying problem areas that would be of subsequent focus in therapy and assessment approaches specific to the development of a behavioral case formulation of the client's presenting complaints. The process of generating a behavioral case formulation from assessment information is more fully described in chapter 3.

Presenting Problem or Complaint

When clients initially discuss their problem areas, it is often useful for the therapist to simply listen to the client without interrupting or probing for a reasonable period of time (up to about 10 minutes in an hour-long session; Morrison, 1995). Doing so allows the client the opportunity to freely describe his or her reasons for coming to therapy, and the nature of his or her problems. Such an approach also conveys to the client a genuine interest in what he or she has to say as well as a willingness to work collaboratively. This approach also provides the therapist with an opportunity to informally evaluate how the client organizes his or her thoughts and explains the events of his or her life. Therapists can also generate hypotheses concerning mood and interpersonal style during this period.

Some therapists who favor a nondirective approach are inclined to start the initial sessions with statements such as "Where would you like to begin?" or "What would you like to talk about?" Other nondirective therapists simply say nothing at all and let the client initiate the process without any prompting. Because CBT is often active and directive, therapists who work within this framework generally begin initial sessions with more focused statements such as "Can you tell me about what brought you to therapy?"

After the period of *free speech* (Morrison, 1995), the therapist might make several inquiries to clarify and assess the problem area. When clients express current problems, descriptions are often somewhat vague. Examples might include, "My relationship with my wife isn't so hot," "I have problems with my nerves," "I've really been bummed out these last few months," or "I just want to die." In such instances, the therapist needs to probe further—and identify manifestations of the problem (e.g., the behaviors, thoughts, and emotions involved), the current contexts within which they typically emerge, and the consequences that follow instances of the problem. It is also useful for the therapist to clarify the history and severity of the problem (e.g., when it first emerged, how long it has been going on, whether it is experienced as continuous or intermittent, the types of contexts that it reliably occurs within).

Ethical issues can arise when clients ask that their problems be treated with techniques with questionable effectiveness (e.g., rebirthing therapy), or when the problems indicated go beyond the realm of therapy (e.g., difficulty resolving past-life traumas; Morganstern & Tevlin, 1981). Similarly, a client may seek assistance with a particular problem area, but other, more significant problems become apparent during initial sessions (e.g., engagement in intentional deliberate self-harm, anorexia or bulimia nervosa, dissociative disorders). In these instances, a therapist must insist that the more serious and severe behaviors be addressed first, or addressed concurrently but regarded as higher priority treatment targets. Ultimately, the therapist may not accept the client's goals for therapy or intervene in the manner suggested by the client. When this occurs, a referral to another mental health professional might be indicated.

Assessment of Response Classes on the Basis of Correlated or Descriptive Features

Behavioral assessors will often collect information about the kinds of behavior clients display. Responses to assessment measures about the types of behavior frequently displayed constitute one method for sampling behavior and might also suggest possible target behaviors for therapy. Topographical classification or assessment methods of these types are primarily concerned with how people behave (Nelson & Hayes, 1986b), whereby individuals are classified according to the forms of behavior they exhibit. Such information can be useful in the behavioral assessment of a person's problem areas (Farmer & Nelson-Gray, 2005; Nelson-Gray & Farmer, 1999). Sole emphasis, however, on topographically defined behavior patterns or response–response relations has limited value from a behavioral perspective, particularly when it comes to altering behavior patterns (Naugle & Follette, 1998). That is, behavioral summaries captured by diagnostic or construct labels do not provide guidance as to how behavior came about or what factors might be influential in the maintenance of behavior, or why people behave the way they do.

Diagnostic Assessments

Shortly before the publication of the third edition of the *Diagnostic and Statistical Manual of Mental Disorders* (3rd ed.; *DSM–III*; American Psychiatric Association, 1980), semistructured diagnostic interviews such as the Schedule for Affective Disorders and Schizophrenia (SADS; Endicott & Spitzer, 1978) were beginning to appear. These were largely used by researchers who were primarily concerned with identifying groups of persons who were similar on some dimension on the basis of symptom presentation. Prior to interviews like the SADS, research in the area of depression, for example, was difficult to integrate and synthesize because studies operationalized and assessed the depression construct differently. What defined a depressed person in one study might have differed from what defined a depressed person in another study.

Since the publication of *DSM–III*, numerous diagnostic interviews have been developed that assess single disorders (e.g., posttraumatic stress disorder; Foa, Riggs, Dancu, & Rothbaum, 1993), a group of related disorders (e.g., the personality disorders; First, Gibbon, Spitzer, Williams, & Benjamin, 1997), or several distinct classes of psychiatric disorders (e.g., L. N. Robins, Helzer, Croughan, & Ratcliffe, 1981). Although still widely used in research, diagnostic interviews are now being used more frequently in general clinical practice, particularly in practices that specialize in the provision of therapies for a limited number of conditions.

The principle use of psychiatric diagnosis from a behavioral perspective is found in its classification and communication function. Because diagnostic concepts are largely defined in terms of behavioral acts, diagnoses may also suggest target behaviors for intervention. As many empirically supported therapies have been evaluated with reference to persons with particular diagnoses (Chambless et al., 1996), knowledge of an individual's diagnosis might also suggest effective treatment approaches.

Questionnaire, Checklist, and Rating Scale Assessments

Similar to diagnostic categories, psychological constructs are also often defined in terms of groupings of behaviors that are endorsed by or evident for an individual. We might conclude, for example, that a person is experiencing excessive levels of anxiety if he or she endorses several moderately or highly intercorrelated items on questionnaires related to the anxiety construct.

Over the past 25 years there has been a surge of published self-report measures that are easy to complete, relatively brief, and highly focused on particular problem areas (Froyd, Lambert, & Froyd, 1996). Questionnaire assessments are usually geared toward understanding the client's experience relative to other persons. To this end, a client's score on a questionnaire is usually referenced to those from a larger normative sample; the client's position within the general population is inferred on the basis of the number of standard deviation units his or her score is from the normative mean. Sometimes cut scores are used to denote the degree of an extremity of a score. These scores are then used to make inferences about the client in certain situations.

Checklists and rating scales are often completed by someone familiar with the client and typically consist of sets of behavioral acts to which the respondent indicates how frequently, if at all, the behavior occurs. Examples of such measures include the parent and teacher rating scales of the Child Behavior Checklist (Achenbach, 1991) and the Conners' Rating Scales (Conners, 1997). Checklist data are often useful in behavioral assessment, as they not only indicate the severity or frequency of behavioral problems but also frequently suggest specific behavioral targets.

Identification of Behavioral Repertoires and Skills Deficits

During the first stages of assessment, it is often useful to initially categorize problematic behaviors within one of two broad categories: behavioral excesses and behavioral deficits. *Behavioral excesses* may take several different forms. By definition, they are apparent when a person displays particular forms of behavior that are excessive in terms of frequency, intensity, or duration. The behaviors also occur to an extent that they become associated with distress or impairment in functioning.

The associated functions that behavioral excesses have for an individual need to be determined on a person-by-person basis. Several behavioral excesses are maintained, at least in part, by positive reinforcers such as pleasant tactile stimulation (e.g., promiscuous sex), intermittent generalized reinforcers (e.g., compulsive gambling), or notice from the social environment (e.g., disruptive attention-seeking behavior). Frequent overt displays of anger, aggression, or coercive behaviors are often maintained by both positive reinforcers (e.g., physical intimidation that results in others' complying with requests) and negative reinforcers (e.g., displays of anger that result in others' withdrawing, retreating, or capitulating). Other forms of behavioral excess are maintained by negative reinforcers and are most evident among persons who display strong avoidance and escape behavioral repertoires. The act of avoidance or escape generally results in the termination or cessation of contexts experienced as unpleasant and aversive. When behavioral excesses are examined, one often discovers some type of associated reinforcement process.

Behavioral deficits are apparent when persons do not demonstrate an adequate range of behavior in a variety of contexts or do not display adequate flexibility when adjusting behaviors in accordance with shifting circumstances. When behavioral deficits are evident, there are generally two reasons. One is that past environments did not adequately model, shape, or reinforce such behaviors. Another possibility is that absent behaviors have been learned at one time and are part of the person's repertoire. They appear deficient, however, because they either have been subjected to punishing contingencies or have been extinguished. Individuals who have significant behavioral deficits in important areas tend to be less skillful in the behavior they display and less successful in obtaining reinforcement from the environment for their behavior.

Evaluating Coping Behaviors

Coping behaviors are often important to assess, as such behaviors reflect how a person responds to adversity. Many of the types of problem behaviors that clients seek help with in therapy are, paradoxically, often the product of coping efforts that worked in the short term but posed long-term problems (e.g., Hayes, Strosahl, & Wilson, 1999; Linehan, 1993a; Martell, Addis, & Jacobson, 2001). When effective and nonharmful coping behaviors are deficient, as is often the case among persons with long-standing problems, CBT-oriented therapists will often assist clients in developing or strengthening alternative and adaptive coping skills. Problem-solving skills, social skills, self-regulation skills, mindfulness skills, and acceptance skills are examples of coping skills that are often targeted for strengthening within CBT.

- *Problem-solving skills* are particularly useful for assisting the client to find effective solutions to problems that arise. Clients who are vulnerable to feeling helpless, or who repeatedly engage in coping responses that also have a number of associated maladaptive qualities, are often deficient in their ability to generate novel or alternative ways of responding to problems.
- *Social skills* are requisite for developing and maintaining social and intimate relationships and for obtaining reinforcement from others. Individuals who have deficit social skills frequently also have deficits in coping, as they are less successful in accessing or mobilizing the social environment and less likely to receive support, aid, advice, or direction from others.
- Self-regulation has been defined as any efforts a person uses to alter inner states or responses (Vohs & Baumeister, 2004, p. 2). *Self-regulation skills*, therefore, refers to skills a person may or may not have developed for exercising control over him- or herself in areas as diverse as emotions, thoughts, impulses, attention, and bodily sensations.
- *Mindfulness skills* refer to several skills or abilities that have in common the fostering of a full awareness in the moment. Component skills include attention, awareness, observation, discrimination, nonjudging, and the maintenance of a present or here-and-now focus. Behavior patterns that are antithetical to mindfulness include rumination, worry, and dissociation.
- Many people who come to therapy have had the experience of growing up in an invalidating environment (e.g., Linehan, 1993a). As a consequence, many clients struggle with issues of self-worth, value as a person, and acceptance of themselves and their experiences. *Acceptance, self-validation,* and *tolerance skills* are often helpful for clients who are overly reactive, highly sensitive, and impulsive (C. J. Robins, Schmidt, & Linehan, 2004). Acceptance as a skill involves the ability to focus on the current moment, or mindfulness, and accurately perceive without

distortion or judgment. Part of acceptance, then, involves a type of openness to and acknowledgement of one's experience, devoid of accompanying evaluations or distortions (C. J. Robins et al., 2004).

A number of behavioral interventions in CBT seek to develop, strengthen, and maintain effective coping behavior. Examples of behavioral interventions designed to foster these skills are reviewed in chapters 5 through 10.

Evaluating Impairments in Functioning

There are several reasons for evaluating the degree of functional impairment associated with the client's problems. First, the degree and pervasiveness of impairment indicate the severity of the problem (Morrison, 1995). When significant impairment is observed in several domains of functioning, the problem likely requires more intensive forms of intervention. When impairments are more focal and limited, therapy might emphasize functioning in the few contexts in which impairment is most pronounced. When a client reports no impairment, time might be taken to clarify why he or she came to therapy.

Second, the level or nature of impairment can have relevance for the choice, course, or emphasis of therapy modalities and interventions. Moderately severe to severe impairments, as indicated by an inability to maintain personal hygiene, suicidal preoccupation, or the influence of hallucinations or delusions on behavior, might suggest more intensive therapeutic modalities such as inpatient psychiatric care or day hospital programs. When impairments are pervasive, longstanding, and affect several areas of functioning—as is sometimes observed among persons with severe personality disorders—long-term therapy might be contemplated. Depending on the client's areas of strength and impairment, therapy might also be offered in multiple modalities (e.g., individual therapy, group skills training, telephone consultations, pharmacotherapy). Because of risks or safety issues associated with some forms of impairment, the emphasis of therapy might also be prioritized according to the potential for harm. Suicidal preoccupation or behavior, when present, would likely take precedence over impairments with less potential for lethality, such as those related to quality of life (Linehan, 1993a). In chapter 4, we provide detailed guidelines for prioritizing client problem areas.

Third, psychological disorders are often defined, in part, by the presence of behavioral patterns associated with subjective distress or impairment in occupational or social functioning. The inclusion of the term *impairment* in the definition of psychological disorders, which is the case for the vast majority of *DSM*-defined disorders, represents an effort to lessen the influence that cultural beliefs, values, mores, and norms have on the judgments about the person. Although it is recognized that concepts of harm or loss of benefit are judged with reference to the standards of a person's culture, the inclusion of the impairment criterion decreases the likelihood that certain behavior patterns will arbitrarily be labeled as abnormal by external observers.

In the following sections, we touch on a number of domains in which impairments are likely to be revealed. In addition, we introduce some issues within each area that might be important for a behavioral assessor to consider. Contemplation of these issues would not only help determine whether current problems are accompanied by impairment or a change in functioning but also help establish aspects of the client's behavioral repertoire that already exist but are not currently evident.

Personal Functioning

In the evaluation of one's personal functioning, it is useful to compare how the person is currently functioning with how well he or she has functioned in the past. This information not only suggests a level of impairment but also might clarify what behavioral skills or coping resources already exist in the person's behavioral repertoire. Examples of questions for evaluating this area include the following:

- "What difficulties has this problem caused you?"
- "Does this problem cause you any discomfort?"
- "Has this problem had any impact on those things that you currently enjoy or have enjoyed in the past?"
- "For the time that this problem has been going on, have you experienced any difficulties taking care of yourself?"
- "Have you had difficulty sleeping? Any changes in your weight or appetite? How about energy level?"
- "Since you have had this problem, have you had periods of feeling out of control? If so, can you tell me more about this?"
- "Has this problem resulted in your avoiding situations or activities that you would not have avoided before?"
- "Have you previously sought help for this problem?"

Family and Social Relations

Solid family or social relationships might protect against the development of many forms of psychological disorder (McLeod, Kessler, & Landis, 1992) and can enhance physical and psychological health (Cohen & Wills, 1985). Impairments in these areas might not only increase one's vulnerability to psychological disorders but also exacerbate any problems that may already exist (Lewinsohn & Gotlib, 1995).

In an examination of family and social relations, it is important to distinguish whether current problems in these areas might be due to avoidance tendencies (e.g., withdrawal from interpersonal relationships); deficits in social skills (e.g., relevant social behaviors have not been learned); suppression of social behavior by the environment (e.g., social behaviors have been learned, but are punished by others when displayed—as exemplified in the case of a person who might experience spousal abuse when she displays assertive and autonomous behavior); or a low rate of positive reinforcement for social behavior (e.g., the individual lives within a context that does not positively support social behavior).

- "Since this problem emerged, have you noticed any changes in your relationships with family? Your spouse or partner? Friends? Coworkers?"
- "Have you had any recent difficulties or conflicts with people?"
- "How would you characterize your current relationships with family and friends?"
- "Is there someone in your life now that you would feel comfortable going to if you had a problem or needed help? Do you see this person often?"

Occupational and School Functioning

For many individuals, the first signs of impairment often emerge in response to the demands of day-to-day living. Work or school life is often filled with daily demands for performance, with the added pressure that performance is constantly evaluated (e.g., by supervisors or teachers).

- "Has this problem had any effect on your work (or studies)?"
- "Have you missed any days from work (or school)?"
- "Have you been reprimanded at work (or school) because of this problem?"
- "In the past, have you had many jobs? If so, what were the circumstances that prompted you to leave your jobs?"

Legal Difficulties or Proceedings

Legal difficulties are more likely when a person's history includes substance abuse, bipolar disorder, and antisocial behaviors (Morrison, 1995). A review of the person's legal history might reveal the presence of psychological conditions that might otherwise not be immediately apparent. In discussing legal issues, it is also useful to explore whether the client is involved in any current or pending litigation. Such knowledge might buffer against any future surprise when one's therapy work and notes are subjected to court review, or when one might be asked to testify during divorce or child custody proceedings. In the event that litigation is likely, and the therapist might be called to supply testimony, it is important to discuss with the client the advantages and disadvantages of providing evidence or opinion during ongoing therapy.

- "Have you ever had any legal difficulties?"
- "Have you ever been arrested?"
- "Are you currently involved in any legal proceedings that might have relevance to our work together?"
- "Do you anticipate any future litigation, such as divorce proceedings or child custody disputes?"

Health and Medical Status

Several studies have indicated that physical health is associated with overall well-being (e.g., Kozma & Stones, 1983). A variety of medical conditions can also produce signs and symptoms that strongly resemble psychological disorders (e.g., Jacob & Rapport, 1984); and certain behavioral and psychological disorders increase risk for health-related problems (e.g., Garner, 1997). Hypoglycemia, hyperthyroidism, or acute caffeine intoxication, for example, are associated with signs or symptoms that can resemble panic attacks (Street & Barlow, 1994). Conversely, some psychiatric disorders increase the risk for health-related problems. In the case of bulimia nervosa, for example, the use of purging compensatory methods can result in electrolyte abnormalities, impaired renal functions, and esophageal weakening or rupture. Before initiating therapy, it is advisable for the client to seek out a medical consultation in the event that there are current untreated medical difficulties or an indication that current symptomatology may be due to or exacerbated by an underlying medical condition.

- "Do you have any current medical problems?"
- "Have you had any medical problems in the past?"
- "What medications are you currently taking?"
- "How would you describe your health currently?"

Current Life Situation and Quality of Life

Quality of life is another factor that can be considered during initial assessments as well as throughout therapy. Quality-of-life factors not only influence one's overall sense of well-being but also can pose threats to ongoing therapy (e.g., no money for housing, arrests for criminal behavior). Behaviors that interfere with quality of life and also threaten the viability of ongoing treatment or are associated with risk and safety issues should be actively targeted in therapy (Linehan, 1993a).

- "Where do you currently live?"
- "Whom do you live with?"
- "What is your financial situation like?"
- "Do you have recreational interests? How often do you participate in these?"
- "Have you had any recent changes in your life?"

- "How would you describe a typical day for you?"
- "Are you satisfied with your current situation? Would you like for anything to be different?"

Suicide Risk and Other Risk Areas

The assessment and evaluation of risk are important aspects of the ongoing therapy of a client. In the initial stages of assessment, suicidal and homicidal ideation and intention should be assessed as well as other indicators of risk such as thinking anomalies (e.g., hallucinations and delusions), substance abuse, and self-harm tendencies. The client's history in relation to these areas should also be evaluated (e.g., past suicide attempts, past acts of aggression). In the event that there is a suggestion of child or elder abuse, or abuse of any vulnerable person, the therapist must thoroughly explore the issue, and take appropriate action, such as notifying appropriate authorities, if such abuse is acknowledged.

If a client reports suicidal or homicidal thoughts or self-harm behaviors, the original plan for the initial session should be suspended, and these areas addressed in great detail. Included within this assessment might be an evaluation of the frequency, intensity, and duration of these thoughts as well as the strength of the urge to act on such ideation. Any plans for action should be evaluated as well as associated means and the availability and potential lethality of such means. In the event that the client is at imminent risk for harming self or others, appropriate action should be taken to ensure the safety of the client or others.

When a situation is not urgent or imminent (e.g., low urge to act on suicidal ideation, ability to tolerate emotional pain, suicidal behavior viewed by client as ineffective coping, unavailability of lethal means, willingness to act in accordance with an established suicidal prevention plan; see Chiles & Strosahl, 1995), further detailed exploration is warranted. For those who report suicidal ideation, for example, one might take time to determine what the client feels hopeless about (J. S. Beck, 1995), or what problems the individual believes suicidal action or parasuicidal behavior may solve (Linehan, 1993a). Protective factors, such as reasons for living, are also important to explore (Linehan, 1993a).

- "Have you had thoughts of wanting to hurt or kill yourself? Have you ever acted on these thoughts? Do you have these thoughts now?"
- "Have you ever wished that you were dead?"
- "Have you had thoughts of wanting to hurt others? Have you ever acted aggressively toward another person?"
- "Sometimes people do things to cause pain to themselves, whether or not they have a desire to kill themselves. Have you ever done anything to intentionally inflict pain on yourself?"

- "Have you ever had feelings of rage to the extent that you lost control?"

THE BEHAVIORAL INTERVIEW

Behavioral interviews are often conducted within the first few sessions by behaviorally oriented therapists as a means for gathering information relevant to the development of a behavioral case formulation. The focus of such interviews is frequently on the designation of the client's problem areas (e.g., problematic emotional responding, ineffective interpersonal or coping behavior), an identification of specific behavioral patterns related to these problem areas, an exploration of possible precipitants and maintaining factors associated with these patterns, and an investigation into the possible commonalities among these problem areas. Although behavioral interviews take many different forms, a number of similarities can be identified (Kanfer & Saslow, 1969; Morganstern & Tevlin, 1981; Peterson, 1968; Spiegler & Guevremont, 2003; Turkat, 1986). An underlying philosophical assumption that guides the interview is that behavior is determined, whereby current behavior is jointly influenced by immediate environmental factors and the culmination of a lifetime's worth of experiences. There is also an emphasis on current behavior and functioning. Relevant aspects of the client's history might also be explored to place problem behaviors in a historical perspective and to aid in the identification of possible current contexts and maintaining factors associated with these behaviors.

During the behavioral interview, the therapist frequently adopts an *active approach*. As the client provides new information about him- or herself, the therapist continuously develops, tests, and refines the case formulation in accordance with existing knowledge (e.g., by predicting a client's responses to questions posed, or predicting behavior in certain situations as recounted by the client). Consistent with this active approach, there is an ongoing evaluation of potential target behaviors. In the initial stages of assessment, a therapist might consider client behaviors in terms of broad, inclusive categories such as excesses or deficits, and strengths or assets (e.g., areas of competence or skill, effectiveness of coping behavior, social support network). In addition to thinking about potential target behaviors in relation to their frequency, intensity, severity, and generality, one might consider the antecedents that precede behaviors of interest and the consequences that follow them.

To evaluate these areas, behaviorally oriented interviewers ask questions that emphasize the what, when, where, how, and how often features of behavior (Spiegler & Guevremont, 2003). Examples of interview questions for investigating areas typically addressed in the early phases of behavioral assessment are outlined in Exhibit 2.1.

FUNCTIONAL ANALYSIS: CLARIFYING THE CONTEXT AND PURPOSE OF BEHAVIOR

A functional understanding of clinically relevant behavior attempts to isolate the conditions under which behavior is most likely to occur and identify the consequences that function to maintain it over time. The products of such an analysis are, in turn, integrated into a hypothetical model about the client's behavior and subsequently used to inform decisions concerning which behavioral interventions might be most appropriate for this client at this time.

In the sections that follow, we describe four essential components of a functional analysis of behavior: (a) antecedent stimuli (i.e., discriminative stimuli and establishing operations), (b) person variables (i.e., physiological makeup, heritable biological characteristics and learning history), (c) behavior (i.e., cognitive–verbal, physiological, emotional, and motor responses), and (d) consequences (reinforcement and punishment, immediate and delayed). These four components represent the foundations of a hypothetical model of a client's problem area, whereby a person's behavior is regarded as a joint function of immediate environmental variables (antecedent stimuli and response consequences) and person variables that the individual brings to a situation (Goldfried & Sprafkin, 1976).

The Antecedents of Behavior

From a behavior therapy perspective, there are two general types of antecedents that set the occasion for behavior. These are *discriminative stimuli* and *establishing operations*.

Discriminative Stimuli

Discriminative stimuli (or S^D) are events that provide information about the likelihood that reinforcement or punishment will follow the engagement in some type of behavior. The informational value of S^D is based on a person's previous experiences for behaving in certain ways in the presence of those or related stimuli. When a given behavior has been typically reinforced or punished in the presence of S^D, those S^D will often acquire influence over behavior by signaling the likelihood of reinforcement or punishment. Displays of disruptive behavior in the classroom, for example, are frequently reinforced and maintained by attention from peers. The presence of peers in a classroom setting, then, is often S^D that occasion disruptive behavior for children who have been previously reinforced for such behavior by peers in similar settings.

Establishing Operations

Establishing operations (EO), sometimes referred to as *motivational operations*, constitute another type of antecedent that sets the occasion for cer-

EXHIBIT 2.1
Examples of Interview Questions Typically
Addressed Early in Behavioral Assessment

For identifying possible target behaviors and the frequency and severity of those behaviors:
"What brings you here today?"
"What is the problem as you see it?"
"Please tell me about types of problems you have been having that you wish to address here."
"Are there things going on in your life right now that make you unhappy?"
"How often does the problem occur?"
"How serious do you see the problem to be?"
"Have others suggested that this is a problem?"
"Are there things that you used to enjoy doing that you no longer do?"
"Are there situations in which you are unsure of how to respond?"
"Has this problem had an impact on your family life? Your work? Your relationships with important persons in your life? Your overall sense of well-being?"
"Has anything important changed in your life since this problem has occurred?"

For establishing antecedents of target behaviors:
"When, or in what situations, does the problem occur?"
"What is happening right before the problem occurs?"
"If you think back to the last time the problem took place, what was going on then?"
"Does this problem typically happen when you are around other people, or by yourself?"
"Prior to the problem occurring, do you typically experience certain thoughts or feelings?"
"Before doing this behavior you regard as problematic, do you have any thoughts about what might happen as a result?"

For identifying possible consequences of target behaviors:
"What happens right after the problem occurs?"
"What do you get from doing this?"
"When the problem occurs, are you aware of any changes in how you feel?"
"If the problem takes place around other people, how do they respond when it occurs?"
"Are there times when the problem gets better? If so, what is going on at that time?"
"Are there long-term effects associated with the problem?"

For evaluating the associations that learning history or person variables might have with target behaviors:
"When did the problem first begin?"
"Do you recall other times in your life when you had this same problem? What was going on in your life then?"
"Is the problem today different in any way from this problem in the past?"
"When you had this problem in the past, was there anything you tried back then that helped?"
"Has anyone in your family, including grandparents and cousins, ever had this problem?"

For assessing the effectiveness of coping behaviors:
"What have you tried to reduce or eliminate the problem? How has that worked?"
"Tell me how you cope with difficult situations. When you do that, does it help? Does this way of coping cause other problems?"
"Do you find yourself coping with the problem through avoiding or withdrawing in any way?"

"Are you more likely to do certain things when the problem is present? If so, what do you do?"

"Is it difficult to deal with those painful feelings when they are there? If so, what do you do when you're feeling them?"

For evaluating the consistency of problem behaviors with values or goals:
"How might life be if this was not a problem for you?"

"If you think about it, are your actions consistent with what you want your life to be about?"

"What might you be doing in your life right now if this was not a problem for you?"

"Is there anything missing in your life right now that is important to you?"

"If therapy is successful, how would things be different for you?"

For assessing the client's ideas about how to address his or her problem areas:
"What do you think might be done to improve your situation?"

"Can you imagine yourself doing anything that would make the situation better?"

"If you didn't have this problem, what would you be doing differently?"

"Do you know of anybody that had problems similar to yours? What did they do?"

"What might contribute to others' feeling satisfied with their lives?"

---

tain behaviors. Establishing operations refers to the influence that environmental events or conditions have on behavior by changing the reinforcing or punishing properties of other environmental events (Laraway, Snycerski, Michael, & Poling, 2003; Michael, 1982, 2000). If, for example, a person is deprived of water for a long time, the reinforcing value of water or similar substances (e.g., juice, soda, beer) increases as a result of the deprivation. Conversely, a person who has just consumed a lot of water might find the act of drinking even more water to be unpleasant. The reinforcing value of water for such an individual has been diminished because of prior satiation.

Internal events that arise from certain environmental events, such as thoughts and emotional states, are common EOs for some behaviors (Michael, 1982; Miltenberger, 2005). Among people who frequently binge eat, for example, common EOs that occasion binge episodes include negative mood states, negative thoughts related to self, sleep deprivation, and food cravings associated with prolonged food deprivation (Farmer & Latner, 2007). The experience of anger, perhaps as a result of painful or aversive stimulation, might serve as an EO for aggressive behavior. Similarly, deprivation of attention might function as an EO that increases the likelihood that the deprived person will enact a variety of behaviors that have in common an attention-obtaining function (Michael, 1982, 2000).

Included among EOs are *rules* that influence behavior (Schlinger, 1993; see also chap. 6, this volume). Rules are verbal stimuli, transmitted through spoken word or writing, which specify consequences or outcomes associated with acting in particular ways. Rules include instructions, commands, demands, "if–then" statements, advice, oral traditions, moral teachings, and modeled behavior (Baum, 1994). Technically speaking, a rule is a verbal description that specifies an antecedent condition or context, a particular behavior or set of behaviors, consequences for behavior, or a combination of these (Anderson, Hawkins, Freeman, & Scotti, 2000). In this respect, rules are regarded as stimuli that, in the presence of which, a response specified by the rule will result in either reinforcement or punishment. *Rule-governed behavior*, then, refers to those behaviors influenced by verbal rules that specify the operating contingencies associated with behavior. A client with fears about public speaking, for instance, might have his or her behavior guided by the following rule: "If I speak [the behavior] in front of a large audience [the antecedent condition or context], I will be evaluated negatively and humiliated [the consequence]." Such a person might avoid public speaking as a result of this rule, even if it is not accurate. The rule-governed behavior concept is used to account for behavior influenced by delayed consequences and provides a framework for how thoughts or self-directed speech might promote goal-oriented actions (Malott, Malott, & Trojan, 2000).

The Consequences of Behavior

Behavior is usually performed to produce particular outcomes. Whether or not behavior is successful in producing that outcome, however, will influence its likelihood of being performed under similar circumstances in the future. In this section, we describe consequences of behavior and the influence that these consequences have on future behavior.

Factors That Increase or Maintain Behavior

Often in CBT, the focus is on behaviors that occur frequently and are problematic. Many of the behaviors dealt with in clinical contexts are reinforced behaviors, which is why they persist and become more frequent or intense over time.

There are two types of reinforcement that increase or maintain behavior: *positive reinforcement* and *negative reinforcement*. The terms *positive* and *negative* in relation to both reinforcement and punishment (described in the following list) do not connote a type of evaluation (e.g., good or bad); rather, they refer to whether behavior results in the application of something (i.e., positive) or the removal of something (i.e., negative). Given the technical definitions of these terms, we can define positive and negative reinforcement as follows:

- Positive reinforcement occurs when behavior results in the application or provision of a reinforcing event, which increases the probability of the behavior in future similar situations.
- Negative reinforcement occurs when behavior results in the removal or termination of an aversive event or condition, which increases the probability of the behavior in future similar situations.

Positive or negative reinforcement processes often maintain *behavioral excesses*, or behaviors that occur with such frequency or intensity that they become problematic. To understand what function the excessive behavior serves for the individual, it is important to understand *why* the person engages in the behavior. Theories on the functional properties of addictive behaviors, for example, have emphasized two processes, both of which Fowles (2001) has conceptualized as an "abuse of reinforcers." When substance abuse is instrumental in producing pleasant or desirable consequences (e.g., euphoria), it is regarded as positively reinforced behavior. Conversely, when substance use produces relief (escape) from aversive states or environments (e.g., negative emotion, social anxiety), it is regarded as negatively reinforced behavior. Although the positive and negative reinforcing effects of substance use are likely instrumental in the maintenance of addictive behaviors, individuals are expected to vary in terms of which type of reinforcing consequence most influences their behavior. Consequently, in the process of understanding the problematic behavior targeted in therapy, we must understand why the person engages in the behavior. Such knowledge will likely inform decisions concerning which interventions are most appropriate for a given individual.

Problematic binge eating is another example of a behavior that might be maintained by different consequences depending on the individual. Some models on the maintenance of binge eating emphasize the avoidance function that binge eating serves for the person. Generally speaking, when we talk about behavior maintained by avoidance, we are usually talking about negative reinforcement processes whereby behavior results in the elimination or removal of something aversive. In relation to binge eating, various theoretical models have emphasized the role that binge eating has on the avoidance of or escape from aversive self-awareness (Heatherton & Baumeister, 1991; McManus & Waller, 1995) or negative emotions (Johnson, Schlundt, Barclay, Carr-Nangle, & Engler, 1995). Other models of binge eating emphasize the positive reinforcing functions that establish and maintain binge eating. Possible reinforcers for binge eating include the taste of desired foods (Loro & Orleans, 1981) and reinforcement provided by others in the social context of eating (Johnson et al., 1995). Additional research suggests that the degree to which the taste and consumption of food might be reinforcing varies as a function of the type of eating disorder a person displays. Those with binge eating disorder, for example, have reported greater enjoyment associated with eating during binges compared with those with bulimia nervosa (J. E. Mitchell et al., 1999).

Factors That Decrease or Extinguish Behavior

There are two types of punishment, both of which decrease the future likelihood of punished behavior under similar stimulus conditions:

- *Positive punishment* occurs when behavior results in the application or provision of an aversive event or condition, which decreases the probability of the behavior in future similar situations.
- *Negative punishment* occurs when behavior results in the removal or termination of a reinforcing event or condition, which decreases the probability of the behavior in future similar situations.

Another type of process that results in a reduction or elimination of behavior is *extinction*. Extinction of behavior over time occurs when behavior is reliably performed without being followed by reinforcing consequences. If a behavior does not produce intended effects or reinforcing consequences then it will simply "drop out" and no longer be displayed over time.

In an example of the role of extinction, some models of depression (e.g., Ferster, 1973; Lewinsohn, 1974) emphasize a low rate of response-contingent positive reinforcement (RCPR) for social behaviors that, in turn, effectively extinguishes these behaviors over time. As behavior frequency becomes reduced because of low RCPR, the opportunities to receive reinforcement for social behavior correspondingly become less and less. This resultant progression is a true downward spiral, whereby a low rate of RCPR for social behavior becomes associated with a low rate of emitted behavior that further reduces the likelihood of reinforcement for behavior.

The consequences that affect behavior are summarized in Table 2.1. In this table, forms of behavioral consequation are compared and contrasted in terms of the type of consequence, the effect the consequence has on behavior (i.e., increase or decrease), and the behavior–consequence relationship.

Additional Considerations Associated With Behavior Consequences

When examining the consequences of behavior, there are two other important considerations. The first is that the definition of what constitutes a reinforcer or punisher is solely determined by the effect the consequence has on future behavior. A reinforcer is, by definition, an operation that increases behavior frequency or intensity over time. A punisher, in contrast, is an operation that decreases a behavior over time. Although an event might appear to be either rewarding or punishing on the basis of its surface features, we can only infer the nature of the consequent event by observing the effect that it has on future behavior. Among some individuals, for example, attention from others can be either a rewarding or an aversive consequence for behavior. For those who consider attention from others rewarding, the behavior that resulted in attention will likely be more probable in the future. In contrast, persons who experience attention as aversive might be less likely to subsequently display behaviors that resulted in attention.

TABLE 2.1
Behavioral Operations and Their Effects

Operation	Type of consequence	Effect on behavior	Behavior–consequence relationship
Positive reinforcement	Rewarding	Increase	Behavior → receive rewarding event
Negative reinforcement	Relieving	Increase	Behavior → removal of aversive event
Extinction	Frustrating	Decrease	Behavior → no reinforcing outcome
Positive punishment	Aversive	Decrease	Behavior → receive aversive event
Negative punishment	Penalizing	Decrease	Behavior → removal of rewarding event

Note. Adapted from *Personality-Guided Behavior Therapy* (p. 60), by R. F. Farmer and R. O. Nelson-Gray, 2005. Washington, DC: American Psychological Association. Copyright 2005 by the American Psychological Association.

A second consideration is whether the consequences are short term or immediate versus long term or delayed. In the case of problematic behaviors, short-term consequences often maintain such behaviors whereas long-term consequences make those behaviors problematic (Nelson-Gray & Farmer, 1999). When conducting a functional analysis, assessments might emphasize both the short- and long-term consequences of problematic behavior.

Person Variables and Learning History Within a Functional Analysis

Person variables, sometimes referred to as *organismic* variables (Goldfried & Sprafkin, 1976), include biological characteristics of the individual and the effects of past learning. Examples of biological characteristics include genetic predispositions, temperament, physical appearance, and the effects of aging. Learning history refers to the influence that a lifetime of environmental learning has on one's behavior, knowledge of which can aid predictions about how a person might behave in particular environmental contexts.

As an example of the potential importance of biological characteristics in developing a functional understanding of problematic behavior, abnormalities in appetitive and metabolic functioning have been suggested to influence overeating among some individuals with bulimia nervosa and binge-eating disorder (Latner & Wilson, 2000). Similarly, many of the symptoms and features of anorexia nervosa and bulimia nervosa can be accounted for by the common long-term physical effects of starvation. An undernourished individual's behavioral and psychological functioning will often be impaired; however, when weight and nutrition return to more normative levels such impairments are often reversed (Garner, 1997).

Many psychological conditions have been suggested to have some genetic influences, such as schizophrenia, bipolar disorder, attention-deficit/hyperactivity disorder, and anxiety disorders (Rhee, Feigon, Bar, Hadeishi, & Waldman, 2001). Although genes cannot themselves be directly manipulated, knowing one's family history with reference to a particular problem behavior might suggest possible biological influences on behavior—such as those that result in an individual being especially sensitive to the reinforcing effects of certain substances or environmental events (Farmer, 2005; Tabakoff & Hoffman, 1988).

With regard to learning history, many forms of problematic behaviors persist for years or decades. Examples of such behaviors include eating disorders (Pike, 1998) and alcoholism (Helzer et al., 1985). High volumes of positive and negative reinforcers often maintain frequent and long-standing behavior problems. Given the abundant reinforcers associated with such behavior, the prognosis for successful treatment is often poor, perhaps because such behaviors are not experienced as especially troublesome or because they provide considerable relief (Vitousek, Watson, & Wilson, 1998).

Knowledge of learning history might reveal the functional development of a person's problem areas, suggest variables that might influence these problem behaviors in current contexts, and imply additional problem areas not readily apparent but consistent with prototypical histories associated with certain forms of psychopathology. In an example of the latter, a majority of individuals with borderline personality disorder (BPD) have histories of deliberate self-harm or suicidal behavior, which are sometimes not readily acknowledged in early interviews. In the event that someone exhibiting BPD features does not volunteer information concerning past self-harm or suicidal behaviors during an initial interview, the therapist might consider exploring these areas given the commonality of this type of behavioral history.

When historical etiological antecedents to problematic behavior can be identified, they might have little or no relevance for the maintenance of those behaviors over time. That is, we cannot assume that factors instrumental in the initial establishment of a set of problematic behaviors exert influence on current behavior. Consequently, to understand current behavior, one needs to identify contemporary influences on behavior.

Now that we have described the four key components of a functional analysis of behavior, we provide in the next section an example of a functional analysis of a clinically relevant behavior. Within this example, we also demonstrate how multiple analyses of single chains of behavior (i.e., chain analyses; Linehan, 1993a) can be combined to derive a broader functional understanding of the key variables that influence the problematic behavior.

Examples of a Clinical Functional Analysis

"Adam," a 24-year-old ranch hand, came to the clinic for assistance with alcohol dependence. Prior to undergoing a medically supervised detoxification as a precursor to a course of CBT, he met with a psychologist who assessed the descriptive and contextual aspects of his drinking behavior, among other areas.

In reviewing Adam's drinking history, the therapist learned that he began episodically drinking at age 12. He cited peer influences as his main reason for drinking at the time (e.g., "All of my friends were doing it"). After a period of drinking, he and his friends would typically go downtown and vandalize property, verbally harass people, and steal items typically worth less than $300. Adam commented that he enjoyed the psychoactive effects of alcohol, felt that alcohol facilitated camaraderie with his mates, and took pleasure in the effects of what he did while intoxicated (e.g., the reactions on faces of people that he harassed, possessing stolen objects). He added that he was always an impulsive individual and enjoyed a good time.

When the therapist sampled several episodes of excessive drinking over the past few weeks, a fairly consistent pattern emerged. Adam's drinking was more or less continuous in that he would drink on four or more occasions during a typical day. Common antecedents to drinking would include reduced tissue concentrations of alcohol and associated feelings of discomfort (nausea, feelings of edginess, lethargy) linked to withdrawal, strong alcohol cravings, and negative drink-related thoughts related to himself ("I'm just a drunk and I'll never amount to nothing"). He also reported that he would also drink immediately before he met with the ranch owner, stating that "It's just easier for me to get along with him if I'm a little crocked" and "When I'm juiced, it's easier for me to joke around with him." Further probing of these disclosures indicated that Adam typically felt some mild to moderate anxiety immediately prior to beginning a social exchange with the ranch owner. He also indicated that when he joked around with the rancher and others, he felt a stronger bond with them. Regarding the latter, he reported that others responded to him more positively when he was intoxicated.

When other consequences of intoxication were explored, Adam described a mixed picture. On the one hand, he reported that he would feel somewhat euphoric once he started drinking, and that his discomfort and cravings would quickly lessen and then go away. Similarly, as the intoxicating effects of alcohol took hold, he reported that he felt less anxious when interacting with others and, in fact, was able to "be himself," which he described as being more socially outgoing and funny. Adam also reported that he enjoyed the taste of alcohol. Whiskey was his favorite; he would typically consume about four standard drinks on each drinking occasion.

On the other hand, within an hour of a drinking episode, Adam reported, "I would start to feel bad again." The euphoria would have lessened or be completely gone, cravings would return, and negative self-thoughts would again surface. As time progressed, physical withdrawal symptoms would intensify. The ability to work would typically be impaired as these aversive effects became more pronounced. On the basis of past experiences, Adam learned that he could terminate the aversive experiences through consuming more alcohol.

Figure 2.1 illustrates the functional analysis of Adam's alcohol use. In this model, dots that appear in between components in the response chain indicate a probability function, and a dot represents a probability that the preceding component will influence the following component. Items listed within the Reinforcing Consequences components that are followed by (+) indicate positive reinforcing consequences whereas items followed by (−) indicate negative reinforcing consequences, both of which maintain or strengthen preceding behavior.

Functional Response Class Assessment

One of the goals of performing functional assessments of problem behaviors is to facilitate the client's attention to the contextual flow within which such behavior is embedded. As a result, clients are more likely to understand the influences on their behavior, and the notion that they do what they do because of the effects that their behavior produces.

When grouping behaviors, behaviorally oriented clinicians typically do so according to the purpose that behavior serves. Functional response classes are groups of behaviors that produce the same or similar outcomes, even through they may assume several different forms (Follette et al., 2000). Phobic behavior, dissociation, intentional self-harm, and substance abuse, for example, are vastly different forms of behavior. They often, however, have a similar underlying function for individuals who engage in them, namely experiential avoidance (Hayes, Wilson, Gifford, Follette, & Strosahl, 1996). Individuals who display these and other forms of avoidant behavior might be regarded as having a strong or excessive behavioral avoidance repertoire. Additional assessments often reveal that such behaviors have powerful short-term negative reinforcing properties, but very harmful long-term associated outcomes (Nelson-Gray & Farmer, 1999).

Functional response class assessment often reveals behavioral repertoires that warrant development, reduction, or refinement. Knowledge of the function or purpose that problematic behaviors serve for the client can often be used in the design of intervention strategies that target the context within which problematic behavior is embedded.

EXAMPLES OF OTHER BEHAVIORAL ASSESSMENT METHODS

Several behavioral assessment methods exist, and depending on the client's presenting problems, some methods might be more appropriate than others. In this section, we discuss two commonly used behavioral assessment methods: self-monitoring and direct observation. Other approaches to be-

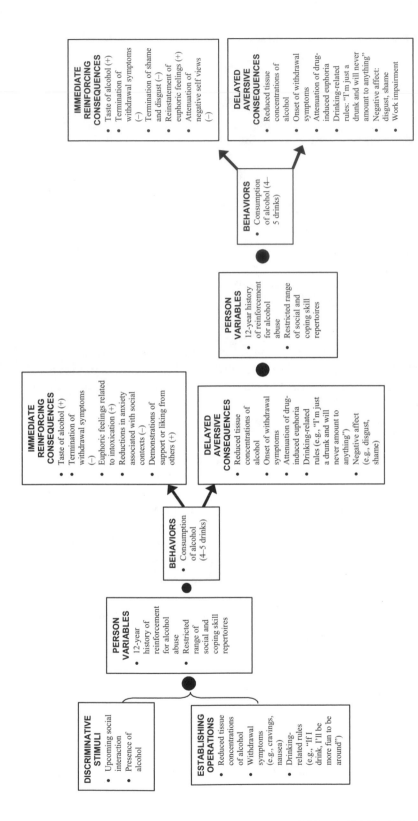

Figure 2.1. Functional analysis of Adam's drinking behavior.

havioral assessment are described in Ciminero, Calhoun, and Adams (1986) and Nelson and Hayes (1986b).

Self-Monitoring

Self-monitoring is an assessment procedure whereby the client collects data on behaviors of interest as they occur within naturalistic settings (Korotitsch & Nelson-Gray, 1999). To engage in self-monitoring, the client must be clear as to what behaviors should be monitored; that is, target behaviors must be clearly defined and the client familiar with the range of exemplars of the behavior. The client must also be able to notice when the target behavior occurs and record it. If the self-monitoring method is somewhat complex, some instruction in how to use the assessment instrument might be required. Although commonly regarded as an assessment approach, the simple act of self-monitoring has also been observed to result in changes in behavior frequency in desirable directions (Korotitsch & Nelson-Gray, 1999).

As an assessment tool, self-monitoring can be used to identify the antecedents that precede behaviors of interest. Such information might be useful for determining the types of contexts in which problematic behavior is most likely. Self-monitoring methods can also be used to monitor the frequency of certain target behaviors. When data on behavior frequency are collected prior to and during active therapy, self-monitoring assessments can be used to evaluate whether therapy is having a beneficial effect. Similarly, when the treatment consists of multiple components, self-monitoring data might reveal which among the treatment components was most useful or effective in producing desirable behavior change.

Methods for self-monitoring vary according to the nature and purpose of the assessment. If the frequency of a specific behavior is the object of assessment, then a tool such as a golf counter or a piece of paper where hash marks are recorded might be sufficient. Perhaps more commonly, self-monitoring forms such as thought records (e.g., Young, Weinberger, & Beck, 2001), mood charts (Miklowitz, 2001), or diary cards (e.g., Linehan, 1993a) might be developed to keep track of the occurrence of clinically relevant behaviors and the contexts within which they occur. In the published literature, self-monitoring methods have been used to keep track of a variety of behaviors including instances of self-harm, hallucinations, alcohol consumption, classroom participation, binge and purge episodes, and insomnia (Korotitsch & Nelson-Gray, 1999).

Direct Observation

When direct observation is used as an assessment methodology, persons other than the client monitor the frequency of target behaviors, the contextual features associated with target behaviors, or some combination of these. The observers can be family or friends of the client, or other persons who enter the client's natural environment for assessment purposes. In the published literature, examples include parents as participant–observers of aspects of their children's behavior, spouses in couple's therapy who monitor the frequency of certain partner behaviors, and assistants who enter the classroom environment to observe disruptive behaviors displayed by a child (Hayes, Barlow, & Nelson-Gray, 1999).

Direct observation methodologies can be devised in such a way that they reveal important information about a client's target problem area. During in vivo exposure for agoraphobia, for example, a therapist will often accompany the client to a number of anxiety-evoking environments such as a town center or shopping mall. During the exposure process, the therapist will often assist the client in monitoring his or her level of anxiety to determine the extent to which the client's anxiety habituated during the exposure session.

As suggested in the previous example, therapists often act as participant–observers of their clients' behavior. The behavioral assessment literature is ripe with instances of therapists entering the clients' natural environments to observe contextual aspects of their problem behaviors. One such approach has been called *ABC recording* (Hawkins, 1986), which refers to the antecedents of behavior, the target behaviors themselves, and the consequences that follow. Observers using this approach may monitor the individual's activity for displays of the target behavior. When the target behavior occurs, the observer notes antecedent conditions that were present immediately beforehand. The observer also notices and records how the social environment responded to the behavior after it was displayed (e.g., responded in a warm or disapproving manner).

Functional analytic psychotherapy (FAP; Kohlenberg & Tsai, 1991), an interpersonally oriented behavior therapy, is premised on the notion that the therapeutic environment is a social context that has some similarities to interpersonal situations that clients participate in outside of therapy. As such, clinically relevant behaviors in FAP are evoked and observed, then responded to in a manner consistent with the client's treatment goals. For behaviors to strengthen, displays of clinically relevant behaviors are responded to with natural reinforcers (e.g., expressions of warmth or support from the therapist). Instances of problematic behaviors are not reinforced and instead placed on an extinction schedule (e.g., the therapist may respond to complaints from the client by ignoring the client, in the event that complaining is a problem behavior of the client's that reliably leads to difficulties in important relationships). In this example, the therapist is acting as a participant–observer because he or she is part of the client's current environment, with one of the roles of the therapist being to notice clinically relevant behaviors.

Other examples in which therapists act as participant–observers include role-play situations. Role plays permit the therapist to observe the client's social behavior in a simulated environment that resembles aspects of his or her natural environment in which the problem occurs. As an example, a client might perform some type of target behavior (e.g., assertive action) in a simulated interpersonal context, with the therapist acting as a significant other might in this situation. After the role play, the therapist can provide the client with feedback on his or her performance and offer suggestions for how to improve the effectiveness of the behavior on future occasions.

CLOSING THE INITIAL INTERVIEW

Before closing the initial interview, it is often useful to provide the client with an opportunity to raise anything else he or she regards as important (e.g., "Is there anything that we have not discussed so far that would be important for me to know?"). It is also helpful to check in with the client to evaluate whether he or she has any questions (e.g., "Do you have any questions for me?"), or whether he or she has any discomfort associated with events that transpired during the session (e.g., "Is there anything that happened or came up during today's session that bothered you?"). In addition to providing the client with an opportunity to express him- or herself in these areas, such questions convey a spirit of collaboration and an interest in the client's welfare. It is also useful to summarize the main points raised during the session and anticipate the next steps in the process with the client (e.g., continued assessment, development of a formulation of the client's problem areas, and generation of a plan for therapy based on this formulation; Sundberg, Winebarger, & Taplin, 2002).

SUMMARY

In conducting initial behaviorally based assessments of a client's presenting complaints, it is often helpful for a therapist to do the following:

- Provide the client with a description of what to expect during the first few sessions, and work with the client to establish a warm and collaborative therapeutic relationship.
- Convey that CBT is an action-oriented therapy, and the client will have an active role in making important decisions about his or her treatment and in carrying out therapy-related activities.
- Broadly assess his or her functioning including strengths and relevant behavioral skills.

- Emphasize what the client does and describe clinically relevant behaviors in behavioral terms.
- Identify the circumstances or situations in which the client is more likely to engage in clinically relevant patterns of behavior.
- Explore the consequences that these behavior patterns typically produce, with attention given to the processes that might account for the maintenance of these behaviors over time.
- Assess the history associated with the client's problem areas; consider any biological conditions that might be associated with such behavior patterns.
- Evaluate the level and pervasiveness of impairment associated with clinically relevant behaviors.
- Consider and implement methods for assessing behaviors of clinical interest.
- Continue to develop, explore, and refine hypotheses concerning how clinically relevant behavior patterns might be related; that is, work toward the development of a case formulation.
- Inquire about the existence of other important areas that were not discussed before closing the initial interview, explore the client's overall sense of the therapeutic process thus far, and anticipate with the client what the next meeting or two might cover.

3

BEHAVIORAL CASE FORMULATION

As we briefly noted in the last chapter, a case formulation consists of the identification of a set of problem areas and the generation of hypotheses about factors associated with their development and maintenance (Eells, 1997). To arrive at these hypotheses, the therapist must first sift through and organize information gathered during the initial assessment phase. Although multiple determinants of behavior are generally assumed, behavioral case formulation approaches tend to emphasize operant and classical conditioning processes and social learning principles in the conceptualization of such influences. A clear understanding of these areas facilitates the therapist's development of a formulation of the client's difficulties that will, in turn, inform the therapist's selection of interventions applied in subsequent therapy sessions.

In this chapter, we primarily address the process of developing a behavioral case formulation. In so doing, we discuss approaches for reducing large amounts of information obtained during initial assessments to a set of problem areas to address in therapy. We also describe approaches for sharing and exploring the validity of this formulation with the client. In the next chapter (chap. 4), we discuss steps to translate the case formulation into a guide for making positive and sustained changes in behavior.

TAILORING ASSESSMENTS AND INTERVENTIONS TO THE CLIENT'S NEEDS, GOALS, AND STRENGTHS

Division 12 of the American Psychological Association (Society of Clinical Psychology) recently created a task force that, among other activities, developed a listing of psychological therapies that have empirical support for their efficacy (Chambless et al., 1996). Therapies included within this list were regarded as either "well-established" in terms of demonstrated efficacy in at least a couple of well-controlled clinical trials or "probably efficacious" on the basis of accumulated clinical trial data (see Chambless et al., 1998, for the criteria used in designating therapies as either "well-established" or "probably efficacious").

Empirically supported therapies (ESTs) are generally listed with reference to diagnostic category. There are now several empirically supported therapies that target single disorders such as major depressive disorder (A. T. Beck, Rush, Shaw, & Emery, 1979), obsessive-compulsive disorder (Steketee, 1993), or panic disorder (Barlow & Craske, 2000). The vast majority of therapies identified as efficacious are cognitive, behavioral, or cognitive behavioral in nature (Chambless et al., 1996).

Perhaps as a result of the demonstrated success of ESTs and standardized therapy protocols used in the treatment of specific disorders, the practice of therapy has increasingly become more protocol-driven. That is, psychological interventions are often assigned to clients on the basis of presenting symptomatology or diagnosis. The guiding rule is something like, "if the client has diagnosis x, then use treatment y," provided that an effective therapy exists for that diagnosis or collection of symptoms. The use of ESTs in this way often results in successful outcomes for persons whose needs are consistent with the therapeutic objectives of the treatment protocol (Tarrier & Calam, 2002).

ESTs often represent a good starting place for clients who have single disorders for which ESTs exist. Often, however, clients present with multiple problem areas. In these instances, there is little guidance regarding the order in which separate protocols should be applied, and insufficient evidence that such a sequential approach is useful. For some disorders such as depression, there is more than one EST (A. T. Beck et al., 1979; Lewinsohn, Antonuccio, Steinmetz-Breckenridge, & Teri, 1984; Martell, Addis, & Jacobson, 2001). It is also common for clients to present with problem areas for which there is no EST. In these instances, the EST list provides no guidance as to which interventions to select.

In contrast to the EST approach, which is variable centered (i.e., on diagnosis or symptom presentation) and protocol driven, the practice of behavioral assessment can be regarded as an approach to assessment that is tailored to the individual client (Hayes, Nelson, & Jarrett, 1986). Individualized assessments are performed in acknowledgement that each person is distinctly different from any other in terms of inherited biological factors and learning history, and that each person exists within a unique context. Diversity among persons is recognized and valued, and client assessments and intervention strategies are tailored to the therapy goals that are best suited to the client's problem areas and strengths. This is evident in the types of assessment modalities that therapists might use, or in the specific goals the client and therapist determine collaboratively to guide therapy.

When behavioral interventions are undertaken in cognitive behavior therapy (CBT), assessments tend to be performed throughout therapy. That is, the assessment process is ongoing, iterative, and adjustable, and can result in modifications of hypotheses concerning factors that influence client behavior. Repeated assessments are also useful to evaluate the impact of interventions and the maintenance of therapy gains over time.

An idiographic or formulation-based approach to therapy is often well-suited for clients with multiple problem areas. Such an approach also provides therapists with greater flexibility in designing interventions, as therapeutic techniques can be selected from many empirically supported protocols (Persons, Roberts, Zalecki, & Breechwald, 2006). The case-formulation approach also suggests alternatives in the event that initial interventions prove unhelpful.

When therapists make individualized decisions about therapeutic interventions for multiproblem clients based on idiographic assessment data, CBT principles, and empirically supported CBT interventions, the therapeutic outcomes are often similar to those reported for clients treated with ESTs for single disorders (Persons et al., 2006). Similarly, a number of studies suggest that treatment gains are often greatest when therapeutic interventions are tailored to the client's specific problem areas (e.g., Iwata et al., 1994; McKnight, Nelson, Hayes, & Jarrett, 1984; Nelson, Hayes, Jarrett, Sigmon & McKnight, 1987).

NARROWING DOWN THE CLIENT'S PROBLEM AREAS

In this section, we discuss phases of assessment. As we note, the initial assessments are quite broad in scope. As the clinical picture emerges, however, the focus increasingly narrows. This process is summarized in Exhibit 3.1.

Broadly Surveying Possible Problem Areas

In some respects, the initial assessment procedure can be likened to a funneling process (Hawkins, 1986). Within the first phase of assessment, for example, several potential problem areas might be screened. In addition to the client's chief complaint, broadband questionnaires (e.g., Brief Symptom

EXHIBIT 3.1
Phases of Clinical Assessment

- *Broad survey of problem areas.* This involves screening possible problem areas in addition to those acknowledged by the client. Broad-bandwidth assessments might be used, such as diagnostic interviews, questionnaires, or symptom surveys. Within this phase, problem areas are conceptualized in general terms, and decisions concerning therapy are generally rudimentary (e.g., "Is therapy indicated? If so, which therapeutic modality or modalities would be most appropriate?").
- *Description of the client's problem areas.* This consists of a conceptualization of the client's primary problem areas within descriptive categories (e.g., diagnostic labels, functional response classes, topographical descriptions of behavior). Ideas for therapeutic approaches are still fairly broad and focused on classes of intervention strategies that might be appropriate (e.g., exposure therapy, skills training).
- *Identification of behavior patterns to target in therapy.* This consists of the delineation of specific behavior patterns to address in therapy, the generation of hypotheses concerning behavioral principles that are relevant to the maintenance of particular behavior patterns (e.g., positive reinforcement, negative reinforcement), and the design of interventions.
- *Implementation of an intervention, and continuous evaluation of intervention effectiveness.* This includes an evaluation of the effectiveness of therapy as it is taking place. Assessment information gathered during this phase indicates whether behavior is changing as therapy progresses, and whether adjustments in the therapeutic approach should be undertaken to increase the likelihood of beneficial therapeutic outcomes.
- *Posttreatment assessment of behavior patterns targeted in therapy.* This consists of posttreatment assessments on behavior patterns targeted in therapy. These assessments might be performed immediately following the conclusion of therapy, and at spaced intervals thereafter (e.g., 1, 3, 6, and 12 months posttreatment). Their main purpose is to evaluate the maintenance of therapy gains over time and to detect instances when targeted behavior patterns reemerge or regain strength, suggesting the need for additional therapy or booster sessions.

Inventory; Derogatis, 1992) or diagnostic interviews (e.g., Structured Clinical Interview for *DSM*; First, Spitzer, Gibbon, & Williams, 1997b) might be administered. Such assessments might reveal problem areas that would otherwise go unnoticed. At this point in the assessment process, decisions concerning treatment are fairly general, such as whether therapy is indicated or whether a referral should be considered.

During the initial assessment phase, exchanges between the therapist and client are typically focused on the problem area itself. Generally, a client's chief complaint or problem area falls within one of the following general areas (Morrison, 1995): problems with thinking or thought content (i.e., cognitive or thought disorders); substance abuse; mood disturbance; general or specific anxiety; physical complaints; disruptions in occupational or social functioning; or personality problems. For clients with multiple problems, several of these areas might be pertinent.

During the early phases of assessment, it may be useful for the therapist to clarify with the client what aspects of his or her behavior are problematic.

Inquiries into this area are often fairly broad at first. The therapist, for example, might ask if the behavior is happening too much, is too intense, or goes on for too long, all of which might suggest behavioral excesses (Follette et al., 2000). If the client wishes to behave in a certain way but does not, this might suggest behavioral deficits, or perhaps reflect the influence of rules related to the consequences of behavior that, in turn, suppress subsequent action (e.g., "If I do ____, nothing good will come from it" or "If I do ____, I'll be humiliated"). Inquiries about the degree of impairment or distress associated with problematic behaviors (or nonengagement in behaviors that are pleasurable or rewarding) are also useful for gauging the severity of the problem area.

Transitioning From Broad Survey to Focal Assessments

In the second phase of assessment, the focus narrows. The end of this phase might include a definition of the client's problem area, a diagnosis, or some other means of classification (Hawkins, 1986). Once the general problem areas have been identified, intervention approaches might be considered in broad terms (e.g., exposure therapy, skills training, medication referral).

In the third phase, the assessment focus narrows further. The basic goals of this phase are the identification of specific target behaviors and the design of intervention strategies linked to assessment information (Hawkins, 1986). The selection of target behaviors, particularly among multiproblem clients, can be a challenge. Multiproblem clients, for example, often display some combination of the following:

- *behavioral excesses* (e.g., anxiety frequently experienced in situations that are objectively nonthreatening, substance misuse, reward-seeking behavior);
- *behavioral deficits* (e.g., impoverished coping skills, limited social skills);
- *difficulties in stimulus control* as evident by displays of inappropriate behavior in specific contexts (e.g., sexual provocativeness in inappropriate settings, inappropriate self-disclosures to strangers);
- *failures to display appropriate behavior in relevant contexts* (e.g., frequent failures to carryout responsibilities at work, refusal to perform household responsibilities);
- *excessively high or low performance standards* (e.g., perfectionism that interferes with task completion, frequent critical remarks directed at oneself); and
- *problems in self-regulation or control* (e.g., poorly controlled or impulsive behavior such as compulsive gambling or binge eating, frequent emotional outbursts).

During the first few phases of this process, it is often useful to consider the potential relevance of general principles of behavior as well as general scientific and clinical knowledge about the behavior patterns displayed by the client. These general, or *nomothetic*, principles can serve as guides for formulating client problems, suggesting ideas about possible influences on the client's behavior, and considering possible effective therapeutic strategies. These nomothetically informed ideas or hypotheses, if implemented, can be evaluated in the context of an ongoing idiographic assessment of the client. As the goals for therapy are also informed by the nature of the client's problem areas; their hypothesized maintaining influences; and the degree to which the problem areas are severe, cause impairment, or pose a risk to the client or others, ongoing assessments would ideally provide information relevant to each of these areas (Goldfried & Sprafkin, 1976).

The last two assessment phases are primarily concerned with the assessment process itself (Hawkins, 1986). In the fourth phase, the effects of interventions on target areas or behaviors are continuously assessed. The main data derived from these assessments might be the severity of the problem area, its frequency, or its pervasiveness. In the fifth phase, assessments are performed posttreatment to evaluate the maintenance of therapy gains over time. In chapter 4 we describe procedures and considerations related to these last two phases.

DEVELOPING THE CASE FORMULATION

In this section, we begin by highlighting basic assumptions that underlie a behavioral case formulation. We then provide a general framework for developing a case formulation grounded in behavior theories and principles. After this we include a section that describes how information collected during initial interviews can be integrated to yield a cohesive case formulation that, in turn, informs the subsequent selection of therapy interventions.

Assumptions Associated With Behavioral Formulations

From a behavioral perspective, there are several central assumptions about the client in relation to his or her problem areas. In behavior assessment and therapy, for example, the primary level of analysis is the whole person in interaction with his or her environment (Follette et al., 2000; Hayes, Strosahl, Bunting, Twohig, & Wilson, 2004; Martell et al., 2001). From this perspective, behavior and the environmental context are not seen as "parts" to be analyzed separately. Rather, behavior and context are analyzed as a unit (Martell et al., 2001).

To make this central concept clearer, we first describe what is meant by the term *context*. Context is the fabric within which behavior occurs, with the fabric defined by prior learning history, physiological makeup, and current situational determinants (the antecedents and consequences of action). Many of an individual's most important behaviors occur within him or her, such as one's thoughts, emotions, or bodily sensations. To understand these behaviors as well as overt behaviors, one needs to understand the contexts both within and outside of our skin. For these reasons one cannot separate "person" from "environment" when it comes to understanding and changing the behavior of another. As summarized by Martell et al. (2001): "A contextual view . . . leads us to focus on changing actions and contexts. We're interested in what people are doing . . . when they're doing it, how they're doing it, and what the consequences are" (p. 16).

A central focus of behavioral interventions has historically been on the current situational determinants of behavior. There are two primary reasons for this. First, volumes of experimental research indicate that behavior varies in accordance with the contexts within which it occurs, and consequences associated with behavior affect its future occurrence (e.g., Catania, 1984). Second, one cannot change the past. That is, one cannot eliminate a client's prior learning and the resultant effects that such learning has had on his or her current actions. Therapeutic interventions, however, can promote new learning. Similarly, there are aspects of one's physiological makeup that one cannot alter (e.g., genetic endowment). Accumulating evidence, however, indicates that brain structures and functions, and possibly gene expressions, can be modified by environmental events (Gottlieb, 1998; Heim & Nemeroff, 1999; Kandel, 1998) and that psychosocial therapies, when effective, can alter brain functioning such as neurochemistry and regional blood flow (Etkin, Pittinger, Polan, & Kandel, 2005).

Another important assumption of behavioral interventions involves the distinction between etiology, or the development of a psychological condition, and the maintenance of the condition over time. Historical factors that are responsible for the development of certain behavioral patterns are not necessarily responsible for the maintenance of those patterns. To understand influences on present-day behavior, one must look to influences found in current contexts. Such a view is consistent with the here-and-now focus of behavioral interventions.

Finally, problematic behavior often indicates the absence of alternative and more effective behaviors in the person's behavioral repertoire or the influence of contemporary environmental factors (e.g., environmental reinforcement for behavioral excesses, environmental suppression of infrequently occurring behaviors). Depending on the situation, therapy might emphasize the teaching of new behaviors (e.g., coping skills, more effective actions), alteration of current environments (e.g., eliminating reinforcement for frequently occurring problematic behaviors, increasing reinforcement opportunities for appropriate or effective behaviors), or modification of faulty thoughts or rules (e.g., helping individuals become aware of the actual contingencies associated with their behavior, supplying more accurate rules related to behavior in certain contexts). Additional assumptions associated with behavioral interventions and therapies can be found in Farmer and Nelson-Gray (2005).

A General Framework for the Development of a Case Formulation

Within CBT, the case-formulation approach involves the development of an in-depth and individualized formulation of the client and his or her problem areas. The formulation approach presented here involves the conceptualization of the client's particular problem areas along *functional* and *structural* domains (Nelson & Hayes, 1986; Persons & Tompkins, 1997). That is, this approach takes into account both the contextual features within which clinically relevant behavior occurs and the topographical (or descriptive) features of these behaviors.

Once established from pretreatment assessments, the therapist and client continually evaluate and refine the initial case formulation. That is, the case formulation is dynamic rather than static and is modified in accordance with new information or observations. The validity of the case formulation is indicated by the following:

- *The ability of the formulation to account for areas on the problem list.* Does the formulation yield a convincing and coherent story about the problem areas in terms of their emergence, maintenance, and manifestation in some situations more than others as well as the client's vulnerabilities that contributed to these problems (Persons, 1989)? If the formulation does not provide a logical account supported by existing client data, additional assessments might need to be performed or additional work on the formulation might be required.
- *The ability of the formulation to predict clinically relevant behavior.* A formulation also has validity to the extent that it helps the clinician accurately predict a client's behavior in specific situations. When new data appear that are inconsistent with the formulation, the clinician and client modify the formulation as needed. The validity of the case formulation, then, is subsequently evaluated in terms of its explanatory power, comprehensiveness, ability to account for items on the client's problem list, and accuracy in predicting future behavior in specific contexts (Persons et al., 2006; Wolpe & Turkat, 1985).
- *The client's reaction to the proposed formulation.* In the event that the client agrees with the formulation and supports it with additional examples or evidence, the validity of the formulation

is supported. If, however, the client disagrees with formulation, it is often useful to take time to understand what aspects of the formulation the client disagrees with, and how he or she would modify the formulation to make it more accurate (Persons, 1989; Wolpe & Turkat, 1985).

- *The effectiveness of the interventions on the basis of the formulation.* The case formulation provides guidance for the selection and adaptation of empirically supported interventions for his or her problem areas (Persons et al., 2006). The effectiveness of the intervention, in turn, is regarded as an indicator of the accuracy of the formulation. In instances in which the intervention is not effective, it is likely that either the formulation was incorrect or the intervention was inappropriate given the factors that established and maintained the behaviors targeted in therapy (Hayes & Follette, 1992). When the therapist believes the formulation was correct, an alternative intervention consistent with the formulation might be tried and evaluated. Alternatively, the therapist might reexamine the underlying hypotheses and assumptions on which the formulation is based.

In this section we provide a model of case formulation influenced by Persons (1989; Persons et al., 2006; Persons & Tompkins, 1997). In keeping with the focus of this book, greater emphasis is placed on contextual factors associated with problem behavior, and the influence of hypothetical cognitive constructs (e.g., schemas, core beliefs) deemphasized. We therefore organize our presentation according to the following formulation elements: (a) the problem list, (b) precipitants and activating situations, (c) hypothesized origins, (d) the working hypothesis, and (e) sharing and exploring the formulation with the client. The last four elements of the case formulation, (f) the treatment plan, (g) establishing a motivation for change and securing a commitment for action, (h) potential obstacles to effective therapy, and (i) procedures for evaluating the effectiveness of therapy, are discussed in detail in chapter 4 of this volume, in which we present an illustrative case example that integrates all elements of the case formulation. Components of this model of case formulation are presented in Exhibit 3.2.

The Problem List

The assessment process begins with the generation of a problem list, which is often defined by a set of topographically defined behaviors that might be subsequently targeted in therapy. This list is often substantially informed by the client's chief complaint but also may include other problem areas that emerge during the assessment process (e.g., from the clinical interview, self-report measures, or behavioral tasks such as the Behavioral Avoidance Test that assess an individual's reaction to feared stimuli).

EXHIBIT 3.2
Steps in the Development of a Behavioral Case Formulation

- *The problem list.* This list contains no more than 10 problematic behavior patterns to address in therapy.
- *Situational determinants of targeted problem areas.* This includes a description of antecedent conditions that reliably set the occasion for problem behavior, as well as the consequences which follow behavior that, in turn, influence its future frequency, intensity, or duration.
- *Hypothesized origins.* This includes a delineation of hypotheses concerning relevant biological characteristics and learning histories associated with the primary problem areas.
- *Working hypothesis.* This is an integrated and cohesive case formulation that addresses interrelations among the various problem areas.
- *Sharing and exploring the formulation.* This involves sharing the therapist's understanding of the client's problem areas, including ideas about factors associated with onset and maintenance of these problems. The client's agreement with formulation is also explored, with the formulation modified in accordance with client feedback.
- *Treatment plan.* This includes the provision of a rationale for the therapeutic interventions suggested, followed by an evaluation of the client's understanding of the rationale. Therapeutic goals in behavioral terms are also specified, as is the therapeutic framework, interventions, and between-session activities that comprise the suggested treatment approach.
- *Establishing a motivation for change and securing a commitment for action.* This involves nonconfrontational and empathic discussions with the client about the effects and consequences of the problem behavior. The therapist and client also explore the potential benefits of change.
- *Potential obstacles to effective therapy.* The therapist offers one or two hypotheses concerning potential therapy obstacles. This increases the likelihood that problems posed by potential obstacles are anticipated and avoided.
- *Procedures for evaluating of the effectiveness of therapy.* Movement toward measurable therapy goals is repeatedly assessed to determine whether sufficient progress is being made as therapy unfolds.

Persons and Tompkins (1997) suggested that problem lists typically consist of five to eight items, and should not contain more than 10 items or the list may become unwieldy. If there are more than 10 potential problem areas, the therapist might work with the client to prioritize potential areas so that therapy will be more focused. Although not all items on the problem list may be actively or explicitly targeted in therapy, it is often useful to monitor nontargeted areas throughout. Nontargeted areas may be discovered to be therapeutically relevant at a later date or subsequently found to rise and fall with changes in other problem areas actively targeted in therapy.

Persons and Tompkins (1997) also suggested that items on the list, whenever possible, be summarized with no more than a few words (e.g., depressed mood, panic attacks, binge eating, marital conflicts) and supplemented with a short topographical description of associated behavioral, cognitive, or mood components of the problem (e.g., frequently sleeps more than 10 hours per day and avoids social interactions, with accompanying negative self-referential thoughts such as "I'll never amount to anything" and feelings of emptiness). Additionally, to monitor change in the problem area as therapy progresses, the therapist needs to quantify the problem area in some way (e.g., frequency counts of problem, problem intensity ratings, scores on a relevant self-report measure, activity log record).

Even though not necessarily identified as problem areas by the client, other areas in which quality of life is adversely affected in some way (e.g., daily alcohol use, unemployment, health-related problems) might represent potential problem areas. These areas should initially be included in the list. An all-inclusive list allows the therapist to consider the wide range of potential factors that might be associated with the client's primary problem areas and may consequently aid in the development of working hypotheses about these areas (Persons, 1989).

Once a problem list is generated and the therapist and client agree on its content, the therapist should take time to consider possible common themes that run through these various problem areas (Persons, 1989). That is, the therapist might question, "What do all of these problems have in common?" Although the list might contain a number of diverse or topographically distinct behaviors (e.g., bingeing, purging, agoraphobic avoidance, dissociation, intentional self-injury), they might all have in common similar functional properties or relations (e.g., experiential avoidance). In addition to listing problem behaviors on the basis of topography, they can also be organized according to their associated functional properties, as behaviors that have similar functions can often be effectively addressed through the same therapeutic interventions.

Situational Determinants of Behavior: Precipitants, Activating Situations, and Behavioral Consequences

Precipitants and activating situations refer to antecedent conditions (e.g., discriminative stimuli, establishing operations) that set the occasion for behavior. Consequences are the events that follow behavior, which influence the frequency, intensity, or duration of future behavior in these situations (e.g., reinforcers or punishers).

Functional analyses, reviewed in chapter 2 of this volume, help identify antecedent and consequent events that influence behavior. Such analyses also facilitate the development of hypotheses concerning a particular form of problem behavior (Sturmey, 1996). The validity of the functional analysis and associated hypotheses concerning behavior will be evident from the outcomes of systematic tests of associated underlying assumptions.

Steps in generating a functional formulation of specific problem areas involve the following (Farmer & Latner, 2007):

- use of questionnaire measures and clinical interviews to obtain information about the form and function of problematic behaviors;

- ongoing self-monitoring and recording of target behaviors and their associated contexts in initial assessments and during therapy; and
- generation of hypotheses about the functions of problem behaviors and the exploration of the validity of these hypotheses with the client. '

In addition to immediate environmental contingencies, there is another class of behavioral determinants that influence behavior. These are verbal rules that specify associations between antecedent events and behaviors, behaviors and consequent events, or a combination of these (Skinner, 1969). In fact, it is quite possible that for most individuals, behavior is more strongly influenced by contingency-specifying rules than actual environmental contingencies.

When verbal rules function as an antecedent determinant of behavior, such behavior is *rule-governed*. Examples of rules that could influence behavior include the following: "If I make myself vomit, I won't get fat," "If I have a few drinks, I'll be less anxious and more funny around others," and "When someone acts like they want to get to know me, they actually are looking for ways to take advantage of me."

Verbal rules in some circumstances are analogous to self-efficacy expectations and outcome expectations in social cognitive theory (Bandura, 1986). *Self-efficacy expectations* are a set of beliefs about one's ability to perform certain behaviors. Such expectations result from personal knowledge concerning actual behavioral deficits. Alternatively, such expectations might be erroneous and underestimate one's actual behavioral capacities. In this latter case, an individual might incorrectly conclude that there are deficits in his or her behavioral repertoire because of faulty early learning (e.g., frequent statements by the client's father that convey the idea "You'll never amount to anything") or inaccurate feedback concerning performance by others (e.g., overly harsh and unrealistic evaluations by a job supervisor). Regardless of the accuracy of one's thoughts about his or her behavioral efficacy, when self-efficacy is low, the likelihood that a person engages in a particular behavior in a certain context is likewise low (e.g., "Why should I try? I know I can't do it").

Outcome expectations refer to a person's estimate that a given behavior will result in certain outcomes. In social cognitive theory, positive outcome expectations function as incentives for behavior (e.g., "If I try, I will succeed" or "If I try, I will get what I want"). Negative outcome expectations function as disincentives and reduce the likelihood that an individual will perform behavior in certain contexts (e.g., "Why should I try? No good will come from it").

Similar to both efficacy and outcome expectations, rules suggest whether certain behaviors are more or less likely under certain circumstances on the basis of consequences associated with actions referred to in the rule statements. Rule statements also have some similarity to A. T. Beck's notion of *primary assumptions* (also referred to as *personal rules* or *core beliefs*) in his cognitive model of therapy:

> During his [sic] developmental period, each individual learns rules or formulas by which he attempts to "make sense" of the world. These formulas determine how the individual organizes perceptions into cognitions, how he sets goals, how he evaluates and modifies his behavior, and how he understands or comes to terms with events in his life. In essence, these basic assumptions form a personal matrix of meaning and value. (A. T. Beck et al., 1979, p. 244)

A review of chapter 12 ("Depressogenic Assumptions") of A. T. Beck et al.'s (1979) landmark work reveals that core assumptions often take the form of rule statements that specify a behavior, a consequence associated with that behavior, an antecedent condition in the presence of which a behavior will produce a specified outcome, or some combination of these (e.g., "If I am nice [suffer for others, appear bright and beautiful], bad things [divorce, poorly behaved children] won't happen to me"). Although there are key differences among behavioral and cognitive accounts of these processes (see Farmer & Nelson-Gray, 2005, for a review), there is a general consensus that rules or assumptions about behavior have significant influence as to whether behavior will be performed in some circumstances and how it is evaluated.

As we discussed in the chapter 2, establishing operations also can affect the likelihood of behavior by altering the reinforcing properties associated with engaging in certain forms of behavior. If, for example, one has not had anything to drink for a long time, the reinforcing properties associated with drinking water or other beverages are much greater. Conversely, if one has just consumed large amounts of water, the act of drinking more water would likely be experienced as aversive. Many forms of problematic behavior are more likely following certain establishing operations (e.g., binge eating after a period of food deprivation, purging following the consumption of large amounts of food, aggressive actions when feeling angry in response to a frustrating event, consumption of a large amount of alcohol when feeling acutely stressed).

When therapists assess precipitants and activating situations with the client, it is often useful to evaluate whether there have been any changes in how the problem has been manifested over time, the antecedent conditions under which it occurs, or the short- and long-term consequences that follow problem behavior. Such assessments will clarify the evolution of the behavior over time as well as the range of influences that have functioned to shape and maintain it.

Hypothesized Origins

Hypothesized origins refer to what we described as person variables in the last chapter; that is, one's biological characteristics and learning history as related to the primary problem areas. These person variables often constitute predisposing or vulnerability factors associated with the development, reoccurrence, or maintenance of problem areas. Clarifying the client's predisposing factors might illuminate why this particular person developed the problem in question, whereas someone else under similar circumstances would not have developed the problem.

Biological characteristics include genetic predispositions, temperament, and other physiological characteristics that might have some relevance for the problem area (e.g., normal effects of aging on cognitive abilities, the effects of disease). Several psychological conditions, for example, have been observed to run in families, a finding that has often been interpreted as indicating a genetic influence (Rhee et al., 2001). Similarly, variations in temperament are often regarded as the result of biological influences (Fowles, 2001) and also observed to run in families (Eysenck, 1983). There is also an indication that variations in temperament partially account for variations in the sensitivity or responsiveness to rewarding and punishing outcomes (Farmer & Nelson-Gray, 2005), factors that might be considered when developing hypotheses about the client's behavior and designing interventions.

Aspects of the client's early learning history also frequently account for the development of current problem areas. Among such potential influences might be modeling experiences, social and cultural values or practices, or a history of reinforcement for engagement in the problematic behaviors. Individuals with more chronic patterns of psychological disorder often have more extensive learning histories, behavioral deficits, and behavioral excesses linked to the problem area. Persons with some forms of personality disorder, for example, often report histories of significant interpersonal loss, neglect, rejection, or abuse (Zanarini et al., 1997). Resultant behavioral deficits or excesses as well as long-standing vulnerabilities associated with such histories might be targeted, particularly if longer forms of therapy are contemplated.

One way to initiate the collaborative process of developing a formulation and, more specifically, to generate hypotheses about the origins of the problem, is to ask the client what his or her thoughts are about how the problem came about. By the time a client comes to therapy, it is likely that he or she has spent a good deal of time thinking about the problem. Questions for exploring this area include the following:

- "When did you first notice this problem?"
- "What was going on in your life when this first occurred?"
- "Do you have ideas about how this problem came about?"
- "How have people responded when this problem is present?"

- "Can you recall a time when this problem helped or benefited you in some way?"
- "Are there other people you know who also have this problem?"
- "Once this problem first occurred, did it have any lasting effects on you? If so, what are they?"

Working Hypothesis

The working hypothesis represents the heart of the case formulation and seeks to tie together each of the client's problem areas into an integrated and cohesive formulation (Persons, 1989). The formulation ideally addresses the interrelations among the various problem areas through the consideration of similarities in etiological, predisposing, precipitating, and maintaining factors.

In relation to behavioral interventions in CBT specifically, a working hypothesis seeks to explain the function of problematic behavior for the individual and to specify the forms or topographies of problematic behavior that share similar functions. The degree of distress or impairment associated with these problem areas might also be specified, as these considerations have implications for what treatment setting or treatment modalities are most appropriate for the client as well as the appropriate duration of treatment. Treatment settings refer to whether the client would best benefit from weekly outpatient sessions or more frequent contacts, if a crisis plan should be developed and whether it can be successfully carried out on an outpatient basis, or whether inpatient or other forms of institutional care (e.g., day hospital) are required. Treatment modalities are exemplified by individual therapies (e.g., weekly outpatient CBT, supportive therapy), group or milieu therapies, biological interventions (e.g., medications, electroconvulsive therapy), or some combination of these.

Psychiatric diagnoses can inform the case formulation and treatment decisions, particularly if there is a high degree of homogeneity of determinants of behaviors that define the diagnosis across persons (Haynes, 1986). Given that diagnostic categories are often defined by collections of covarying behavior, cognition, and emotion, they are not necessarily incompatible with cognitive or behavioral approaches to assessment. Diagnostic concepts, however, are nomothetic. That is, they are group or variable centered, whereas behavioral assessments within CBT tend to be idiographic, or centered on the individual and his or her uniqueness (Nelson-Gray & Paulson, 2003). A diagnosis without an accompanying individualized formulation leaves the therapist with little guidance on how to best provide symptom relief (Persons, 1986). Consequently, from a CBT perspective, a diagnosis is largely regarded as a supplement to, not a substitute for, an individually focused case formulation that includes consideration of contextual factors associated with the problem area.

Similar to psychiatric diagnoses, psychological test findings are a useful supplement to, but not a substitute for, an individualized case formulation. Test findings can, for example, be used to validate a client's diagnosis or aspects of the formulation. Tests, such as self-report measures, can also be used to index pretreatment functioning in clinically relevant areas and to assess any progress or gains during treatment as well as maintenance of therapeutic gains posttreatment.

EXPLORING THE PROBLEM FORMULATION WITH THE CLIENT

Behavioral assessment and intervention are collaborative endeavors in which the client and therapist work together to understand and ameliorate problems that are important to the client. As the case formulation serves as a road map for subsequent therapeutic interventions, it is important for the therapist to give the client a clear description of this road map as well as the opportunity to add to it or modify it. The following are several tasks for the therapist related to communicating the formulation to the client: (a) presenting the formulation in an open and collaborative manner, (b) distinguishing the client from the problem, (c) using effective communication strategies, and (d) dealing effectively with the issue of diagnosis.

Presenting the Formulation in an Open and Collaborative Manner

When exploring a formulation of the problem area with the client, the therapist may find it useful to describe his or her understanding of the etiology of the problem area; any hypothesized predisposing factors; a description of the development of the problem over time; and how manifestations of the problem may have changed in terms of expression, antecedent triggers, or consequences. Primary emphasis, however, should be placed on factors that currently function to maintain problems (Wolpe & Turkat, 1985).

When the therapist offers his or her views, it is ideally done in a manner that conveys openness to exploration. The presentation should be done at a level easily understandable to the client, and the use of technical terms (e.g., negative reinforcement, automatic thoughts) should be kept to a minimum. Often, however, a formulation that is grounded in core CBT principles and concepts will require the use of associated terminology. When using technical terms, the therapist should define key concepts clearly and use actual examples from the client's life to illustrate their application. Educating the client about the rationale of behavioral approaches to treatment is, after all, part of the therapeutic process.

If the client disagrees with the formulation, the therapist must take great care to clarify why before proceeding (Wolpe & Turkat, 1985). Given that the formulation is based on a wide variety of information obtained during pretreatment assessments, it is likely that disagreements will be based on small details that can be easily clarified rather than on larger, differing views of core assumptions.

Distinguishing the Client From the Problem

When reviewing the formulation, the therapist should distinguish the client from the problem. Doing so conveys to the client the idea that the problem area, not the client him- or herself, is the focus of therapy. Such an approach often conveys that the client's problems are understandable and that both the client and the therapist are united to solve the problem (Wolpe & Turkat, 1985). It is also important for the therapist to continuously seek feedback regarding the client's understanding of the formulation and his or her views of the formulation's accuracy.

Using Effective Communication Strategies

To facilitate the client's understanding of the formulation, the therapist may find it helpful to supply a diagram that summarizes the overall model, or to develop a diagram while discussing the formulation (Persons & Tompkins, 1997). Such a diagram can take several forms, such as a time line that represents the onset of critical events, or a functional representation of the client's problem behavior (as exemplified in chap. 2, this volume). Ideally, the emphasis of the diagram should be on factors that can be changed or modified as a result of therapy, assets of the client's that can be strengthened, or a combination of these. In addition, once a formulation has been developed and discussed, it is often useful to check the client's understanding by asking him or her to explain it (Persons, 1989). One way to do this is to ask a client to imagine that he or she is discussing his or her problem and formulation with a friend or family member.

Dealing Effectively With the Issue of Diagnosis

A question often arises as to whether the labels ascribed to the client's problem areas, such as diagnoses, should be shared with the client. Often a client can feel significant relief and optimism if the therapist tells him or her the name of their problem (Addis & Carpenter, 2000). Some diagnostic labels, however, are not always appropriate to share. In particular, personality disorder diagnostic labels might not be appropriate to share given the many conceptual and psychometric difficulties associated with these concepts (Farmer, 2000; Farmer & Chapman, 2002) in addition to their associated stigmatizing properties. The label that the therapist provides the client for his or her problem does not necessarily need to be a diagnostic label. Rather, the label can refer to the collection of behaviors the client exhibits that will be targeted in therapy (e.g., chronic pain, excessive stress, intentional self-harm, marital distress).

SUMMARY

When developing a behavioral case formulation, it is often useful for therapists to do the following:

- Broadly assess the client's functioning and then continuously narrow the focus of assessments as problem areas become clearer.
- Develop a problem list that identifies behavior patterns likely to be addressed within therapy.
- Consider basic behavioral principles that might apply to the client's problem areas, particularly with reference to behavior maintenance.
- Give thought to how behavior patterns on the problem list and current contexts interact as a unit and emphasize this level of analysis when developing the case formulation.
- Share with the client the working hypothesis of his or her problem area and explore his or her perceptions concerning the accuracy and completeness of this hypothesis.
- Continuously evaluate and refine the case formulation, particularly with reference to whether the formulation accounts for areas on the client's problem list, predicts clinically relevant behavior, and explains the effectiveness of therapeutic interventions.
- Consider how problem areas will be assessed before, during, and after treatment, as assessment data will provide useful information concerning the effectiveness of therapy and the maintenance of therapy gains once the active phase of therapy has concluded.

4

TREATMENT PLANNING

In some respects, the process of treatment planning and formulation is like an exercise in problem solving and decision making (Kanfer & Busemeyer, 1982). Whereas problem solving involves coming up with alternative approaches for responding to problems, decision-making processes involve using rules or guides to make selections among available alternatives. When viewed from this perspective, the client and therapist first work together to identify problems. Upon reaching consensus as to the nature of the problem areas, the therapist and client decide collaboratively how to best approach these areas on the basis of a detailed understanding of the client's problems and knowledge of the most effective treatment guidelines available.

In this chapter, we outline guidelines for translating the case formulation into a plan for therapy. This discussion includes suggestions for collaboratively establishing therapy goals, guidelines for prioritizing problem areas identified by the client, and considerations for deciding which interventions to select. We also address related issues such as determining an appropriate framework for therapy, steps in the collaborative exploration of the therapy plan with the client, establishing or enhancing client motivation and commitment for therapy, and identifying and preparing for potential obstacles to therapy. This is followed by an overview of methods for evaluating intervention effectiveness. We conclude this chapter with a detailed illustrative case example.

INITIAL STEPS IN DEVELOPING
A COLLABORATIVE PLAN FOR THERAPY

A number of factors influence which interventions are optimal for a particular client with a given problem area. Among these are characteristics of target behaviors, characteristics of the client, social–environmental factors, diagnosis, treatment history, and characteristics of interventions (Haynes, 1986). Client characteristics include motivation for therapy, goals for treatment, personal resources and skills, and thoughts about whether the social environment will positively support therapeutic change. Behaviors that compete with therapeutic goals may also reduce the likelihood of successful treatment and thus should be targeted in therapy. Social–environmental factors are important to consider, particularly if the problem behavior coincides with particular social or environmental contexts. When situational influences on behavior are apparent, they might be addressed as part of the overall intervention program. Characteristics of interventions include features that define the interventions as well as associated qualities such as cost-efficacy; side effects; and the magnitude, generalizability, and maintenance of treatment effects.

In this section, we provide general guidelines associated with developing a collaborative plan for therapy that uses behavioral interventions within a cognitive behavior therapy (CBT) framework. In doing so, we are cognizant that there is currently no single method or empirically supported approach for integrating an array of assessment data and, from this, designing an effective intervention. We also note that prior to coming to therapy, clients often have already tried many ways of coping with the problem. If a client has been in therapy before, it is often useful to clarify why he or she previously entered therapy, what issues therapy primarily addressed, how these issues were approached in therapy, and to what effect. Interventions that were previously tried and appropriately administered but failed to produce desirable outcomes might be considered only after alternative interventions are tried.

Reaching Consensus on the Goals of Therapy

In planning treatment, it is important for the therapist and client to clarify and explicitly agree on the goals of therapy. Goals may include the content focus of therapy (e.g., what topics will be of central importance), which target behaviors to pursue, which interventions or strategies will best realize therapy goals, the within-session structure of therapy, engagement in therapy-related activities in between sessions, the duration and frequency of therapy, and the use of follow-up or maintenance sessions. Reaching agreement in these areas not only establishes an implicit therapy contract but also ascribes the client's and therapist's roles, tasks, and responsibilities (Otto, Reilly-Harrington, Kogan, & Winett, 2003).

For clients who participate in therapies that have a cognitive behavior focus, therapists may find it useful to discuss up front that therapy will largely focus on current behaviors and problems areas and the rationale for this emphasis. The expected number of sessions to reach therapy goals is also important to review. Finally, CBT should be described as an active approach to therapy within which the therapist and client participate together.

When the client's goals for therapy are not explicitly conveyed by his or her chief complaint, therapists can ask about how therapy might ideally be helpful. Questions such as the following, taken from Persons (1989, p. 327), can help the client identify goals:

- "How will you know when you have solved this problem?"
- "How might your life be different when you solve this problem?"
- "What will you do differently once this problem is solved?"

Suggesting Areas to Address That the Client Does Not Acknowledge as Problems

Although clients often come to therapy for assistance with relatively specific problems (e.g., mood disturbance, lingering effects of trauma), therapists sometime learn about other behaviors that are problematic. Examples include suicidal behavior, self-injury, binge–purge behavior, substance abuse, or other behaviors that interfere with the client's quality of life. When such behaviors are evident, the therapist might highlight them, assess their impact on the client's functioning, and ascertain whether the client wishes to change these behaviors. Clients may not wish to change some problem behaviors (e.g., non-life-threatening substance abuse), and it might be reasonable for these behaviors not to be targeted in therapy. In other cases, some behaviors (e.g., suicide attempts or self-injury) are likely to be life threatening or to significantly interfere with the quality of the client's life, and the therapist might make them high priority treatment targets out of necessity. Generally, the client is more likely to accept the inclusion of these behavioral targets if the therapist is able to provide a cogent rationale for doing so.

The Overarching Therapeutic Goals of Developing Psychological Flexibility, Freedom, and Effectiveness

Whenever possible, therapists should emphasize in therapy the development of effective behaviors or behavioral repertoires and place less emphasis on the elimination of behaviors (Goldiamond, 1974; Hawkins, 1986). This approach is in contrast to other approaches that primarily emphasize eliminating something, such as emotional distress, rather than acquiring something.

Behaviorally oriented clinicians, in contrast, often find it helpful to build behavioral repertoires and skills that provide the client with more behavioral options and greater flexibility for responding to situations that arise (Hayes & Strosahl, 2004; Linehan, 1993a). Rather than eliminate emotional distress, for example, a therapeutic goal might be to assist the client in coping more effectively when distress is present. A benefit of building behavioral repertoires (e.g., coping skills) is that it often lessens the frequency, intensity, or duration of the problem area (e.g., emotional distress). By strategically developing or strengthening certain behavioral repertoires, therapists simultaneously provide the client with more behavioral options and greater flexibility for responding that often result in the reduction or elimination of the target problem.

Albert Bandura (1986, p. 39), the primary developer of social learning and social cognitive theories, regards freedom as having choices among options, with available options determined by prior learning experiences. As the client gains more behavioral options and, correspondingly, greater flexibility, his or her freedom also becomes that much greater. Behavioral interventions in CBT seek to increase an individual's freedom by providing him or her with more skills, abilities, and options for responding to the events in his or her life than were previously available (Kazdin, 1984). Multiple abilities, capabilities, and behavioral alternatives increase an individual's opportunities for greater flexibility in responding and increase likelihood for effective action across varying contexts. Similarly, therapists often attempt to facilitate clients' sense of personal freedom by helping them understand contextual factors that influence their behavior, articulate their goals and values, and realize that problem behaviors or dysfunctional ways of coping are often inconsistent with these goals and values (Kazdin, 1984).

Prioritizing Problem Areas

Most clinicians agree that high-risk behaviors, such as suicidal or parasuicidal behaviors, should receive immediate priority. In her description of dialectical behavior therapy (DBT), for example, Linehan (1993a) outlined a schema for prioritizing behaviors to attend to during individual therapy sessions. Her within-session hierarchical framework during the first stage of therapy prioritizes treatment targets in terms of their potential to threaten the life of the client, disrupt or reduce the effectiveness of therapy, or interfere with the client's ability to attain a reasonable quality of life.

In Linehan's (1993a) hierarchical arrangement of Stage 1 treatment targets, behaviors regarded as most urgent or of the highest priority are *life-threatening behaviors*, including suicidal behaviors and nonsuicidal self-injury. Examples of behaviors that fall within this class are suicide crisis behaviors, suicide attempts, suicidal ideation and communication, suicide-related expectancies and beliefs, and nonsuicidal self-injury. On similar footing in terms of urgency and priority are homicidal plans or indications of aggressive, neglectful, or otherwise abusive actions toward individuals who are unable to protect themselves (e.g., children, elderly adults).

The next class in her schema consists of *therapy-interfering behaviors* on the part of the client or therapist (Linehan, 1993a). Examples of such behaviors for the client include frequent missed sessions, chronic lateness, strong emotional outbursts or aggressive behavior directed at the therapist, or failure to complete homework assignments; examples of behaviors for the therapist include routinely starting sessions late or frequently gazing at the clock during sessions. Behaviors that fall within this class would likely undermine therapy, result in therapy being less effective, lead to therapist burnout, or diminish the interest that the therapist or client has in continuing therapy.

The third class consists of *quality-of-life interfering behaviors* and includes substance abuse, unprotected sexual behavior, financial problems, criminal activities, and dysfunctional interpersonal behaviors. Finally, the last class consists of *behavioral skills to increase*. In DBT, skills training usually takes place within a separate skills training group. Individual therapy sessions, however, might facilitate the integration of these skills into the client's daily life.

Linehan (1993a; see also Koerner & Linehan, 1997) proposed other classes of treatment targets within her sequential stage model. Once the Stage 1 treatment targets have been adequately addressed the focus of therapy shifts to Stage 2 targets, or *posttraumatic stress responses*. Among the areas addressed within this stage are the facilitation of acceptance that trauma or abuse occurred, lessening of self-blame and stigmatization associated with trauma and abuse, and attenuation of intrusive stress responses (e.g., through exposure-based therapies for trauma, as exemplified by Foa & Rothbaum, 1998). Because therapy for trauma is often emotionally evocative and somewhat difficult for the client, it is important to ensure that the likelihood for risk has been substantially reduced and coping skills have been enhanced as a result of Stage 1 interventions. Other Stage 2 targets might include work on reducing emotional suffering, addressing "quiet desperation," and dealing with unresolved grief.

Stage 3 interventions in DBT are geared toward ordinary problems in living (e.g., problems with work, relationship difficulties), with a focus on increasing self-respect, as evident by the ability to value, believe, validate, trust, and cherish oneself. Any remaining issues associated with quality of life are also addressed. Finally, Stage 4 specifically addresses the sense of incompleteness or emptiness that many persons experience, synthesis and integration of many areas of life (e.g., past with present, present with future, self with others), and acceptance of reality the way that it is. An outcome associated with success in these areas would be the ability to experience a sustained sense of joy and freedom.

The stages of therapy in DBT we have outline are provided as examples for how a therapist might think about sequencing therapy in relation to treatment targets over time. Even though the specifics of this approach may not be applicable to all clients with multiple problems, some sort of hierarchical and sequential approach is usually indicated.

With clients who have fewer problem areas or problems of a more acute nature, other guidelines for target behavior selection might be considered (Hawkins, 1986; Nelson & Hayes, 1986b). These include selecting behaviors for attention in therapy that

- are given priority by the client,
- are widely regarded as desirable by others,
- have the greatest likelihood of being reinforced in natural environments,
- facilitate entry into natural environments in which other important behaviors might be taught or reinforced (e.g., hygiene; appropriate conduct for maintaining job),
- have a high degree of general utility across situations or contexts (e.g., problem-solving skills),
- maximize the flexibility of the client's behavioral repertoire and promote long-term benefit to the person,
- belong to a similar functional response class as the primary problem behaviors, and
- occur lower in a skill hierarchy (i.e., foundation skills) and are necessary to establish before modifying skills higher in a hierarchy.

DECIDING WHICH INTERVENTIONS TO SELECT

In chapter 3 of this volume, we reviewed the concept of empirically supported therapies (ESTs) and noted that the majority of ESTs are referenced to specific diagnostic concepts. When clients have specific and limited problem areas for which an EST exists, and when therapists' select an appropriate EST for such clients, therapeutic outcomes are often very positive (Tarrier & Calam, 2002).

Whereas disorder-specific EST protocols might be useful for individuals who have a single and specific problem area or diagnosis, they might be less applicable to individuals who have multiple problem areas. With such clients, a therapist might elect to administer several relevant ESTs simultaneously or sequentially; however, such an approach can be cumbersome and have many redundancies. There is also little in the way of guidance as to which problem area to target first (Persons, Roberts, Zalecki, & Breechwald, 2006).

Additionally, some clients who have a specific problem area with an associated EST do not require all therapy components in the EST protocol. A client with panic disorder, for example, may not engage in shallow and rapid breathing when anxious. For such an individual, treatment components on breathing retraining may not be particularly relevant or helpful. As this example illustrates, therapy selection based on diagnosis alone might result in the application of therapeutic approaches that are not optimally effective, or might result in the application of more therapy interventions than are necessary (Eifert, Schulte, Zvolensky, Lejuez, & Lau, 1997). Ultimately, this may result in lengthy and costly treatment interventions, when a briefer and more targeted course of therapy could have been equally effective. In addition, when the relevance of particular interventions is not apparent to the client, he or she may lose interest in or become pessimistic with regard to therapy, and consequently drop out prematurely.

Finally, many problem areas do not have an associated EST. In these circumstances, a strict empirically informed protocol-driven approach is not available. When confronted with such a situation, a therapist is left with several options: (a) do not treat the client, (b) refer the client to another provider, (c) use a collection of techniques or components of ESTs for problems that are similar to those of the client, or (d) employ evidence-based cognitive and behavioral principles in the development of a client formulation that subsequently informs the selection of interventions. We suggest that strategies (c) and (d), when combined, are more likely than other options to address important idiographic features of the client and his or her life context that influence treatment outcome. In essence, behavioral case formulation and treatment planning are *principle-driven* rather than protocol-driven endeavors.

In this section, we highlight two principle-driven case formulation approaches to the selection of interventions: clinical functional analysis and the case formulation-driven modular approach. These approaches contrast with the client-matching-to-EST approach as they are both idiographic and guided by behavioral and cognitive principles, or formulation driven, and not exclusively protocol driven. Although we present these approaches separately, they are not necessarily exclusive and can be combined to produce a formulation that takes into account both functional and topographical aspects of the client's problem areas.

The Role of Functional Analyses in the Selection of Interventions

Findings from a clinical functional analysis or behavioral chain analysis (Koerner & Linehan, 1997; Linehan, 1993a) are examples of approaches that are ideal to identify the sequence of events that precede and follow problem behavior. Knowledge of such influences can, in turn, inform the design of an intervention that is conceptually linked to the assessment findings.

The components of a clinical functional analysis are reviewed in chapter 2 of this volume. Procedurally, the therapist and client might first work together to clearly identify links or sequences between antecedent events and problem behaviors as well as immediate and delayed reactions to the problem behavior displayed by the client and others. Once these have been defined in reasonable detail, specific junctures in the sequence are identified in which opportunities exist for alternative responses that might, in turn, produce more desirable outcomes and avert conditions that occasion the problem behavior (Koerner & Linehan, 1997).

Findings from such analyses can also be used to facilitate a cost–benefit analysis of specific problem behaviors. With this approach, the cost of current problem behaviors is analyzed in terms of their consequences, both positive and negative, and the extent to which such outcomes are consistent with long-term goals or values. Once established, alternative behavioral routes are explored that have a high likelihood of producing similar reinforcers as problematic behaviors, but without the associated negative costs. By building competencies and behavioral repertoires, the likelihood that therapy will produce lasting gains is much greater, as effective behaviors should be instrumental in producing their own reinforcing consequences that function to maintain them over time.

As suggested by Haynes (1986), the selection of interventions based on a clinical functional analysis should be strongly influenced by a client's therapeutic goals, as interventions that result in outcomes incongruent with the client's goals are often doomed to fail. A well-designed intervention takes into account the client's skill and ability level and other strengths and resources that he or she brings to the therapeutic situation (Haynes, 1986). Strengths can facilitate the acquisition of more adaptive behaviors, or help the client succeed in environmental contexts that are different from those in which the problem emerges.

Evaluating the Functional Similarity of Different Forms of Problem Behavior

Upon performing a set of functional analyses for different problem areas, a therapist might notice that several behaviors that a client engages in (e.g., excessive and ritualistic house cleaning, binge eating, excessive alcohol consumption, dissociation) often occur under similar circumstances (e.g., when feeling stressed, after a disagreement with a partner) and produce similar outcomes (e.g., a reduction in the intensity or frequency of unpleasant thoughts or emotions). Such diverse behaviors might constitute a *functional response class*. Functional responses classes consist of groups of behaviors that, although different in form or expression, share functional relatedness as they are often influenced by similar classes of environmental variables, including the outcomes or consequences they produce (Farmer & Nelson-Gray, 2005; Follette, Naugle, & Linnerooth, 2000).

Experiential avoidance, for example, has been described as a functional response class characterized by an unwillingness to remain in contact with private experiences such as painful emotions, thoughts, or memories, as evidenced by a tendency to actively alter these experiences through some other behavior (Hayes, Wilson, Gifford, Follette, & Strosahl, 1996). Behaviors used to alter these experiences (e.g., substance use, dissociation) are often effective as they attenuate or terminate these experiences and are consequently maintained over time as a result of the relief they produce (negative reinforcement) or other associated reinforcing outcomes (e.g., the experience of euphoria in the case of substance use, which might positively reinforce drug consumption). Farmer and Nelson-Gray (2005) and Follette et al. (2000) describe several examples of functional response classes.

An awareness of the similarity in functions that multiple problem behavior patterns serve can help pinpoint the core processes that maintain their occurrence. These similar core processes, in turn, can be addressed therapeutically through the same intervention strategies. If common functions exist among diverse patterns of behavior, it is also important to establish what, if any, alternative behaviors are present in the client's repertoire that have similar functions and are more adaptive, health promoting, and consistent with the client's personal goals. As therapy works to reduce or eliminate the problematic behavior patterns, adaptive alternative behaviors might be targeted for strengthening. When the client's repertoire is deficient of behavioral alternatives, therapy might be focused on teaching new skills that can eventually substitute for problematic behavior patterns.

A Case-Formulation-Driven Modular Approach to Intervention Selection

A modular approach to intervention selection has been described as a strategy for developing an individualized approach to treatment planning based on assessment information (Hennin, Otto, & Reilly-Harrington, 2001; Overholser, 2003; Van Brunt, 2000). With this approach, empirically supported CBT interventions are dismantled into their associated components. The selection of CBT modules for clients is individualized, with selection based on pretreatment assessments, a consideration of the client's needs, and the client's therapy goals.

Compared with an EST protocol-driven approach, this case-formulation approach is more individualized and flexible. Rather than using all treatment components within a single EST protocol, a therapist instead uses intervention strategies from several different EST protocols that have particular relevance for the client's problem areas (Persons et al., 2006). Similarly, intervention decisions might be guided by nomothetic formulations and approaches that most closely correspond to the unique characteristics of the individual client (Haynes, Kaholokula, & Nelson, 1999; Persons et al., 2006).

When a client's depression is associated with social withdrawal and corresponding social skills deficits, for example, effective social skills training interventions might be selected.

Prior to selecting appropriate modules, the therapist ideally performs detailed assessments within a given area (e.g., does a client who is depressed demonstrate highly negative views of self, excessive worry, social skills deficits, problem-solving deficits, nonengagement in previously enjoyable activities, or some combination of these?). From these assessments, a problem list is developed that outlines areas tied to the overall problem area that is of greatest concern. Following the collection of pretreatment assessment information, a treatment approach is constructed by assembling modules that are relevant to the client's needs and goals, with between-session therapeutic activities (e.g., self-monitoring of target areas, repeated assessments of areas related to treatment goals, therapy related homework) as the "glue" that holds the modules together and provides continuity across treatment elements (Van Brunt, 2000).

If, for example, a depressed client displays negativistic views of self and future, he or she might be assigned to a cognitive restructuring model. Another client who is depressed and displays primary deficits in the area of social skills might undergo a skills training module. Similarly, a third depressed client, who has become withdrawn and stays at home and worries a good part of the day might undergo a therapy program that initially emphasizes worry reduction and behavioral activation. Rather than receiving a complete CBT treatment package that might involve cognitive restructuring, social skills training, and behavioral activation, a client would receive only those components that are most appropriate for him or her from an all-inclusive treatment package.

Some General Intervention Guidelines

Within chapters 5 through 10, we describe several different behavioral interventions and the circumstances under which they are most appropriate and likely to be effective. In this section, we briefly discuss some general considerations in the design of therapies that use behavioral interventions. Behaviorally oriented therapists should, however, seek to establish the relevance of these nomothetic guides for a given client before selecting interventions to use in therapy.

Interventions for Behaviors Maintained by Positive Reinforcement

Problematic behavior maintained by positive reinforcement processes is often effectively addressed by interventions that involve environmental change. To support new or infrequent positive behaviors (e.g., socially affiliative behaviors, abstinence from illicit drug use), one might also seek alternative environments that naturally reinforce behaviors one wishes to increase and do not support or reinforce behaviors one wishes to decrease (Cunningham, 1998; Farmer & Nelson-Gray, 2005). Chapter 5 describes approaches to changing behavior by changing the environment.

Interventions for Clients Who Are Depressed or Who Experience Behavioral Inertia

Some clients engage in a low rate of behavior, particularly behaviors he or she previously found enjoyable or pleasurable. This is especially true of individuals who are depressed (Martell, Addis, & Jacobson, 2001) or who experience low self-esteem (Bednar & Peterson, 1995). Many persons who come to therapy also display a low sense of self-efficacy, or do not believe that they are capable of engaging in certain forms of behavior. Similarly, many clients do not believe that behavior they are capable of performing will lead to positive outcomes; that is, they have low outcome expectations. In chapter 6, we discuss behavioral experiments as a method for increasing behavior and testing thoughts about behavioral capacities and behavioral outcomes. In chapter 8, we discuss behavioral activation strategies for individuals who engage in avoidance behaviors that, in turn, negatively affect one's mood by reducing his or her opportunities to access positive reinforcers.

Interventions to Increase Effective Behavior and Ameliorate Behavioral Deficits

Therapy goals often include learning to be more effective through one's behavior, to increase both objective and subjective mastery, or to enhance behavioral skills. Invention strategies that are intended to develop, increase, or strengthen behavioral repertoires often involve direct instruction, advice, modeling, behavioral rehearsal, and skills training. Examples of behavioral interventions that develop or strengthen behavioral repertoires in these ways can be found in chapter 7.

Interventions to Target Unhelpful Thinking Patterns

Clients with a variety of psychological conditions often display "overly rigid rule governance"; that is, they are strongly influenced by thoughts or statements from others that inaccurately specify associations between behaviors and consequences. This reduces flexibility in responding to certain environmental events and results in ineffective or aversive outcomes. For such clients, the accuracy of these rules or assumptions can be challenged, or clients might be encouraged to attend to and bring behavior more in line with the actual contingencies associated with behavior. Other clients may have uncertain or ambivalent long-term goals, or for whatever reason may not act in accordance with their own goals or values, and instead respond more strongly to immediate environmental contingencies. In chapter 6, we describe intervention approaches for altering faulty assumptions or appraisals, modifying inaccurate rules that influence behavior, and developing awareness of and bringing behavior more in line with long-term goals and values.

Interventions to Target Emotional Difficulties

Many clients also evidence problems with excess negative emotions, particularly anxiety. Among these persons, some respond to a range of situations with high levels of anxiety, panic, behavioral avoidance, avoidance of private experiences (e.g., emotions, memories, physiological sensations), or some combination of these. Exposure-based therapies are often effective interventions for addressing excessively high anxiety maintained by avoidance or conditioning processes. These therapies are reviewed in chapter 9.

A common feature in the history of many clients is the experience of growing up in an invalidating environment (Linehan, 1993a). Persons with such histories, as adults, frequently invalidate themselves or others. There are many ways in which self-invalidation is manifest, including pervasive experiential avoidance, substance abuse, dissociation, strong self-dislike, and impaired interpersonal relations. Acceptance and mindfulness interventions are particularly useful when a client wishes to increase acceptance of him- or herself, others, or his or her experiences. Such interventions are also useful for clients who have great difficulty staying in the moment—that is, persons whose thoughts are focused either on the past or on anticipated future events. These interventions are described in chapter 10.

Additional Intervention Considerations

Before closing this section, we also note that it is frequently useful to consider whether a medication evaluation referral or a medical examination would be appropriate for some clients. The latter would be especially important for severe psychological disorders (e.g., psychotic disorders), behavior problems that can adversely affect biological functions (e.g., substance abuse, anorexia nervosa, bulimia nervosa), or behavioral or emotional problems that might have their origins in physiological functions (e.g., hypothyroidism in the case of depression, hypoglycemia in the case of anxiety or panic).

DEVELOPING A FRAMEWORK FOR A COURSE OF THERAPY

Clients vary in terms of the number of problem areas they have and the degree of severity and impairment associated with problem areas. For clients with multiple and severe problems, it is often useful to establish an organizational plan for therapy given the many areas that would likely be targeted for therapy and the many therapeutic challenges and complexities that are likely to arise with such individuals.

Deciding Which Therapy Modes to Use

Earlier in this chapter we provided some guidelines suggested by Linehan (1993a) for prioritizing target behavior selection. Although these were suggested as hierarchically arranged treatment targets over four stages of her dialectical behavior therapy (DBT), we are of the view that the scope and hierarchical arrangement of Stage 1 targets are relevant for the treatment of many psychological conditions (i.e., ensuring safety and decreasing risk, taking steps to increase the likelihood that therapy will succeed, enhancing quality of life, helping with skills training and skills application). Such a framework provides guidance for what areas might be addressed, and in what order, within individual therapy sessions. In this section we discuss another consideration related to the establishment of a therapeutic framework, particularly for multiproblem clients: a structural framework within which treatment modalities are embedded.

In DBT, there are four primary treatment modalities (Linehan, 1993a). *Individual outpatient therapy* usually consists of one or two weekly sessions, each 1 to 1.5 hours in length. The primary focus of these sessions is on problem areas targeted for therapy (e.g., self-injury, therapy-interfering behaviors, substance misuse, repeated entry into harmful environments). The *skills training group* is a separate treatment modality and primarily involves instruction in coping skills. Groups are typically composed of six to eight clients, and sessions take place weekly for about 2 hours during Stage 1. The third treatment modality, *telephone consultation*, involves contact between the therapist and client by phone in between sessions. Either the client or the therapist can initiate contact, with conversations intended to be opportunities for therapist consultation concerning methods and approaches for coping with difficult situations (other than through self-injury or suicidal behaviors), promoting the use of behavioral skills to everyday situations, and repairing any disruptions in the therapeutic relationship prior to the next session. *Case consultation meetings* constitute the fourth treatment modality, and this is explicitly for therapists working within the DBT framework. These meetings are analogous to supervision meetings and usually take place on a weekly basis.

Even though the inclusion of each therapy modality may not be necessary for many clients, they provide an example of the various levels and methods of therapy. As clients display more chronic and severe forms of behavior, more modalities of therapy are often indicated.

DISCUSSING THE THERAPY PLAN WITH THE CLIENT

As noted by Addis and Carpenter (2000), clients often have a variety of reactions to therapist's suggestions for a treatment plan and description of the therapy rationale. Among these are hope and optimism, self-doubts, expectations of failure, uncertainty about whether one is able to carry out the therapy, and apprehension as a result of not fully understanding the process of therapy in the initial stage.

A credible therapeutic rationale provided by the therapist can promote a client's hope and optimism about subsequent therapy (Addis & Carpenter, 2000). Doing so might convey to the client that the problem is understandable, that he or she is not the only one who has struggled with this problem, and that there are effective therapies for his or her problem areas. If a client is hopeful that change is possible, he or she might be more willing to try something new or persevere in the face of obstacles. In this section, we discuss two primary areas therapists frequently review with the client before initiating therapy: the rationale for the therapy and the rationale for between-session activities (e.g., homework).

Discussing the Therapy Rationale

Discussing the rationale for therapy and the selection of specific therapeutic interventions with the client can be a delicate task. As noted by Addis and Carpenter (2000), such discussions usually involve issues such as etiology of the client's problem area (or why the problem came about), and why this problem is perhaps best addressed by the modes of therapy suggested by the therapist. As reviewed by Addis and Carpenter (2000), a client's acceptance of the treatment rationale is usually associated with greater therapeutic benefits.

When the interventions selected for therapy have been empirically evaluated and found to be useful for persons with problem areas similar to those of the client, it is important to convey this information. For many clients, knowledge that the therapeutic approaches planned for use have been widely tested and found to be effective for many, and that they are grounded in scientific research, can promote a sense of optimism about therapy and its prospects for success (Kazdin & Krouse, 1983).

Because the treatment rationale is an important aspect of therapy, it is useful for the therapist to spend time verifying that the client understands the rationale and assess whether he or she agrees with it. Addis and Carpenter (2000, p. 151) provided examples of questions that a therapist might ask the client once the rationale has been discussed:

- "What are your reactions to what you know about this therapy so far?"
- "What parts concern you?"
- "What parts seem positive or potentially helpful?"
- "If you were to explain to a friend or family member how this therapy works, what would you say?"
- "What is your understanding of why you are having this problem?"
- "What are your ideas about the best way to overcome or cope with this problem?"

When the client does not accept the therapy rationale, or if he or she voices doubts, the therapist might take time to carefully explore the client's doubts in a nonthreatening and validating manner. The therapist should objectively consider the client's view and, if relevant, incorporate his or her perspectives into a modified plan. Among the more common client reactions is that CBT interventions are superficial and do not deal with the "real problem" (Addis & Carpenter, 2000). One way for the therapist to respond to this reaction is by distinguishing for the client between etiology and maintenance. That is, the therapist takes time to acknowledge that the reasons why certain problem areas develop are often multifaceted and complex. Why these problems take hold and persist over time might be completely different issues, however, and therapy will likely be more effective if it addresses current determinants of the problem area. The therapist might also note that there is presently no evidence to suggest that an underlying problem, if present, must be solved to get one's life back on track (Addis & Carpenter, 2000). Providing the client with a summary of research findings on the effectiveness of the approach suggested might also be helpful, as would the adoption of a "let's give it a try and see" approach. Regardless of the approach taken, it is important to first hear the client and consider the potential kernel of truth that can, in turn, be incorporated within the CBT framework and treatment plan.

Discussing Between-Session Activities as an Integral Part of Therapy

CBT interventions typically involve between-session activities carried out by the client. Examples of typical activities include self-monitoring, completing questionnaires, filling out thought records, or engaging in self-initiated exposures. Studies that have examined the association between carrying out such between-session activities (or homework) and therapeutic outcome often show robust positive associations (Burns & Spangler, 2000; Kazantzis, Deane, & Ronan, 2000). Therefore, if homework is part of a therapy plan, it should be regarded as an integral part of the therapeutic process.

The likelihood that a client will carry out homework in between sessions is greater if the therapist provides a detailed rationale, including an explanation of how the activity is tied to therapy goals. Time should be dedicated to an exploration of the client's reaction to this activity being a part of his or her ongoing therapy and his or her views as to whether there are potential obstacles that might interfere with performing such activities.

When clients carry out what was asked of them in between sessions, the therapist must take time to review these activities with the client during therapy sessions. The therapist might inquire about how the activity went, explore what the client learned from the activity, or query whether he or she had any difficulties in relation to the activity. A failure on the therapist's part to acknowledge and reinforce the client's efforts in this regard will likely lead to less adherence to prescribed activities in the future and, in turn, result in a less efficacious therapy (Bryant, Simons, & Thase, 1999).

When clients do not participate in homework activities, the therapist might set aside time in a session to carefully explore the reasons why. Some reasons, such as not having time to do the homework, can be addressed through problem-solving strategies. In these instances, not having the time to carry out important parts of the therapy might be the identified problem, and the therapist and client might collaboratively generate a list of solutions to facilitate homework participation (e.g., setting aside specific time intervals during the week to carry out these activities). Other reasons offered might signal, directly or indirectly, that the homework is too difficult or complex. In these instances, homework activities might be broken down into smaller components, and the client asked to select a subset of activities to carry out over the week. Clients may also not participate in between-session activities because they believe the exercise will be unhelpful. In such cases, a behavioral experiment might be set up to evaluate whether a client's belief in the nonhelpfulness of the exercise is accurate (see chap. 6). Alternatively, a client might be asked to take a greater role in designing between-session activities to potentially assist him or her in realizing important therapeutic goals.

ESTABLISHING A MOTIVATION TO CHANGE AND SECURING A COMMITMENT FOR ACTION

If the motivation to be actively involved in therapy is low, the likelihood for therapeutic change is similarly low. The association of level of distress with motivation for change often follows an inverted "U" function. That is, too little distress might contribute to a perception of an absence of benefit associated with therapy. Too much distress, however, might make it difficult for the client to participate in therapies that challenge him or her to examine and modify sources of distress, particularly if coping resources are also low. Having a moderate degree of discomfort about one's problem areas, in contrast, might motivate one to try out new and different ways of responding as a way to lessen this distress.

One strategy for facilitating motivation for therapy is motivational interviewing (Miller & Rollnick, 1991; Sobell & Sobell, 2003). In essence, motivational interviewing is a nonconfrontational, empathic, and minimally intrusive approach for discussing the effects and consequences of the problem behavior and exploring the benefits of change. It is done in such a way that the likelihood of eliciting resistances or defensiveness is minimized. Such an approach is particularly indicated if motivation for therapy is low (e.g., client comes to therapy solely at the request of family members) or the client is motivationally conflicted or ambivalent.

Components of motivational interviewing frequently include (a) challenging the client to identify reasons for changing, (b) providing the client with feedback about personal risk or impairment associated with problem behavior, (c) teaching the client problem-solving strategies for promoting change, (d) helping clients identify their own strengths and resources, (e) providing advice, and (f) facilitating the client's sense of self-efficacy and optimism (Miller & Rollnick, 1991; Sobell & Sobell, 2003).

The following are examples of motivational interviewing-consistent questions or statements associated with problem drinking provided by Sobell and Sobell (2003, pp. 218–219):

- "Tell me about your alcohol use."
- "What would you like your drinking to be like a year from now?"
- "Tell me about the good things and less good things about your drinking."
- "It sounds like you might have some ambivalence about changing your drinking."
- "If you continue drinking like you have in the past year, where do you see yourself in two or three years?"
- "You have managed to cut down your drinking considerably. How did you manage to do that?"

In using motivational strategies, it is important not to come across as judgmental or threatening (e.g., "You don't seem to be taking your drinking very seriously" or "You have a serious drinking problem that you are denying"; Sobell & Sobell, 2003, p. 219). Although motivational interviewing is not typically regarded as a behavioral intervention, it is often a useful strategy for helping clients evaluate the consequences of their behaviors, formulate more accurate rules related to their behavior, and identify goals or values that might function as guides for altering the direction or course of behaviors targeted for change (see chap. 6, this volume, for detailed discussions of strategies for developing new rules and for bringing behavior under the influence of values or distal goals). In these respects, the therapeutic goals of motivational interviewing are both complementary to and compatible with the goals frequently associated with behavioral interventions.

A low motivation for therapy is sometimes associated with severe forms of psychological disorder (e.g., severely depressed mood or a thought disorder). In such instances, consideration should be given to medical consultation to evaluate the possible use of medications. When distress is high, thus making it difficult for the client to fully participate in therapy, therapy might also include the development of coping skills for reducing distress.

Another strategy for enhancing motivation for treatment as well as for establishing early intervention or prevention strategies is the use of treatment contracts (Otto et al., 2003). Once the client and therapist collaboratively establish the goals and parameters for therapy, a formal treatment contract might be developed. Such a contract is usually written and typically specifies the responsibilities and expectations of all parties within the contract (Otto et al., 2003).

Otto et al. (2003) suggested three benefits associated with therapy contracting. First, therapy contracts promote motivation for change and adherence with therapy procedures by solidifying goals for the client. The client can subsequently refer to these written goals during times of stress or setbacks. A written contract also constitutes a public stand on what the client is working toward. Second, particularly during times of stress, it provides the client with a reminder of therapy options, therapeutic principles, coping skills, and treatment contingencies. When used in this way, the therapy contract might consist of a checklist of coping strategies the client may use in stressful situations or a sequence of steps the client can take to resolve crisis periods. A contract might also delineate specific and centrally important therapeutic procedures (e.g., methods for monitoring mood and steps to take when a client's mood begins to elevate or his or her sleep becomes impaired, as in the case of bipolar disorder) or specify consequences for the client's engagement in some sort of target behavior (e.g., a client receiving treatment for substance abuse cannot come to a session intoxicated). Third, in times of crisis, the contract can provide a framework for crisis resolution, and a consent form for treatment team members, family members, and support services (e.g., crisis agencies, social work agencies) to act for the benefit of the client. This is of particular relevance for clients who have difficulty taking appropriate action themselves during times of heightened stress. When contracts serve these purposes, they often include a suicide crisis plan and a checklist that family members can follow to help protect the client during particularly vulnerable periods. An example of this is a client's agreement to refrain from actively engaging in suicidal behavior and instead contact a family member or caregiver if other coping efforts have not succeeded. If a treatment contract is used, the client ideally is the person who actively develops the contract. An example of a treatment contract can be found in Otto et al. (2003).

When therapists use contracts, they should continue to be vigilant and periodically check in with their clients about the behavior patterns targeted in the contract (Otto et al., 2003). Just because a client signs a contract indicating that he or she will not attempt suicide during the active phase of therapy, for example, a therapist cannot assume that the client will automatically adhere to this agreement or that the contract alone will produce beneficial changes in this area. Therapists might also examine their own motivations for developing and entering into contracts with their clientele. If, for example, a client's signing of a no-suicide contract occasions a considerable sense of relief in the therapist, then the therapist might question who is best being served by the regulating functions of the contract.

Securing a commitment for change in the early stages of therapy might simply involve a client's willingness to participate in a set of therapeutic procedures for a short period of time and to reevaluate progress during and after the initial stages. Such a commitment does not ask a lot of the client and allows the client and therapist the opportunity to review the therapy plan and the commitment to it if necessary.

POTENTIAL OBSTACLES TO EFFECTIVE THERAPY

Persons (1989) suggested, and we agree, that the case formulation can assist in generating hypotheses about potential obstacles that might challenge therapy. Anticipation of such obstacles allows for the opportunity of preplanning and increases the likelihood that the therapist can prevent or solve the problems that obstacles pose.

Following the sharing of the case formulation, the therapist might suggest one or two potential obstacles that might adversely affect therapy (Persons, 1989). These can be suggested as potential problems, and the therapist might (a) explore with the client the degree to which he or she also perceives these as obstacles; (b) examine whether other potential obstacles are anticipated by the client; and (c) invite the client to brainstorm with the therapist about how these obstacles should be addressed if and when they occur, or how related issues might be addressed in therapy so that the anticipated obstacles do not arise.

The client, for example, who holds the view "I'm not able to cope with stress" will likely experience difficulty completing between-session activities and will likely offer stress as a reason. Similarly, such a client will be more likely to present to therapy sessions with a series of crises and will demand that the therapist assist in resolving those. With such clients, difficulty in effectively responding to stress may represent a potential obstacle to therapy. When such obstacles are anticipated, however, they can be translated into therapeutic goals and represent opportunities for genuine change.

PROCEDURES FOR EVALUATING
THE EFFECTIVENESS OF THERAPY

Therapy goals agreed on by the client and the therapist prior to the initiation of therapy suggest the nature and type of outcome measures that might be repeatedly assessed prior to the initiation of therapy, during therapy, and after active therapy has concluded. Ideally, therapy goals should be measurable so that the therapist and client can determine together whether sufficient movement is being made toward the realization of treatment goals as therapy progresses (Persons et al., 2006).

The process of evaluating therapy effectiveness includes the selection of an appropriate assessment framework and appropriate dependent measures

(Nelson & Barlow, 1981). For most clients, the A–B or A–B–C assessment framework is generally the most appropriate. The "A" phase is the baseline phase, in which the frequency, intensity, or duration of a particular behavior is monitored and recorded prior to the application of an intervention. The "B" phase represents the intervention phase. The "C" phase covers a period of time after the active phase of therapy has been discontinued. Intermittent assessments during the "C" phase are often useful for evaluating the degree to which therapy gains have been maintained, or whether there is any evidence suggestive of a lapse or relapse (e.g., a decrease in treatment gains, or a return to baseline or "A"-phase levels of functioning).

When desirable change is observed between "A" and "B" phases, it is possible that the therapy contributed to this change. We cannot necessarily conclude, however, that therapy was the cause of this change. That is, change may have been influenced by factors that, although independent of the intervention, occurred during the intervention phase. Stated another way, we cannot infer causation from correlation. Despite this limitation in inference, we strongly suggest that therapists repeatedly collect data related to the client's main problem areas throughout therapy. Repeated assessments not only help inform or guide treatment, they also promote responsible clinical practice. If the client is having a negative reaction to a given therapeutic intervention, the therapist may not be aware of this unless data were collected during therapy. Similarly, it would not be ethical to continue a therapy over an extended period of time when it is not producing any therapeutic gains or benefits.

Repeated assessments not only provide information as to whether an intervention is effective but also suggest whether an intervention will be effective in the future. In A. T. Beck's cognitive therapy for depression, for example, clients are unlikely to show significant improvement in mood over a 20-session course of therapy if they do not indicate some improvement by the fourth session (Ilardi & Craighead, 1994; Persons & Tompkins, 1997). In such instances, a therapist might consider switching therapy approaches if there is no evidence of prompt therapeutic change. Assessments during therapy also provide guidance as to whether therapy should be discontinued as planned. Emerging research suggests that the likelihood of relapse is greater when therapy is discontinued before a full recovery has been achieved (Thase et al., 1992).

Nelson and Hayes (1986b) provided some guidelines to evaluate therapy efficacy. Among these are recommendations that measures should accurately assess the primary behavior(s) targeted in therapy, measurement should occur frequently, and, if possible, before initiating treatment. Repeatedly administered measures should be convenient to take or complete, and data obtained should be graphed by either the client or the therapist and regularly reviewed as part of the therapeutic process, with significant events that might account for marked variability noted on the graph. Dependent measures can include data collected through self-monitoring, direct observation, or repeated questionnaire assessments or checklists.

For some problem areas, it is useful to assess target behaviors or experiences at least a few times a day. Some depressed clients, for example, report that they are depressed all the time. They may not discriminate variations in their mood over the course of a day and, correspondingly, variations in environmental contexts that influence such mood fluctuations. For such clients, it may be useful to self-monitor mood at prescribed points during the day (e.g., morning, early afternoon, late afternoon, and evening), with the self-monitoring perhaps as simple as making a rating along a 7-point scale indicating the degree or intensity of depressed mood experienced at the time of self-assessment (from 1 = *not at all depressed* to 7 = *the most depressed I ever get*). Many persons, even those with relatively severe psychological disorders, evidence considerable variability in mood when assessed repeatedly during waking hours (Farmer, Nash, & Dance, 2004). Variations in mood ratings might help the client identify factors that influence mood as well as provide a challenge to the view that some clients have that they are depressed or distressed all the time.

EXTENDED CLIENT ILLUSTRATION

In the case example that follows, we illustrate elements of the behavioral case formulation and treatment planning process outlined previously. The formulation approach presented here is primarily informed by the work of Persons (1989; Persons & Tompkins, 1997; Persons et al., 2006) and Haynes (1986; Haynes et al., 1999; Haynes & O'Brien, 1990).

Background Information

"Robert" is a married 24-year-old accountant who lives in the Pacific Northwest region of the United States. His primary physician referred him for a psychological evaluation and possible therapy related to a fear of heights.

Chief Complaint

During the initial interview, Robert reported his primary problem as a long-standing fear of heights, which has become more pronounced in the past few years. The main reason Robert cited for seeking therapy now is that he was recently awarded a job promotion that necessitates travel to another office in a neighboring city. Commuting to the new job requires that he travel across a long, steel bridge that spans a wide river and gorge. Robert estimated that the bridge was some 500 feet above the water and about a mile long. He further reported that the only alternative routes to his new office would add about 100 miles roundtrip to his commute each day. Because of his intense fear of being on the bridge and the associated avoidance of it, Robert has taken vacation leave and delayed the start of his new job, as he believes that it is currently impossible for him to drive over the bridge.

Psychological and Psychiatric History

Robert reported a largely unremarkable psychological and psychiatric history. The only problem area he acknowledged was a fear of heights. He reported falling from a second-story patio deck at age 5. Apart from a mild concussion, Robert reported no significant injuries from the fall.

After the incident, Robert recalled that his mother seemed overly protective and typically did not allow him to go out and play without her close supervision. She also had a tendency to exhort caution frequently (e.g., "If you get too close, you'll fall and break your neck!" and "Be careful or you're going to get hurt!"). Although Robert denied any lasting psychological impact from the fall (e.g., no troubling memory flashbacks), he reported that as a child he found himself mentally imagining and rehearsing the hypothetical consequences described in his mother's admonishments (e.g., imagining himself falling and seeing himself with a broken neck or head injuries). In relation to his present-day fear of heights, Robert reports that as he approaches heights, many of the same type of images come to him and exacerbate his level of distress. When in or approaching high places, Robert also reported that he experiences recollections of seeing one of his friends fall from a bike. This incident occurred when Robert was about 12 years of age. His friend experienced a moderate gash in the head that produced a lot of blood. Robert added that he tends to only recall this incident when in or around high places.

A timeline analysis of the development of his fear of heights revealed that since the fall at age 5, he has been more apprehensive when in high places. Within a few years of the incident, however, Robert reported that he would occasionally climb on trees and playground equipment, although he also described incidents during this time when he refused to approach high locations. Avoidance of heights and escape from high places gradually increased over the years and became well entrenched by his middle adolescent years. By then, Robert reported that he avoided almost all high places, including airplane travel as well as open-view elevators.

Robert reported that he has always been somewhat "jumpy." As an example, he reported that sharp, loud, and unexpected sounds, such as a car backfire, cause him a very strong physiological reaction. Robert added that many of the sensations he experienced immediately after being startled are the same type of experiences that he has when he is on or near a high location (i.e., panic, palpitations, depersonalization, dizziness, feeling frozen and unable to move, and shortness of breath). When Robert experiences these sensations around heights, they reportedly only go away, and only gradually, once Robert has left the situation. He had difficulty recalling when he last stayed in a high location when feeling panicky, adding that he fears that he might go crazy or do something that would be embarrassing to him in those situations (e.g., shout out loud or faint).

Other reports from Robert suggested some dependent characteristics. These included difficulty making everyday decisions without first seeking advice, difficulty expressing disapproval out of fear of losing support or approval, and feeling helpless when alone. When asked, Robert said that he felt he overly relied on others, particularly his wife, which he believed caused some strain on his relationships. He added that he wished he were more independent.

Robert received therapy on one previous occasion, principally for his fear of heights. This occurred 4 years ago for about 3 months and took place at his university student counseling service. Robert reported that counseling largely consisted of talking, mostly about his past and particularly about his relationship with his mother. He reported that his fear of heights did not improve as a result of this therapy.

Family and Social Relations

Robert grew up in an intact home. His father worked as a long-haul truck driver and was home about one third of the time when Robert was growing up. His mother worked at home and primarily took care of Robert and his two younger siblings. She maintained a small home business that centered on the crafts she made. Robert described his siblings as "more anxious than most." He indicated, however, that he was the only one with a phobia. Robert described a history of good relations with family members, which continues to this day.

Robert recalled some periods of anxiety during his elementary school years. He felt non-height-related anxieties most acutely when his mother dropped him off at school each day. He reported that although there was a twinge of anxiety upon being dropped off, this usually passed within a few minutes. Although he reported not having many friends during his school years, he indicated that he has always had two or three close friends.

During late high school, Robert began dating and met his future wife during his 2nd year at university. The most significant strains in their relationship currently are related to Robert's fear of high places, as they have not pursued activities and interests together that involve heights (e.g., traveling in a plane, dining on upper-level restaurants in the downtown area). Other aspects of his social and family history are unremarkable.

School and Occupational Functioning

Robert reported that his academic performance was above average, typically near the top of the class. Since graduating from university with a bachelor's degree, he has been steadily employed as an accountant by the same firm. His performance reviews have always been good. His recent reassignment to the main office was regarded as a promotion for his good work.

Health and Medical Status

Robert's health status is unremarkable. A medical evaluation carried out by his physician ruled out any significant vestibular influence on phobic symptomatology or any other medical problem (e.g., impairments in visual acuity) that might account for Robert's experience.

Impairment, Distress, and Coping

Robert's current primary impairments are anxiety related and associated with his fears concerning traveling to places he would like to go. This situation has become more acute in recent weeks as a result of a change in work setting that requires daily travel over a bridge. He also acknowledged that he relies too much on others, particularly his wife, and that his fear of heights has caused some strain on their relations as he avoids participation in some leisure activities as a result. Although Robert has always had some degree of distress related to his fear of heights, this distress has increased markedly in recent weeks because he sees no viable way to cope with his fear other than through avoidance.

Case Formulation

Following two sessions of clinical interviews as well as between-session self-monitoring assessments and a number of questionnaire assessments, Robert's therapist came up with the following formulation.

The Problem List (Identifying Problematic Behavior in Terms of Its Descriptive and Functional Features)

1. *Exaggerated fear of heights.* When in high places, he experiences panic-attack like symptoms.
2. *Catastrophic thoughts and images related to being in high places.* Thoughts and images often involve personal injury as a result of falling from high places.
3. *Avoidance of high places.* Passive avoidance of high places is associated with an absence of fear and panic; escape from high places is associated with a reduction of fear and panic as well as images and thoughts related to personal injury.
4. *Avoidance of travel when heights are involved.* He is unable to participate in some leisure activities (e.g., plane travel) or commute to new job; he experiences relief when travel or some leisure activities are no longer considered.

5. *Frequent reliance on others for advice and support.* He has difficulty making decisions or taking action without advice or reassurance; he has difficulty tolerating being alone and tends to "go along" with others rather than experience disapproval.
6. *Strained marital relations related to height phobia.* Difficulty in traveling and engaging in some leisure activities with wife have contributed to some marital discord and resentments.

Situational Determinants of Behavior on the Problem List: Precipitants, Activating Situations, and Behavioral Consequences

Problem Areas 1 through 4 previously described constitute behavioral excesses and are all related to situations that involve heights. Avoidance and escape behavior is reinforced behavior as it produces immediate relief (i.e., reductions in anxiety or panic, lessening of unpleasant physiological sensations, attenuation of catastrophic thoughts and images). These functional properties of escape and avoidance behavior likely maintain their occurrence as well as Robert's fears and catastrophic thoughts and images. Problem 5 also includes some behavioral excesses (e.g., frequently asking others for advice, acting in an overly compliant manner). The reassurance provided by others appears to result in a lessening of apprehension and anxiety, thus making advice-seeking negatively reinforced behavior. The social support and reassurance provided by others is also pleasing to Robert and suggests that this reaction from others also positively reinforces his reassurance-seeking. "Going along with others" similarly results in a reduction of anxiety associated with conflict and is likewise negatively reinforced. Robert's tendency to seek out others or distracting activities (e.g., TV watching) when alone is similarly associated with a reduction in and relief from feelings of helplessness.

Hypothesized Origins (Person Variables and Learning History)

Robert's fall from the patio decking at age 5 was associated with a change in his mother's behavior. In particular, his mother became more vigilant for potential dangers that might cause injury to Robert, notably heights. She would frequently be physically present and watchful when he played. She also relayed a number of verbal rules that implied serious injury if care was not taken around high places (e.g., "If you get too close, you'll fall and break your neck"). In response to these statements, Robert stayed away from high places and also mentally rehearsed the behavior–consequence relations implied in these statements (e.g., he imagined himself falling and badly injuring himself). This mental imaging, plus recollections of his friend's bleeding face after he fell from a bike, might have further covertly conditioned associations between certain environmental situations (high places) with certain behaviors (falling) and associated consequences (serious physical injury or death).

Also during his childhood, Robert learned that one way to make un-comfortable emotions and physical sensations go away is to passively avoid or actively escape from the situations that evoked them. Although this method of coping was effective in reducing anxiety and fear, it did little to facilitate the development of alternative responses that would allow him to cope and perform effectively in anxiety-evoking situations.

There is also a suggestion that Robert might be temperamentally prone to anxiety. That is, there are some indications that he shows a higher degree of autonomic reactivity to unexpected events than persons typically experi-ence. He also appears to have been more anxious than other children follow-ing separation from his parents. These, in combination with the observation that his other siblings are also somewhat overly anxious and that Robert scored high on a trait measure of anxiety, suggest that he might be tempera-mentally predisposed to the experience of anxiety.

Working Hypotheses

Dominant themes present among Problem Areas 1 though 5 include coping with anxiety-evoking situations (e.g., heights, conflict, uncomfort-able inner states) through escape and avoidance behaviors. Although escape and avoidance are associated with immediate reductions in anxiety and fear, such behaviors prevent the extinction or habituation of unjustified anxiety and fear in the environments in which they are experienced. Problem Area 6 appears to be long-term aversive consequence associated with Problems Ar-eas 1 through 5. Robert indicated that he very much loves his wife and would like to share a close and satisfying life with her.

High levels of fear and panic, exaggerated estimations of danger associ-ated with high places, and escape and avoidance from these places appear to be accounted for by three primary processes: (a) experiencing a fall from a high area at age 5 that resulted in some injury and observing a friend sustain an injury at age 12 after falling from a bike; (b) learning rules from his mother that convey heights are dangerous (e.g., "If you get too close, you'll fall and break your neck"); (c) covert conditioning processes that repeatedly linked certain environmental contexts (high places) with particular actions (fall-ing) and associated aversive consequences (serious bodily injury), and a his-tory of reinforcement for avoidance or escape from high places. Figure 4.1 graphically represents several aspects of the working hypothesis of Robert's fear of heights.

Robert also revealed that he finds emotions such as anxiety and associ-ated physiological reactions such as elevated heart rate, depersonalization, shortness of breath, and dizziness to be very unpleasant. Robert added that he actively seeks to get away from situations that produce these experiences, in part, because the experiences themselves are aversive and associated with unpleasant outcomes (e.g., going crazy).

ANTECEDENTS

- A high area
- Height-related rules (e.g., "If you get too close, you'll fall and break your neck")

PERSON VARIABLES

- 11-year history of reinforcement for avoidance/escape
- Fall from patio deck at age 5
- Observing effects of friend's fall from bike at age 12
- High physiological reactivity
- Anxious temperament
- History of mentally rehearsing catastrophic outcomes associated with falls from high places

BEHAVIORS

- Anxiety
- Panic
- Palpitations
- Depersonalization
- Dizziness
- Frozen in movements
- Shortness of breath
- Images of self falling and resultant bodily injury
- Images of injured friend
- Images of self being injured while falling
- Passively avoid high places
- Actively escape from high places

IMMEDIATE REINFORCING CONSEQUENCES

- Reduction of anxiety and panic following escape or avoidance (−)
- Reduction of unpleasant physiological sensations following avoidance or escape (−)
- Cessation of catastrophic images of injury due to falling following avoidance or escape (−)
- Cessation of fear of going crazy following avoidance or escape (−)
- Receive reassurances from others that high areas are safe (+ and −)

DELAYED AVERSIVE CONSEQUENCES

- Marital tension and discord associated with having to limit activities to accommodate avoidance
- Does not participate in some leisure activities that are enjoyable (e.g., travel)
- Work impairment (cannot travel to new job)

Figure 4.1. Functional analysis of Robert's fear and avoidance of heights. Dots between components of the response chain indicate a probability function, whereby a dot represents a probability that the preceding component will influence the following component. Items listed within the *Immediate Reinforcing Consequences* components followed by (+) indicate positive reinforcing consequences and items followed by (−) indicate negative reinforcing consequences, both of which maintain or strengthen preceding behavior.

The anxiety-reduction function of avoidance and escape behaviors was hypothesized as the primary maintaining factor for Robert's phobic anxiety. Robert continues to avoid and escape in the presence of heights because doing so works. These actions provide immediate relief and are consequently effective means of short-term coping. The cost, however, is that overreliance on escape and avoidance as a method of coping has resulted in the avoidance of an increasingly wider range of situations or contexts over time that is now beginning to adversely affect Robert's marriage and work.

From a diagnostic perspective, Robert met the *Diagnostic and Statistical Manual of Mental Disorders* (4th ed., text rev.; American Psychiatric Association, 2000) criteria for Specific Phobia, Natural Environment Type (Heights). This type of phobia has historically been referred to as acrophobia. As with most phobias, exposure and response prevention is widely regarded as the treatment of choice given its high effectiveness rate in eliminating phobic fears. This intervention also conceptually maps onto the individualized working hypothesis of Robert's fear of heights (see Figure 4.1).

It was hypothesized that a therapy program that exposes Robert to high places but blocks associated escape and avoidance behavior would reduce or eliminate the fear and unpleasant physiological sensations and images he currently experiences in these settings. Skills training elements will also be included, such as diaphragmatic breathing, to provide Robert with coping alternatives to escape and avoidance. While acknowledging a desire to reduce his interpersonal dependency on others, Robert indicated that he would rather focus therapy on his fear of heights, particularly given the urgency to resolve this problem. The therapist agreed and noted that some of the approaches used to overcome his fear of heights might also be applicable to situations in which overly dependent behavior is more probable, as such behavior also appears to include an anxiety-reduction function.

Treatment Plan

Goals include the following:
- eliminate fear of heights;
- reduce the intensity and incidence of physiological sensations (e.g., palpitations) and unpleasant images (e.g., falling and injuring oneself);
- eliminate avoidance of and escape from high places;
- facilitate and support approach behavior to high areas;
- teach and support alternative coping methods when anxious in high situations; and
- participate in pleasant or necessary activities not currently engaged in because of avoidance of heights (e.g., drive car over bridges, travel in airplane).

Therapeutic framework:

- two 1.5-hour assessment sessions;
- two 1-hour sessions of preexposure preparation (includes development of fear hierarchy with commonly encountered high situations or places ordered in terms of level of associated distress; training in diaphragmatic breathing); and
- five 1.5-hour sessions of in vivo exposure sessions that will consist of the following:
  - meeting at a mutually agreed on public location that corresponds with items on the client's fear hierarchy,
  - review of between-session therapy-related activities,
  - in vivo exposure,
  - debrief of exposure session, and
  - planning next session and between-session activities.
- between-session activities that largely involve skills practice, self-monitoring, and self-initiated graded exposures;
- three monthly follow-up sessions after discontinuation of active therapy; and
- one 6-month follow-up after the last monthly follow-up session.

Interventions include the following:

- self-monitoring;
- breathing retraining and mindfulness training;
- therapist modeling of skill and mastery associated with being in and coping with high situations;
- exposure plus response prevention;
- "think aloud" procedure during exposure sessions (i.e., say out loud what one is thinking and covertly experiencing during exposures);
- hierarchically ordered in vivo self-initiated exposures in between sessions; and
- going on "dates" with wife, which include exposure to high places (e.g., dining in a top story restaurant and intentionally sitting by a window).

Motivation for Therapy and Commitment to Therapy Goals

Robert recognizes the negative effect avoidance coping has on his life. He further recognizes that if he does not do something about it now, it may have irreversible effects on his job, his relationship with his wife, and his goals of traveling. His motivation for therapy appears to be high.

Potential Obstacles to Effective Therapy

On the basis of his self-reports, it is possible that Robert might excessively seek reassurance from the therapist or from others during exposure sessions. To reduce the likelihood of this, Robert and the therapist reached an agreement that he may ask the therapist only once during an exposure session if the situation is safe and the therapist will honestly reply. In the event Robert asks again, his query will go unanswered and he will be encouraged instead to focus closely on his experiences during the exposure. Robert also agreed to relay these instructions to any persons present (e.g., his wife) during self-initiated exposures in between sessions.

Given Robert's history of avoidance and escape, and that a small but significant proportion of persons who undergo exposure therapy prematurely quit, Robert and his therapist agreed to spend some time during preexposure sessions discussing this possibility. During these discussions, the tasks include a priori problem solving, whereby Robert and the therapist have a plan in place to put into action if and when Robert considers leaving therapy in response to the exposure sessions. Other preexposure therapeutic activities are geared toward the development and practice of skills that Robert can use during exposures to cope with anxiety and distress (e.g., diaphragmatic breathing, mindfulness skills).

Procedures for Evaluating the Effectiveness of Therapy

Two sets of assessments were used. One set consisted of measures that were administered prior to the initiation of therapy and immediately following the discontinuation of active therapy as well as at follow-up assessments conducted 3 and 9 months after therapy. Robert completed another set of measures on several occasions during active treatment. Measures from both of these assessment sets are listed in the following section.

Assessment Measures Administered Pre- and Posttherapy, and at 3- and 9-Month Follow-Up Assessments

- Behavioral Avoidance Test (BAT; Borkovec, Weerts, & Bernstein, 1977). Both before and immediately following active treatment, and at 3- and 9-month posttreatment assessments, Robert will be asked to approach and enter into the same anxiety-evoking situation. The setting he and the therapist agreed on for this assessment is the footpath on the bridge that he will eventually need to drive over to get to work. The following will be evaluated during the BAT at both pre- and posttherapy: (a) whether Robert will be able to walk onto the footpath at all, (b) how far along the footpath he will walk, (c) how long he will be able to remain on the footpath, and

(d) his peak levels and duration of subjective distress as intermittently assessed during the test.

- Individualized Fear and Avoidance Hierarchy. Prior to the initiation of the in vivo exposure sessions, an individualized fear and avoidance hierarchy will be developed. This includes a list of situations that Robert often encounters that are associated with anxiety or panic, with items on the list arranged in order of the amount of distress that the situation typically evokes using a scaling system in which 0 = *no anxiety or avoidance at all* and 100 = *very severe anxiety or avoidance*. Pretreatment ratings of associated distress will be used to hierarchically organize the content of exposure sessions, with the less distressing situations being those that Robert is exposed to first. Following the discontinuation of active treatment, Robert will be asked to provide distress ratings for situations listed on the hierarchy, with between-pretreatment ratings used as referents to evaluate therapy effectiveness at posttreatment and follow-up.

- Dyadic Adjustment Scale (Spanier, 1976) is widely used to assess marital distress. Both Robert and his wife will be administered this test pre- and posttreatment, and again at 3- and 9-month follow-ups.

- Pleasant Events Schedule (MacPhillamy & Lewinsohn, 1974) consists of a listing of 320 activities that are potentially enjoyable to a wide range of individuals. On this measure, individuals are asked to indicate the frequency of engagement in each activity over the past month and the degree to which such activities were experienced as pleasant. A subset of these activities involves participating in enjoyable activities with other people.

Measures Administered Repeatedly (Before, During, and Following Active Therapy)

- Subjective Units of Distress Scale (SUDS; Wolpe & Lazarus, 1966) ratings are self-report ratings of overall distress that Robert feels during exposure sessions, with 0 = *no anxiety or panic* and 100 = *extremely intense anxiety and panic*. SUDS ratings will be collected every 3 minutes during exposure sessions. Change in SUDS ratings during exposure sessions will be used to index the degree of habituation or extinction of anxiety during exposure sessions and will also provide a guide to the therapist as to when it is appropriate to discontinue the exposure (e.g., not before the several consecutive ratings are 50% below baseline or preexposure levels of self-rated distress).

- The Trait Scale of the State–Trait Anxiety Inventory, Form Y-2 (Spielberger, Gorsuch, Lushene, Vagg, & Jacobs, 1983) will be completed by Robert once a week and will reflect the degree of anxiety he has generally felt over the past 7 days. Printed on a set of 5- by 7-inch index cards is a table within which Robert will record behaviors of clinical interest and associated features for each day of the week. On each diary card, Robert will be asked to indicate if he approached or entered a high place that day, identify the high place, record his SUDS rating immediately following approach or entry, write down how long he remained in the situation, indicate his SUDS rating at the time he left the situation, and record a mastery rating related to his ability to skillfully remain in the situation. He was also asked to list any coping skills that he used that were helpful in that situation. Data corresponding to between-session planned self-initiated exposures are recorded on this card, as are any unplanned exposures that Robert initiated.

SUMMARY

When designing a treatment plan, it is often helpful for therapists to:

- Reach consensus with the client as to the problem areas that therapy will address, the specific goals of therapy, and how therapy might be structured to increase the likelihood of realizing these goals.
- Consider prioritizing problem areas when a client presents with multiple problems, whereby the highest priority areas would be those associated with the greatest risk of harm to self or others.
- Consider treatment goals primarily in terms of building behavioral repertoires or skills whenever possible (rather than goals that primarily involve the elimination of already established behaviors).
- Consider whether there is an effective empirically supported therapy (EST) available for behavior patterns targeted for therapy and, if so, whether such a treatment approach would be appropriate for this particular client.
- Contemplate designing an individually tailored therapeutic program based on the case formulation if there is no EST for a client's problem areas or a relevant EST is not appropriate for the client.
- Collaboratively evaluate the proposed treatment plan with the client, including a provision of a rationale for suggested treat-

ment elements and a discussion about the role and possible therapeutic benefit of activities carried out by the client in be-tween sessions.

- Work to establish a motivation for change and secure a commit-ment for action in case either of these are minimal or lacking.
- Suggest a couple of potential obstacles to effective therapy, and explore with the client how these might be effectively addressed should they arise.
- Reach consensus on the procedures used in the evaluation of therapy effectiveness (i.e., how change will be monitored over the course of therapy).

5

CHANGING BEHAVIOR BY CHANGING THE ENVIRONMENT

A fundamental set of behavioral intervention strategies involves helping people change their behavior by changing aspects of their environment. This group of behavioral interventions, collectively referred to as *contingency management strategies*, involves altering environmental conditions that occur prior to (antecedents) or following (consequences) behaviors of clinical interest. These procedures primarily target two classes of environmental events: (a) signals that influence or direct behavior and (b) consequences that motivate behavior (Boyce & Roman, 2003). Contingency management procedures have been most commonly used in modifying behavior among children, individuals with developmental disabilities, persons with severe psychological disorders, and institutionalized adults (e.g., long-term inpatient mental health facilities, correctional institutions). Among cognitively normal adults, contingency management procedures and programs have been used most successfully with persons who display behavioral excesses or deviations maintained by primary reinforcers. These include drug, alcohol, and tobacco use or abuse; sexual promiscuity and sexual deviations; and eating-disorder-related behaviors (Boyce & Roman, 2003).

We begin this chapter by describing key concepts and assumptions associated with the use of contingency management strategies. This is followed by the presentation of guidelines for implementing these interventions. We also describe several examples of contingency management interventions commonly found in many cognitive behavior therapies.

OVERVIEW OF CONTINGENCY MANAGEMENT PROCEDURES

In this section, we first discuss the concept of contingency management as well as some of the important assumptions, concepts, and considerations associated with the use of these procedures to change behavior. Next, we describe general guidelines for implementing contingency management procedures.

Key Terms and Concepts

One central concept associated with contingency management is the *behavioral contingency*. A behavioral contingency is a relationship between events that occasion a behavior, the behavior itself, and the consequences that the behavior produces (Malott, Malott, & Trojan, 2000). "June" struggled with heroin use. Whenever she was at her friend Fred's house, he would urge her to use heroin with him. If she used heroin, he would stop bugging her. Shortly after using heroin she would experience a mellow euphoria. The behavioral contingency consisted of (a) events that occasion heroin use, such as being at Fred's house, being urged by Fred to use drugs, the availability of heroin, and the presence of gear to prepare and inject heroin; (b) the behavior of using heroin; and (c) the consequences of using heroin, such as negative reinforcement (termination of "bugging" by Fred) and positive reinforcement (euphoria). A behavioral contingency, then, is a causal relationship that links the events that occasion behavior, the behavior, and the outcomes of the behavior; the outcomes occur only if the behavior specified in the relationship is performed (Malott et al., 2000).

Another important concept is *stimulus control*. Stimulus control procedures primarily work by altering the antecedents to behavior. Recall that in chapter 2 of this volume, we briefly described two general classes of antecedents: *discriminative stimuli* and *establishing operations*. Discriminative stimuli (S^D) are events that signal the likelihood of reinforcement or punishment for behavior. A behavior is under stimulus control when it occurs in the presence of a particular stimulus, but not in its absence (Kazdin, 2001). In the case of June, she typically used heroin only when her friend Fred urged her to use, and when drugs and paraphernalia were available.

The following is another example of stimulus control that illustrates coercive control practices. "Edith" and "Sam" are a married couple. Sam frequently physically abuses and insults Edith. Over time, Edith has learned through operant learning processes that if Sam asks her to engage in sexual activity on certain occasions (S^D), and if she agrees and participates in sexual relations (behavior in presence of S^D), she will avoid being hit and insulted by Sam (negative reinforcement for behavior in the presence of the S^D, as her behavior results in the termination of the husband's threats and avoidance of physical abuse). If she refuses, however, Sam may hit or insult her. Edith's behavior of acquiescing to Sam's sexual requests has come under the control of antecedent stimuli (S^D).

As is often the case, S^D are quite complex, and the consequences that they signal can vary considerably as a function of other contextual variables. Various aspects of Edith's husband's behavior, the time of day, or other features of the current situation may, for example, signal that negative reinforcement is more or less likely if Edith agrees to engage in sexual activity. If Sam appears to be calm or in a good mood, is in a hurry to get to work, or asks for sex in a casual, offhand manner, the S^D might indicate that physical and verbal abuse is not forthcoming if Edith refuses his request. In contrast, if Sam appears agitated, has nothing else to do, or asks in a demanding manner, these S^D may signal that physical and verbal abuse will follow Edith's refusal, and negative reinforcement will follow acquiescence. On these occasions, Sam is resorting to coercive control practices to get his needs met.

It is important to note that a discriminative stimulus (S^D) in operant learning is different from a conditional stimulus (CS) in respondent or classical conditioning. The key difference is that, in the framework of operant learning, the individual is not responding in an automatic manner to stimuli in the environment. Whereas in classical conditioning a CS automatically elicits a response in a reflexive manner, S^D in operant conditioning set the occasion for certain behaviors by signaling the likelihood of reinforcing or punishing consequences. S^D and other contextual variables, in the aggregate, influence whether an individual will or will not respond to S^D in a particular manner but do not automatically or reflexively elicit a response.

In chapter 2, we defined another class of antecedent stimuli, establishing operations (EOs), as events or biological conditions that alter the reinforcing or punishing properties associated with consequences. To illustrate the influence of S^D and EOs on setting an occasion for a particular behavior, we refer to the example of Edith and Sam again. Edith has a history of not receiving adequate care and attention from loved ones. In her childhood, her caregivers neglected her physical and emotional needs, often locking her in her bedroom for days at a time. Let us say that a few days ago, her best friend moved across the country, resulting in a loss of social and emotional support. Now, Sam is her primary source of emotional (or physical) intimacy, and she feels deprived of physical closeness and intimacy. In this case, Edith's current state of deprivation constitutes an EO. As she arrives home, Sam asks her to have sexual intercourse with him (S^D). He seems calm and asked in an offhand manner, indicating that the threat of physical abuse is low even if she says "no." Even though she does not really want to have sex, her probability of saying "yes" might be somewhat elevated, as deprivation from intimacy (an EO) increases the positively reinforcing properties of sexual activity. If her best friend had not just left town, and she was not in a state of emotional deprivation (EO), she may be less likely to say "yes."

In chapter 2, we also discussed and defined reinforcement, punishment, and extinction, and we reiterate the key points here. There are two different categories of consequences that influence behavior: (a) consequences that increase the likelihood that similar behaviors will occur in the future in a similar context (i.e., reinforcers) and (b) consequences that decrease the likelihood that similar behaviors will occur in the future in a similar context (i.e., punishers). When describing the type of reinforcement or punishment, a further distinction is made. A consequence, either a reinforcer or a punisher, is characterized as "positive" when the behavior results in the application of consequences. Conversely, a consequence is considered "negative" when the behavior results in the removal, cessation, or termination of some event. Extinction is another procedure for decreasing behavior and involves the removal of reinforcers that previously maintained the behavior. When the behavior no longer leads to reinforcers, it becomes less frequent over time and may extinguish entirely.

Key Assumptions of Contingency Management

The primary assumption underlying contingency management interventions is that the target behavior in question is under the influence of direct-acting environmental antecedents or consequences. This is in contrast to behavior influenced by rules, which may operate differently than actual environmental contingencies. A woman with anorexia nervosa, for example, might deprive herself of food to achieve a slim appearance. The behavior of food avoidance might be under the influence of a rule, such as "If I don't eat, I'll lose weight and I'll be more attractive to others." Implied in this rule is the idea that extreme weight loss and an overly thin appearance will result in a variety of social reinforcers (e.g., comments by others that convey an attractive or healthy appearance, greater acceptance or valuation by others). When the behavior–consequence relations specified in this rule are contrasted with the environmental contingencies, there is usually a discrepancy. Indeed, the social environment often regards people who are emaciated as unattractive and unhealthy and is more likely to shun, criticize, or avoid persons who are severely underweight as a result of self-starvation practices. Contingency management procedures are most effective when behaviors targeted in therapy are under the influence of direct environmental contingencies, not verbal rules that specify environment–behavior relations.

When contingency management procedures are used to increase certain behaviors, another important assumption is that the client has the targeted behaviors within his or her behavioral repertoire. If the client has not previously learned the target behaviors, no amount of contingency management will increase them. Other reinforcement-based strategies used to establish and develop novel behaviors, such as shaping (discussed later in this chapter), might be used first until the novel behavior becomes part of the individual's repertoire.

Steps in Applying Contingency Management Interventions

There are several important steps to using contingency management procedures. We outline these steps as a general guide for clinicians, but therapists may elect to use some or all of these steps in light of the circumstances of particular clients. These steps include (a) specifying and defining target behaviors and relevant contextual factors, (b) orienting the client to contingency management, and (c) being alert to the occurrence of target behaviors.

Specifying and Defining Target Behaviors and Relevant Contextual Factors

Before using contingency management procedures, a therapist needs to clearly specify and operationalize the target behaviors. *Target behaviors* are those behaviors that are to be altered, either increased or decreased in frequency, intensity, or duration. As discussed in chapter 2, a thorough behavioral assessment involves collecting detailed data on the various target behaviors. Contingency management strategies generally work best when the target behavior is clearly defined, directly observable, and can be recorded or monitored.

In using contingency management, a therapist must remember that a behavior cannot be divorced from its context. Indeed, the context is the primary focus of contingency management. For a client who displays certain behavioral excesses, such as heroin use in the case of June, it is important to precisely specify which drugs she uses, how frequently and in what quantities she uses the drugs as well as when, where, and with whom she uses drugs. As contingency management interventions modify the context of behavior (antecedents and consequences), it is important to specify the contextual variables associated with drug use.

For June, relevant S^D might consist of the presence of drug-using friends (Fred), the presence of drugs or drug paraphernalia, certain areas of the city (e.g., those related to drug use), or other such factors. EOs might consist of withdrawal symptoms or drug cravings. EOs, S^D, and the effectiveness of potential reinforcers for drug abstinence (e.g., vouchers, cash, privileges) are quite idiographic and problem specific and must be clearly specified for each individual client before embarking on a contingency management program.

Orienting the Client to Contingency Management

As outlined by Linehan (1993a), it is important to first orient the client to the use of contingency management strategies. Clients often come to therapy with some understanding that positive consequences or rewards might increase certain behavior, whereas negative consequences or punishment might decrease certain behavior. Often, however, clients need more information to fully consent to and engage in the process of modifying their behaviors through contingency management procedures. In our experience, it is helpful to make two key points about learning principles.

The first point is that reinforcement, punishment, and extinction procedures are defined by their effect on behavior. A reinforcer is not a reinforcer if it does not increase the likelihood that a behavior will occur again under similar circumstances. Similarly, a punisher is not a punisher if it does not reduce behavior. Some clients believe that they are "reinforcing themselves" just because they are engaging in pleasurable activities or "punishing themselves" by intentionally harming themselves in some way because of what they did (e.g., cutting their arm with a razor in response to a situation associated with the emotions of guilt or shame). It is often useful for the client to understand, for example, that pleasurable activities themselves are not reinforcers unless they occur contingently on particular behaviors and increase the likelihood of these behaviors over time.

The second point is that persons do not always participate in behavior with the intention of receiving reinforcement from the environment. In fact, persons are often unaware of many of the factors that influence their behavior (Nisbett & Wilson, 1977). This is a particularly important point to make with clients who have a history of being called "manipulative" for engaging in unpleasant interpersonal behaviors. Consider the following example of a client who engages in frequent self-injury. In this example, the only time the client received any focused attention from her mother was when she was talking about her struggle to stop self-injuring. Otherwise, her mother spent most of their phone conversations talking about herself or her new husband. Even though this client had no intention of engaging in self-injury to get attention from her mother, over time, she and her therapist observed that her self-injury tended to occur a day or two prior to phone calls or visits with her mother, and her self-injury increased in frequency commensurate with increases in the frequency of conversations with her mother. As an experiment, this client was asked by her therapist to make self-injury an "off limits" topic with her mother, and a plan was generated for garnering her mother's attention that did not involve talking about self-injury. Please see Exhibit 5.1 for an example of how a therapist might communicate these points to a client.

Being Alert to the Occurrence of Target Behaviors

Positive therapeutic outcomes are more likely if the therapist remains alert to occurrences of the target behavior(s) both within and outside of ses-

EXHIBIT 5.1
Educating the Client Regarding Reinforcement

One way to get closer to reaching your goals in therapy is to use reinforcement. Have you ever heard of the word *reinforcement*? Reinforcement is any consequence that increases the likelihood that you will do a particular behavior again in the future. For example, let's say you took yourself out to your favorite place for coffee every time you exercised each day for a whole week. You noticed that, over time, you had more and more weeks of exercising everyday. In this case, going out for coffee would be a reinforcer, actually what's called a *positive reinforcer* for exercising. If, however, you found that going out for coffee had absolutely no effect on how often you exercised, then going for coffee would not be a reinforcer. A reinforcer has to be something that actually increases a behavior—it's not just something that is enjoyable or pleasant.

Another important point is that reinforcement can work without your even knowing it. Also, just because your behavior leads to positive results doesn't mean that you did it with the intention of getting those results. For example, I know that when you ask your children to do something and they say "no," yelling at them works to get them to say "yes" and do what you ask. The thing is that, you may have no interest, intention, or desire to yell at them at all. In fact, from what I know about you, you feel badly about yelling, and you would rather not do so. But, unfortunately, yelling actually works. Your yelling is reinforced by your children saying "yes" and doing what you have asked them to do.

---

sions. The therapist can facilitate this task by using self-monitoring or observational methods, consistently inquiring about key behavioral targets each week, and observing in-session behavior to determine whether target behaviors are occurring during sessions. Being alert to the occurrence of target behaviors has a useful purpose in both the assessment (e.g., for determining the contexts that reliably occasion these behaviors, and for establishing the frequency of these behaviors) and treatment stages of therapy. In treatment, when the therapist notices a target behavior, he or she has the opportunity to respond in an effective manner that will influence the frequency of these behaviors over time.

CHANGING BEHAVIOR BY ALTERING ANTECEDENTS

Intervention strategies described in this section involve altering antecedent events to change behavior. These strategies involve arranging, modifying, or otherwise altering the amount of contact clients have with particular stimuli to increase the likelihood of desired behaviors; reducing the likelihood of undesired behaviors; or both of these strategies. There are several different specific approaches for modifying antecedents, and examples of these procedures are provided subsequently.

Removing or Avoiding Antecedents

One approach to altering antecedents involves the removal, elimination, or avoidance of cues that occasion certain target behaviors. This approach, sometimes referred to as *cue elimination*, is especially useful for reducing problematic behaviors occasioned by certain environmental cues, such as addictive behaviors. When applied for this purpose, cue elimination involves having the client remove all drug-associated stimuli from his or her environment, and having the client completely avoid environments in which drugs are used (Cunningham, 1998). In more severe instances in which drug use has become associated with a large number of environmental stimuli in an individual's community, relocating to another location might be the only effective way for eliminating a substantial number of cues that occasion drug use.

Cue elimination is a common intervention in treatments for clients with substance use problems. Avoiding (or removing) "high-risk" situations is a central feature of relapse prevention for alcohol use problems (Marlatt & Gordon, 1985), and for cognitive behavior therapy (CBT) for alcohol problems in general (McCrady, 2001). Dialectical behavior therapy (DBT; Linehan, 1993a) for borderline personality disorder has also been adapted for use with persons who are dependent on opiates and other substances (Linehan et al., 2002). DBT for substance use problems involves a strategy called "burning bridges," which essentially involves having the client cut off his or her contact with drug-using people and drug dealers, thereby reducing the likelihood that he or she will encounter stimuli that signal that drug use will lead to reinforcement (Dimeff, Rizvi, Brown, & Linehan, 2000).

In an example of cue elimination procedures for reducing deliberate self-harm, "John" was a client who cut and burned himself a couple of times per week. He typically burned himself when he was feeling angry or ashamed, was overwhelmed with work obligations, or had experienced a recent conflict with his partner. It quickly became apparent, however, that he only burned himself when he was in a situation in which burning implements were readily available, or when he could see candles, incense, or matches nearby. As soon as he saw burning implements or the places in which they were stored, he experienced intense urges to burn himself, and he often acted on these urges. When he was ashamed, overwhelmed, or afraid, but burning implements were not easily attainable, or when he was in a place or situation in which burning was not an option (e.g., work), John typically found another way to cope with his emotions. The urges to self-injure were under the control of antecedent stimuli, consisting of the burning implements or, more broadly, situational stimuli that occasioned mental images of John burning himself.

In John's case, therapy initially involved stimulus control strategies to reduce his contact with burning implements. John, for instance, came up with a list of implements that he typically used to harm himself and then noted whether they were household necessities. He threw these nonessential items (e.g., incense candles) into the trash and placed essential items in a hard-to-reach place in the garage. Once these items were no longer visibly available in the house, John noticed a reduction in the frequency of his urges to self-harm. In addition, this strategy had the added benefit of making it time consuming and difficult for him to obtain burning implements when he had urges to harm himself.

Modifying Antecedents

Another strategy involves *modifying the antecedents* for problematic behaviors, which entails making changes in attributes of stimulus situations that are related to the occurrence of the undesired behaviors. For some people who struggle with alcohol or drug abuse, certain people or places become so strongly associated with substance use that it is almost impossible to avoid using substances in the presence of these people or at these places. Modifying drug use cues might involve encouraging the client to ask drug-using peers to stop using or offering drugs in his or her presence. "Heather" was a client who struggled to stop binge drinking. She effectively abstained from alcohol use in most contexts; however, she almost always drank when she was out with her friends at restaurants. Heather had become quite adept at refusing alcohol when the waiters or service staff offered it to her. When she was at a restaurant or pub with friends, however, they would often encourage her to drink, and when she said "no," her friends would badger her until she gave in. As she valued her friends and did not want to alienate or end her relationship with them, therapy involved helping her find ways to communicate to friends that she values their friendships but would prefer if they did not encourage her to drink. Although it took several attempts, Heather's friends eventually stopped asking her to drink, thus altering some of the key antecedents for drinking.

Introducing Stimulus Cues to Alter the Frequency of Behavior

In some instances, the therapist might help the client rearrange cues in his or her environment in a manner that increases the likelihood of desired behaviors or decreases problematic behaviors. These strategies can be especially helpful when the client is motivated to change particular behaviors or engage in new behaviors but forgets to do so, has not established a routine of practicing new skills, or is busy and overwhelmed with life.

Cues, for example, might be introduced into a client's typical environment to increase target behaviors. Cues might include items such as sticky notes placed in key places around the home to serve as "reminders" for the client to engage in or practice particular behaviors. Similarly, a client might carry around a "coping card" that lists new behaviors to use in certain situations (e.g., in a crisis, use the following skills to cope with emotions), or use mnemonic or other strategies (e.g., the "method of loci") from cognitive psychology to enhance recall of details regarding specific behaviors and when to use them.

"Dan" wished to lose weight and wanted to reduce the amount of food that he ate while he was at home. His therapist worked with him to introduce several cues into the environment to decrease his overeating of fatty and sugary foods. These alterations included increasing the availability and salience of healthy foods not associated with overeating and the introduction of small plates, bowls, and utensils to occasion smaller amounts of food consumption. Dan also decided to reward himself once per week with a tall "mocha" if he had avoided overeating for the whole week. To increase the salience of the contingency between avoiding overeating behavior and the reinforcer (the mocha), Dan placed a piece of paper on his refrigerator on which he had written, "Tall mocha on Thursday if I stick to the eating plan."

Discrimination Training

Discrimination training involves the delivery of reinforcers for behavior in a given stimulus situation (S^D) but not in other stimulus situations (S^Δ). As used here, S^Δ denotes a discriminative stimulus that signals the unavailability of reinforcement or punishment for a particular behavior. When such training is successful, an individual learns to discriminate between situations in which certain behavior is appropriate (e.g., results in reinforcement) or not appropriate (e.g., does not result in reinforcement). As a result, the client will more likely attend to relevant cues (S^D) in a given situation and ignore irrelevant cues (S^Δ).

Persons with some forms of anxiety disorder, for example, may associate many stimuli with aversive events or outcomes and hence experience many aspects of the world as threatening. Therapy might, therefore, involve helping the individual learn cues that reliably signal aversive outcomes. That way, the client only engages in avoidance behavior in the presence of cues that signal actual or probable threats or dangers (S^D). When cues that are not associated with actual threats or danger (S^Δ) occur, the client either ignores them or responds in a manner that does not involve avoidance.

As a therapeutic tool, discrimination training is probably most appropriate when the client's problem behaviors result from inappropriate *stimulus generalization*. Technically speaking, stimulus generalization occurs when a behavior that has been reinforced in one context increases in frequency or intensity in other contexts in which the behavior has not been previously reinforced. As a general rule, previously neutral stimuli that have similarities with the physical or sensory qualities of the established S^D are especially susceptible to stimulus generalization.

Stimulus generalization can become problematic when individuals experience different environmental features as functionally similar when they are not and respond in a rigid, inflexible, and ineffective manner. When discrimination training is used to reduce stimulus generalization, behavior that has generalized to inappropriate cues becomes more narrowly confined to situations in which it is appropriate and less likely in situations in which it is not.

One central feature of posttraumatic stress disorder (PTSD) is the generalization of trauma-related cues to cues that were previously neutral. As a result, individuals with PTSD often respond to sets of cues that do not actually signal forthcoming dangerous events. Individuals who have developed PTSD as a result of events experienced during combat, for example, might sometimes respond to aspects of current environments as if they were in a combat situation (e.g., ducking for cover when a helicopter flies overhead; experiencing intense fear or panic, accompanied with a strong desire to flee or escape, upon hearing a car backfire). As a result of stimulus generalization, the individual acts as if large numbers of stimulus cues in his or her typical environments signal a danger or threat.

Behavioral therapies for persons with PTSD often involve discrimination training to reduce stimulus generalization that has occurred since the traumatic events. This might include, for example, noticing and discriminating other contextual features in the environment that indicate it is not a dangerous situation. When such training is successful, the client responds to common environmental cues that are not associated with an increased risk or danger as S^Δ rather than S^D.

Sometimes individuals demonstrate deficits in discriminating among different emotional states. For instance, a person might apply the word "anger" to an experience that is more appropriately labeled "anxiety." As a result of mislabeling the experience of anxiety as anger, a person might behave in a manner that is incongruent with the actual emotional experience but consistent with the misapplied label, such as verbally or physically attacking another person. Follette, Naugle, and Linnerooth (2000) and Linehan (1993a) described other problems associated with discrimination deficits, such as emotionally responding to events or people, inappropriately expressing to others the emotional impact of their actions, difficulty regulating one's emotions, or trouble "motivating" appropriate action (whereby the mislabeled emotion state serves as an EO for a different emotion that the client does not experience). In short, the functional potential associated with emotions cannot be fully realized among persons who have deficits in their ability to discriminate and accurately label their emotional experiences.

Several clinical problems are defined, in part, by difficulties in accurately discriminating among and labeling private events. Behavioral interventions for such deficits include discrimination training of emotions and training in the accurate application of feeling–state words to various emotional experiences. *Self-labeling training*, for example, involves teaching the client skills that assist him or her in accurately identifying and labeling emotional experiences. Components of this form of discrimination training include (a) an identification of the events that occasioned the emotional experience; (b) a description of the nature of the emotion, such as quality, intensity, and the physical sensations or thoughts that accompany it; and (c) a delineation of types of behaviors that might be used to express the emotion, or the types of behaviors that the emotion might motivate (Linehan, 1993a). Reinforcing the accurate application of labels to private events such as emotions is considerably more difficult than it is for overt events, and requires attentiveness and empathy on the part of the therapist.

Arranging Establishing Operations to Decrease Behavior

Some behaviors can be reduced by altering EOs. Many of us have, for example, learned to avoid grocery shopping on an empty stomach after discovering that we end up purchasing highly caloric "junk" foods, or go beyond our intended grocery budget. When we are feeling somewhat satiated on food, perhaps as a result of having a meal beforehand, the reinforcing qualities of the fattening foods on the grocery shelves is lessened.

One example of arranging EOs to decrease behavior is the use of methadone to decrease heroin use. Among other properties, methadone suppresses narcotic withdrawal symptoms, reduces drug cravings, and blocks the high from heroin while not producing euphoria itself. Methadone, then, reduces EOs that occasion heroin use and reduces the positive reinforcing properties of heroin. Given these effects, methadone use results in a decrease in behaviors that have historically been used to obtain heroin as well as a reduction in heroin use (Poling & Gaynor, 2003)—in part because of the influence it has on altering EOs (biological conditions) that historically occasioned heroin use.

Satiation therapy, perhaps more appropriately termed "oversatiation therapy," involves the delivery of more reinforcers than is optimal or preferred (Bowers, 2003). The provision of an excessive amount of reinforcers might eventually make them less desirable or less effective in terms of influencing behavior. With this approach, reinforcers are delivered in a manner that is not contingent on the occurrence of a target behavior.

Ayllon (1963) published the first description of satiation therapy. In this case study, a psychiatric inpatient frequently hoarded towels. Initial attempts to suppress this behavior by hospital staff were ineffective. When satiation therapy was implemented, hospital staff provided towels noncontingently over several weeks, with more towels delivered to the client's room each successive week. As the program progressed, the client's towel hoarding decreased in frequency. In fact, she frequently attempted to give back or remove towels given to her by hospital staff.

Other examples of satiation therapy can be found in sexual deviance treatment literature. One such approach, called *masturbatory satiation*, has as a therapeutic goal the reduction of sexual arousal to inappropriate stimuli, such as children. This procedure involves prolonged masturbation while engaging in inappropriate sexual imagery. Because masturbation is prolonged

(1–2 hours) and extends beyond ejaculation to the point that it no longer produces pleasurable sensations, inappropriate sexual stimuli eventually lose their erotic or stimulating qualities. Examples of this approach with pedophiles can be found in Marshall (1979) and Johnston, Hudson, and Marshall (1992).

One strategy for reducing behaviors that are maintained by positive reinforcement, especially social reinforcement, is the noncontingent delivery of events, actions, or objects that normally reinforce problematic behavior. This means that reinforcers are delivered on the basis of the passage of time and are independent of displays of the target behavior (Vollmer & Wright, 2003). As this intervention does not involve the establishment of alternative behaviors, it is not a particularly useful technique by itself. Rather, it might be part of a larger treatment package geared toward the reduction of a specific set of behaviors.

Chiles and Strosahl (1995) outlined a comprehensive approach for treating and managing individuals who are chronically suicidal. One intervention element in their treatment model, the "random support call," involves the noncontingent delivery of attention and support from the therapist. This intervention is based on the idea that some clients have a history of receiving attention and support from others (positive reinforcers) when they engage in self-injurious acts (target behavior to decrease). These phone calls involve the therapist telephoning the client from time to time just to check in and inquire how things are. Phone calls are brief, just a couple of minutes, and convey the message that the therapist is engaged in and genuinely supportive of the client's therapy.

> I care about how you're doing. I hope the behavioral homework assignment is going well. You were going to pay particular attention to x. How is that going? I really look forward to seeing you next week. Take care. (Chiles & Strosahl, 1995, p. 137)

The rationale for this intervention is that noncontingent support and attention from the therapist lessens the association between suicidal behavior and the provision of support (e.g., attention and caring by the therapist). In this way, noncontingent attention might also be an effective strategy because it provides the client with valued social support that has been primarily accessible only by talking about suicide or engaging in suicide attempts. Random support calls might also reduce EOs that occasion suicidal behaviors (e.g., deprivation of support and attention) by providing the support and attention that he or she is deprived (similar to the example above regarding Edith). From the perspective of an EO, if the deprived reinforcer is already being provided noncontingently, there is less of a need to engage in the problematic behavior to obtain the reinforcer. In the case of deliberate self-harm, why would a person intentionally physically injure him- or herself to gain attention when attention is freely and abundantly available (Vollmer & Wright, 2003)?

Arranging Establishing Operations to Increase Behavior

Later in this chapter, we discuss behavioral contracting as a contingency management procedure. For our purposes here, we note that behavioral contracts are sometimes used to make explicit a client's goals, the behavioral steps that facilitate the realization of those goals, and the consequences of acting toward a goal (e.g., delivery of specified reinforcer) or away from a goal (e.g., loss of specified reinforcers, or response cost). Contracts also represent a publicly expressed commitment to act in the manner outlined in the contract. When thought of in this way, the contract can possibly function as an EO that increases the frequency of behaviors specified in the contract (Miltenberger, 2004). The contract, for example, might occasion an aversive state (e.g., anxiety, tension) when the client observes that he or she is not behaving in a manner consistent with the provisions of the agreement, contemplating the therapist's reaction to his or her failure to follow through with agreed-on provisions, or thinking about what it would be like not to realize personal goals. Acting in accordance with the contract under these conditions, then, would be negatively reinforced behavior, as doing so would reduce any anxiety or tension elicited by the contract (Malott et al., 2000; Miltenberger, 2004).

In another example of arranging EOs to increase behavior, consider a client who is depressed, reports having little energy, and takes lengthy naps (2–3 hours) during the day. At bedtime, however, the client typically has great difficulty falling asleep and usually lies in bed restlessly for several hours. As part of the client's treatment for sleep disturbance, the therapist instructs him or her to avoid naps during the day, even if he or she feels very tired. The therapist reasoned that the extended naps during the day might have removed an important EO (feeling tired or desiring sleep) that makes falling asleep a reinforcing activity. Falling asleep is not reinforcing when the client is not tired. Blocking sleep during the day might increase feelings of tiredness at nighttime, thus increasing the likelihood that at bedtime (S^D), the client will fall asleep (Miltenberger, 2004).

ALTERING CONSEQUENCES TO INFLUENCE BEHAVIOR

Applying or altering consequences to effect behavior change primarily involves reinforcement, punishment, or extinction-based strategies. As noted previously, when the goal is to increase behavior, the best therapeutic strategy is to use reinforcement. In contrast, when the goal is to decrease behavior, therapy may involve extinction or punishment. There are several ways to incorporate the modification of consequences into treatment, but across many different behavioral and cognitive behavior treatments, the most common strategies often boil down to three essential steps: (a) determine which contingencies are under the control of the therapist and the client; (b) establish ways to block or prevent the reinforcement of maladaptive or undesirable behaviors, or extinguish or punish these behaviors; and (c) establish ways to reinforce adaptive or desirable behaviors.

Issues in Reinforcement Contingencies

When using contingency management strategies, a therapist needs to be aware of several issues that are particularly applicable to reinforcement, punishment, and extinction procedures. One important point about reinforcement strategies is that reinforcement is idiographic. What is reinforcing to one client may not be reinforcing, and indeed may be punishing, to another client. Praise for therapeutic progress, for example, may actually decrease therapeutic progress for a client with a learning history in which praise has typically been followed by punishment or an increase in demands for continued improvement.

The timing of reinforcement influences the degree to which it will effectively increase behavior. Generally, reinforcement that occurs very soon after the behavior of interest (i.e., immediate reinforcement) is more likely to lead to behavior change, compared with delayed reinforcement. For instance, if a parent is helping his daughter learn to say "please" when asking for treats at a party, the child may be more likely to say "please" if the parent gives her a treat immediately after she says please. If, however, the parent gives his daughter a treat the next day, the treat is less likely to influence the child's likelihood of saying "please." Similarly, if a client comes in after completing an arduous therapy homework assignment and the therapist waits until the following week to acknowledge the client's completion of it, attention from the therapist will likely not influence or maintain "homework behavior."

In addition to timing, the scheduling of reinforcement influences the extent to which it increases future behavior. There are several different types of reinforcement schedules and two that are particularly relevant for the following discussion:

- A *continuous schedule* involves providing reinforcement after each instance of a particular behavior. The therapist might provide praise, attention, or other forms of reinforcement every time the client, for example, successfully completes his or her therapy homework, avoids using drugs (for drug-abusing clients), or spends time outside the home (for agoraphobic clients).
- A *variable ratio schedule* involves providing reinforcement following a varying number of responses. In this case, the therapist on occasion provides reinforcement after a couple of effective responses; on other occasions, the therapist waits until the client has emitted the behavior several times. For a client with

anorexia, for example, a therapist might provide reinforcement after the client has eaten three healthy meals. At other times, however, the therapist might provide reinforcement only after the client has eaten five or six healthy meals.

When considering the use of reinforcement schedules to influence client behavior, a therapist should remember four important principles:

- Continuous reinforcement is most effective at helping a client learn a new behavior and will initially lead to the highest frequency of responses.
- Behavior on a continuous reinforcement schedule is vulnerable to extinction when the reinforcement schedule is thinned (made less frequent).
- The variable ratio schedule is associated with the most resistance to extinction.
- The best way to help a client learn new behaviors and maintain them in the face of low or absent reinforcement (i.e., to produce "extinction-resistant" behavior) is to first reinforce a new behavior continuously and then thin reinforcement to a variable ratio schedule.

The characteristics of the reinforcer also influence the extent to which reinforcement influences behavior. Generally, reinforcers that are larger in magnitude are more effective than reinforcers that are smaller in magnitude. If, for example, a gambler wins $1,000 at the slot machines, he or she is more likely to play the slots again than if the winnings are more meager (e.g., $1). However, sometimes reinforcers can be too large. Overly enthusiastic and emotionally intense praise by the therapist, or an unrealistically large reward for performance on schoolwork (e.g., providing an A+ for C+ level work), may actually be less effective than reinforcers that are more realistic and moderate.

There also has been some suggestion that using *natural reinforcers* (when available) is preferable to using arbitrary reinforcers (Kohlenberg & Tsai, 1991). Natural reinforcers have an inherent connection with the behavior of interest. In contrast, arbitrary reinforcers are not naturally connected with the behavior and generally would not occur in the client's natural environment. Rewarding a client with praise (e.g., "Thank you so much for opening up to me about your past trauma") for open self-disclosure often represents arbitrary reinforcement, as it is quite unlikely that people would respond this way to the client in his or her natural environment. In contrast, natural reinforcement might involve leaning toward the client, conveying interest, listening empathetically, nodding, and other such behaviors that are likely to represent adaptive reinforcing responses in the client's natural environment.

As we noted earlier, satiation (an EO) is another factor that can influence the effectiveness of reinforcement. The client may simply not respond to S^Ds that signal a type of reinforcement that has already been delivered at a high volume. In fact, after satiation, stimuli that would have previously functioned as reinforcers might, in fact, function as punishers.

Determine Which Consequences Are Under the Influence of the Therapist

Often it is helpful for therapists to be aware of the types of consequences they can use in reinforcing desirable behaviors or extinguishing or punishing undesirable behaviors. The therapeutic relationship offers many opportunities to use principles and practices of reinforcement, punishment, and extinction. Among contemporary behavioral therapies, functional analytic psychotherapy (Kohlenberg & Tsai, 1991) and DBT (Linehan, 1993a) perhaps most explicitly use reinforcement, punishment, and extinction in the context of strong therapeutic relationships. Exhibit 5.2 includes a list of different therapist behaviors that may reinforce, extinguish, or punish client behaviors. This is not an exhaustive list, but it does include many of the most frequent strategies therapists use in standard outpatient CBT.

Prevent the Reinforcement of Dysfunctional or Undesirable Behaviors

Once the therapist and client have decided to work on reducing particular target behaviors, it is important for the therapist to avoid reinforcing these behaviors when they occur. If a socially anxious client is working on increasing social activities, and he or she avoids attending a group therapy session, the therapist may want to avoid behavior that might reinforce such avoidance. As another example, in DBT, therapists are encouraged to use a neutral, matter-of-fact tone of voice and restrict their display of warmth and support after a client has made a suicide attempt or has injured him- or herself (Linehan, 1993a). The rationale is that it is critical to avoid reinforcing these behaviors.

Not all target behaviors are amenable to reinforcement from the therapist, however, and not all clients will increase behavior in response to presumably "reinforcing" actions on the part of the therapist. For some clients, if the therapist provides attention, praise, support, and warmth following the occurrence of maladaptive behaviors, these behaviors may increase. For other clients, attention, praise, support, and warmth may have no effect on certain behaviors. Nevertheless, in the case of suicidal or deliberate self-harm behaviors, the therapist might err on the side of caution (assuming that attention and support may function as positive reinforcers), as the last thing a therapist wants to do is reinforce harmful behaviors, or behaviors that move the client away from his or her goals.

Reinforce Adaptive Behaviors and Progress

The therapist can use contingency management strategies in a variety of ways. As illustrated by Linehan (1993a) and Kohlenberg and Tsai (1991), two key ways for doing this are (a) to use consequences within the therapeu-

EXHIBIT 5.2
Consequences Under the Control of the Therapist

Reinforcement strategies	
Positive reinforcement	Negative reinforcement
Increasing session length Increasing session frequency Praise, encouragement Increasing eye contact Validation Contact in-between sessions Warmth Expressing caring and positive regard Doing things for the client Making changes in the therapy when asked Attentiveness Therapist self-disclosure Prosocial chit-chat	Decreasing session length (for clients who find longer sessions aversive) Decreasing session frequency (for those who prefer long sessions) Reducing or withdrawing demands (e.g., homework) Making changes to aspects of the therapy that the client does not like Not talking about a behavior that a client feels ashamed of (e.g., self-harm) when it is not happening

Punishment strategies	
Positive punishment	Negative punishment
Expressing disappointment Expressing disapproval Expressing frustration Nonverbally expressing disapproval Confronting the client Increasing demands on the client Talking at length about the maladaptive behavior Increasing session length, frequency, or contact in-between sessions (for clients who find contact aversive)	Withdrawing warmth Withdrawing validation Reducing session length Reducing session frequency Reducing contact in-between sessions

Extinction strategies
Ignoring dysfunctional behavior Using a neutral voice-tone Using a matter-of-fact tone of voice Being less available to the client after dysfunctional behavior Limiting or withdrawing warmth Sticking to the treatment plan despite the occurrence of distress or maladaptive behavior

Note. Whether events listed in this exhibit actually reinforce, punish, or extinguish behavior would need to be idiographically determined for each client. We are indebted to Marsha Linehan, as several of these strategies have been either outlined in her text on dialectical behavior therapy (Linehan, 1993a) or demonstrated or communicated to the second author (Chapman) during his postdoctoral training with her.

tic relationship and (b) to set up formal or informal reinforcement, extinction, or punishment systems, or assist the client in doing so.

If the therapist notices that undesirable target behaviors are occurring during the session, or have occurred since the last session, the therapist might use extinction procedures. There is a variety of ways to use extinction. One method is to simply ignore or restrict the degree to which the therapist responds to the target behavior. As another example, a therapist treating an angry client who displays outbursts in sessions might ignore the angry behavior and respond to the client as if he or she is behaving in a "normal" manner (if it is possible that the behavior has inadvertently been positively reinforced in the past by the therapist or other people).

An important point regarding reinforcement and punishment is that providing reinforcing responses within sessions is more likely to reinforce in-session behavior than it is to reinforce behavior that occurs outside of sessions (Kohlenberg & Tsai, 1991). As previously mentioned, the closer in time that the reinforcement occurs to the behavior, the more effective it is in increasing the probability of a particular behavior being repeated in the setting within which it was reinforced. Sometimes verbal praise, encouragement, or other such therapist behaviors may increase the client's *verbal report* of progress or positive behaviors but may not reinforce the behaviors themselves.

There are several examples in the clinical literature of reinforcing adaptive behavior and progress. In their behavioral intervention for cocaine dependence, Higgins et al. (1991) evaluated the effectiveness of a treatment approach that offered reinforcement for cocaine abstinence. When clients produced clean urine specimens at scheduled meetings, they earned points that were worth the equivalent of 15 cents per point. Points were redeemable for retail items. The first negative specimen was worth 10 points, or $1.50. Each successive negative specimen was worth an additional 5 points, with an additional $10 bonus offered after each set of four consecutive negative specimens. Urine samples were collected four times per week, and the maximum an individual could earn if consecutively abstinent over the 12-week course of therapy was $1,038. A dirty urine sample indicative of cocaine use would reset the point scale back to the initial $1.50 level. In this study, 11 of 13 (85%) clients completed the 12-week intervention. Of these, 10 (91%) achieved abstinence for 4 continuous weeks, 6 (55%) were abstinent for 8 continuous weeks, and 3 (27%) were abstinent for the entire 12 weeks. Overall, persons who received this contingency-based behavioral intervention produced a significantly larger number of clean urine samples compared with control participants who received 12-step counseling. Although treatment programs that offer monetary incentives for progress can be expensive, they are often much less expensive than several weeks of inpatient treatment.

Other examples of this approach are presented in Petry et al. (2001). In their case examples, Petry et al. described the use of a "prize bowl" to reinforce drug abstinence. In one example, a client with opioid and cocaine dependence was allowed one draw from the prize bowl for each urine specimen that was clean of one of the substances, and four draws if the specimen was clean of both substances. The prize bowl contained slips of paper, on half of which was written "good job" with no additional prize. Forty-four percent of the slips indicated a "small prize" (e.g., $1 food vouchers, lipstick, nail polish), 6% a "large prize" (e.g., sweatshirt, watch, a voucher for books or CDs), and 0.4% a "jumbo prize" (e.g., television, VCR). Urine samples were collected 2 to 3 times per week, and for each week of consecutive abstinences of both substances, bonus draws were awarded (e.g., 5 bonus draws for the first week, 6 bonus draws for the second week, 7 bonus draws for the third week, etc.). A total of 200 draws were possible when the client was completely clean of substances for the 12-week study period.

Behavioral Interventions for Developing, Increasing, or Strengthening Behavior

In this section, we describe several different behavioral interventions that use reinforcers to develop, increase, or strengthen behavior. These strategies largely involve shaping and modifying reinforcement contingencies.

Shaping

Shaping is a procedure that is most appropriate for developing a skill or establishing a behavior not currently in the person's repertoire. Shaping is reinforcement of successive approximations to a final, desired response. Once a complex behavior or behavior sequence is specified for development, the sequence or components of the behavior is broken down into smaller elements. During shaping, a reinforcer is delivered on each occasion that the client engages in the initial behavior in a sequence of behaviors. Once the client has established the initial behavioral element, the therapist prompts the next behavior and withholds reinforcement until the client engages in that next behavior or makes an effort to engage in it. Each time, it takes a closer approximation to the desired behavioral sequence for the client to get the reinforcement. This process continues until the client reliably performs the target behavior. At that point, the emphasis shifts from the acquisition of behavior to the maintenance of behavior (Ferguson, 2003). During this maintenance phase, the therapist might deliver reinforcement not for each instance of the target behavior but instead for some variable number of instances of the target behavior (e.g., reinforcement is delivered every fourth time the behavior is displayed).

As a primary method of teaching new behaviors, shaping has been successfully illustrated in several clinical investigations (e.g., Kazdin, 2001; Miltenberger, 2004), including studies in which persons with schizophrenia were taught appropriate social behaviors (Pratt & Mueser, 2002). In most applications of CBT, however, shaping processes tend to be more informally carried out. When teaching new or alternative social behaviors, for example, behavior therapists might use *behavioral rehearsal*, otherwise known as *role playing*. This approach is most useful for teaching new behaviors or skills, or demonstrating how to perform a particular behavior, and consists of the following components (Goldfried & Davison, 1976):

- willingness of the client to learn new and relevant behaviors in areas of skill or ability acknowledged as currently deficit or non-effective;
- identification of situations in which deficit or noneffective responding is a source of distress or impairments in functioning;
- participation in role plays in a clinical context, which involves the enactment of behaviors aided by instruction (e.g., telling the client what to do), therapist modeling, or shaping process and feedback provided by the therapist; and
- performance of rehearsed behaviors in natural environments, coupled with self-evaluating whether the behavior was performed skillfully and resulted in desirable consequences.

Other considerations and guidelines associated with shaping procedures can be found in Ferguson (2003), Goldfried and Davison (1976), Kazdin (2001), and Miltenberger (2004).

Increasing Reinforcement for Desired Behaviors That Occur at a Low Rate

In some instances, desired or adaptive behavior occurs at a low rate because reinforcers are unavailable from the client's natural environment. The absence of reinforcers for behavior over time might result in extinction. Low rate of reinforcement for behavior has figured predominantly in some theories of depression and has been used to account for the low rate of activity often observed among depressed persons (Lewinsohn & Gotlib, 1995). Low rates of reinforcement for certain behaviors, particularly social behaviors, are also common among people who overuse escape and avoidance coping strategies, such as those who experience excess amounts of anxiety.

Gaining access to potential reinforcers might involve entering into new environments that potentially offer more reinforcers than current environments, avoiding punishing or aversive environments that decrease or suppress behavior, becoming more behaviorally active, or some combination of these strategies. One approach for realizing these therapeutic goals might involve having the client reenter situations that he or she avoids but that were previously associated with reinforcement. Another approach might involve pleasant events scheduling, with emphasis placed on increasing the frequency of behaviors that were previously associated with pleasure and enjoyment (Lewinsohn, Antonuccio, Steinmetz-Breckenridge, & Teri, 1984). In chapter 8 of this volume, we describe strategies for increasing behavioral activity.

A related issue is a focus on a *restricted range of reinforcers*. Substance abusers, for example, have a tendency to spend a good deal of time engaged in behaviors that are linked to substance use. "Jordan," for example, spent much of his time begging, stealing, or searching for money to buy drugs with, seeking out the "perfect" drug paraphernalia, using drugs, getting high, and recovering from the effects of drugs (e.g., hangover, fatigue, difficulties in concentration). Treatment with Jordan might, therefore, involve expanding the reinforcing consequences for behaviors unrelated to or incompatible with drug use. Such behaviors might involve participation in alternate pleasant activities or the development of skills that can be used to access reinforcers that are not currently available (e.g., vocational skills, social skills). As a result of such interventions, Jordan might rediscover that behaviors other than those associated with drug use can also produce reinforcing outcomes.

One important behavioral principle to keep in mind is the *matching law*, originally demonstrated by Herrnstein (1961). According to the matching law, the frequency, intensity, and time that an individual spends engaging in a particular behavior is directly proportional to the reinforcement value of the behavior. Essentially, people "match" their behavior to the available schedule of reinforcement. Lejuez and colleagues (Hopko, Lejuez, Ruggiero, & Eifert, 2003; Lejuez, Hopko, & Hopko, 2001, 2002) applied this principle to the treatment of depression. If reinforcement is more frequent, accessible, or immediate for engaging in depressive behaviors (e.g., staying in bed all day, avoiding people, watching hours of television) than it is for engaging in nondepressive behaviors (e.g., going out, socializing, working, engaging in enjoyable recreational activities), the individual will devote more time and effort to engaging in depressive behaviors. When we apply the matching law to the example of Jordan, his therapist must find some way to make the reinforcement value of prosocial, adaptive behaviors stronger than the reinforcement value for drug-use related behaviors. Please see Figure 5.1 for an illustration of how this might work in the case of Jordan's drug use.

Another approach for increasing low-rate behaviors is to make engagement in high-frequency behaviors contingent on engagement in the low-frequency behaviors targeted to be increased. This procedure is sometimes referred to as *Premacking*, named after the individual who first described the procedure (Premack, 1959). An assumption underlying this approach is that a behavior that occurs with low frequency (or less preferred) becomes more probable when high-frequency behaviors (or more preferred) are contingent on performance of the low frequency behavior. In DBT (Linehan, 1993a), for example, high-risk behaviors such as suicidal behavior and deliberate self-harm represent the highest priority treatment targets. When a client in DBT reports current suicidal or self-harm ideation, or reports engagement in suicidal or self-harm behavior since the last session, the therapist gives these behaviors the most attention and the largest amount of session time. Many clients who routinely engage in such behaviors, however, do not particularly like talking about them (and would like to avoid doing so). In DBT, however, one way to use Premacking is to defer other topics of discussion until high-priority behaviors such as those associated with self-harm and suicide have been addressed. In this respect, discussion of quality-of-life issues that are important to clients (more preferred topic area) is contingent on com-

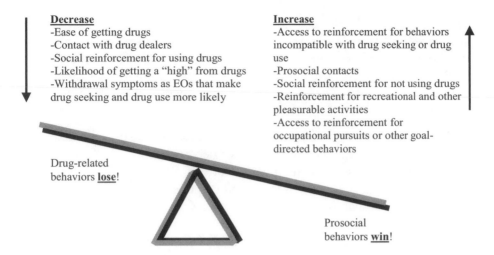

Decrease
-Ease of getting drugs
-Contact with drug dealers
-Social reinforcement for using drugs
-Likelihood of getting a "high" from drugs
-Withdrawal symptoms as EOs that make
drug seeking and drug use more likely

Increase
-Access to reinforcement for behaviors
incompatible with drug seeking or drug
use
-Prosocial contacts
-Social reinforcement for not using drugs
-Reinforcement for recreational and other
pleasurable activities
-Access to reinforcement for
occupational pursuits or other goal-
directed behaviors

Drug-related
behaviors **lose**!

Prosocial
behaviors **win**!

Figure 5.1. Interventions based on matching law in the case of Jordan's drug use.
EO = establishing operations.

plete and through discussions about self-harm and suicidal behaviors (less preferred area), when relevant (see Naugle & O'Donohue, 1998, who observed the similarity of this procedure in DBT to Premacking). Among other applications, Premacking has been used to increase activity levels among individuals with schizophrenia (W. S. Mitchell & Stoffelmayr, 1973) and time spent walking for a person with conversion disorder (Kallman, Hersen, & O'Toole, 1975).

Procedures for Decreasing or Weakening Behavior

In this section, we describe several behavioral interventions that use extinction and punishment procedures to decrease or weaken behavior. These interventions include extinction and differential reinforcement, covert sensitization, and response cost procedures.

Extinction and Differential Reinforcement

One way to decrease the frequency of problematic target behaviors is to eliminate the reinforcers that maintain them. When a behavior previously maintained by reinforcement no longer produces reinforcing outcomes, the behavior will likely decrease in frequency and perhaps be eliminated (or extinguished) altogether.

An important first step in using extinction procedures is to identify the reinforcers that maintain the behavior. Functional analyses of the problem behavior will often identify the reinforcers that support the behavior. Once the therapist and client have decided to eliminate reinforcers that maintain the problem behavior, the next step is to consider how to respond when the target behavior does not occur, if at all. When extinction procedures are used to reduce the frequency or intensity of a target behavior, some type of reinforcement contingency is usually added to establish a behavioral alternative to the behavior targeted for elimination. Examples of reinforcement contingencies that might accompany extinction procedures include the following:

- *Differential reinforcement of other behavior (DRO)* is delivered when the target behavior does not occur within a specified interval. Reinforcement, then, is contingent on the target behavior not occurring over a specified period, or the absence of the target behavior.
- *Differential reinforcement of alternative behavior (DRA)* is delivered following the display of an alternative behavior that is functionally similar to the target behavior but different in topography (form). This method is used when the therapeutic goal is to replace problematic target behaviors with more adaptive behaviors that produce similar outcomes.

In the case of DRO, the therapist and client determine how long the client must go without engaging in the target behavior to obtain the reinforcement. When DRA is used, the client and therapist need to agree on the alternative behavior or acceptable range of behavioral alternatives. Under ideal circumstances, the alternative behavior is already within the client's behavioral repertoire and is naturally supported (reinforced) by the client's social environment (Wallace & Robles, 2003). If the alternative behavior is not currently in the client's repertoire, the therapist might first use shaping or other contingency management procedures to establish the behavior prior to embarking on the DRA approach. The therapist and client also collaboratively decide on the nature of the reinforcer. In the case of DRA, the same natural reinforcers that supported the target behavior ideally are accessible through the alternative behavior. In the case of DRO, an ideal reinforcer is one that is just as potent or even more so than the reinforcers that maintained the target behavior. Reinforcers are most effective when they occur immediately and continuously after displays of the desired alternative behavior (e.g., with DRA) or after the client does not display the undesired behavior within a specified interval (e.g., with DRO; Wallace & Robles, 2003).

In an example of DRO and DRA procedures for reducing drug use (Iguchi, Belding, Morral, Lamb, & Husband, 1997), three interventions were compared: voucher reinforcers for clean (i.e., negative for targeted drugs) urinalyses (UA group), voucher reinforcers for the completion of treatment-plan-related tasks (TP group), and standard treatment (STD group). In the UA condition, participants earned $5 in vouchers for each clean urine sample (collected 3 times per week). In the TP condition, participants earned up to

$15 in vouchers each week for completing therapy-related tasks assigned by their therapists. The STD condition consisted of individual counseling sessions and medication-administration-related privileges.

The reinforcement contingency for the UA group was based on DRO principles, as avoiding drug use during a specified period (between urine samples collected at regular intervals) resulted in the delivery of a reinforcer ($5 voucher exchangeable for goods). The reinforcement contingency for the TP group was based on DRA principles, as the delivery of vouchers was used to reinforce instances in which the client engaged in behaviors consistent with his or her individual long-term treatment goals, which were also inconsistent with drug use. When a client did not have some of these behaviors within his or her repertoire, planned activities often involved a shaping component designed to help the client learn the behaviors. In the case of a jobless person who wanted to achieve full-time employment, the goal for an initial week might involve contacting two vocational training programs during the week and bringing literature on class offerings to therapy. The next week's activity might be to schedule an evaluation for eligibility for admission to a training program. The subsequent week's activity might be to supply proof (e.g., paperwork) of participation in an assessment meeting, and so on.

All participants were opiate dependent, and the main outcome variable for all groups over 12-weeks of therapy was the percentage of drug-free urine samples. Study results indicated that the TP condition was associated with proportionately more clean urine samples than either the UA or the STD conditions. Treatment gains for persons in the TP condition were also maintained during a 6-week follow-up period. These findings suggest that reinforcing alternate behaviors consistent with long-term goals and inconsistent with drug use can facilitate drug abstinence among dependent persons.

Remember Edith, who had difficulty saying "no" to her husband Sam's sexual advances? In therapy with this couple, one of the first steps would be to identify the husband's behavior as coercive sexual behavior. Before embarking on further treatment, the therapist might assess whether each partner is committed to remaining in the relationship and working on these problems. If so, therapy might first involve clarifying for the couple exactly how coercion works in their relationship. In doing so, it is often helpful to define positive and negative reinforcement and illustrate how each partner is caught in a coercive behavioral trap. As an example, the therapist might state, "Sam, you would like to have sex with your wife more often, and you have learned that if you act in a threatening manner she will usually give in. So, you get positive reinforcement for 'threatening' behavior. Edith, you have been hit by your husband in the past, so when he acts in a threatening manner, this is a signal for physical danger. You have learned that if you do what he wants you to do, you get negative reinforcement because your actions stop his threats and protect you from being hurt. What we have to do is work on getting you both out of this trap. . . ."

Therapy with this couple might involve a combination of DRA procedures, shaping, and perhaps skills training. Extinction-oriented interventions might involve removing positive reinforcement of threatening behavior on the part of the husband (extinction) and removing the negative reinforcement for the wife's acquiescence. One approach for accomplishing this would be to assess whether the husband has the skills to express his needs or wishes in a noncoercive manner, or in such a way that he does not violate the rights of his wife or others. If the husband has deficits in this area, therapy with him might first emphasize instruction in relationship-enhancing communication skills, perhaps using skills training (see chap. 7) and shaping strategies. Another strategy would be to work individually with the wife to help her find ways to decline sexual requests and yet remain safe from physical abuse. Additional ancillary anger management interventions or individual treatment for spousal aggression might help the husband learn how to regulate his anger and reduce the threat of physical aggression in the relationship. Finally, another approach might be to clarify the sexual interests and needs of each partner and come up with effective strategies for both partners to communicate these needs. In each case, the therapist would focus on making sure that both partners are reinforcing relationship-enhancing behaviors on the part of the other partner (e.g., noncoercive communication on the part of the husband), and not reinforcing relationship-damaging behaviors. These latter strategies would involve DRA, through extinction of maladaptive behaviors and reinforcement of alternative, relationship-enhancing behaviors.

One important consideration in using extinction procedures is that the undesired target behavior sometimes temporarily increases in frequency or intensity after positive reinforcement is withdrawn. This common, temporary side effect of extinction procedures is referred to as an *extinction burst*. In the example of Edith and Sam, if Edith is working on declining Sam's sexual advances, he might actually increase the intensity of his verbal or physical abuse when she first starts to say "no." He might also change his strategy and desperately try other ways to convince her to engage in sexual activity with him. The same type of phenomenon happens all the time at vending machines. If a person puts money into a vending machine and it does not produce the soda or treat, he or she might press the buttons harder, hit, or kick the machine. This is not particularly good for the vending machine but is much less of a concern than the threat of an escalation in Sam's coercive behaviors. Therefore, it is important to remember that, often, the initial response to the implementation of the extinction procedure is a sudden increase in the frequency or intensity of the target behavior, which gradually declines as reinforcers continue to be withheld.

When a behavior is placed on an extinction schedule, reinforcement for the behavior under extinction must be continuously withheld, even within the period of an extinction burst (if it is safe to do so). A behavior that is incompatible with or alternative to the behavior undergoing extinction could also be reinforced, which might further facilitate the extinction process while establishing a different, and perhaps more adaptive, behavior. Additional procedural guidelines concerning extinction and differential reinforcement can be found in Miltenberger (2004), Malott et al. (2000), and Wallace and Robles (2003).

Covert Sensitization and Other Positive Punishment Procedures

Positive punishment procedures (i.e., those that involve the application of an aversive event or stimulus following the performance of a behavior targeted for weakening) are infrequently used in CBT. Aversion therapies based on the principle of positive punishment historically included mild electric shocks and the use of chemicals or drugs to produce nausea. These techniques have largely been abandoned because of their equivocal effectiveness and a host of unintended negative side effects such as the dehumanization of the client, fear or mistrust of the therapist, and impracticality when applied in natural client settings (Kearney, 2006).

Covert sensitization is an alternative behavioral intervention based, in part, on positive punishment principles. This approach has been primarily used to reduce some behavioral excesses (e.g., abuse of substances, gambling, sexual deviations such as pedophilia or exhibitionism, nail biting, overeating). With this procedure, the therapist instructs the client to imagine participating in the target behavior. As the client does so, the therapist asks him or her to imagine the cooccurrence of some type of aversive event (e.g., becoming nauseous to the point of vomiting, the experience of ridicule or horrified stares from others). The aversive event the client imagines acts as an aversive consequence or punisher for engagement in the maladaptive behavior. Although the consequence itself is covert, occurring in imagination, there is some indication that behavior change as a result of this process occurs at the overt or publicly observable level (Kearney, 2006; Upper & Cautela, 1979). The following are some of the key steps in covert sensitization (see also Exhibit 5.3 for an extended example of this procedure).

- The therapist first identifies the behavior, contexts in which it occurs, and the reinforcing consequences associated with it.
- The therapist orients the client to the procedure and begins by inducing a state of relaxation (e.g., through progressive muscle relaxation or deep breathing exercises).
- The therapist instructs the client to close his or her eyes and imagine him- or herself beginning to engage in the problem behavior (e.g., reach for a pack of cigarettes, begin to pull a cigarette from the pack).

EXHIBIT 5.3
A Covert Sensitization Scenario

Close your eyes, and imagine that you are walking down the sidewalk, when you see a convenience store up ahead on your left. It is a lovely day, with a slight breeze, and you can feel the warmth of the sun on your face. You look over at the convenience store, and you feel the urge to buy a pack of cigarettes. You start to get a funny feeling in your stomach, and you feel very slightly dizzy, but you keep walking toward the store, and you head inside. As you ask the person at the counter for a pack of cigarettes, you notice that she pauses and looks at you quizzically, slightly raising her eyebrows. As she hands the pack of cigarettes to you, you also notice that the woman next to you is whispering to her daughter. You grab the pack of cigarettes, and the feeling in your stomach gets worse. You start to feel a little queasy, and you feel a slight, cold sweat breaking out on your forehead. As you walk outside and open the pack of cigarettes, and smell the faint odor of tobacco, you feel (and hear) a gurgling sensation in your stomach. Your throat starts to tighten, and you feel acid moving up your esophagus. You are even dizzier now, and the cold sweat has spread to your neck and arms. You also feel jittery and shaky. As you grab a cigarette and begin to light it, food particles and fluid from your stomach come up into your throat, and you have to lean against the wall and take a deep breath to stop yourself from vomiting. As you take a drag on the cigarette, stomach acid and food particles rush, acrid and warm, into your mouth, and you vomit all over the sidewalk. You see particles of green pepper, tomato, and other such foods that you ate during your lunch at the pizza place, and people around you have stopped and are staring, aghast. You quickly drop the cigarettes, and walk away from the storefront. As you get further and further away, you feel better and better. The taste in your mouth diminishes, you feel less dizzy and shaky, and you start to feel relaxed, happy, and relieved.

- The therapist instructs the client to imagine him- or herself experiencing some aversive consequence.
- The therapist instructs the client, through very graphic and vivid instructions, to imagine these consequences worsening.
- At the point when the specific target behavior is first covertly enacted (e.g., taking the first puff from the cigarette), the aversive consequences peak.
- Subsequently, the therapist instructs the client to imagine him- or herself escaping the situation in which the target behavior occurred.
- As he or she escapes or gets further away from the situation, feelings of relief and euthymic mood become more pronounced.

This latter aspect of covert conditioning, relief upon escape, is designed to strengthen avoidance responses to cues typically associated with the target behavior, thus increasing the likelihood that avoidance behavior will be substituted for approach behavior in natural environments in which the problem behavior frequently occurs (Kearney, 2006).

In clinical practice, clients typically undergo numerous covert sensitization sessions with the therapist (e.g., between 5–10 imagined scenes per session over 30 sessions). After sufficient practice with the therapist, the client might be given between-session assignments to practice the covert imagery (Kearney, 2006). Other procedural considerations are reviewed in Kearney (2006) and Upper and Cautela (1979).

Olfactory aversion is another positive-punishment-based procedure that has limited demonstrated effectiveness for reducing sexually deviant behaviors. When used in clinical contexts, an aversive odor from a noxious substance (usually ammonia or valeric acid) is self-administered immediately after the onset of a target behavior (e.g., sexual arousal to child stimuli). Examples of the application of this procedure can be found in Laws, Meyer, and Holman (1978) and Earls and Castonguay (1989).

Response Cost

When punishment procedures are used in CBT, they are most frequently based on the principle of negative punishment, or the removal of a rewarding or desirable event following the enactment of behavior targeted for weakening. Behavioral interventions based on this principle and carried out for this reason are described as *response cost* interventions. An assumption associated with response cost procedures is that the client already has access to reinforcers and that the therapist or some other person (e.g., a participant–observer) is in a position to remove reinforcers contingent on displays of targeted behavior. Whenever a punishment procedure is used, including those based on response cost, it is often useful to simultaneously reinforce a desired behavior while the target behavior is being weakened.

Examples of response cost in nonclinical settings are quite common. These include fines for engaging in a behavior that violates a relatively minor social code or law (e.g., speeding ticket, fine for the late return of a library book). Similarly, some parental discipline strategies are based on this principle, such as *time out*. A shorthand label for "time-out from positive reinforcement" (Friman & Finney, 2003), time out is a procedure that involves the removal of an individual from a reinforcing context contingent on the display of an undesired target behavior. In the application of this procedure, a child might be immediately removed from a situation in which the targeted problematic behavior occurred and placed for a period of time (e.g., 1 minute per age in years) in a situation in which the reinforcers that maintain problematic behavior are absent (e.g., attention) and there is nothing to do (children often experience doing nothing as aversive; see Friman & Finney, 2003). Once the child associates engagement in the target behavior with a change in situation, from preferred to nonpreferred, the frequency of the problematic behavior usually decreases.

Another example of the use of response cost includes the use of a "donation jar," wherein an individual who is seeking to decrease a behavior (e.g., cigarette smoking) contributes to the jar (e.g., $1) for each instance of the targeted behavior beyond that day's goal (e.g., number of cigarettes smoked in excess of the goal amount for that day). To make the response cost procedure aversive, the therapist or other person donates all contributions in the jar at the end of the intervention period to a charitable organization whose actions or values are offensive to the client (e.g., the campaign committee of a political candidate whom the client opposes).

In another example involving DBT (Linehan, 1993a), deliberate self-harm and suicidal behaviors fall within the highest priority treatment targets. To reduce such behaviors, the individual therapist uses multiple strategies, including the availability of telephone consultation in between sessions. Before engaging in acts of deliberate self-harm, clients are encouraged to call their therapist and ask for help in coping if their own efforts are not effective. One rule associated with this privilege, however, is that the client must call before he or she engages in deliberate self-harm. If the client calls following deliberate self-harm, the therapist keeps the telephone call short, with the main purpose being to determine whether injuries are life threatening and whether medical emergency services should be summoned. It is also understood between the therapist and the client, on the basis of agreements reached during therapy orientation, that if the client calls after he or she has engaged in self-harm behavior, then the client is not allowed to call the therapist for the following 24 hours.

The 24-hour prohibition against further phone contact is primarily designed to prevent therapist reinforcement for self-harm and suicidal behaviors (e.g., through increased attention, demonstrations of caring or concern). In this respect, the 24-hour prohibition period is consistent with the principle of extinction. Also associated with this procedure is the removal of opportunities for reinforcement from the therapist by not being allowed to call for a period of time. That is, there is a response cost associated with commission of the target behavior (e.g., engagement in deliberate self-harm before calling the therapist). In this respect, the 24-hour rule is somewhat analogous to time out, as reinforcement from the therapist is no longer available (or is taken away), contingent on acts that are targeted for reduction and subsequent elimination.

ADDITIONAL APPROACHES FOR CHANGING BEHAVIOR THROUGH CONTINGENCY MANAGEMENT AND SELF-MANAGEMENT STRATEGIES

In this section, we describe four different strategies for modifying behavior through contingency or self-management procedures. As we note in the following subsections, each procedure involves some sort of alteration of the context within which targeted behavior occurs or does not occur to influence the frequency of behavior in desirable directions.

Self-Management Strategies

Some individuals seen in clinical contexts demonstrate impulsive behaviors. Often, clients engage in impulsive acts to obtain short-term rewards, often with apparent disregard for the immediate or delayed aversive long-term outcomes that accompany such behavior.

One approach for reducing the influence of immediate reinforcers on behavior in favor or long-term goals involves the use of *self-management strategies*. Self-management is evident when a person engages in a behavior or set of behaviors to influence the occurrence of another behavior (i.e., the target behavior) on a later occasion (Miltenberger, 2004). To illustrate, a client wishes to reduce the amount of cigarettes he or she smokes and eventually stop smoking altogether. Cigarette smoking in this example is the target behavior. To reduce the target behavior, the client engages in several other behaviors (e.g., self-monitoring of cigarette use, goal setting, regular exercise, healthier food choices) to increase the likelihood that he or she will successfully decrease his or her use of cigarettes.

Within laboratory-based studies, *self-control* has been defined as "choice of a larger but more delayed outcome over a smaller but less delayed outcome" (Logue, 1998, p. 252). Impulsivity is regarded as the opposite of self-control, whereby smaller immediate outcomes are preferred over larger delayed outcomes. Within these definitions, there is a conceptual correspondence to the terms *immediate gratification* and *delay of gratification*. When considered from this perspective, self-control would likely be enhanced if an individual engages in cost–benefit analyses of outcomes associated with behaving in particular ways. That is, the act of reflecting on possible courses of action before acting, and contemplating likely outcomes of each action based on previous experience, might increase the salience of possible aversive outcomes associated with impulsive actions.

Behavioral (or Contingency) Contracting

Behavioral contracting is a method for formalizing agreements reached between a client and therapist concerning the client's behavior. When using behavioral contracts, the client and therapist first collaboratively establish goals for particular behaviors. "Monique," for example, struggles with anger management and engages in angry outbursts. She and her therapist might identify "reducing angry outbursts" as a therapy goal. They might also specify "practicing anger management skills 4 times per week" as a goal that is consistent with reducing angry outbursts. In coming up with a behavioral contract, Monique and her therapist might specify that if she goes for 1 week without engaging in an angry outburst, she will reward herself by renting a video that she has been hoping to watch. Alternatively, they might specify that if she practices her anger management skills 3 times per week for 2 weeks in a row, she can have an extra long therapy session (if therapy is reinforcing), buy herself a small gift, or obtain some other type of reinforcer. The therapist might also agree, as part of the contract, to be available by phone to assist Monique in inhibiting angry outbursts or to perform some other action to facilitate Monique's movement toward her goals.

Behavioral contracts can be written or established through a verbal agreement. As summarized in Houmanfar, Maglieri, and Roman (2003), behavioral contracts have at least four central functions:

- formalization of behavioral goals;
- provision of an accessible reference that serves as a reminder of behavioral goals, and a means to monitor progress toward the realization of those goals;
- specification of the responsibilities of each individual involved in the contract; and
- a public statement signifying a commitment to the goals specified in the contract.

There are several important ingredients for effective behavioral contracts. First, it is important to clearly specify some threshold level of performance (e.g., in terms of frequency or duration) required for certain positive consequences. Second, the consequences associated with reaching specified levels of performance involve some form of positive reinforcement or negative punishment (i.e., response cost). Third, it is helpful if the behavioral contract specifies how consequences will be administered and by whom as well as the duration of the contract period. Fourth, it is also important for the therapist and the client to establish methods for monitoring progress, such as behavior charting or some other form of self-monitoring or participant observation. A final consideration has to do with focusing on the positive aspects of the client's behavior (Houmanfar et al., 2003). The contract would ideally identify what the client should do, not what he or she should not do. This might involve, for example, reconceptualizing a client's problem area in terms of goals (Heinssen, Levendusky, & Hunter, 1995). Once a behavioral threshold specified in the contract is reached, the reinforcer specified in the contract should be delivered as soon as possible. Houmanfar et al. (2003, pp. 43–44) provided an example of a behavioral contract used in family therapy, and Heinssen et al. (1995) provided guidelines for the use of contracts in institutional or milieu setting for clients with severe psychological disorders.

Habit Reversal Procedures

Habit behaviors generally fall into one of three categories: nervous habits (e.g., nail biting, skin picking, hair pulling, teeth grinding, mouth biting), motor or vocal tics, and stuttering (Adams, Adams, & Miltenberger, 2003;

Miltenberger, 2004). Habits such as these are often maintained by negative reinforcement processes linked to anxiety or tension reduction or to automatic reinforcing processes associated with self-stimulation. Stuttering, however, is linked to interrupted airflow through the vocal cords and is often reduced through regulated breathing methods (Miltenberger, 2004).

Several different methods have been used to effectively reduce nuisance behaviors associated with habit disorders (Miltenberger, 2004). According to Adams et al. (2003), two features associated with habit control procedures are most strongly linked to positive treatment effects. The first of these is *awareness training*. This involves training in the ability to detect and discriminate instances of the habit behavior when it occurs. Various manifestations of the habit behavior are clarified, as are the conditions that typically occasion such behavior.

The second component is *competing response training*. This involves instruction in ways to immediately stop the target behavior as soon as the client is aware that it is happening. This is immediately followed by performing an alternative behavior that competes with the target behavior. When nervous habits and tics are the target behaviors, competing behaviors appear to primarily operate as punishers for the target behaviors (Miltenberger, 2004).

To decrease nail biting, for example, a client might first self-monitor instances of nail biting. This includes discriminating among the various forms and manifestations that nail biting might have and also noticing the situations in which nail biting is most likely to occur. Once the client has demonstrated adequate awareness of his or her nail biting and the antecedents associated with its occurrence, competing behaviors that can be used in these situations might be identified. Depending on the situation, this might include putting on gloves, placing lotion on one's hands, or grasping a pencil. Regardless of the form of the competing behavior, it functionally should result in the hands being unavailable for nail biting (Adams et al., 2003).

Token Systems

Token systems (sometimes called *token economies*) have been used in diverse therapeutic contexts (e.g., hospitals, prisons, schools, community mental health centers, family households) with persons from varied clinical populations including inpatients, outpatients, children, adults, students, and family members (Ghezzi, Wilson, Tarbox, & MacAleese, 2003). In a token economy, a system is devised whereby individualized behavioral goals are identified, and persons within the economy receive conditional positive reinforcers (e.g., tokens, points, vouchers) when behaviors consistent with personal or institutional goals are enacted. Because of its complexity and artificiality, token economies are frequently regarded as treatment options when either other approaches are ineffectual or other alternatives are not available (Ghezzi et al., 2003).

Steps for designing, implementing, and evaluating a token economy are outlined by Ghezzi et al. (2003) and are summarized here:

- *Clear specification of the target behavior(s).* The target behaviors selected are ideally consistent with individual member's goals, are specific and concisely defined, and are readily observable by others. When behaviors would result in response cost, these should also be specified in a similar manner.
- *Clear definition of where the token economy will take place.* All participants in the token economy system should clearly understand when and where the contingencies associated with the program are in effect and when and where they are not.
- *Careful selection of tokens.* The tokens used should not be readily subject to counterfeiting or duplication.
- *Careful selection of back-up reinforcers.* Back-up reinforcers are those events, objects, privileges, or activities for which tokens can be exchanged. Back-up reinforcers should be tangible and deliverable immediately at the point of exchange and have value to or be enjoyed by persons who participate in the system.
- *Clear specification of the reinforcement schedule.* This involves the establishment of guidelines for how many tokens will be awarded for a given behavior, or how many times a behavior would need to be performed for a token to be delivered. Generally, for behaviors that the client already engages in frequently, relatively few tokens are necessary to reinforce the client's behavior. In contrast, for behaviors that the client normally performs infrequently, more tokens are necessary. Early in the establishment of a token economy system, tokens might be awarded for each instance of the behavior and then thinned in accordance with the relative frequency of the behavior.
- *Development of an exchange-rate menu.* This menu would be a written (and perhaps publicly posted) list of how many tokens would be required for a given reinforcer.
- *Establishment of parameters for when and how tokens will be exchanged.* This would include notice of where and when persons could go to redeem their tokens.
- *Recordkeeping.* This would involve maintaining a record on the various elements of the token economy system. Specifically, this would minimally include noting how many tokens an individual earned over a short interval of time (e.g., a work shift, a 24-hour period) for each target behavior, the number of tokens exchanged for back-up reinforcers, and the back-up reinforcers that were selected by the participants.

Although token systems activate and initially support new behaviors, they are not particularly effective in promoting long-term maintenance of behavior in the client's natural environment. For this reason, if behaviors initially established through token systems are to generalize to situations outside of the therapeutic context, they will eventually need to be sustained by naturally occurring contingencies present in the client's environment.

SUMMARY

- One set of contingency management procedures involves changing antecedents to increase or decrease particular behaviors, including stimulus control strategies (e.g., cue elimination, discrimination training) and procedures for arranging or modifying establishing operations.
- Interventions that involve altering consequences to influence behavior include reinforcement, punishment, or extinction-based strategies.
- Natural responses on the part of the therapist can function as reinforcers for client behavior targeted to be increased.
- A variety of therapist behaviors can weaken or reduce problematic client behavior targeted to be decreased.
- When using the forms of contingency management outlined in this chapter, the clinician or therapist must clearly specify the target behavior(s), orient the client to the contingency management procedures, and be alert to the occurrence of target behaviors.
- Knowledge of and facility with the application of learning principles can complement the use of therapeutic interventions designed to bring the client's behavior in line with his or her personal goals and values.

6

TARGETING THE FUNCTIONAL ASPECTS OF THOUGHTS AND THINKING PATTERNS

Cognitive therapy has traditionally emphasized the importance of altering inaccurate or biased thought content to bring about therapeutic change. Recent research reviews, however, have questioned whether cognitive interventions in cognitive behavior therapy (CBT) that explicitly target thought content are important for facilitating symptomatic improvements (e.g., Longmore & Worrell, 2007). When it is not clear that belief change causes symptom change, a question arises as to whether there are other aspects of thinking patterns that might be associated with psychological symptoms. One behavioral perspective on this question, which we develop in this chapter, emphasizes the *functional properties* associated with particular patterns of thinking.

The behavioral intervention strategies reviewed in this chapter explicitly attempt to alter functional aspects of harmful thinking patterns by reducing avoidant or detrimental modes of thought and increasing goal- and value-directed behavior. To illustrate the functional approach, we describe intervention strategies for reducing worry and rumination as well as for testing the validity of thoughts that associate behavior with anticipated (usually aversive) outcomes. Then we discuss strategies for altering or inhibiting problematic behavior by promoting the development of sustained patterns of behavior consistent with one's goals and values. We conclude the chapter with a client illustration that demonstrates several of the intervention strategies reviewed.

THINKING AND THOUGHTS FROM A
BEHAVIORAL PERSPECTIVE WITHIN CBT

In addressing how thinking processes and thoughts are handled from a behavioral perspective within CBT, we first need to distinguish between the content of thoughts and the function of thinking behavior (Addis & Martell, 2004). The *content* of thinking refers to what a person is thinking about. Consider the example of an executive who has been worrying about the presentation she is going to give at work tomorrow. The content of thinking would refer to the actual images, scenarios, and covert verbal statements she experiences as she worries. The *function* of thinking, however, refers to why a person is thinking in terms of the purpose it serves or the consequences it produces. In this instance, worrying might be a form of avoidance behavior, similar to procrastination, that is negatively reinforced on the basis of the consequences that worrying produces. This executive, for example, might worry because doing so minimizes or blocks contact with self-doubts she has concerning her competencies in the areas that she will present. The act of worrying can also be a way to avoid expending the effort required to put the presentation together. Similarly, worrying may provide relief from feelings of frustration associated with having to do something she would rather not do (i.e., develop and deliver a presentation). Although worrying might be associated with some discomfort (e.g., anxiety), it may also provide relief from a number of other experiences that, in the aggregate, are even more uncomfortable.

Traditional cognitive therapy is primarily concerned with the content of thinking. This includes the content of moment-to-moment thoughts; memories; underlying assumptions that guide the interpretation of ongoing experiences; and mental representations of the self, others, and the world. As suggested by Sacco and Beck (1995) and Young, Weinberger, and Beck (2001), the primary goals of traditional cognitive therapy involve

- identifying examples of maladaptive thoughts;
- helping the client identify relationships between maladaptive thoughts, emotion, and behavior;
- objectively evaluating the content of the client's maladaptive thoughts by
  - examining the evidence for or against that thought,

- appraising the value of thinking in a particular way,
- searching for alternative explanations for an event to which the thought is related,
- evaluating what the real implications are if the thought is accurate, and
- regarding maladaptive beliefs as hypotheses to be tested rather than as "facts";
- challenging the client to substitute more reasonable beliefs in place of maladaptive automatic thoughts; and
- identifying and evaluating core underlying assumptions or schemas that globally influence the client's perceptions and interpretations of persons and events.

The primary focus of cognitive therapy, then, is on the content of thinking, and this content is targeted for change to bring about additional changes in emotion and behavior.

Behavioral approaches, in comparison, typically emphasize the purpose or functions associated with the client's thinking. Is a person, for example, who is thinking about how to solve a problem in his or her life, or ruminating or in some other way, distracting him- or herself as a way to avoiding something? Is this individual trying to figure out how to most effectively respond in this situation by weighing the likely consequences associated with responding one way versus another way? Or, is he or she applying a rigidly held rule that may or may not apply in this situation? In comparison to traditional cognitive therapy, behavioral interventions place less emphasis on altering the content of one's thinking and more emphasis on understanding what thinking is doing for the individual in a given moment (Addis & Martell, 2004).

From a behavioral perspective, the act of thinking is a form of behavior, and similar to other behavior, thoughts can have any of the following functions (Miltenberger, 2004):

- A *discriminative stimulus* for behavior (e.g., the thought, "I'm beginning to feel overwhelmed. I had better slow down my breathing" might be followed by the behavior of breathing more slowly and deeply).
- An *establishing operation* that alters the consequences for behavior (e.g., "If I eat that delicious looking cake, my blood sugar levels will go up and I'll probably feel sick").
- A *conditioned stimulus* for an emotional response (e.g., when the act of imagining a dog produces anxiety-related autonomic arousal for someone with a fear of dogs).
- A *reinforcing or punishing consequence* for another preceding behavior (e.g., after dropping a favorite coffee mug onto the tile floor and watching it break, a person covertly exclaims to her-

self, "You're such a klutz sometimes. You need to be more careful!").

In this chapter, we discuss several behavioral interventions that are primarily directed at altering the functional aspects of clinically relevant patterns of thinking.

REDUCING WORRY, RUMINATION, AND OBSESSIONS

Borkovec (1994) and others (e.g., Addis & Martell, 2004) have conceptualized habitual worry and rumination as a style of thinking that is negatively reinforced as a result of the escape or avoidance function it serves in relation to the suppression of anxiety. Worry and rumination also preclude opportunities for dealing with problems directly and actively (Addis & Martell, 2004). To determine, however, whether someone who is worrying or ruminating is actually avoiding (rather than some other alternative such as problem solving), it is important to first understand why the person is thinking about certain events over and over at this particular point in time.

Rumination is often different in form than problem solving (Addis & Martell, 2004). When persons ruminate, they mentally repeat some event, circumstance, or issue, and the actual or hypothetical associated negative consequences. In problem solving, however, the focus is on identifying the problem, generating solutions to the problem, choosing one or two potential options that are most likely to be effective in the given situation, acting on the selected solution option, and evaluating the consequences of the approach. Rumination often involves few, if any, of these elements. Instead, rumination is often a way to avoid taking actions that might potentially solve the life problems that occasion rumination (Addis & Martell, 2004).

Worrying, obsessing, and ruminating are strongly associated with anxious, depressed, and angry moods. One important commonality across ruminating, worrying, and obsessing is that each form of thinking involves focusing on the past or a hypothetical future. As a result, the individual who is ruminating, worrying, or obsessing is not focused on the present moment and may have difficulty responding to what is happening in his or her immediate environment (Martell, Addis, & Jacobson, 2001). From a behavioral perspective, central questions in relation to this process are, "Why is this person psychologically disconnecting from the environment now?" and "How is disconnecting through rumination helping this person?"

If rumination is a form of avoidance, and if the outcomes of rumination are more harmful than beneficial, therapy might target rumination. This is perhaps best accomplished by coming up with alternative coping options for tolerating anxiety associated with the problem, identifying what the client is avoiding through rumination, preventing avoidance behaviors, and taking action to solve the problem (even if anxiety is present; Addis & Martell, 2004).

In behavioral activation interventions (Addis & Martell, 2004; see also chap. 8, this volume), once clients can identify instances of unproductive rumination, they are encouraged to label it as such (i.e., "this is ruminating"), and use the act of ruminating as a cue for alternative and more effective actions. As a part of this approach, the client and therapist might generate a list of alternative activities, with activities selected on the basis of their associated mood-enhancing features or potential effectiveness for dealing directly with the problem at hand.

In addition to responding to rumination by labeling it and using it as an occasion to take action, other behavioral interventions have been developed and evaluated for their effectiveness in reducing rumination. These include exposure-based interventions (e.g., Steketee, 1993), reviewed in chapter 9 of this volume, and acceptance- and mindfulness-based interventions (e.g., Hannan & Tolin, 2005), which are reviewed in chapter 10 of this volume.

ALTERING FUNCTIONAL ASPECTS OF THINKING THROUGH BEHAVIORAL EXPERIMENTS

Behavioral experiments constitute one approach for modifying both the form (i.e., content) and function (i.e., effect) that thinking has on emotion and behavior. A central tenet of behavioral experiments is that the explicit or implicit rules or assumptions that underlie one's thinking are regarded as hypotheses to be tested. Take, for example, the following thought that a depressed client might express: "Nothing makes a difference. I feel equally terrible all day" (A. T. Beck, Rush, Shaw, & Emery, 1979, p. 125). There are at least three assumptions associated with this thought: (a) mood or some other physiological sensation is invariant over the course of an entire day, (b) these sensations are consistently and persistently negative to the extreme (i.e., "terrible"), and (c) nothing can be done to alter this negative mood or physiological sensation. Such thinking also conveys both hopelessness and helplessness for the possibility of eventual relief from painful emotions or sensations. Functionally, such a thought might be associated with passivity, submission, avoidance, and withdrawal, all of which result in reduced access to positive reinforcers for behavior. If the client expresses this thought, other people might get the impression that they cannot help, or they might avoid the individual because some persons experience expressions of intense suffering or hopelessness as aversive. Unfortunately, such loss of social support might result in a further intensification of depressive experiences.

When rigidly held and untested, a single thought such as the one just discussed can have a wide-ranging detrimental impact. Such thoughts, however, are often premised on a number of assumptions that may not be valid. When thoughts are viewed as hypotheses to be tested rather than as "facts," new opportunities arise as a result of being freed from the constraints associated with such thinking.

Bennett-Levy, Westbrook, et al. (2004) defined *behavioral experiments* as "planned experiential activities, based on experimentation or observation, which are undertaken by patients in or between cognitive therapy sessions" (p. 8). In traditional CBT, behavioral experiments are often used to evaluate the therapist's cognitive formulation of the client's problem areas or to help the client test his or her dysfunctional thinking content and develop more accurate thoughts (A. T. Beck et al., 1979; Bennett-Levy, Westbrook, et al., 2004).

Among cognitive therapy practitioners, behavioral experiments are regarded as effective means for changing thoughts and behavior. In a study by Bennett-Levy (2003), cognitive therapists who participated in a training seminar that involved the practice of CBT techniques on themselves rated behavioral experiments as more useful in producing cognitive and behavior change than self-monitoring and recording thoughts on an automatic thoughts record. Although such findings suggest that behavioral experiments have face validity among practitioners of CBT, only indirect evidence currently exists on the effectiveness of behavioral experiments as a therapeutic tool.

Types of Behavioral Experiments Within CBT

Bennett-Levy, Westbrook, et al. (2004) distinguished between two types of behavioral experiments: (a) those that resemble true experiments and involve the manipulation of the environment through action (i.e., the *hypothesis-testing approach*) and (b) those that are akin to an observational study, in which information is gathered that is either consistent or inconsistent with a specific belief (i.e., the *discovery-oriented approach*). In an example of the hypothesis-testing approach, a client might have the thought that she cannot eat ice cream, a desired but forbidden food, because of the immediate impact that doing so might have on her shape and weight. A CBT-oriented therapist would approach this thought as a hypothesis, and a test might be constructed to evaluate the validity of the assumptions associated with this thought. When at home, for example, the client might be encouraged to weigh herself and measure her stomach or hips with a tape measure prior to eating a standard portion of ice cream. Soon after eating the ice cream, she might weigh and measure herself, and perhaps again several hours later in the day, as a means to evaluate whether the initial thought was accurate.

In an example of the discovery-oriented approach, the question of "Will I gain weight if I incorporate sensible portions of ice cream into my regular diet two to three times a week?" can be investigated by seeking out relevant information, such as from a nutritionist or a physician. For clients who do not wish to conduct a hypothesis-testing oriented behavioral experiment, a discovery-oriented experiment might be a good starting point, and the resultant information might be sufficient to allay unwarranted fears and concerns.

Behavioral experiments can experientially demonstrate to clients that activities or events can influence mood, thinking, and behavior. Behavioral experiments can also be helpful with clients who demonstrate low self-efficacy expectations (Bandura, 1986), or those who have doubts about their ability to carry out a behavior or sequence of behaviors (e.g., "If it weren't for my anxiety I would be able to go to the shopping mall"). When clients doubt that they can carry out a behavior, they will often not try and will avoid the activity altogether. A behavioral experiment (e.g., having the client go to the shopping mall despite anxiety) can demonstrate that these doubts are unfounded and that the client can engage in effective action despite the presence of doubts.

Behavioral experiments can also be especially useful for clients who exaggerate the potential for negative outcomes associated with certain actions. Bandura (1986) defined ideas concerning the outcomes or consequences of behavior as outcome expectations. When anticipated consequences are negative, aversive, punishing, ineffectual, or unpleasant, there is less incentive to engage in behaviors that could result in those consequences. Behavioral experiments can be arranged to evaluate whether certain behaviors, in fact, result in negative outcomes or, alternatively, result in desirable or effective outcomes in certain situations.

Procedures for Conducting Behavioral Experiments

When behavioral experiments are used to test hypotheses linked to specific thoughts, generally one of two types of interventions are used: in vivo experiments and simulated experiments such as role plays (Rouf, Fennell, Westbrook, Cooper, & Bennett-Levy, 2004). With either approach, the overall therapeutic goal is to test and evaluate the validity of certain thoughts. Features can also be built into the behavioral experiment whereby the validity of an alternative thought—one that might serve as a more accurate substitute—is simultaneously tested. A moderately depressed client, for example, might think that he is too depressed to clean his house. The specific thought regarded as a hypothesis to be tested might be, "I cannot clean my house so long as I'm depressed." In working with the client around this thought, his therapist might suggest an alternative belief, such as "I am capable of cleaning a portion of my house even when I am feeling depressed." An experiment might subsequently be devised for testing this competing thought. Such an experiment should be well planned prior to implementation and include a detailed description of the activity (e.g., pick up and put away clothes on bedroom floor, make bed, and pick up and put away papers and books scattered throughout bedroom between 7:00 p.m. and 7:30 p.m. on Wednesday evening) as well as guidelines for evaluating performance (e.g., rating mood quality both before and after engagement in a specified task, rating the degree to which the activity was effectively carried out and accomplished).

When behavioral experiments are performed to obtain information or gather evidence in relation to a specific thought (a discovery or observational experiment), primary emphasis is placed on assisting the client to discover the processes that maintain a problem or to find out what happens when one acts in a novel or different way (Rouf et al., 2004). Observational strategies used to promote discovery include direct observation of models, survey or data gathering, and obtaining information from other public sources (Rouf et al., 2004).

One type of observational experiment involves the therapist modeling a behavior that would be highly anxiety evoking to a client. In such an exercise, the client's role is to simply observe or to gather information (Rouf et al., 2004). At this point in the process, the client would not be an active participant in the experiment. For a client with obsessive-compulsive disorder who has excessive and debilitating fears of contamination, for example, the therapist might model the competent handling of a can of insecticide while the client watches (Steketee, 1993). Similarly, for those with intense anxiety reactions when in the presence of certain stimuli, such as dogs, simply observing the therapist interact with the dog without fear often produces change in phobic behavior among clients (Bandura, 1986).

Observational strategies associated with surveys and data gathering involve collecting factual information or opinions concerning some matter of interest (Rouf et al., 2004). A client with body dysmorphic disorder, for example, might believe that physical attractiveness is the primary determinant of relationship satisfaction and long-term relationship stability. For such a client, a survey task might be devised whereby the client informally asks friends what they see as the most important determinants of satisfying and close interpersonal relationships. Information related to a client's thoughts could also be accessed via public informational sources, such as library resources or the Internet.

Rouf et al. (2004) stressed the importance of planning as a precursor to conducting behavioral experiments to maximize the likelihood of success. Included among their considerations for adequate preparation are the following:

- Is the rationale and purpose of the experiment clear to the client?
- Have relevant and specific thoughts been identified for examination during the behavioral experiment?
- When appropriate, have more realistic alternatives to the problematic thought been explicitly identified?
- Have the specific elements of the experiment been identified (e.g., setting, time, place, resources required, activities to be performed)?

- Have the possible outcomes of the experiment been discussed, and how these might be interpreted in relation to the target thought?
- Have possible problems that might arise during the experiment been anticipated and addressed through problem solving or through perspective taking?
- Have the client's reservations about carrying out the experiment been solicited and responded to?
- Is the level of exposure required by the experiment consistent with what the client can effectively tolerate at this time?

In addition to the previous considerations, Rouf et al. (2004) also suggested that when active experiments are undertaken, clients should record the outcomes of the experiment. The client might, for instance, record ratings of how strongly he or she believed the target thoughts both prior to and after completion of the experiment (e.g., where 0% = *do not believe the content of the thought at all* and 100% = *complete and total agreement with the content of the thought*). Similar self-ratings might be collected on the level of emotional intensity associated with the thought, given that one of the primary objectives of behavioral experiments is to facilitate emotional change. Records of such information can provide direct evidence as to whether the experiment weakened the influence of the targeted thought.

For clients to achieve maximal benefit from behavioral experiments, they should also be aware of and focused on their environment and experience during the exercise (Rouf et al., 2004). This includes full attention to the stimulus features of relevant environmental cues present when carrying out the experiment, awareness of internal reactions (e.g., cognitive, emotional, physiological, behavioral) during the experiment, and any shifts that might take place in these areas as the experiment progresses. Also important is the blocking of any avoidant or escape behaviors during the exposure (e.g., distracting, dissociating, scanning for safety signals from the environment), as full immersion in the experiment will likely produce greater therapeutic effects.

Once the experiment is complete, clients should be encouraged to verbalize and discriminate what happened (Rouf et al., 2004), with special attention given to antecedent–behavior and behavior–consequence links. Such an emphasis helps reinforce the contextual focus on behavior and promotes new learning when the experiment produces outcomes inconsistent with targeted thoughts.

A final component of the behavioral experiment is the promotion of rule generalizability to other relevant situations (Rouf et al., 2004). This might be enhanced through discussions with the client about what he or she has learned from the experiment that could be applied to future situations. Contrasting the outcomes of the experiment with preexisting expectations may help the client develop alternative and more accurate rules to influence future behavior. The therapist might also take time to discuss plans for following up on the experiment (Rouf et al., 2004). That is, how might the client expand on his or her progress gained from the experiment? What other assumptions need to be evaluated or tested for further progress to be possible? What might constitute the next experiment? Quite often several experiments are required before a primary belief is sufficiently weakened or contradicted to the point that the client is ready to abandon it. Other guidelines and additional coverage of behavioral experiments in CBT can be found in Bennett-Levy, Butler, et al. (2004).

Hypothesized Mechanisms of Change Associated With Behavioral Experiments

From both cognitive and behavioral perspectives, the primary therapeutic benefit of behavioral experiments is derived from the client actually doing something different from what he or she did before (Addis & Martell, 2004; Bennett-Levy, Westbrook, et al., 2004). In cognitive therapy, the act of doing something differently is believed to result in cognitive change that, in turn, is regarded as the underlying basis for therapeutic change (A. T. Beck et al., 1979). From a cognitive perspective, then, behavioral experiments produce cognitive change by establishing the validity (or lack thereof) of specific beliefs or in helping clients develop more accurate beliefs. Cognitive change is thought to directly influence emotional states and facilitate more effective means for confronting life's problems (Rouf et al., 2004).

Another mechanism of change associated with behavioral experiments may involve *decentering*. Decentering refers to shifting one's perspective on aversive thoughts and feelings, whereby they come to be viewed as transient or passing events that are neither necessarily valid reflections of reality nor the central core feature of the self (Segal, Williams, & Teasdale, 2002). Segal et al. and others have speculated that this process of altering one's relationships within one's inner experiences, as opposed to changing the content of one's thoughts, is more strongly associated with therapeutic change in cognitive therapy. Decentering is evident in behavioral experiments, in which thoughts are viewed as hypotheses to be tested and not necessarily as valid facts. Decentering is also a feature of attentional and mindfulness-based interventions, which are reviewed in chapter 10 of this volume. These interventions help facilitate an awareness that thoughts and emotions are transient and ever-changing as well as the perspective of a self separate or distinct from the experiences of the self (e.g., "the person who observes your experiences, your thoughts and feelings, is different from those experiences").

From a behavioral perspective, the simple act of changing aspects of one's behavior allows for change in other cooccurring behaviors (e.g., thinking and emotion). Such changes in behavior may, in turn, alter how the environment responds to the individual, such as by making sources of reinforcement more accessible or available (Martell et al., 2001). Behavioral experiments often encourage the client to confront avoided activities and events through action. Acting rather than avoiding involves doing something different and allows for the possibility of outcomes that are different from what the client expects.

PROMOTING BEHAVIORAL FLEXIBILITY BY ALTERING THE FUNCTIONAL ASPECTS ASSOCIATED WITH ONE'S THINKING

As we discussed in chapter 5, environmental antecedents that have been associated with reinforcement for certain behaviors in the past often set the occasion for similar behaviors when present in current situations. *Verbally represented rules* are another important class of antecedent conditions that influence behavior. In this section, we discuss the influence of verbal rules, their potential clinical relevance as establishing operations, and various behavioral interventions used to alter their influence. We also discuss strategies for developing desirable behavior patterns that are more strongly influenced by distal consequences (e.g., goals, values) implied in rule statements.

An Overview of Rule-Governed Behavior

A *rule* is "something that tells us what to do, when to do it, and what will happen when we do it" (Forsyth & Eifert, 1998, p. 53). Rules can consist of statements that an individual applies to him- or herself (e.g., "If I get this job, then I'll be a worthwhile person") or aspects of his or her world (e.g., "It's impossible to get ahead in life if one is honest and plays by the rules"). Rules can assume several different forms, including instructions, advice, commands, demands, propositions, laws, moral injunctions, myths, and modeled behavior (Baum, 1994).

How Rules Might Influence Behavior

Rules can have several different functional features (Barnes-Holmes et al., 2001; Baum, 1994). Rules might specify, for example, the consequences of acting in a certain way (e.g., "Mom said if I eat all of my dinner tonight I'll get a special dessert"). Rules also may strengthen, weaken, or otherwise alter the influence of the environment on a person's behavior (e.g., "Although I usually end up losing on the slot machines, today I have my lucky gemstone pendant so things should go better"). Rules may also influence sequences of behavior over time by specifying distal consequences (e.g., "If I do nice things for Melissa and spend a lot of time around her maybe she'll eventually go out with me"). When rules are accurate, they can result in efficient and effective forms of behavior as they eliminate the need for trial-and-error learning. If one is told, for example, "Do not touch the stove when it is hot because you will be burned" and one adheres to this rule, one does not need to discover for him- or herself through actual experience that touching a hot stove is painful.

When behavior is under the influence of verbal stimuli such as rules (rather than immediate environmental contingencies), the behavior in question is said to be *rule-governed*. From a functional perspective, the rule is technically regarded as an antecedent, typically an establishing operation (Malott, Malott, & Trojan, 2000; Schlinger, 1993). Rules are verbal descriptions of a behavioral contingency within which a behavior is specified, as well as a consequence associated with that behavior, or an antecedent condition in the presence of which the behavior will produce the specified outcome (Anderson, Hawkins, Freeman, & Scotti, 2000). A rule, then, might take the form of something like, "When it is x, y is the right thing to do" or "If I do y, then z will occur" where x is some type of antecedent condition, y refers to some behavior, and z is some outcome that could be reinforcing or punishing.

Among persons with sufficiently developed verbal repertoires, most behavior is under rule control rather than immediate contingency control. If it were not, our behavior would be haphazard, erratic, and highly changeable from one situation to the next. The fact that much of our behavior is under rule control accounts, in part, for the stability evident in behavior across time and situations. The principal of rule-governed behavior also accounts for why behavior might be influenced by distal outcomes. In these instances, however, it is not the actual distal outcome that directly influences behavior. Rather, it is the rule statement that describes the behavior–consequence contingency that exerts direct influence on behavior (hence the term *rule-governed*). The rule statement, then, directly influences behavior, whereas the consequence implied in the rule indirectly influences behavior (Malott et al., 2000).

A person, for example, might feel reasonably confident on the basis of prior experiences that if he mails a subscription card with a check for a magazine, about a month later the magazine will begin to arrive at his house (Malott et al., 2000). The act of mailing in the subscription card and check caused the magazine to be received a month later, and receiving the magazine may have functioned as a reinforcer. The delivery of the magazine is not, however, a reinforcer for the act of mailing in the subscription card and check, as the outcome of this behavior is too delayed. In this example, then, the person who subscribed to the magazine might have said to himself when filling out the subscription card, "If I fill this card out and enclose a check, I'll start receiving this magazine in 1 month." This rule statement is what is directly influencing the act of filling out the card and check, whereas the reinforcer implied in the rule (i.e., receive the magazine) has only an indirect effect. Whether an outcome of an action carried out under the influence of a rule subsequently confirms or contradicts the rule will, however, influence whether one acts in accordance with that rule in the future (Malott et al., 2000).

Although rule statements often have a direct influence, and the outcomes implied or specified in the rule have an indirect influence, there are some conditions under which rules might affect behavior in other ways. When an individual, for example, verbalizes a rule statement to him- or herself, and when that statement implies negative outcomes if the rule is not followed, an aversive physiological state such as tension or anxiety can result (e.g., "If I don't work on this project tonight I'll be so far behind I'll never get it done before tomorrow afternoon's deadline"). In this instance, rule following might represent a form of escape behavior when rule-adherence results in a lessening of the aversive physiological states of anxiety or tension (Malott, 1989).

Individual Differences in Rule-Following

Individuals vary according to the extent to which their behavior is influenced by rules, and this is, in part, influenced by the extent to which rule following has been previously reinforced and rule statements have been historically proven to be accurate. As a result of experience, people will often generate and verbalize rules about possible behavioral contingencies. Behavior guided by such rules might accurately describe behavior–consequence relationships. Sometimes, however, individuals are overly influenced by rules, to the extent that they become relatively insensitive to immediate environmental contingencies that operate differently than the environment–behavior relations characterized in the rule statement (Follette & Hayes, 2000). That is, some individuals may be overly concerned about rule following and correspondingly less observant of what behavior actually works in their current situations. Excessive or overly rigid rule adherence in such instances can result in excessively inflexible and noneffective behavior.

Deficits in rule following, conversely, can also be problematic. This deficit, in turn, might be associated with problems in other areas, including the following:

- deficits in verbal ability, attentional skills, or concentration skills, all of which are requisite abilities for discriminating features of a rule statement (e.g., the specified behavior, consequence, or both);
- hypersensitivity and responsiveness to immediate environmental cues, as is evident among members of some groups such as those with attention-deficit/hyperactivity disorder (Johansen, Aase, Meyer, & Sagvolden, 2002);
- deficits in the skill of discriminating behavior–consequence relations, as individuals who do not discriminate the effects of their actions are less likely to have future behavior influenced by their outcomes, with subsequent behavior less effective as a result (Farmer & Rucklidge, 2006; Patterson & Newman, 1993); discrimination of behavior–consequence relations might also

facilitate the rule-generation process or contribute to the refinement and accuracy of rules and thus occasion more effective behavior (Barkley, 1997);

- failures to generate self-rules, which often take the form of prepo-
sitional statements that link particular forms of behavior to
outcomes (e.g., "If I study hard, I'll likely get good grades and a
higher paying job once I graduate") and are important for self-
management and self-regulation; and

- substance intoxication, which interferes with all forms of behavior, including thinking and language use.

Generally speaking, overly rigid rule governance is more characteristic
of internalizing disorders, whereas deficits in rule generation and adherence
are more strongly associated with externalizing disorders. Individuals who
are elevated in both internalizing and externalizing features, such as those
with borderline personality disorder, often demonstrate rigid rule adherence,
difficulties in self-management, and strong reactivity to immediate environmental experiences, among other areas.

Assessment of Rules That Influence Behavior

One initial approach for working with problematic thinking patterns is
to monitor and record them. Self-monitoring not only provides information
relevant to ongoing therapy but also has associated therapeutic functions.
Research suggests that the act of simply noticing and recording behavior
often results in beneficial changes in the frequency of the behavior being
monitored (Nelson, 1977). Monitoring one's thought patterns, in particular,
might assist clients in identifying the types of rules that influence their behavior, help them evaluate the degree of correspondence between their rules
and actual behavior–consequence relations, and facilitate the development
of more accurate rules that influence future behavior.

A first step in working with patterns of thinking often involves the
identification of underlying rules and an examination of the effect that rule
adherence has on the individual. A therapist might use traditional cognitive
therapy techniques, such as the daily thought record, to identify automatic
thoughts. From a behavioral perspective, however, the functional aspects of
one's thinking are more important than the content or the type of logic-error
evident in one's thinking. In the case illustration provided at the end of this
chapter, we suggest some modifications in the thought-recording process that
provides additional information on the function of the client's thinking.

Therapeutic Interventions for Altering Rigid Adherence to Faulty, Inaccurate, or Harmful Rules

Sometimes rules may not accurately state the true relation between
behavior and consequences. Even when actions are guided by inaccurate rules

that repeatedly result in ineffective outcomes, they are nonetheless resistant to change (Hayes, Brownstein, Zettle, Rosenfarb, & Korn, 1986), and consequently, can become quite problematic. In this section, we discuss therapeutic interventions for reducing the influence of rigidly held rules and modifying rule statements so they more accurately reflect actual behavior–environment relations.

Rule following or adherence can become problematic when it is overly excessive and rigid. Some clients, for example, might be overly conscientious as evident by persistent efforts to not disappoint or offend, please others or be good, or be overly compliant. Self-rules for such overly conscientious persons might include statements such as, "If I am good to others, then I will be liked and valued" and "If I make waves, I'll disappoint others." Similarly, some clinical groups are primarily defined by their tendency to rigidly adhere to rules, such as those with obsessional, perfectionistic, workaholic, and paranoid tendencies.

There are two general therapeutic approaches that can be used to reduce overly rigid rule following: (a) strengthening the influence of immediate reinforcement contingencies on behavior or (b) weakening the influence of rigidly held rules. Chapter 5 discusses methods for strengthening the influence of immediate reinforcement contingencies. For weakening rules that result in rigid and maladaptive behavior patterns, traditional cognitive therapy techniques might be helpful, such as behavioral experiments described earlier in this chapter. In this section, we describe additional therapeutic approaches that can be used to weaken the influence of maladaptive or inaccurate rules.

In cognitive therapy, *cognitive distortions* refer to persistent errors in reasoning or systematic misinterpretation of situations (Sacco & Beck, 1995). Another way to view these distortions from a behavioral perspective is to regard them as faulty rules defined by inaccurate associations between antecedents and behaviors, or behaviors and consequences. Examples include the following:

- *All-or-none thinking, dichotomous thinking, black-or-white thinking* is evident when thinking patterns are polarized, and outcomes are only possible at the extreme ends of a continuum (e.g., "You're either with me or against me"; "I'm a complete loser").
- *Personalization* is the tendency to inaccurately relate events or circumstances to oneself (e.g., "My boss didn't smile at me when I walked by his desk today; I bet he's thinking of firing me").
- *Overgeneralization* involves making broad and sweeping conclusions based on outcomes of single events. The use of certain words in some contexts might suggest the presence of overgeneralization. These include *all, none, every, always,* and

never (e.g., "All men cannot be trusted" or "Whenever I try to get ahead, nothing good ever comes from it").

- *Disqualifying the positive* involves minimizing or negating positive experiences or outcomes that conflict with rules that are negative (e.g., after a junior colleague offers praise following the delivery of a presentation, the presenter concludes, "She's saying this only because she wants to get in good with me").
- *Should statements* consist of a group of inflexible rules about oneself or others concerning how one should act. The presence of "should" rules results in a greater tendency to judge, often against unrealistic or inflexible standards (e.g., "I should never make mistakes"). Other words that suggest the presence of inflexible rules for action include *ought*, *must*, and *have to*.
- *Catastrophizing* involves predictions of highly negative outcomes related to small events rather than viewing these events in perspective. Catastrophizing is often revealed by the use of words such as *awful*, *dreadful*, *terrible*, *horrible*, and *horrendous* to denote an anticipated outcome (e.g., "It would be horrible if people noticed I was anxious").

Perhaps the most direct way to approach such inaccurate or faulty ways of thinking is for the therapist to appeal to the client's actual experience, that is, examine instances from the client's life to see if these rigid rules are uniformly accurate. When approached in this way, the therapeutic issue becomes whether the client's rule fits the events of the context to which it refers. To this end, we do not recommend that clients learn the complex skills of labeling by name the type of cognitive distortion evident. More important, we believe, is the skill of accurately matching up thinking related to a given context to the actual events of the context itself; that is, the therapist describes antecedent–behavior–consequence relations as they actually occurred or unfolded.

Another related way for therapists to respond to these thoughts is to examine with the client the effect that such thinking has when present. That is, when the client distorts actual experience, what does he or she do in relation to the distortion? Does avoidance or escape behavior follow? Does the client characteristically withdraw or give up? Does the client ruminate or become passive? If maladaptive behaviors accompany distorted modes of thinking, then a therapeutic goal might be to (a) heighten awareness of such modes of thinking and the effects that such thoughts characteristically have on behavior, (b) block any maladaptive behavior patterns that are associated with such thinking, and (c) engage in an alternative behavior that is more directly geared toward solving the problem that occasioned the distorted thought. Another approach is for the therapist to test the thought through behavioral experimentation. Doing so involves the therapist taking action, testing the underlying assumptions of the thought, or collecting factual information related to the thought that is either consistent or inconsistent with it.

Perfectionistic thinking is another example of a thinking pattern that often contributes to overly rigid rule-governed behavior. With this pattern of thinking, there is a tendency for the client to see oneself or world in dichotomous, black-and-white, or all-or-nothing terms. In addition to reducing the client's evaluation of one's behavior to the narrow categories of "success" or "failure," excessively high self-standards for performance often result in frequent disappointment, a consequence of an inability to realize unattainable goals (Bandura, 1986). Such a frame of reference also makes alternative evaluations of one's behavior more difficult, such as from the perspectives of "partial success" or "effectiveness." Excessively high performance self-standards are common among persons with certain psychological characteristics or disorders, such as obsessive-compulsive personality disorder, Type A personality, anorexia nervosa, or depression.

Evidence of perfectionistic thinking might be revealed by thoughts such as "I cannot make any mistakes on this" or "I have to accomplish at the very highest of my abilities" or "If I'm not at the top of the class, then I'm a failure." Burns (1980) has described several strategies for challenging the effectiveness or benefit of perfectionistic thinking. These include the following:

- An *objective evaluation of the utility of perfectionistic thinking.* Does such thinking result in more effective outcomes, or does it result in negative emotions and self-appraisals?
- *Participation in behavioral experiments geared toward the exploration of outcomes related to lower standards.* The purpose of these types of experiments is to see what effect, if any, acting in accordance with lower performance standards has on personal or performance satisfaction. Such experiments might also evaluate the effects of intentionally making a mistake or acknowledging personal flaws to others. When a mistake is made, for example, are the outcomes as negative as expected? When flaws, vulnerabilities, or potentially embarrassing information about oneself is disclosed to others, does that result in ridicule or negative evaluation, or does it promote a deepening of relationships?
- *Explore other ways of representing naturally occurring events other than through dichotomous categories.* This type of experiential exercise might involve the client intentionally taking notice of situations, events, or objects to see if they can all be categorized in a certain way. That is, can one point of view be completely correct, and another competing view be completely wrong? Are there some arguments within both perspectives that ring true to some degree, whereas others come across as weaker? Do other

persons appear all one way in some area, such as calmness, intelligence, attractiveness, or competence? Do such individuals shine in some areas, but have weaknesses in other related areas?

Another therapeutic approach to perfectionistic thinking or excessively stringent rules for self-reinforcement is to shift the focus of behavioral evaluation away from the topography (or form) of behavior (e.g., "Was the threshold for performance reached?") to a consideration of behavioral effectiveness (i.e., "What are some of the positive outcomes that resulted from my actions?"). When such a shift in orientation occurs, the emphasis moves away from getting the form of behavior correct, or doing the "right" thing, or realizing of some end-state goal. From this alternative frame of reference, the focus is instead on the evaluation of behavior in terms of the outcome it produces (Follette & Hayes, 2000).

In another example of behavior under the influence of faulty rules, the hallmark of paranoid modes of thinking is "an intense, irrational, but persistent mistrust or suspicion of people, and a corresponding tendency to interpret the actions of others as deliberately threatening or demeaning" (Fenigstein, 1996, p. 242). As paranoid thinking often persists even when there is frequent evidence to the contrary, it is likely that such thinking is under the influence of faulty rules. As with other forms of rigid thinking, a client might be asked to consider alternative explanations (e.g., "Are there any other possibilities that might explain why she acted this way toward you?" or "Is there any evidence that is inconsistent with this way of viewing the situation?"). Along these lines, a feature of therapy might emphasize the development of hypothesis-generation skills, whereby the client is challenged to come up with more than one possible explanation for events that occasion suspicious thinking (Magaro, 1980). Alternatively, the content of the thinking may not be as important as the feeling that accompanies the thought. Rather than directly challenging the thought, it might be useful for the therapist to directly focus on the accompanying emotion in a reflective and validating manner (e.g., "It sounds like you were very angry when the attendant did not respond to your question. Tell me more about what you did when you were having the feeling of anger in this situation").

Inaccurate rules held by people who are especially vulnerable to depressed or anxious moods tend to be evident by their overly negative thinking patterns. Often, this process involves formulating more accurate rules that incorporate some positive aspects of a situation. A cognitive technique geared toward the development of *alternative or balanced thinking* can be used to identify more accurate ways of thinking about the situation (Greenberger & Padesky, 1995):

- If a rule statement does not appear to be accurate because it is not supported by objective evidence, then generate an alternative rule that is more consistent with what has been observed.

- If a rule statement is partially accurate, identify the aspect of it that is supported and note the specific evidence that is consistent with it. Then identify the aspect of the rule statement that does not appear to be accurate and generate an alternative statement in its place that is more consistent with the evidence.
- Rate the degree to which you think the new rule is accurate (on a 0%–100% scale).
- Practice or apply this new rule in situations within which it might apply. As an aid, new rules can be written down on index cards, carried in a pocket or purse, and referred to when indicated.

"William," for example, had the self-rule, "If I am among a group of people, I will have a panic attack and do something uncontrolled that will be embarrassing [90%]." After considering occasions when he was among groups of people, William acknowledged that this statement was too absolute, as he was able on several occasions to be with a group of people and not have an attack. He also could not recall any occasion when he had a panic attack and did something uncontrolled that drew attention to him. Consequently, he revised the self-rule to be, "Sometimes when I am among a group of people, I get panicky. When I'm panicky, I often feel that I'll lose control but so far I have not acted in an out-of-control way during a panic attack [85%]." As he reflected on his therapy experience, he decided to revise the self-rule even further: "Sometimes I get panicky when I'm in a group of people. If this should happen in the future, I know what I can do to cope with my panicky feelings and to reduce their intensity. Given my past history, it is unlikely that even if I do have a panic attack that I will lose control and draw attention to myself [95%]." The goal of such an exercise is to develop more accuracy in one's thinking, which does not necessarily mean the same thing as being more positive in one's thinking. Rather, this process involves the development of a skill for seeing oneself or the world the way it actually is.

Other clients might have rules that suggest that certain types of events or private experiences are threatening. Examples of such rules might be, "Anxiety is bad because it might cause me to lose control or freak out" or "I can't go to the party because I won't know what to say to people and I'll come across as a dolt." Avoidant thinking is often associated with avoidant behavior, whether it be external (e.g., passive avoidance, active escape) or internal (e.g., dissociation, rumination, distraction). Individuals who regard certain private experiences as threatening might take dramatic steps to avoid coming into contact with them such as by engaging in ritualistic compulsive behavior, intentional self-injury, and substance misuse. Paradoxically, however, although such avoidance often provides short-term relief, the avoided experience usually becomes more common or frequent in the future (Hayes, Strosahl, & Wilson, 1999). In recent years a number of behavioral interventions have been developed that target the avoidance of private events. One such intervention is acceptance and commitment therapy (ACT; Hayes, Strosahl, et al., 1999). In ACT, the therapist emphasizes the verbal functions that contribute to experience avoidance. These include evaluation (e.g., "Thoughts about sex are bad and should be avoided at all costs"), reasongiving (e.g., "If it wasn't for my anxiety I would go to the concert tonight"), and literality ("I feel like I'm an evil person so I must be").

Modeling and observational learning are other means by which rules or behavioral prescriptions may be transferred. Modeling processes involve observing another person's (i.e., the model's) behavior and discriminating features of the behavior. Whether or not an observer is likely to imitate a model's behavior is dependent on a number of features, including the capability of the observer to physically perform the behavior, the extent to which component skills related to the modeled behavior are in the observer's repertoire, and whether the model was reinforced for enacting the behavior that was modeled (Bandura, 1986; Catania, 1994). When a model is reinforced for his or her behavior, the likelihood that the observer will imitate modeled behavior is increased, whereas imitation will be less likely if the model's behavior is punished. Once the imitator acquires the model's behavior through observational learning, the behavior can be further refined and adapted as a result of shaping processes. Observational learning, just like learning through verbally transmitted rules, is a very efficient way to learn, as one does not require several instances of trial-and-error learning to acquire a new behavior.

Establishing Rules That Bring Behavior in Line With Desirable Distal Outcomes

In this and in the following sections we discuss therapeutic interventions for transcending the influence of immediate environmental events in favor of bringing behavior in line with desirable distal outcomes. As we previously noted, distal outcomes only influence current behavior indirectly; the direct-acting influence is a rule that associates current behaviors with distal outcomes. In the next two sections we are primarily concerned with two general classes of verbal rules: those related to goals and those related to values. Before describing intervention strategies for increasing goal- and value-directed behavior, we first distinguish the concepts of goals and values from a behavioral perspective.

Distinguishing Goals and Values From a Behavioral Perspective

When people speak of goals and values, they generally do so in terms of what an individual has. From a behavioral perspective, however, both goals and values are evident in one's action. That is, goals and values are regarded as verbal rules that are associated with verbally constructed consequences that make some behaviors more appetitive and others more aversive (Twohig,

Masuda, Varra, & Hayes, 2005). Evidence of the influence of goals and values is seen in one's behavior that is, in turn, influenced by contingency-specifying rules for behavior.

As used here, *goals* refer to concrete events, situations, or objects. They can be realized, achieved, or completed (Hayes & Smith, 2005). Goals are attainable and can specify a directional course that has value for the individual. Ideally, goals that an individual pursues should be consistent with or complementary to his or her values. *Values* refer to areas of life that one cares about or regards as important (Twohig et al., 2005). Unlike goals, values are not something to be achieved or completed; rather, a person's values are made manifest in his or her day-to-day actions (Hayes & Smith, 2005). In this respect, values are choices or selections among alternatives, and they, too, suggest a directional course. Values often represent the outgrowth of cultural teachings or practices. One's values, however, might diverge from cultural practices as a result of personal experience.

In an example from Twohig et al. (2005), a client with obsessive-compulsive disorder might value being a good mother and wish to be free of the anxiety that occasions compulsive behavior. Being free of anxiety might be a goal that is temporarily realized through engagement in ritualistic behavior. Participation in compulsive actions, however, takes time away from living in accordance with the value of being a good mother, as time spent on rituals is time that is not available for being with her daughter.

In another example, Hayes and Smith (2005, p. 159) illustrated the distinction between goals and values with reference to a person with a drug addiction. Such an individual might take drugs to "feel good," or for its immediate positive reinforcing effects. Although this might represent the goals of drug use, being high and feeling good may not necessarily be valued outcomes for such an individual. Rather, this person might actually value being physically with and psychologically close to other people. Taking steps in the direction of establishing, maintaining, and deepening relationships, though, might occasion significant anxiety. Because such feelings are experienced as aversive, the person stops moving forward and instead takes drugs to deal with the anxieties associated with moving in a valued, yet frightening, direction. Initial movements in a valued direction, then, might not "feel good" in the short term, whereas drug consumption might produce immediate "good feelings."

In the next section, we describe techniques for realizing goals, or potentially achievable outcomes that result from a series of actions. After discussing techniques associated with goal setting, we offer examples of values-based intervention strategies in a following section.

Goal Setting and Time Management

Goal setting in behavior therapy is always individualized in accordance with the needs and therapeutic objectives of the client. Selected goals are ideally related to one's values or ideals and should represent something that the client is willing to spend time and effort working toward (Hayes, Strosahl, et al., 1999). Goals should also be achievable within a practical time frame, and progress toward the realization of goals should be evident in each step taken. Goals also might be conceptualized in terms of things to work toward rather than away from (M. Davis, Eshelman, & McKay, 2000). In the case of goals related to alcohol abuse, a practical goal might be complete abstinence or controlled drinking, with the parameters of what constitutes "complete abstinence" or "controlled drinking" clearly defined. This would be more desirable than the goal of "avoiding alcohol."

Goal setting is often carried out in conjunction with self-monitoring and some type of contingency-management program. Consequently, a list of goals might be drawn up and subdivided into short-term goals (e.g., goals that one might work toward in the days and weeks ahead) and long-term goals (e.g., goals that will require sustained effort over longer periods of time to achieve). Once goals are clearly identified, the therapist and client might consider together how to go about realizing these goals. Thought might also be given to what rewards will be made available for efforts directed toward the realization of goals, or what the cost might be when efforts are not made. Consideration might also be given to the inclusion of other people. The addition of others often increases the likelihood that the program will be effective and reduces the likelihood that some parts of a behavioral contract will not be carried out (e.g., response–cost provisions). Social reinforcement from others is also often a potent influence on behavior. Addis and Martell (2004) summarized the steps associated with goal setting:

- *What are the steps for working toward a goal?* The path to realizing a goal is more likely to be followed if the points along the way are clearly spelled out. As a rule, smaller and clearly defined steps are better than bigger and vague ones.
- *In what sequence should these steps be organized?* Once steps have been clearly identified and delineated, they should be arranged in a logical sequence that maximizes the likelihood for reaching the goal. Consideration should be given to what needs to be completed first before another step can be taken. In this regard, steps can be thought of as separate actions that, in the aggregate, link up to a chain of actions that collectively move one toward the realization of a goal.
- *Commit to carrying out each of the identified steps.* This involves specifying the day and time that the first step will be taken. In doing so, thought should be given to what the step would involve in terms of resources or time, and arranging for these in advance. Consideration should also be given to potential ob-

stacles that might arise and how these will be overcome as well as how progress at each step will be monitored.

- *Work through any barriers.* Regardless of mood, inhibiting thoughts, or other psychological barriers, the goal is to take a step, one at a time.
- *Reward oneself.* This involves acknowledging one's efforts and what one has accomplished after the completion of each step by providing a reward or pat on the back.

Part of goal setting and working toward goal realization is *time management.* Effective management of one's time is a necessary skill if one is to get one's work done and have time left over to do elective enjoyable activities. A related goal might be to manage one's time so that time and energy is spent on valued activities, and not on procrastination or avoidant activities.

The effective use of time requires prioritizing activities, clarifying one's values, and comparing the worth of activities on the basis of their relationship to those values. This also involves daily planning, in which one makes a specific plan each day to accomplish goals and activities that are highest in priority. *Time logs* can be used to organize one's daily plan. A time log is a listing of activities that one plans to carry out over the course of the day, an estimate of how much time is required to carry out each of the activities, and a priority rating for each activity. Priority ratings might be based, for example, on the degree to which the activity is tied to important to goals or values, or the significance of consequences associated with carrying out or not carrying out the activity (M. Davis et al., 2000).

As observed by Hayes, Strosahl, et al. (1999), persons who attempt to shift their behavior from immediate contingencies to long-term goals are often confronted with a challenge: the immediate outcomes that follow goal-directed behaviors. In some instances, the immediate consequences that some persons might experience for acting in a valued direction might be experienced as aversive, even though the behavior performed is related to desirable goals. Take, for example, an individual who wishes to no longer passively avoid or actively escape from situations that occasion anxiety. To accomplish this, she will likely experience immediate significant anxiety as she enters into and remains in anxiety-evoking situations. For her to remain in such situations, she must value the nonimmediate or distal outcomes associated with exposing herself to situations that evoke such uncomfortable experiences.

Behavioral intervention strategies designed to facilitate action toward valued or long-term goals include *acting toward a goal* (Martell et al., 2001). Related therapeutic goals are the facilitation of the client's engagement in previously established behaviors that have been extinguished or the acquisition and enactment of new behaviors. For individuals whose behavior is often guided by immediate contingencies or experiences, such as current emotions, a therapeutic goal would be to help them shift their behavior away from responding to immediate events. That is, clients might be encouraged to act in accordance with values or long-term goals rather than with immediate emotional experiences. Expressed a different way, "the goal is the action itself, rather than the outcome of the action" (Jacobson, Martell, & Dimidjian, 2001, p. 261). Helping the client find a good job, for example, may not be the focal goal of therapy; rather, a goal consistent with a behavioral activation approach would be to help the client develop and maintain a pattern of behavior (or routine) that increases the likelihood of finding a good job, regardless of how he or she might feel while doing so (Jacobson et al., 2001).

Long-term goals often involve valued outcomes related to health, career, family, relationships, finances, leisure and personal interests, and general satisfaction. Acting in accordance with long-term goals, then, often involves acting in accordance with what one values. In the next section, we discuss intervention strategies that facilitate the development of behavioral habits or routines that are consistent with one's values.

Values-Based Intervention Strategies

Although *values-based intervention strategies* have been central features of therapies developed from the human potential movement during the 1950s through the 1970s, they are only now beginning to surface within CBT therapies. Values connote what holds meaning for the individual, what is good versus bad, or what is moral versus immoral (Baum, 1994). One's values are often apparent in how someone responds to questions such as the following (Hayes, Strosahl, et al., 1999):

- "What do you want your life to stand for or be about?"
- "What are your hopes, aspirations, or wishes for yourself during your lifetime?"
- "How do you want people to think about you once you're gone?"

Values can be regarded as a special form of verbal behavior in the form of rules that specify, either directly or indirectly, the contingencies of behavior linked to the value. As related to their directional or purposive qualities, values can be considered as "verbally construed global desired life consequences" (Hayes, Strosahl, et al., 1999, p. 206). This quality coordinates and maintains values-related behavior over long periods of time.

In ACT, as with other behavioral interventions, the act of valuing is regarded not as a feeling or even thought. Rather, the act of valuing is manifest through action (Hayes, Strosahl, et al., 1999). ACT interventions facilitate taking action in a manner consistent with one's values. Because values, in contrast to goals, are not fully realizable or permanently achievable, they have greater potential applicability across time and situations and are less likely to give way to satiation or change (Hayes, Strosahl, et al., 1999). An associated therapy goal within ACT is to assist clients in developing behavioral trajectories that move and sustain behavior in a direction consistent with their values. To this end, a good deal of therapeutic activity in ACT is directed toward helping clients identify their values and act in accordance with these even in the face of psychological obstacles.

Motivational interviewing or *motivational enhancement therapy* is an approach to therapy that has primarily been associated with the treatment of alcohol abuse and dependence (Miller, Zweben, DiClemente, & Rychtarik, 1995), although it has recently been applied to several other psychological conditions (Burke, Arkowitz, & Menchola, 2003). When interpreted from a behavioral perspective, motivational interviewing helps the client establish connections between current harmful behavior patterns and more distal outcomes as a way to lessen the influence of immediate environmental contingencies. In the first phase of therapy, the primary objective is to establish a motivation for change. Among the techniques used to accomplish this is the provision of information to the client about the level of his or her alcohol use, and the likely effects it will have in the future if current use patterns continue (Miller & Rollnick, 1991). Within this phase, the therapist provides the client with information about his or her personal risk and degree of impairment and emphasizes the client's personal responsibility for bringing about a change in drinking behavior.

In the second phase, emphasis is placed on the facilitation of a commitment to change. During this phase, the therapist explores with the client his or her readiness for change and whether a decision to change has been made. The therapist, in an empathic and supportive manner, provides clear advice that encourages a change in drinking behavior. When the client expresses an interest in change, various change options are discussed and considered. A significant other might be included within change plans to increase the likelihood that action plans will be carried out. Consequences associated with taking action toward change versus inaction are also contemplated.

In the last phase, the client and therapist discuss and test out change-oriented strategies. Also within this phase, any progress or gains are reviewed, and the client's motivation and commitment for change are frequently reassessed and reaffirmed.

Inhibiting Problematic Behaviors Through Rule Generation and Adherence

Rules can also be useful for promoting restraint (Alessi, 1992). Societies, for example, often enact laws that demarcate the division of what constitutes acceptable and unacceptable behavior. Other examples of cultural rules that frequently restrain behavior include values, warnings, taboos, and admonishments, all of which imply negative social consequences for instances of noncompliance.

Some persons' behaviors are inordinately influenced by immediate environmental cues, resulting in behavior that is primarily stimulus driven and influenced by short-term contingencies. Such individuals may appear to be impulsive, erratic, and pleasure seeking. For individuals who are overly reactive to immediate environmental cues, one therapeutic task might be to shift the influence of behavior away from immediate environmental contingencies to the influence of rules that specify alternative distal outcomes. One consequence of this might be that individuals will be in a better position to develop and sustain behavior patterns that assist in achieving long-term objectives.

To facilitate this, the therapist might direct early work toward goal or value identification. Once identified, the therapist and client might work together to identify patterns of behavior that would be required to realize such values and goals. Once so identified, the client might be encouraged to act in a manner that is consistent with his or her values (Hayes, Strosahl, et al., 1999; Martell et al., 2001). Included among these techniques is acting *"as if,"* which we describe in greater detail in chapter 8 of this volume. In short, acting "as if" involves acting in line with how one would ideally like to be. Approaches such as this make distal consequences of one's actions more salient and increase the likelihood that behavior will be brought more in line with these distal goals, thus resulting in a decrease in the salience of immediate environmental influences.

Another approach is *behavioral contracting.* A behavioral contract is a rule or statement, often written, that specifies a behavior to increase or decrease, when the behavior should or should not take place, the method used to monitor behavior, and the consequences associated with either performing the behavior or not performing the behavior (Malott et al., 2000; Miltenberger, 2004). In this respect, the contract serves as an establishing operation that brings behavior in line with the parameters set forth in the contract. Rules that are easier to follow describe immediate outcomes that are both sizable and probable. In contrast, rules that describe immediate outcomes that are relatively small in magnitude or very improbable are more difficult to follow (Malott et al., 2000). In dialectical behavior therapy (Linehan, 1993a), variations of the basic behavioral contracting strategy are used during the process of orienting the client to therapy, clarifying therapy-related expectations for the client and therapist, and establishing guidelines for responding to crisis situations.

CASE ILLUSTRATION

"Jenny" is a 24-year-old married woman who is employed as a retail clerk at a local department store. All of her adult life, she has exhibited a pattern of behavior consistent with generalized anxiety disorder. This is most evident in her persistent worry about something bad happening. The content of her anticipatory thoughts ranges from doing things incorrectly or making mistakes to being negatively evaluated by others, to a preoccupation with her own faults and shortcomings, and to exaggerated pessimism about the future. Worrying is related to sleep disturbance (particularly in getting to sleep at night), fatigue, difficulty concentrating and sustaining attention, and feelings of tension most of the time. Jenny also reported some features consistent with major depressive disorder, social anxiety disorder, agoraphobia, and avoidant and dependent personality disorders, but not to the level of diagnostic threshold for these conditions.

In her initial explorations of the function of Jenny's worrying patterns, her therapist inquired about how worrying might be helpful. The therapist made the assumption that worrying was helpful in some way, as it occurred with high frequency, suggesting that some sort of reinforcement process functioned to maintain worrying. Jenny offered several reasons for worrying (listed in the "Establishing Operations" section of the functional formulation provided subsequently), including the view that "worrying helps me figure out what to do" and "worrying calms my mind a bit." As she and her therapist examined this further, Jenny's additional disclosures were consistent with the view that worrying is sometimes associated with a short-term reduction in anxiety or other negative emotions; however, worrying did not solve her problems. Rather, Jenny reported that she characteristically tends to replay various scenarios of how negative events might unfold and how they will affect her, with little time spent considering how to solve these problems if they actually arose.

Jenny disclosed that she sought therapy at this time because she sees herself becoming increasingly avoidant of situations or places, particularly those in which other people are present. Her worrying is also associated with impairment as it interferes with her sleep and takes time away from other activities. Although reassurances from others often provided her with limited short-term relief, they had little long-term effect on her worrying patterns. Jenny described that she was tired of going to people, particularly to her husband, over the "small matters."

During the assessment phase of therapy, Jenny's therapist asked her to self-monitor situations that accompany worrying. A self-monitoring form was developed based on the daily thought record used in cognitive therapy. Slight modifications in this form were made to assess Jenny's behavior in the context of worrying and the consequences associated with such behavior.

Jenny's recordings over 3 days are displayed in Exhibit 6.1. Upon giving the completed form to her therapist, Jenny indicated that this record was fairly representative of her worrying patterns. As they reviewed the form together, several observations were noted:

- Jenny is more vulnerable to worrying when time is unstructured, that is, when she is alone, uncertain what to do, or bored.
- Sometimes emotions that accompanied worrying decreased in intensity while she worried.

EXHIBIT 6.1
Jenny's Functional Daily Thought and Feeling Record

Situation	Feelings	Thought	What Is Troubling About This Thought	Action	Consequences of Action
What happened? Where were you? Who were you with?	Label your feelings in this situation and rate its intensity (from 0 = no feeling to 10 = most intense feeling possible).	What were you thinking in this situation around the time you had the unpleasant feeling?	What does this thought mean to you? If the thought is true, what are the implications? Also, rate the degree of evidence for this thought (from 0 = no evidence to 10 = clear objective evidence).	What did you do in this situation after you had the feeling or thought? (If you did nothing, just write "nothing.")	What happened after you acted? (If you did not act, did the situation change, or did your thoughts or feelings change? Were your actions helpful or unhelpful? If so, how?
1 At home, sitting, and largely doing nothing but thinking.	Anxious (8)	I am going to be evaluated negatively in quarterly job evaluation.	I might get fired. (3)	Nothing (just continue to worry).	Anxiety went down a little. Did nothing about problem.
2 Argument with husband at home (regarding finances).	Angry (5) Anxious (7) Sad (4)	Sometimes we just don't seem compatible.	We might drift apart or divorce. (3)	Went to husband and suggested we need to work this out rather than leave situation as is.	We worked out disagreement. Anxiety and anger gone. Feel more positive toward him.
3 At work, boss frowned at me when I walked by.	Anxious (7)	He's got it in for me.	I'll be fired for sure. (4)	Nothing (continued to worry).	No changes until customer came along.

	Situation	Emotion	Automatic thought	Response	Outcome
4	At work, manager is teaching me a new inventory method.	Anxious (7) Pressured (8)	Why can't I get this? I must be stupid or slow.	I'm not competent or very intelligent, and won't amount to much. (6)	Told manager I need to go to the bathroom (but I really didn't need to).	Went to bathroom. Felt less anxious. Came back and afterward was able to learn method.
5	At home, watching TV, bored because there is nothing good on.	Bored (7)	My mother's going to fall and break her hip.	She might have to be hospitalized, or she might die. (6)	Called mother to talk (really to see if she was okay).	Relieved. Mother says she's getting around fine.
6	In bed, trying to sleep.	Anxious (9)	My mother's going to fall and break her hip.	She might have to be hospitalized, or she might die. (5)	Tried to stop worrying. Went on to imagine myself at her funeral and the sadness that I felt.	Couldn't stop worrying. More anxious, and now sad and more worried. Didn't get to sleep for 3 hours.
7	Getting ready for work by myself, thinking about finances.	Anxious (8) Sad (6)	If I lose my job, we won't be able to make mortgage payments.	We'll be homeless, and I won't have a job. (4)	Continued to get dressed and think about these possibilities.	Felt a little less anxious, worrying decreased. Finished getting dressed.
8	At home by myself (husband away for poker night), don't know what to do.	Bored (7) Anxious (5) Uncertain (7)	This world is really falling apart. Wars, terrorism, crime, corruption.	The world isn't a safe place anymore.	Nothing. Just thought about these issues.	Still alone. Boredom went down, but anxiety and feelings of uncertainty went up. Also feel pessimistic and sad now.

- Her "emotion intensity" ratings were consistently higher than her "evidence" ratings, suggesting that her degree of emotional reactions were considerably stronger than the evidence in support of her thinking in these situations.
- Even though Jenny thought she was addressing her problems through worrying, much of her rumination involved amplifying unlikely negative outcomes associated with the scenarios she worried about, with little time actually spent on constructive problem solving.
- In situations in which she worried, Jenny often did "nothing" in response to her worries or the contexts that occasioned them.
- In one instance in which she actively responded to a situation that occasioned worry, an argument with her husband (see Situation 2 in Exhibit 6.1), she observed that actually doing something about the problem helped resolve it, whereas worrying alone usually does little to address her concerns.

As a result of the clinical interview, self-monitoring, and other pretreatment assessments, Jenny's therapist developed the following functional formulation of her pattern of worrying.

Antecedent conditions included the following:

- *discriminative stimuli*, which are situations in which there are few pressures for alternative behavior to worrying (e.g., when alone or when there are no customers to attend to); situations in which there is no clear indication of how to respond or what to do; situations that require a response that is not clearly established within Jenny's behavioral repertoire; the presence of other people, particularly persons in positions of authority; and
- *establishing operations*, which include the experience of anxiety, boredom, or uncertainty regarded by Jenny as aversive as well as rules related to worrying, such as the following:
  - "My worrying prevents bad things from happening."
  - "Worrying is a useful way to solve my problems."
  - "Worrying calms my mind somewhat."
  - "If something bad happens that I didn't anticipate, I won't be able to handle it (with "it" referring to the intensity of her anxiety and the situation she is in)."
  - "I can't manage this situation by myself."
  - "Forcing myself to stop worrying is the only way to make worries go away."

Person Variables

Jenny had a family history of various problems related to anxiety; a long personal history of anxiety and worry, with some indication of a history of negative reinforcement for worry (e.g., occasionally results in an immediate decrease in anxiety level and some reductions in catastrophic thoughts and images); a lifelong hypersensitivity and responsiveness to cues associated with punishment, threat, and danger; and a lifelong history of excessive behavioral inhibition and hypersensitivity to other's evaluations.

Responses

Jenny's responses included worry, with content of worries tending to shift from one domain to the next and occurring often in a continuous flow that can go on for relatively long periods of time; disengagement from the immediate environment to attend to worries. Agitation and restlessness, difficulties going to sleep, muscle and psychic tension, and problems with concentration and attention accompany periods of worry; she excessively seeks out reassurance and support from others.

Consequences

Reinforcing outcomes associated with worrying include the following:

- *Negative reinforcement*: Jenny experiences an immediate reduction in anxiety, boredom, or uncertainty as well as reductions in catastrophic thoughts and images as worrying progresses over time.
- *Positive reinforcement*: She receives support and reassurance from others and is accompanied by others when she expresses uncertainty as to whether she can perform a particular activity or engage in a certain event.

Immediate aversive outcomes include the following:

- Because worries are attended to when present, her behavior is less effective in relation to immediate environmental events; she is unable to sleep even though she feels tired and fatigued.

Delayed aversive outcomes associated with worrying include the following:

- Jenny experiences fatigue after periods of worry, increasingly avoids places where others are present, loses time for valued activities because of time spent worrying, notices impairment with performance at work, and experiences ongoing distress related to the current situation.

Therapy with Jenny included several behavioral interventions not further described here, such as diaphragmatic breathing to promote present moment awareness and reduce tension; exposure to specific reccurring worries (presented in her own voice via a cassette tape); response prevention (cessation of reassurance and support seeking as well as seeking the physical accompaniment of others as a means of coping with anxieties and worries); and the promotion of decentering, or the perspective of thoughts and feelings as separate from self, through experiential and mindfulness exercises. The following summary describes her therapy as it relates to techniques explicitly used to alter the functional aspects of her worrying behavior.

In therapy, Jenny and her therapist first discussed features that distinguish unproductive rumination from problem solving. With some assistance, Jenny was able to identify several features, and she listed these on an index card as they were discussed. Her therapist suggested that when she notices herself worrying on the basis of the presence of these features, she was to correctly label her behavior (e.g., "this is unhelpful rumination"). On the basis of the hypothesis that worrying was a form of avoidance behavior that helped Jenny cope with certain contexts or situations, Jenny and her therapist developed a list of activities other than rumination that Jenny could do if she catches herself ruminating. These were written down on a separate index card, and Jenny was encouraged to refer to this card for ideas for alternative behavior when she found herself worrying and unsure about what else she could do. The act of worrying, then, was transformed to the status of a cue that signaled alternative action. Alternative behaviors listed on the card were chosen on the basis of their likelihood of producing positively reinforcing outcomes. Because these alternatives were listed on a small index card, she could carry this list with her wherever she went and consult it when needed.

In initial sessions, Jenny and her therapist devised some behavioral experiments to test some of the rules that served as establishing operations for worrying. Some of these rules, such as "Worrying is a useful way to solve my problems," were already revealed to be inaccurate through the self-monitoring exercise depicted in Exhibit 6.1. As a result of self-monitoring, Jenny revised this rule to suggest, "Worrying does not solve my problems."

One behavioral experiment targeted the rule, "Telling myself to stop worrying is the only way to make worries go away." The experiment was based on the assumption present in Jenny's statement that suggested verbal control is an effective means for suppressing private events such as thinking (i.e., "Telling myself to stop worrying. . . "). An experiment was set up whereby Jenny's rule was tested against an alternative rule, "Trying to stop myself from thinking or feeling something only makes it 'there' more." The experiment involved noticing what happened when she took part in the Chocolate Cake Exercise from ACT, and then deciding whether what she noticed was more consistent with her rule or the alternative rule. For this exercise, Jenny was asked to do the following (from Hayes, Strosahl, et al., 1999):

> Suppose I tell you right now that I don't want you to think about something. I'm going to tell you very soon. And when I do, don't think about it even for a second. Here it comes. Remember, don't think about it. Don't think of . . . warm chocolate cake! You know how it smells when it

first comes out of the oven. . . . Don't think of it! The taste of the chocolate icing when you bite into the first piece. . . . Don't think of it! . . . It's very important; don't think about any of this! (p. 124)

Jenny acknowledged that the more she tried not to think about the chocolate cake, the more it was "there" for her, and that the image became increasingly more threatening as she was unable to get rid of it despite all efforts. Her therapist appealed to Jenny's other experiences with suppression of private events, and whether it was true that such efforts generally worked that way. Jenny eventually concluded that trying to get rid of thoughts and feelings really does not work. After the exercise and when reflecting on her past experiences, Jenny accepted the alternative rule and discarded the old one.

Another behavioral experiment targeted the rule, "The world is threatening and dangerous," which, when further dissected, was refined to suggest, "People are threatening and will harm me." For this experiment, Jenny and her therapist agreed that to test the validity of this thought, she would sample various downtown locations where people congregated. They agreed that this would be a therapist-guided activity, whereby the therapist would join Jenny on a walk to several predetermined and nearby locations where people gather: a shopping mall, grocery store, city park, central city square, and bus station. They set aside 2 hours for this exercise, with the goal being to look for evidence either in support of or inconsistent with the view that people are threatening and will inflict harm. The therapist's role in this exercise was to provide support and encouragement, to monitor and discourage the use of any safety behaviors (e.g., rushing through the experiment, reassurance seeking, distraction), and to guide the exercise to ensure that Jenny took in available information relevant to her rule.

As they visited these predetermined spots, Jenny was encouraged by her therapist to notice the people, their movements and actions, their posture, the expressions on their faces, the tones of their voices, and the content of their speech. Her task was to detect whether there were any indications of danger or threat originating from the people she observed, and whether others she watched appeared fearful or threatened. During these experiments, her therapist also monitored her level of anxiety and sampled her thinking in alternating 2-minute intervals. As the experiment went on, Jenny reported that she became less and less anxious. She noticed that others did not come across as threatening or appear to be threatened. Rather, she observed that most people appeared to be having a good time as they went about their business. Prior to the experiment, Jenny's belief in the rule, "People are threatening and will harm me" was 70%. Upon the conclusion of the experiment, she rated it at 20%.

As therapy progressed, increasing emphasis was placed on identifying Jenny's values, or what is centrally important to her, and what she wanted to be known for or her life to be about. Values identification was subsequently emphasized on the basis of her expressed wish to "Do things that I'm not doing because of all of the time I spend worrying." When asked, Jenny indicated that she would be willing to experience tension and anxiety if it meant no longer having her life sidelined by worries. For Jenny, this represented a shift away from the predominant short-term goals of reducing tension and anxiety and toward a life direction that had importance to her, even if this meant experiencing some degree of discomfort.

As a starting point, Jenny and her therapist focused on relationships, something that she very much valued but an area that she regarded as largely neglected. In her relationship with her husband, for example, she wanted to increase the level of intimacy, as she felt that many of their day-to-day interactions revolved around her anxieties and worries (e.g., reassurance seeking). Although the idea of working toward the development of intimacy in her relationship with her husband was somewhat threatening, she speculated that doing so would not only enhance her relationship with her husband but also eventually shift her away from being preoccupied with her worries.

Initial steps in the process of deepening her relationships with others, starting with her husband, involved setting goals that moved her in a valued direction (Hayes & Smith, 2005). Short-term objectives involved doing more leisure activities with her husband (e.g., going out to a restaurant once a week, going for walks in the park). Time logs were used to organize these events. Long-term goals included having children and establishing a family environment that was consistent with their wishes and aspirations. Jenny also expressed a commitment to spend a little time each day—time that she would typically take up with worrying—to consider ways to enhance the quality of her life with her husband. She also committed to experimenting with being more open and vulnerable with her husband and sharing her values with him. Although the thought of doing so occasioned worries related to rejection, Jenny maintained that she would not be alienated from her values by her unfounded concerns in this area of her life. By the time therapy ended, Jenny had taken steps to shift her life away from entanglements with her worries and anxieties to building the type of life she wanted to have.

SUMMARY

When the functional aspects of thoughts and thinking patterns are considered for targeting in therapy, it is often useful for the therapist to do the following:

- Evaluate possible functional relations between certain patterns of thinking and the client's problem areas.

- Investigate whether certain patterns of thinking preclude opportunities for dealing with life problems more directly and actively.
- Assist the client in noticing and labeling occurrences of unproductive thought, and use such occasions as cues for engaging in alternative actions.
- Devise behavioral experiments that have potential for modifying both the form and function that unproductive thinking has on behavior and that might challenge the client to do something different from what he or she has done before.
- Consider the possible utility of other intervention approaches for altering adherence to inaccurate, faulty, or harmful rules.
- Identify goals and values that might suggest alternative behavior patterns that are incompatible or inconsistent with the client's problem behaviors.
- Design and implement intervention strategies that facilitate engagement in behavior patterns consistent with one's goals or values.

7

CHANGING BEHAVIOR
BY BUILDING SKILLS

Another important class of behavioral interventions, often referred to as *skills training*, helps clients acquire and strengthen new behaviors. Skills training is largely based on the assumption that if the client does not engage in specific behaviors or particular classes of behaviors (e.g., coping behaviors, emotion regulation behaviors, social assertiveness behaviors), there is a deficit in his or her behavioral repertoire. A common and frequently implicit assumption is that if the client were to engage in these behaviors, then his or her life would improve in some way. For instance, a professor who has not demonstrated the behaviors required to deliver an effective lecture would benefit from learning these behaviors. A client for whom suicide attempts and self-harm are the only ways she knows how to manage her intense emotional pain may have a more fulfilling life if she were to learn emotion regulation skills. Skills training is a general intervention approach used to help clients acquire and strengthen particular behaviors (called *skills*) to help them achieve goals and desired outcomes or move forward in a valued direction in life.

Within this chapter, we describe and discuss skills training. We begin by covering some background and historical information on the application of skills-training approaches as well as some research findings on skill-oriented treatment approaches. We define the concept and goals of skills training and discuss when to use skills training and how skills training interventions work. In the latter part of the chapter, we provide some practical guidance on how to apply skills training interventions to help clients acquire and strengthen skills and achieve their goals.

BACKGROUND

In the sections following, we provide a brief history of skills training interventions in behavior therapy and cognitive behavior therapy (CBT). We highlight examples of how these interventions originated and mention some contemporary treatments in which skills training plays a prominent role. In addition, we outline some of the research evidence on the efficacy of skills training.

A Brief History

Skills training has been a feature of behavior therapy practically since its inception. Mary Cover Jones (1924a), a student of John B. Watson, described an early application of skills training used in conjunction with exposure therapy, called *social imitation*. Originally reported in a case study, social imitation involved having peers demonstrate the handling of feared objects for a phobic child ("Peter"). Subsequently, in the 1930s, mental health workers began to use social skills training to increase the social competence of individuals who were transitioning from psychiatric institutions back into the community. Phillips and Zigler (1961) are credited for their seminal work on social skills training in the 1950s, which has evolved and been adapted quite effectively for a variety of clinical problems, with notable examples including depression (Becker, Heimberg, & Bellack, 1987; Rehm, 1979) and schizophrenia (Benton & Schroeder, 1990; Mueser, Levine, & Bellack, 1990).

In the current field of behavior therapy, skills training is potentially applicable to several clinical problems and areas of life, including everything from parenting difficulties to anger management problems, sexual problems, and job functioning, among other domains. In fact, there are probably as many potential applications of skills training as there are clinical problems. Any given problem for which a client seeks therapy involves a set of behaviors to be taught or changed (e.g., deliberate self-harm) and a set of effective behaviors for the client to implement (e.g., emotion regulation and problem-solving skills). Any of these effective behaviors could be conceptualized as behavioral skills (e.g., the skill of coping effectively).

Empirical Basis of Skills Training Interventions

Skills training interventions have demonstrated effectiveness for a variety of clinical problem areas. Generally, evidence-based treatments involve skills training in two primary ways: (a) as a stand-alone treatment and (b) as a component of a larger treatment package. As a stand-alone treatment, social skills training interventions have demonstrated especially strong efficacy for reducing depression (Becker et al., 1987; Rehm, 1979) and for reducing relapse rates of psychotic episodes and rehospitalization among persons with schizophrenia (Bellack, Mueser, Gingevich, & Agrista, 1997). A couple of treatments for substance abuse with strong empirical support use skills training focused on enhancing skills in the areas of interpersonal communication and management of emotions (Higgins, Budney, & Sigmon, 2001; Monti et al., 1990). In addition, anger management skills training programs have demonstrated efficacy in terms of reducing anger as well as overt anger-related behavior (Novaco, 1975; see also Novaco, 1995, for a review).

Skills training interventions also constitute components of larger CBT treatment packages that have considerable evidence of efficacy. Progressive muscle relaxation and diaphragmatic breathing skills, for example, are key components of panic control therapy (PCT; Barlow & Craske, 1994). Up to 78% of persons who complete the full course of PCT in clinical outcome studies are free of panic by the follow-up assessment phase (Craske & Barlow, 2001). The research is unclear, however, as to whether training in relaxation or diaphragmatic breathing skills is an essential component of PCT, or whether these skills improve the efficacy of PCT beyond exposure-based interventions. Similarly, stress inoculation training (Meichenbaum, 1985), cognitive-processing therapy (Resick & Schnicke, 1993), and prolonged exposure (Foa & Rothbaum, 1998) all have demonstrated efficacy in treating posttraumatic stress disorder and include training in muscle relaxation and diaphragmatic breathing skills.

Other evidence-based treatment packages include skills training as a key component. The treatment for couple discord and dissatisfaction that has the strongest empirical support is an approach called behavioral marital therapy (BMT; Jacobson & Margolin, 1979), which heavily emphasizes training couples in effective communication and problem-solving skills. Dialectical behavior therapy (DBT; Linehan, 1993a) currently is the psychosocial treatment with the most empirical support for treating women with borderline personality disorder. DBT includes a weekly outpatient skills training group that teaches skills in mindfulness, regulating emotions (*emotion-regulation skills*), tolerating distress and surviving crises (*distress-tolerance skills*), and navigating interpersonal situations with an effective degree of assertiveness (*interpersonal-effectiveness skills*). Again, as with panic disorder and posttraumatic stress disorder, it is unclear whether skills training is an essential component of BMT or DBT; nevertheless, it is firmly embedded in these evidence-based treatments.

Another issue with regard to skills training has to do with whether simply providing a person with information rather than training in skills constitutes a sufficient intervention. A couple of studies have addressed this question. In one study, clients with schizophrenia were randomly assigned to a group CBT skills-oriented program or to a group psychoeducation program that involved education on mental health and schizophrenia but no formal training in skills (Bechdolf, Knost, & Kuntermann, 2004). Both the CBT-skills program and the psychoeducation program were related to improvement in problems related to schizophrenia, but the CBT-skills group demonstrated lower relapse and higher treatment adherence at posttreatment and follow-up as well as a lower rehospitalization rate at follow-up. In another study, investigators randomly assigned substance-abusing, dually diagnosed adolescents to a CBT-coping skills group or a psychoeducation group. Both conditions were associated with reductions in substance use, but only those clients in the CBT condition demonstrated fewer positive urinalyses at follow-up (Kaminer, Burleson, & Goldberger, 2002). Although the research in this area is somewhat sparse, at present, it appears that simply providing information in a psychoeducational format is not as effective as actually teaching skills.

DEFINING SKILLS TRAINING

Within this section, we provide definitions of skills training as it is currently used in CBT. In considering how to define skill, a few concepts are important, including skill, performance, effectiveness, and flexibility. Ultimately, the goal of skills training is to help clients behave more effectively and sometimes assist them in developing flexibility in terms of how they behave and respond.

Concepts of Skills, Capabilities, and Abilities

There is a large variety of definitions of the word *skill*, with most definitions including terms such as *proficiency*, *capacity*, *capability*, and *ability*, among others. O'Donohue and Krasner (1995) have suggested that whether a person has skills is related to whether he or she has the capacity to perform specific behaviors or *subskills* that fit within a general class of skills. The general class of *social skills*, for instance, includes a large variety of subskills such as displaying polite, courteous, and assertive behavior, among others. According to many definitions, to say that a client has social skills would mean that he or she possesses the capability to perform these behaviors.

There are advantages and disadvantages to conceptualizing skills as capabilities. In terms of advantages, terms such as *capabilities*, *capacity*, and *abil-*

ity have heuristic value and are pragmatic. Some people simply cannot perform certain tasks. Similarly, some clients have never learned the behaviors necessary to function effectively in certain environments. In addition, when assessing and conceptualizing a client's problem areas, it is important to determine what the client is incapable of doing versus what he or she is capable of doing but does not do. When a client is incapable of engaging in a certain behavior (e.g., the client does not know how to be assertive with her boss), then skills training is an appropriate intervention choice. However, if the client is capable of engaging in the behavior but does not do so, then treatment might involve finding ways to remove the barriers to effective action (e.g., motivational issues, fears, or other factors that might interfere with being assertive with a boss).

Terms like *capacity*, *capability*, *abilities*, and other such constructs, however, can be rather nonspecific. It can be misleading to say that a person *possesses* the *capability* to engage in a particular set of behaviors, as it is not clear what is meant by the words *possesses* or *has*. A person does not "have" or "possess" behaviors in the same manner as he or she would "have" or "possess" a tool such as a screwdriver. The only index of whether a client has a particular ability is whether he or she actually demonstrates the behaviors assumed to go along with the ability. Saying that a client is "able" to do something rarely provides any more information than saying that a client "does" something. In our experience, therapists frequently conflate actual behaviors with assumptions about a client's abilities to perform these behaviors (e.g., the use of the term *abilities* in lieu of simply describing the actual behaviors in which the client engaged). One such example is evident in the following statement: "She was 'able' to get out of the house and avoid being physically abused by her partner." This statement actually means, "She left the house before she was abused."

Another disadvantage of appealing to abilities or capabilities is that doing so can obscure contextual changes in behavior. A client may be capable of performing particular behaviors, but he or she does not do so because of contextual factors that inhibit the behavior or support alternative, less effective behaviors, or because of emotional reactions (e.g., fear) or other factors that interfere with effective behavior. In the previous example, the client may effectively leave the house and avoid physical abuse (i.e., she is capable of leaving the house) when the discussion centers on household finances, but she may not leave the house when the conversation centers on a recent affair that her partner had with his secretary. Saying that the client has the "ability" to leave the house obscures the issue that leaving the house depends largely on the context of the discussion or conflict. Therefore, in considering and implementing skills training and other behavioral interventions, it is important for the clinician to be aware of the assumptions, advantages, and pitfalls associated with different ways of describing client problems.

Skills Versus Performance

In contrast with skills, which are the specific target behaviors for skills training, *performance* is the individual's actual display of the skills. The distinction between skills and performance is quite important. "Regina" was a client who displayed very effective interpersonal behavior, in both individual and group therapy sessions. On the one hand, she was among the most polite, courteous, and socially adept members of her therapy group. She often helped other clients with their therapy homework and responded in an effective manner during role plays of difficult interpersonal situations. On the other hand, her interpersonal performance completely fell apart when she was admitted briefly to an inpatient psychiatric unit after a suicide attempt. She acted in a belligerent manner toward staff members and a psychiatrist, refused treatment, and was nonresponsive to her fellow patients.

As illustrated in this example, sometimes clients engage in effective behaviors in one context but do not perform them in other contexts. This client emitted effective interpersonal behaviors in one set of contexts (therapy groups, individual therapy, and generally, in her daily life) but did not perform these behaviors in other contexts and instead performed ineffective behaviors. In this case, her therapist focused on various factors that interfered with the performance of effective behaviors in certain contexts (e.g., the hospital) rather than teaching the client new skills. During therapy sessions, for instance, emphasis was placed on ways to engage in effective behavior despite intense emotional distress, ways the client might generalize effective behaviors she demonstrated elsewhere to the hospital setting, and situations in which reinforcement contingencies that maintained ineffective behaviors could be altered (e.g., being left alone by staff appeared to negatively reinforce this client's unpleasant behavior).

Goals of Skills Training: Effectiveness and Flexibility

Skillful behavior does not occur in a vacuum; rather, it occurs within particular contexts, which brings us to a third concept: *effectiveness*. The notion of effectiveness refers to the extent to which the skill performed helped the client realize his or her behavioral goals in a particular context. Effectiveness is similar to *competence*, defined by O'Donohue and Krasner (1995) as the extent to which the individual fulfills his or her own rights, needs, and goals while "honoring the similar rights, needs, goals, and duties of others" (p. 3). Whereas *skills* refers to the particular behavior or set of behaviors, and *performance* has to do with whether the client executes the behavior, *effectiveness* directly pertains to the effect of the client's behavior on his or her environment.

Situations that impinge on clients in their daily lives are often in a state of flux, and one of the key challenges for clients involves adapting to changes and applying skills effectively. Along these lines, a final concept regarding skills training is the notion of *flexibility*. Whereas effectiveness refers to the degree to which behavior resulted in preferred outcomes within a particular context, flexibility is the extent to which the client adapts to differing contexts or changes in contexts and performs behavioral skills effectively. The concept of flexibility is useful for practitioners because it highlights the need to avoid the trap of carrying out skill-oriented guidelines in a lockstep fashion in such a way that the procedure fails to take into account changes or differences in contextual factors. When therapy involves social skills training, for example, emphasis tends to be placed on teaching topographies or forms of social behavior. A client might be taught, for instance, one assertive response that might be effective in a particular situation. Often, however, several alternate responses produce similar and effective outcomes (Follette & Hayes, 2000). For this reason, effectiveness should be emphasized in skills-training programs, perhaps more so than the performance qualities of the behavior. There may be many roads to Rome, so to speak.

Another example further illustrates the utility of placing emphasis on effectiveness. Skills training often involves providing clients with rules for behavior, such as the following: "When you are asking someone to stop doing something that bothers you, and he or she responds by engaging in verbal attacks, sometimes the best strategy is to avoid responding to those attacks and calmly restate your wishes." This strategy is the "broken record" strategy within the interpersonal effectiveness skills in Linehan's (1993b) DBT skills-training manual. There are many situations in which following this strategy or rule might be effective; however, in other situations, the "broken record" strategy may backfire. Perhaps the recipient dislikes it when people repeat themselves and responds in an irate or aggressive manner as a result (of course, this may just be an *extinction burst*). Hence, it is critical for the client to notice the effect of his or her behavior on others and to adapt and shift his or her approach to changing circumstances and contingencies. As discussed in chapter 6 of this volume, sometimes rule following might result in reduced sensitivity to direct contingencies in the environment (Zettle & Hayes, 1982). It is important, therefore, not only to provide clients with a potentially useful toolbox of skills and the rules needed to use them but also to help them track and adapt their behavior in response to changes in the environment.

WHEN DOES A THERAPIST USE SKILLS-TRAINING INTERVENTIONS?

As with any behavioral intervention, therapists most optimally use skills training after a thorough assessment of the client's problem areas. The primary assumption of skills training is that the client has deficits in the behaviors required to achieve preferred outcomes or goals within particular contexts. Additionally, an often implicit assumption of skills training is that the client would be better off in some way if he or she were to engage in these behaviors.

In determining whether skills training is appropriate, a therapist first needs to establish whether the client has already learned the skills that appear to be deficient. As outlined by Dow (1994), there are at least three hierarchically organized considerations for establishing that a behavioral deficit, in fact, accounts for nonoccurring behaviors.

The first consideration is whether the client can demonstrate the relevant skill or behavior in the protected therapeutic environment. If not, this suggests a skill deficit that might be effectively addressed through skills training. A client may have a deficit in his or her repertoire for several reasons. Parents or other caregivers, for example, may not have been in a position to teach these skills because they had not learned these skills themselves. Alternatively, caregivers may have learned these skills but did not teach the client these skills during his or her development or taught them in an ineffective or incorrect manner. Opportunities for learning these skills later in life may not have been available to the client, particularly if his or her typical environment was impoverished or did not offer reinforcement to establish or support such skills.

If the client can effectively demonstrate the skill or behavior in the therapeutic environment but not in the targeted situation, then two additional considerations might be explored. The first has to do with the issue of response generalization. Although the client may have learned the relevant skills and how to apply them in certain contexts, he or she may not have learned how to generalize these skills to targeted situations. In this circumstance, therapy might emphasize the generalization of these skills to relevant situations. This might involve helping the client identify contextual features that, when present, suggest that such behavior would be appropriate and likely reinforced. Similarly, therapy might include instruction in how to perform the particular behavior in the targeted setting.

The other consideration has to do with the possible suppression of the skill by contextual factors. Antecedents that might inhibit behavior include establishing operations such as the presence of certain emotional states (e.g., anxiety) in the client that may further intensify upon enacting the skill. Faulty rules could also inhibit the behavior in question (e.g., "Why should I try to get what I want? No good will come of it"). Similarly, the client may have been previously punished for displaying skillful behavior in a targeted situation. Assertive action, for example, in the presence of an abusive spouse is rarely reinforced and frequently punished. Other relevant factors include the possible influence of disability or disease on an individual's capability to carry out certain forms of behavior.

Each possibility for infrequent or absent behavior suggests different therapeutic approaches. Most generally, skills training may be an appropriate intervention when (a) the client rarely or never engages in particular behaviors; (b) the infrequency or absence of behavior is not due to environmental constraints (e.g., punishment for displays of particular behaviors, low rate of reinforcement for effective behaviors); and (c) the behaviors would lead to the attainment of personal, therapeutic, or situation-specific goals, or an increase in quality of life. Skills training, then, can be an important intervention when it is clear that the client would benefit from learning new behaviors.

HOW DOES SKILLS TRAINING WORK? MECHANISMS OF CHANGE

Although there has been a proliferation of skills-oriented approaches over the past several decades, there has been relatively little emphasis on how or why skills training as a general intervention works. We discuss next some potential mechanisms of change for skills training. We suggest that there are two different levels of potential mechanisms of change in skills-training interventions: (a) mechanisms associated with skills training as a general class of interventions and (b) mechanisms associated with specific types of skills.

Skills Training as a General Class of Intervention

At the most basic level, skills training is a general class of interventions designed to ameliorate behavioral deficits and increase the client's repertoire of effective behaviors. As such, one mechanism of change may involve expanding the client's repertoire of potential responses in particular contexts. "Christine," for example, was a client who tended to push people aggressively to get what she wanted. If she wanted her boyfriend to spend time with her, for example, she would ask him to do so in a loud manner and would provide details on the horrendous negative consequences that might ensue if he were to say no. Needless to say, this particular set of behaviors burned out members of her social network. Through in-session role plays, it became apparent that the client simply had never learned any other way to ask for what she wanted. After several sessions of training in effective assertiveness skills, this client learned a broader set of methods she could use to make requests of other people. She learned to use a softer tone of voice, to act in a kind and pleasant manner, and to tell the other person how it would positively affect her if he or she were to comply.

Another potential mechanism of change in skills training may involve reinforcement. If skills training is successful in expanding the client's repertoire of effective behaviors in various contexts, the client's ability to access reinforcers may be enhanced. Christine found that her boyfriend was much more likely to say "yes" to her requests when she made them in an easy and kind manner, and he was more likely to enjoy spending time with her. It appeared that her effective behavior came under the control of natural positive reinforcement (i.e., the "yes" and the pleasant behavior of the boyfriend), and as a result, she continued to use effective assertiveness skills. Eventually, she found that her quality of life increased as her interactions with coworkers, friends, and other members of her social network became increasingly pleasant and satisfying. She also developed an increased sense of social competence. In another example, "Juan" was a client who engaged in self-injury as a way to escape or avoid unwanted emotions, most notably anger and anxiety. After several months of skills training, he learned several alternative ways to regulate his anger and anxiety that did not involve harming himself. Eventually, these behaviors came to be associated with negative reinforcement in the form of reductions in unwanted emotional arousal and shame associated with self-injury and also associated with positive reinforcement from others in his social environment when they responded favorably to displays of these new behaviors.

Skills Training as a Specific Set of Skills With Unique Effects

Beyond the mechanisms associated with skills training as a general intervention, several different types of mechanisms may be associated with specific skills taught in different treatment protocols. For instance, as discussed in chapter 10 of this volume, mindfulness and acceptance skills work primarily through increasing the client's repertoire of responses to aversive situations as well as through operant and classical extinction. Interpersonal assertiveness skills work by increasing the likelihood that positive (or negative) reinforcement follows the client's interactions with other people. Skills designed to regulate or manage aversive emotions work by enhancing the client's repertoire of effective responses to unwanted emotions. Effective emotion regulation also leads to negative reinforcement in the form of reduced frequency or intensity of the aversive emotions. In addition, some suggest that diaphragmatic breathing skills, often taught to clients with panic disorder or posttraumatic stress disorder, may reduce anxiety by altering the ratio of carbon dioxide to oxygen in the blood (Craske & Barlow, 2001). Given the plethora of skill sets taught in contemporary CBT, it is impossible to review mechanisms associated with all of the specific skills. It is important to note, however, that the common mechanisms detailed previously (e.g., broadening the client's repertoire and reinforcement) likely apply across diverse sets of skills.

APPLYING SKILLS TRAINING INTERVENTIONS

Within this section, we provide information and instructions regarding how to implement skills training in practice. Sometimes the key ingredients of skills training may be modified to best suit different settings and client populations. With this in mind, we propose that skills training generally involves most or all of the procedures discussed subsequently. These procedures include (a) defining and structuring skills training, (b) orienting the client(s) to skills training, (c) skills acquisition procedures, and (d) skill strengthening procedures.

Operationalize

Before teaching a client a new skill, an important first step is to identify and operationally define the skill or set of skills. Labels for different types of skills abound in various therapy approaches, such as anger-management skills, emotion-regulation skills, sexual skills, job skills, assertiveness skills, employment skills, empathy skills, social skills, and coping skills, among others (O'Donohue & Krasner, 1995). Knowing the general class of skills required by a particular client can point the therapist in the right direction; however, precisely defining the specific behaviors to be taught gives the therapist a clearer picture of which skills to teach. Anger-management skills, for example, may include a variety of specific behaviors involved with managing anger, such as identifying physiological and other cues for anger, correctly labeling the state of anger, discriminating between higher and lower intensity states of anger, devising effective coping strategies to deal with anger in the moment, diverting attention to non-anger-eliciting stimuli, and using diaphragmatic breathing and other relaxation strategies, among others (Novaco, 1975). When embarking on the task of teaching a client skills, it is essential to operationally define the specific skills to be taught.

Determine and Define the Structure and Format

The next step is to determine the format and structure of the skills training. For some clinical problems, evidence-based skills treatment protocols already exist that follow a defined format and structure. In this case, it is often best to stick with the format and structure used in the research to keep the clinical procedures as close as possible to the treatment package that has demonstrated efficacy.

In other cases, various factors make it difficult to apply an evidence-based skills training package. For some clinical problems, established skills-oriented protocols may not exist, may not be tailored to the characteristics of the client, or may not have demonstrated efficacy for problems similar to those experienced by the client. In addition, providing skills training in the manner specified in a treatment manual is at times not feasible because of resource or time limitations or challenges within particular clinical settings. In these cases, the therapist may need to decide on the most effective format for teaching skills given the context of therapy, the client's skill deficits, and the client's characteristics and learning history. Some key related considerations might include the following:

- Will the therapist conduct skills training him- or herself or refer the client to another provider for this intervention?
- Will skills training occur within a formal format or informally as needed within therapy sessions? How often will skills training occur?
- How will the therapist integrate skills training and skills learned into typical therapy sessions?
- Will skills training occur in an individual or a group format?

Perhaps the most common decision has to do with whether skills should be presented in an individual or a group format. Skills training is most often conducted in groups, and there are several potential advantages to a group format. Groups can, for example, be more efficient than individual sessions, in that they reach a larger number of clients in a briefer period. Groups can be more cost effective compared with individual therapy sessions, for both treatment providers and individual clients. In addition, groups can offer opportunities for modeling, social connectedness, role playing, and active practicing of skills that might be limited in individual therapy. Persons with social anxiety or performance problems may also benefit more from group therapy than individual therapy.

There are some advantages of conducting skills training on an individual basis, however. Individual skills instruction allows the therapist to tailor skills training to the issues, difficulties, and characteristics of the individual client. In a group format, clients in the group receive less individualized skills instruction and attention than they would if they were learning skills in an individual format. In addition, the individual therapist is likely to know more about the client (compared with a skills trainer who does not individually work with the client) and may be more likely to offer suggestions regarding skills that fit the client's idiosyncratic life difficulties, wishes, goals, strengths, and weaknesses. Ultimately, the therapist and client may collaboratively determine the format and structure of skills training.

There are a couple of additional factors to consider in deciding whether to conduct skills training through an individual or group format: (a) problem severity and complexity and (b) benefits to group treatment. One question that the clinician may ask is, "Is this a multiproblem client who experiences crises?" If the client has a large array of problems that are the focus of clinical attention and tends to experience relatively frequent crises or intense life stressors, conducting skills training in an individual format may be challenging for the therapist. The therapist may spend so much time addressing crises and acute stressors that there is little time to teach new skills (Linehan, 1993a). Moreover, within therapy sessions that address crises or acute stressors, the client may feel too overwhelmed and distressed to effectively learn new skills.

This is particularly the case if the skills trainer is the same person as the primary individual therapist. In this case, we suggest that group-based skills training with a different therapist may be the most effective approach.

A second question might be, "Would the client benefit most from group or individual therapy?" In some cases, the client's clinical problems and deficits fall within the interpersonal realm. For instance, persons with social anxiety disorder not only may fear social situations (i.e., they have behavioral excesses—an excess of fear) but also may not engage in effective behaviors in these situations (i.e., they have behavioral deficits). As a result, the exposure to interpersonal situations that occurs within a group context along with the opportunity to learn and practice new social behaviors may be quite beneficial. In addition, for some clients, the validation, normalization of difficulties, and feeling of social connectedness that occurs within a group are quite advantageous.

In some cases, however, teaching skills in individual therapy may work best for a particular client. If the client has a strong need for individualized attention and validation, individually administered skills training may be more capable of addressing this need while teaching new skills. When a client's problems involve severe depression and behavioral inertia, he or she may have considerable difficulty maintaining active participation in a group. In addition, if the client experiences recurrent hallucinations, delusions, disordered thinking, or features of psychopathy or antisocial personality disorder, a group setting may not be the most effective mode for teaching skills.

Orienting the Client to Skills Training

Perhaps the very first step in skills training involves orienting the client to several aspects of skills training, including the rationale for skills training and the structure, format, timing, and expectations of skills training. When orienting clients to skills training that occurs within a group, we found it helpful to meet with each new client individually for a brief period (e.g., 10–15 minutes) to provide the client with information on these topics and to address any of his or her questions or concerns. As noted later in this section, skills training sometimes occurs in an informal manner, in which case orienting also may occur in an ad hoc manner. Nevertheless, in all cases, a clear orientation to the skills and their rationale provides the client with a road map of where the treatment intervention is going and how it relates to his or her specific goals, problems, and desires.

Provide a Rationale

One of the first steps in orienting a client to skills training involves providing a rationale. It is generally most effective if this orientation provides a compelling rationale for learning new skills that fits with the client's goals. A central therapy component in DBT (Linehan, 1993a) for suicidal individuals with borderline personality disorder is the skills training group. One of the central skill sets within this treatment is mindfulness (described in more detail in chap. 10 of this volume), which often involves the client observing the experience of the current moment. When asked at the end of treatment which skills were most helpful, many clients who participate in DBT often indicate the mindfulness component. At the beginning, however, clients commonly say something like, "So, how is observing my bodily sensations supposed to help me? I spend most of my time trying not to notice what's going on with me!" Although a clear rationale for learning certain skills arguably is especially important for particular types of clients (e.g., clients in extreme distress, clients court mandated for anger-management training, clients in forensic settings), it is always critical to link skills training (or any other intervention for that matter) directly to the client's desires and goals. Later in this section, we provide an example of how to give a client a clear and cogent rationale for skills training.

Structure, Format, Timing, and Expectations

Often it is helpful to inform the client about aspects of the structure, format, timing, and expectations of skills training. Some of this information involves when and where skills training occurs, how many and what type of clients are in the group, how long skills training sessions are, and the length of the entire skills-training program. Frequently, there are also some specific expectations and agreements a therapist needs to clarify. Some skills-training groups for persons who struggle with substance use, for example, have a rule specifying that clients are not permitted to attend group while inebriated or to talk about using drugs with other group members. Many skills-training programs give regular homework assignments and expect that clients will have completed them prior to the next session. In addition, skills-training groups may have specific rules and expectations about conduct between group members (e.g., no sexual relations, issues regarding forming friendships outside of group) as well as the confidentiality of material discussed during the group. Providing specific orientation to these aspects of skills training gives the client a clear road map of his or her skills-training experience and prevents misunderstandings.

Informal Skills Training

In some cases, skills training occurs in a less formalized manner. For instance, sometimes within particular therapy sessions, it is apparent that a client needs to learn a new skill, and the therapist might highlight this issue, provide brief instruction and orientation on the skill, have the client practice the skill, and then fine-tune it by providing feedback and coaching (discussed in greater detail later in this chapter). In this case, the orientation is quite brief and primarily captures the essence of the skill and a rationale as to why the skill might be helpful to the client.

Clinical Example of Orienting

The following is an example of how a therapist might orient a client to a skills-training group for persons who struggle with substance use. This example illustrates several of the main components of effective orienting that we discussed earlier in this chapter. These include orienting the client to (a) the rationale for skills training; (b) the specific skills that will be taught; (c) the goals, structure, and format of the skills-training group; and (d) the rules and expectations that guide the group.

> As we have discussed, many things seem to keep your drug use going. One thing that stands out, though, is that you haven't appeared to learn a couple of key skills that people use to help themselves stay off drugs. One of these skills is coping with and managing intense emotions and urges to use drugs. Another important skill is dealing with people who ask you to use, such as saying "no" to drugs and meaning it, as well as staying away from people who use drugs [*rationale for skills training*]. These skills—regulating emotions and coping with urges—along with interpersonal and drug-refusal skills, are what we teach in this group [*orienting to the specific skills*]. I think that this group is a great fit for you and you will have an easier time staying off drugs and building the life you want if you learn these skills [*rationale for skills training: connecting skills with the client's goals*].
>
> The group happens every Tuesday evening from 6:00 p.m. to 8:00 p.m. for 6 months and includes about 5 to 10 other clients who also struggle with drug problems. So, you definitely won't be alone in this group [*orienting to the structure and format of the group*]. Now, on the other hand, being in a group with a bunch of people who have drug problems requires some rules. The first rule is that you are not allowed to use or sell drugs right before, during, or right after the group. Another rule is that you are not to come to the group high or drunk. A final important rule is that you are not to share war stories about using drugs with other members. Doing this could lead others into temptation! [*orienting to the rules and expectations of the group*] OK, how does that sound? What kinds of questions or concerns do you have about this group?

Helping the Client Acquire Skills

Helping clients acquire skills requires a variety of behaviors on the part of the therapist. As skills training basically involves instruction in new behaviors, clear and effective teaching is essential. Skill acquisition also involves using behavioral principles of shaping, chaining, and reinforcement to help clients increase their repertoire of effective skills. In addition, skill acquisition often involves a variety of exercises designed to provide clients with opportunities to model and demonstrate effective behaviors. We describe these exercises (using didactic strategies, behavioral principles, and modeling) as well as other skill-acquisition strategies in the following sections.

Use a Variety of Didactic Strategies

As skills training essentially involves teaching, an effective skills trainer performs a range of effective teaching strategies. Although effective teaching involves many component skills and behaviors, we highlight some of the most important skill-teaching behaviors in the following sections. We have organized these skills into the following three categories: (a) conveying information, (b) effective skill-teaching strategies, and (c) effective skill-teaching styles.

Conveying information involves the therapist communicating when, how, and why the skill works and the specific circumstances under which a client should use the skill (i.e., the contexts in which the skill may be effective). To help the client determine the effectiveness of his or her behavior, the therapist can provide him or her with information on how to determine whether or how well a skill has worked. The therapist might, for example, point out the likely results of effective assertiveness behavior. In DBT, for example, skills training involves teaching the client to evaluate the effect of his or her behavior in view of three different types of goals: objectives (specific goals in a situation, such as getting a ride home from work), relationship factors (whether the behavior resulted in a positive effect on a relationship), and self-respect (whether the behavior resulted in an increase or a decrease in the client's self-respect).

One frame of reference that therapists bring to the table in their work with clients is a knowledge base on basic and clinical psychology research. A therapist effectively communicating information from research that is relevant to a client's problem areas or particular skills can enhance the client's understanding of how he or she may effectively use skills outside of therapy. Articles on coping resources and inhibiting impulsive actions, for example, suggest that the resources persons need to inhibit impulsive actions are limited (much like muscular strength) and may fail in the presence of other concurrent demands to exercise self-control (Muraven, Tice, & Baumeister, 1998; Tice, Bratslavsky, & Baumeister, 2001). When teaching a client how to use new skills (e.g., emotion-regulation skills) as an alternative to drugs, a therapist might find it quite helpful to convey this type of information about impulse control to his or her client. As a result, the client may find ways to reduce demands and stressors (e.g., household demands) that use up coping resources at times when his or her struggles with drug use urges are particularly strong. Additionally, it can be helpful to shape a client into his or her "own therapist" by the therapist providing information about the his or her own theoretical perspective on the client's problems.

In addition to conveying relevant information, an effective skills trainer also uses a variety of *effective skill-teaching strategies*. Particularly in group settings, it is important to recognize that different clients learn skills at different rates and have differing preferences in terms of learning styles and learning activities. Some clients prefer to sit and listen to information and instructions about skills and may learn best by doing so. Other clients learn best when they are actively engaged in experiential exercises or active practice. Therefore, in group settings, it can be useful to use a variety of teaching strategies to ensure that some of these strategies will resonate with each client in the group. Such strategies might involve posing interesting questions, commenting on the applicability of the material to an individual client's situation, or using humor to facilitate learning or involvement. Other strategies include preparing or devising on-the-spot experiential exercises that illustrate important points about particular skills or providing interesting examples or metaphors to illustrate key points. In addition, an effective skills trainer times the presentation of material such that neither too much material nor too little material is presented within a particular period, breaks complex concepts and ideas down into concrete and easily understandable components, and presents the material in a manner that is neither over the heads of the clients nor overly simplistic.

An effective skills trainer also must use effective *communication styles*. Some effective communication behaviors include conveying interest and enthusiasm in the skill-related material; using humor; making interesting, unexpected, or off-beat or irreverent comments; or offering vivid or gripping examples of important points. An effective communicator both grabs the attention of his or her audience (even if it is just an audience of one) and conveys information in a manner that sticks with the audience well after the skills-training session. Another effective strategy is to display a range of intensity in terms of voice volume, tone, and include variability in the rate and rhythm of speech.

Provide Modeling Opportunities

Another way to facilitate skill acquisition is to use modeling strategies. Modeling falls under the category of *observational learning*, through which people can "acquire cognitive skills and new patterns of behavior by observing the performance of others" (Bandura, 1986, p. 49). A driving instructor may, for example, demonstrate a variety of component skills involved with driving a stick shift, such as the correct way to hold the gear shift, the correct placement of the right and left foot, how to press down on the clutch with the left foot, and how to move the gear shift into different positions. The instructor might also tie all of these behaviors together with rules that specify when and how to perform these actions effectively (e.g., shift from first to second gear when the RPM gauge approaches 3000, the car is traveling at 10–15 miles per hour, or the car makes a noise that indicates the need to change gears).

The strategy of simply instructing someone on how to use a new skill often has considerable limitations (O'Donohue & Krasner, 1995). Imagine how difficult it would be to verbally instruct someone who has never driven a stick shift without providing any demonstration of how to do it. Some research has suggested that modeling strategies are particularly needed when the skill is very complex or the client has significant deficits in his or her repertoire (Rakos, 1991). One specific advantage of modeling includes the fact that through demonstrating a skill, the therapist can demonstrate an entire chain or sequence of behavior (Bandura, 1986).

Consider the example of teaching assertive communication skills to a client. Assertive communication involves a variety of complex behaviors that occur in a sequence. For example, saying "no" to a coworker who is asking for money might involve making direct eye contact, using body language to communicate confidence and certainty, listening to the individual's request, responding to the request, using a neutral or kind tone of voice, and stating (for example), "I wish I could help you, but I don't have any cash and I am very strapped for money these days. Is there anything else you can do to get the money you need?" It would be quite difficult to capture the complexities and nuances of this sequence of behaviors through verbal instruction alone. In addition, modeling can capture both verbal and nonverbal behavior. This advantage can be particularly important for therapists who are teaching social skills because how a client says something (i.e., tone of voice, eye contact, body language) often is just as important as what the client is saying.

There are a couple of primary ways to provide modeling experiences during skills training. One method involves *demonstrating component behaviors* that comprise the skill or skills. With this method, the therapist might demonstrate a component of a skill by providing an example while describing the skill. For instance, a therapist might say, "One of the most important aspects of assertively asking for what you want from someone involves first describing the situation that you are in. If I wanted to ask a friend for money, I might say 'I'm stuck without any money for the bus, my car has broken down, and I live 40 miles from the clinic. Is there any way that you could lend me some money to get a bus home?'" Another way to demonstrate a skill is to display the physical movements involved with the skill. When therapists, for instance, teach clients with anxiety problems how to use diaphragmatic breathing to modulate the physiological experience of anxiety, they often place their hands on their diaphragms and demonstrate how the diaphragm, rather than the chest, moves when they breathe in and out.

A second method of modeling entails a *demonstration of a chain of behaviors* that is involved in the skill or skills. There are several ways to demonstrate chains of behavior, but one common method is to role play the situation. For instance, a therapist teaching assertiveness skills might role play a situation in which these skills are called for with a cotherapist, the target client, or another client. Role playing allows for flexibility in terms of presenting stimuli and modulating the difficulty of the situation. Role playing also gets the client involved in actively observing and practicing the skills.

Often, however, it is more difficult to role play noninterpersonally oriented skills (e.g., anger-management skills, anxiety-management skills). Another method of demonstrating chains of behavior involves constructing an imaginary scenario (e.g., his or her boss just fired the client) and acting out particular behaviors (e.g., diaphragmatic breathing to attenuate anger) as if they are occurring in the present, while the therapist describes what he or she is doing (e.g., "OK, now, I'm paying attention to my breathing while looking at my boss. . .").

A third, and more formalized, approach to modeling is called *self-instructional training* (SIT), developed by Meichenbaum and Goodman (1971). SIT involves five steps. The first step, called *cognitive modeling*, involves having the client observe while a model performs a task and having the client make statements about the task out loud. A client learning progressive muscle relaxation, for example, might observe a model demonstrate this skill by saying, "Now, I'm tensing my muscles in my foot, and now I'm relaxing my muscles in my foot." The second step in SIT involves *cognitive-participant modeling*, in which the client performs the skill while the model verbalizes instructions. A third step, called *overt self-instruction*, involves having the client perform the new skill while instructing him- or herself aloud. The fourth step, called *fading overt self-instruction*, involves having the client perform the skill while he or she whispers instructions to him- or herself. Finally, the fifth step involves having the client perform the skill while instructing him- or herself, but not aloud (*covert self-instruction*).

A fourth method of modeling involves *disclosure regarding skill use.* When this method is used in a group context, the therapist might elicit examples of when and how clients have used particular skills. The therapist might select clients who are "veterans" in the use of particular skills (if the group involves both beginners and more advanced clients) and have them discuss times during which they applied these skills as well as the consequences of doing so. The therapist or other clients might provide examples of when and how other people have used specific skills. In addition, the therapist also might disclose his or her own use of a particular skill in a difficult or challenging situation.

There are several ways to enhance the effects of modeling. For instance, findings from several studies have indicated that modeling is most effective when the model is similar to the target individual (i.e., the client) in terms of sex and age. Findings also suggest that individuals who are high in status, prestige, or expertise are also effective models. (Baron, 1970; McCullagh, 1987; Mischel & Grusec, 1966; Paradise, Conway, & Zweig, 1986; Zimmerman & Koussa, 1979). Modeling is also effective when positive consequences follow the model's behavior and when the client's attention is directed toward the most relevant elements of the skillful behavior (Bandura, 1986). Findings from some studies have also suggested that modeling coping skills for overcoming challenges or difficulties is more effective than modeling mastery or expertise (Schunk & Hanson, 1985).

This research has important implications for how a therapist might use self-disclosure as a modeling procedure. For instance, a therapist normally qualifies as a high-status person with expertise, so he or she already is in a good position to be an effective model. This research also suggests that therapists would want to avoid disclosing or providing examples of failures in using skills. In addition, it may be more effective for a therapist to describe a scenario in which he or she coped with and overcame some difficulty (i.e., coping modeling), rather than a scenario in which the therapist effortlessly engaged in effective, skilled behavior (i.e., mastery modeling). In addition, we urge therapists to avoid modeling failure experiences. We have found it helpful to model the skill of coping effectively with adversity, but at times, therapists make the mistake of simply modeling the fact that they have experienced adversity, struggled with it, and then failed to cope effectively. When using self-disclosure or other forms of modeling, it is important to think, "What am I trying to demonstrate?" The answer is effective behavior.

Use Reinforcement and Shaping

In addition to effective teaching and modeling, skills training often involves the application of basic behavioral techniques, such as reinforcement, and in particular, shaping. Most of these techniques are discussed in chapter 5, but we nevertheless briefly highlight the importance of shaping. Shaping involves reinforcing successive approximations of a desired behavior. In skills training, the desired behavior could be anything from effective assertiveness, to coping behaviors to manage emotions, to behaviors that involve refusing drugs or tolerating urges to use drugs, among others.

At the beginning stages of teaching a new skill, the client may be unfamiliar with steps for learning new behaviors. Shaping involves breaking complex skills into smaller subskills, teaching those subskills, and then providing reinforcement for small steps or approximations toward the desired behaviors. The therapist requires the client to keep upping the ante or displaying more and more of the desired behavior before he or she provides reinforcement. In working with a client who has not used drugs, for example, the therapist might first provide reinforcement for 1 week of no drug use. But, once the client has gone 1 week without using drugs, the therapist might require 2 consecutive weeks before providing any reinforcement, and so on. Once the client has displayed a particular level of approximation toward the ultimate desired behavior (e.g., 6 months of abstinence from drugs), that particular level is no longer enough to warrant reinforcement. Eventually, the client has to perform the entire desired behavior or sequence of behaviors before the therapist provides reinforcement. At that point, as we discussed in chapter 5, the therapist shifts the focus toward interventions that will maintain the behavior.

"Heather" was a client who had great difficulty saying "no" to others' requests. As a result, she ended up taking on large, overwhelming tasks at work with very little notice or preparation time. Heather wanted to learn how to balance the need to perform well at work (and receive good performance evaluations) with the need to avoid getting into situations that involved overwhelming amounts of work. At the beginning of skills training, she was not yet at the point where she could effectively refuse requests made by persons in authority positions. Therapy with Heather used shaping techniques, which in this instance involved breaking down the behaviors associated with balancing performance with avoiding being overwhelmed into smaller subcomponents, the first of which involved simply saying, "Let me give that some thought and get back to you." Initially, the therapist would reinforce (in the form of warmth, enthusiasm, and praise) this behavior. The next task was for Heather to think through the person's request and then say "no" to him or her if it was reasonable and effective to do so. The next time someone asked Heather to take on a task that she did not wish to perform, and she said, "Let me give that some thought. . .", the therapist held off on providing any reinforcement until Heather followed through with declining the request. Heather eventually worked up to refusing or delaying requests that were unreasonable or overwhelming.

Helping Clients Strengthen Skills Through Practice, Feedback, and Coaching

In the initial stages of teaching a new skill, the therapist's job often includes communicating the essence of the skill through effective teaching methods, modeling the skill, and using shaping and reinforcement strategies to establish the skill within the client's repertoire. Once the client is capable of performing the skill, however, it is time to start honing and sharpening the skill. Strategies for accomplishing this generally fall within the following categories: (a) those that involve helping clients practice skills and (b) those that involve coaching and providing feedback regarding skills. A therapist might also use contingency management strategies to strengthen effective behavior, increase the rate at which effective behavior occurs, or extinguish behavior that interferes with implementing newly developed skills. Although we focus here on skill practice strategies, coaching, and feedback, it may be helpful to review chapter 5 for information on the application of contingency management procedures for strengthening behavior.

In-Session Practice Strategies

One of the primary strategies for strengthening skills is practice. Practicing skills can help the client become more fluid and proficient with effective new behaviors and can increase the likelihood that the client will engage in these behaviors in an automatic manner in relevant contexts. Therapists encourage skill practice in two primary ways: (a) through in-session practicing of skills and (b) through homework assignments.

There are several ways for therapists to promote in-session skill practice: (a) the therapist can have the client engage in the skill or approximations of the skill in individual or group sessions, (b) the therapist and client might role play various skills, or (c) the therapist might have the client repeat the behavior over and over again, essentially helping the client "overlearn" the effective behavior. Other in-session practice strategies involve having the client imagine him- or herself engaging in effective behavior in a variety of different situations. This type of "covert" or "imaginal" practice can be quite helpful for some clients. As with other imaginal strategies, we have found that it is important to help the client imagine in vivid detail what it is like to be in the difficult situation.

The therapist also may promote in-session practice by purposely presenting cues or behaviors that are related to the situation in which the client is struggling or by not removing these cues when they occur incidentally. "Maria" was a client who refused to accept that she had married a man. Maria had a history of watching her father mistreat her mother and observing her parents' marriage slowly and painfully dissolve. She also had very strong beliefs in the importance of being independent and not relying on men. Toward the beginning of therapy, Maria was undergoing a separation from her husband. She reported that he frequently physically assaulted her and often exhibited highly coercive behavior (e.g., he threatened to kill himself if she were to leave him). Maria had great difficulty accepting the fact that she "let herself get married" and that she was still married to this man who had mistreated her. At the time, therapy involved teaching the client the skill of radical acceptance (discussed in chap. 10), which involved simply accepting that she was, indeed, currently married to this person but that she also has the option of divorcing or annulling the marriage. After collaboratively determining with the client that acceptance would be a helpful skill to practice in this domain, the therapist would purposely state in a matter-of-fact tone of voice that she had married this man. After repeatedly practicing the skill of acceptance, Maria was able to acknowledge that she was married on paper (although perhaps not in her heart) while she continued to actively pursue separation.

Therapy Homework Strategies

Homework assignments can be particularly helpful in encouraging skill practice in clients' natural environments. As described by Lindenboim, Chapman, and Linehan (2006), there are several different types of homework assignments in behavior therapy. Many of these assignments fall within the three following categories: (a) discrete homework assignments, (b) self-monitoring homework assignments, (c) skills practice assignments, and (d) conditional homework assignments. Discrete homework assignments involve explicitly assigning the client a discrete task, sometimes for a specified period. A therapist might give a client with binge-eating disorder who is learning the skill of eating slowly and mindfully, for example, the discrete homework assignment of eating mindfully three times per week for the next week. A therapist might give a client who is dependent on heroin a discrete homework assignment that involves practicing drug-refusal skills (e.g., refusing offers for drugs; Higgins et al., 2001; McCrady, 2001) with a supportive friend or partner. In another example, a therapist might encourage a client with panic disorder to practice interoceptive exposure (exposure to feared bodily sensations) to bodily cues each day for 10 minutes over the next week. Often, in structured skills-training programs, discrete homework assignments involve completing homework forms, reading or completing handouts, or other such activities.

Another type of homework assignment involves self-monitoring skill practice. Self-monitoring assignments involve clients' monitoring and recording various behaviors on an ongoing basis, usually daily. Self-monitoring forms, for example, might involve the client keeping track of occasions when skills are practiced by noting the specific skill practiced, how often or how long practice took place, and the level of mastery achieved during the practice. One advantage of this type of assignment is that it encourages the client to move toward increasing the regular practicing of skills, especially when the therapist also encourages and reinforces skills practice.

The third type of homework involves skills practice assignments on the part of the client that encourage the continual practice of skills. This type of assignment is designed to strengthen skills to the point that they become overlearned and are emitted with little effort on occasions in which they are most needed, such as during crises. Indeed, learning and strengthening skills requires time and repeated practice under conditions that support new learning. Some clients experience repeated crisis and chaos in their natural environments, such as interpersonal conflict, employment difficulties, suicidal crises, and other such difficulties. Learning a new skill in a time of crisis is akin to running a marathon while having pneumonia. Therefore, one key benefit of homework assignments that promote ongoing practice is that they assist the client in becoming an expert in new skillful behavior to the point that he or she can skillfully and effectively handle even the most challenging situations.

Last, the fourth type of homework assignment is the conditional type. Conditional homework assignments are those that the client performs only when certain events happen. As such, conditional homework assignments involve "if, then" rules for homework practice, such as, "If you are feeling anxious and panicky, then practice diaphragmatic breathing skills." One example of a conditional homework assignment comes from DBT (Linehan, 1993a). In DBT, the client monitors various problem behaviors on a daily basis and brings to each session a self-monitoring form (called a "diary card") that shows the extent to which these target behaviors occurred each day over the past week. As DBT typically is applied to suicidal clients with borderline personality disorder, some of the key target behaviors involve suicide attempts, suicidal crises, and self-injury. The therapist and client select the highest priority behaviors (e.g., suicide attempts) and typically conduct a functional (or chain) analysis that involves a detailed discussion of the events surrounding a single instance of dysfunctional behavior, with the goal of determining the establishing operations, vulnerability factors, and prompting events for the behavior as well as the consequences of the behavior.

After conducting a functional analysis, the therapist and client often generate solutions that involve implementing new behaviors or skills. Subsequently, the therapist and client may agree on a conditional homework assignment that involves implementing these skills when necessary (e.g., "If you are having thoughts of suicide, then use the skill of distress tolerance"). "Jacob," for example, struggled with intense, episodic suicidal ideation, most commonly in response to feeling shame about perceived inadequacies and transgressions. As his shame typically was not justifiable by the situation, one of the skills that the therapist taught him involved opposite action, or acting in a manner opposite to the action tendencies that are related to shame (see chap. 9). The homework assignment, therefore, called for the client to practice opposite action every time he experienced (unjustified) shame that was above 2 on a scale from 0 (*no shame at all*) to 5 (*the maximum amount of shame possible*) in intensity. This is an example of a conditional homework assignment because the instruction was for the client to use the strategy in a manner contingent on the occurrence of an emotional experience.

Provide Coaching and Feedback

Another way to strengthen skills is to provide coaching and feedback. The therapist might begin by asking the client to emit a particular skill-related behavior. Afterward, the therapist might provide feedback on a variety of aspects of the behavior, including (a) how closely the behavior approximated the desired skill; (b) the likely effect of the behavior, as enacted by the client, on his or her environment (i.e., the effectiveness of the behavior); and (c) various aspects of the topography of the behavior, including frequency, duration, intensity, tone of voice, body posture or language (if it is a verbal skill), or other similar features. In conjunction with such feedback, coaching would involve the therapist offering suggestions, instructions, or recommendations to the client on how to improve skillful behavior. There are many ways to provide coaching, but there are three useful ways to think about coaching: (a) timing, (b) density, and (c) specificity. In terms of timing, it is most helpful for the therapist to provide coaching as close in time to the occurrence of the behavior as possible. Recall from chapter 5 that reinforcement is most effective when it occurs close in time to the behavior. In terms of density of coaching, it is often most effective for the therapist to make one or two suggestions on how the client can improve his or her behavior rather than make numerous suggestions that are likely to overwhelm the client, or that the client is likely to forget.

In terms of specificity, there has been some debate in the literature regarding whether it is more effective to provide very specific feedback and coaching or feedback that simply suggests whether the behavior was effective or ineffective (for issues related to specific vs. general feedback in training therapists, see Follette & Callaghan, 1995). One potential pitfall of very specific coaching is that it might encourage rigid, rule-governed behavior that the client does not flexibly modulate according to shifting contextual demands. However, encouraging effective rule-governed behavior may be helpful to the client in that it provides a road map that specifies what to do in particular situations.

SUMMARY

In summary, when using skills training, we recommend the following strategies:

- Clearly define the skills or sets of skills that the client needs to learn.
- Determine an effective structure and format for skills training. Consider whether it would be most effective to teach skills in a group or individually, and how often, where, and with whom skills training will occur.
- Orient the client to the rationale, structure, expectations, and goals of skills training as well as the nature of the skills that he or she will learn.
- To help clients acquire skills, use a variety of didactic strategies, take the opportunity to demonstrate or model skills (or have other clients do so), and use the principles of reinforcement with an emphasis on shaping.
- To strengthen skills, use homework assignments to encourage clients to practice skills regularly, and provide appropriate feedback and coaching to help clients refine their new skills.
- Have clients practice skills inside and outside of therapy sessions and in as many relevant contexts as possible.

8

ACTIVATING BEHAVIOR:
THE EXAMPLE OF DEPRESSION

Although behavioral activation interventions for the treatment of depression are not new (e.g., Lewinsohn, Biglan, & Zeiss, 1976), they have undergone considerable refinement in recent years (e.g., Addis & Martell, 2004; Martell, Addis, & Jacobson, 2001) and have accumulated strong empirical support (e.g., Cuijpers, van Straten, & Warmerdam, 2007; Dimidjian et al., 2006). Even though behavioral activation interventions are being developed for several psychological conditions (e.g., Hopko, Lejuez, & Hopko, 2004; Hopko, Sanchez, Hopko, Dvir, & Lejuez, 2003), their demonstrated effectiveness has, to date, been limited to the depressive disorders.

Because depressive episodes are common, with as much as 17% of the general population estimated to experience a major depressive disorder at some point during a lifetime (Kessler et al., 1994), and because depressed mood is a common complaint among persons seeking psychological treatment, this chapter is dedicated to the description of the most recent iterations of *behavioral activation* therapy. Behavioral activation is a stand-alone treatment approach for depression that is both relatively parsimonious and simple to implement. As we describe, the unique combination of therapy elements in a coherent and integrated package in contemporary behavioral activation represents a substantial innovation, as is the emphasis on the reduction of avoidance behavior and the comparatively minimal emphasis placed on skills training or modification of thought content.

HISTORY AND THEORETICAL FOUNDATIONS OF BEHAVIORAL ACTIVATION THERAPY FOR DEPRESSION

In a component analysis of cognitive therapy for depression, Jacobson et al. (1996) identified a treatment element that aided individuals in becoming more behaviorally active. This component involved assisting persons with depression in approaching and accessing potential sources of positive reinforcement while avoiding unpleasant and punishing events. Therapists also identified obstacles to behavioral activation, including the client's use of avoidance coping strategies such as withdrawal, inactivity, social isolation, and rumination. Behavioral activation therapeutic components centered on the identification of avoidance coping and the blocking of this avoidance through engagement in actions that have the potential for being positively reinforced. Within this framework, the act of approaching and accessing positive reinforcers was regarded as having natural antidepressant functions (Jacobson, Martell, & Dimidjian, 2001). Subsequent to the component analysis findings reported by Jacobson et al. (1996), behavioral activation was developed into a stand-alone therapy for depression and is comprehensively outlined in Martell et al. (2001) and Addis and Martell (2004).

The roots of behavioral activation can be found in several theories of depression. One theoretical influence was Charles Ferster's (1973) functional analytic account of depression. Ferster's model causally linked depression to environmental factors and highlighted the role of passive responding, avoidance, escape, and withdrawal in the development and maintenance of depression. Another theoretical influence, Peter Lewinsohn's (1974; Lewinsohn & Libet, 1972; Lewinsohn, Biglan, & Zeiss, 1976) behavioral theory of depression, emphasized a low rate of response contingent positive reinforcement (RCPR) in the development and maintenance of depressive symptoms. Lewinsohn and colleagues hypothesized that low rates of RCPR result in low rates of behavior, thus further reducing opportunities to receive positive reinforcement. As a consequence, the vulnerable person's behavior is on a reinforcement schedule that facilitates the extinction of some classes of behaviors and the narrowing of behavioral repertoires. One consequence of this extinction process is the experience of depressive symptoms.

MacPhillamy and Lewinsohn (1974) subsequently developed a clinical measure for evaluating participation in pleasant activities (the Pleasant Events Schedule) and a multifaceted therapeutic strategy (the coping with depression course) for promoting alternative behaviors that are likely to produce positively reinforcing consequences from the environment (Lewinsohn,

Antonuccio, Steinmetz-Breckenridge, & Teri, 1984). When compared with Lewinsohn et al.'s (1984) protocol-driven approach to the therapy of depression, however, the behavioral activation approach is more idiographic (Jacobson et al., 2001). Individualized assessments of activity and avoidance are centerpieces of behavioral activation, and information derived from these assessments informs subsequent therapeutic work. Whereas Lewinsohn's approach assumes that certain events or activities are intrinsically pleasant and reinforcing for all persons, the behavioral activation approach classifies events as reinforcing only when they clearly influence the individual's behavior (e.g., by increasing the frequency of behavior or enhancing mood).

Problem-solving-based formulations and approaches to therapy (D'Zurilla & Nezu, 2001; Nezu, 1989; Nezu & Perri, 1989) also informed developments in behavioral activation. Consistent with behavioral theories of psychopathology, behavioral activation assumes that depression is primarily the result of problematic life events and circumstances, not the result of deficits or dysfunctions that reside within the person (Jacobson et al., 2001).

SUPPORT FOR BEHAVIORAL ACTIVATION AS AN EFFECTIVE THERAPY FOR DEPRESSION

Emerging findings from treatment research suggest that behavioral activation may be among the most important active ingredients of cognitive behavioral treatments for depression. In the cognitive therapy of depression, behavioral interventions predominate within the first few sessions. Component analyses of treatment effects associated with cognitive therapy for depression reveal that most changes in mood occur within the first three to four sessions, prior to any formal introduction of cognitive restructuring techniques (Ilardi & Craighead, 1994). These observations have raised questions as to what constitutes the "active ingredients" of cognitive behavior therapy (CBT) for depression. These analyses suggest, for example, that altering schemas or modifying core assumptions—hypothesized to be the main agents of change in some forms of cognitive therapy (e.g., Young, Weinberger, & Beck, 2001)—add little to the overall efficacy of CBT for depression beyond the behavioral interventions.

Additional research suggests that the behavioral activation component of CBT for depression is primarily responsible for facilitating therapeutic change. Jacobson et al. (1996), for example, reported that the behavioral components associated with CBT for depression were just as effective in promoting therapeutic change as the entire treatment package that included both behavioral and cognitive interventions. The behavioral components largely involved behavioral activation; the addition of cognitive treatment elements to the behavioral activation interventions did not result in any additional significant therapeutic benefit. In addition, 2 years following the discontinuation of active therapy, the relapse rates associated with behavioral activation interventions were no greater than those for the full CBT treatment package (Gortner, Gollan, Dobson, & Jacobson, 1997).

Dimidjian et al. (2006), in a randomized pill placebo-controlled study, evaluated the effectiveness of behavioral activation, cognitive therapy, and antidepressant medication (i.e., paroxetine) in the treatment of depression among adults. Among persons with more severe forms of depression, outcomes associated with behavioral activation were similar to antidepressant medication, and both interventions were superior to cognitive therapy. All three therapies, however, were effective in reducing depressed mood over time. Among those with low-severity depression, all therapies reduced depression, and there was no significant difference among the three treatments in overall effectiveness. Antidepressant treatment was associated with a greater overall attrition rate (44%) compared with behavioral activation (16.3%) or cognitive therapy (13.3%), and there were no significant drug effects relative to pill placebo for those with low-severity depression.

There is also some evidence that behavioral activation is effective for reducing depression among hospitalized inpatients when compared with standard supportive treatments (Hopko, Lejuez, LePage, Hopko, & McNeil, 2003). In addition, researchers have proposed modifications of behavioral activation approaches for different populations, such as clients with depression, co-occurring anxiety disorders (Hopko et al., 2004), and borderline personality disorder (Hopko, Sanchez, et al., 2003).

CENTRAL ASSUMPTIONS OF THE BEHAVIORAL ACTIVATION APPROACH

A central assumption of the behavioral activation theory of depression is that factors that contribute to the development and maintenance of depression reside in the environment, not within the person, and are related to the outcomes of the person's actions. Specifically, depression often arises when an individual's behavior is more frequently responded to with punishment rather than positive reinforcement, or when a person has reduced access to positive reinforcers because of behavioral avoidance (Martell et al., 2001). When viewed from this perspective, depression is regarded as an experience that results from person–environment interactions. The focus in behavioral activation, then, is on the life context, not inner causes, flaws, or defects.

A related risk factor for depression emphasized in behavioral activation is *contextual change* (Addis & Martell, 2004), which involves increases in situations that place an individual at greater risk for depression. Contextual changes may include life stressors such as a divorce, job change, or physical illness. Sometimes these shifts occur very gradually (e.g., increasingly more hours spent on work-related activities and correspondingly less time available for doing enjoyable activities with friends and family), whereas at other times these shifts occur abruptly (e.g., the experience of a job loss and relocation to another city all within a short period of time). In many instances, depression is the cumulative effect of several contextual changes or shifts over time and has resulted in the client's engagement in more activities associated with negative mood and less participation in activities associated with positive moods.

On the basis of these central assumptions, behavioral activation for depression aims to increase activity, counteract avoidance behavior, and increase the individual's access to positive reinforcers (Martell et al., 2001). Activation strategies are precisely targeted and influenced by findings from functional analyses of the contexts within which the client's depression is experienced. The client's thinking patterns are also attended to in behavioral activation therapy. The content of the client's thoughts, however, is regarded as being less important than the context and consequences associated with those thoughts (Martell et al., 2001). That is, attention is primarily focused on where and when thoughts occur, and the effects that they have on how the client feels and what he or she does next.

BEHAVIORAL ACTIVATION APPROACH TO THERAPY FOR DEPRESSION

A primary goal of behavioral activation is to facilitate engagement in activities or entry into contexts that are reinforcing, mood enhancing, or congruent with an individual's long-term goals or values. Doing so often involves the client's blocking avoidant coping patterns that eliminate opportunities for solving his or her life problems or that paradoxically increase vulnerability to depressed moods.

Behavioral activation therapy for depression typically lasts between 16 and 24 weeks. In Dimidjian et al. (2006), clients participated in two 50-minute sessions each week during the first 8 weeks and one weekly 50-minute session during the following 8 weeks. The therapist primarily serves as a consultant who assists clients in becoming skilled observers of the relationships between behavior and associated consequences. The therapist also acts as a coach by encouraging clients to become active, even when they believe that they cannot engage in life-enhancing actions, or they predict that they cannot derive pleasure from their own behavior. Therapists also assist clients in developing life routines that function to maintain behavior consistent with their long-term goals and values.

In the sections that follow, we summarize the components of behavioral activation therapy for depression. Within this therapeutic framework, treatment components generally follow a sequential format. There is room, however, for the therapist to be flexible in his or her approach, particularly given the idiographic nature of the therapy. Our summary of behavioral activation is primarily based on Jacobson et al. (2001), Martell et al. (2001), and Addis and Martell (2004).

Phase 1: Self-Monitor Activities and Moods and the Associations Between the Two

In the behavioral activation model, getting to know oneself involves more than noticing what is occurring on the inside. Acquiring self-knowledge also involves detailed and careful analyses of what is taking place on the outside. Noticing how one acts in certain situations is centrally important (e.g., what is going on at work, what one does at home, what one does when confronted with tedious or unpleasant tasks), as are the emotional and environmental consequences associated with one's actions. In this therapy, primary emphasis is placed on what one does in certain situations because it is often difficult—if not impossible—to change one's personality or genetic endowments. In contrast, it is much easier to change one's activities that, in turn, directly influence how one thinks and feels.

In behavioral activation, the identification of behavioral patterns associated with depressed mood is a precursor to changing those patterns. This process involves the therapist and client working together to identify what to change in a structured and systematic way. To accomplish this, the therapist and client closely examine positive and negative current life events, with special emphasis placed on understanding how the client's life is different when he or she is depressed compared with other occasions when depressed mood is not present. Examples of questions therapists can ask for getting at the latter include, "What is your life like when you are not depressed?" or "Are there things that you are not doing now that you would do if you weren't depressed?"

Detailed self-monitoring is also an important part of identifying behavioral patterns associated with depressed mood. A central assessment tool in behavioral activation is the activity monitoring form, a self-monitoring form that involves keeping track of one's activities and associated moods on an hour-to-hour basis each day for at least 1 week. Generally, the more detail a client can provide in relation to his or her activities, the better. It is more informative, for example, to record "ruminated about my day at work while home alone" than simply "home alone" or "ruminated." Information recorded on the activity monitoring form helps reveal the client's current level of activity, connections between his or her activity level and mood, and level of engagement in avoidance behaviors.

After recording activities and associated moods, the next step is to look for patterns. Over the days that the client made recordings, is there an indication that mood fluctuates according to the client's activities? Is there any evidence suggesting that some frequently occurring events are associated with the client's negative moods? Are some events typically associated with the client's positive moods? What about time slots? Are some times of the day characterized by the client's low mood? If so, does this correspond to an activity that often occurs during that time, or is the client's low mood present during these times regardless of the client's activities?

Monitoring one's activities at this level of detail and noticing patterns over the course of at least a week may also have the benefit of dispelling beliefs some depressed persons experience that suggest that they are depressed all of the time. Such monitoring can also reveal *depression loops*, or instances in which efforts to cope with depressed or negative moods actually result in a further worsening of mood. Some people, for example, cope with depressed mood or stressors by drinking alcohol. For many individuals, consumption of alcohol might result in an immediate shift in mood, perhaps from stressed to relaxed or euphoric. When the immediate psychoactive effects wear off, however, the individual's mood can actually end up being worse than it was prior to drinking. Many clients also report that drinking does not help solve the problems that contributed to their stress in the first place. These examples illustrate how the depression loop can become manifest and might signal that current efforts at coping are actually more unhelpful than helpful.

A Client Illustration: Diane

"Diane" is a 42-year-old recently divorced mother of two children (ages 7 and 9) referred to therapy by a coworker who was concerned about the progressive worsening of her mood. During the clinical interview, Diane reported that she has "been depressed all of the time over the last year," adding that "I cry most days because of how things are." She went on to state that "my life's off track and I just don't know how to pick up the pieces and go on" and "it seems that I worry all of the time now."

Diane reported that she has become increasingly depressed during the past 3 years. She associated the onset and worsening of her depression with the growing realization that she no longer loved her husband and that "his disinterest in the kids and me was becoming more and more apparent." She reported that she had been "persistently sad over the last year, with the depression getting more severe as time goes on." Diane and her husband agreed to divorce last year, with the divorce finalized 9 months ago. She described the associated process as "generally amicable."

Following the finalization of their divorce, Diane's husband of 17 years relocated to another state, leaving her primarily responsible for child care. Diane reported that she and the children frequently talk with each other about the changes that have taken place and the struggle to adapt to their new life circumstances. She added that she maintains an upbeat and optimistic stance when talking with the children, even though she privately views her future with more uncertainty.

Diane reported that her marital difficulties and depressed mood have affected her work as a bank teller. She described difficulty concentrating on her work, as her thoughts are often focused on her current life situation and how bad it is. As of last week, Diane reported that she decided to take sick leave because "it was all getting to be too much and I really have to do something about this."

Questionnaire assessments conducted after the first session were consistent with Diane's reports. Her responses on the Beck Depression Inventory—II (BDI–II; A. T. Beck, Steer, & Brown, 1996) administered after her first session indicated moderate to severe depressed mood (score = 28). On the Penn State Worry Questionnaire (PSWQ; Meyer, Miller, Metzger, & Borkovec, 1990), her score was 52, a score similar to those often observed among people with anxiety disorders characterized by rumination (Fresco, Mennin, Heimberg, & Turk, 2003). Her score on the short version of the Interpersonal Support Evaluation List (ISEL; Brummett et al., 2006; Cohen, Mermelstein, Kamarck, & Hoberman, 1985) was 21, which is generally regarded as a very low score on this measure (Brummett et al., 2006).

Other indications of impairment come from Diane's report that her work has been steadily affected by her worsening mood to the point that she has taken sick leave because she felt she could no longer function adequately. She has also become increasingly distant and isolative at work and has adopted the habit during the past few years of having a couple of glasses of wine at night to "wind down" before going to bed. Several other examples suggest that Diane has been coping largely through avoidant coping strategies.

Before discussing possible approaches to therapy for depression, Diane's therapist asked her to participate in daily self-monitoring by listing her activities and associated moods each waking hour on an activity monitoring form. A description of these events would include not only the activity itself but also a brief description of the context within which the activity took place, the days on which the activity occurred as well as the typical times when the activity was carried out. Activities she participated in between the first and second session, associated moods, (1 = *very low or negative*; 10 = *very positive*) and the degree of pleasure derived from participation in the activity (1 = *very aversive or unpleasant*; 10 = *very pleasant or enjoyable*) are listed in Exhibit 8.1.

As Diane and her therapist reviewed this form together, Diane commented that she was surprised to see how much her mood varied over the course of a typical day. This realization contrasted with her previously held view that she was depressed all of the time. Another pattern she and her therapist discussed is that mood and pleasure ratings tended to rise and fall together. Her therapist speculated that engaging in activities that are pleasurable might be mood enhancing, and they agreed that this hypothesis should be further explored as therapy continued. They also noticed that Diane's mood appears to be consistently low in the evening during times that she watches news on television and sips wine. Diane reported that the events of the world are really getting her down, and that she perhaps overidentifies with the suffering of others. She also observed that she tends to ruminate a lot about her own life situation during that time of the day and that even though she is watching television, "my thoughts are usually somewhere else."

As the therapist learned more about Diane's history, he shared the view that her current episode of depression appears to be strongly linked with several contextual shifts in her life, including a relocation 10 years ago to a new town and the subsequent loss of important relationships because of this move. Outside of coworkers, Diane did not establish new relationships, and she developed routines that largely involved staying at home and caring for her family.

Since moving to her present home 10 years ago, Diane acknowledged that she has not made many friends. Time outside of work had been taken up by child care responsibilities, and she reported having no energy left over for doing other things. Outside of her coworkers, Diane reported that she really does not regularly associate with anyone other than family members. Although there are a couple of people at work she feels close to, Diane noted that she rarely participates in activities with these people outside of work.

Diane's therapist also suggested that more proximally, her divorce and increased child care responsibilities signified another contextual shift that further increased her vulnerability to depressed mood. These contextual shifts coupled with her historical overreliance on avoidant coping strategies appear to have maintained her depressed mood while leaving some of her current life problems largely unsolved.

Between her second and third sessions, Diane completed the activity monitoring form for Thursday through Sunday. The patterns for these days were generally consistent with those observed for Monday through Wednesday. On the basis of information derived from the activity monitoring forms, questionnaire assessments, and clinical interviews conducted over the first three sessions, Diane's therapist generated the following problem list:

1. *Sad mood.* Her mood was generally worse in evening, often accompanied by the consumption of wine.
2. *Persistent worry and rumination.* Thought content is generally focused on negative occasions from the past, negative events that might occur in the future, or on negative evaluations concerning current situation. Rumination periods are more concentrated in the evening and appear to have an associated avoidance function.
3. *Restricted social support network.* Her social network largely consists of family and coworkers (at work only), and she very rarely engages in leisure activities with persons outside of family.

EXHIBIT 8.1
Diane's Activity Monitoring Form for Days Between First and Second Session

Hour	Monday	Tuesday	Wednesday
7:00 a.m.	Wake, prepare breakfast, eat breakfast with kids *Mood*: 3 *Pleasure*: 4	Wake, prepare breakfast, eat breakfast with kids *Mood*: 4 *Pleasure*: 4	Wake, prepare breakfast, eat breakfast with kids *Mood*: 2 *Pleasure*: 2
8:00 a.m.	Dressed, dropped girls off at school *Mood*: 3 *Pleasure*: 4	Showered, dressed, dropped girls off at school *Mood*: 4 *Pleasure*: 4	Dressed, dropped girls off at school *Mood*: 2 *Pleasure*: 2
9:00 a.m.	Tidied kitchen *Mood*: 3 *Pleasure*: 4	Watched TV (old movie) *Mood*: 3 *Pleasure*: 2	Walked in the park *Mood*: 5 *Pleasure*: 4
10:00 a.m.	Napped *Mood*: (asleep) *Pleasure*: (asleep)	Watched TV (old movie) *Mood*: 3 *Pleasure*: 2	Looked through bills at home (did not pay) *Mood*: 3 *Pleasure*: 1
11:00 a.m.	Cleaned house, laundry *Mood*: 4 *Pleasure*: 2	Watched TV (talk show) *Mood*: 3 *Pleasure*: 2	Read newspaper, drank tea *Mood*: 5 *Pleasure*: 4
12:00 p.m.	Prepared and ate lunch, sat outside and listened to radio *Mood*: 6 *Pleasure*: 7	Ordered a pizza, cleaned house, ate lunch *Mood*: 4 *Pleasure*: 3	Ate lunch (dinner leftovers)/ watched TV (news) *Mood*: 3 *Pleasure*: 3
1:00 p.m.	Went grocery shopping *Mood*: 4 *Pleasure*: 4	Napped *Mood*: (asleep) *Pleasure*: (asleep)	Phoned work/read newspaper *Mood*: 5 *Pleasure*: 2
2:00 p.m.	Grocery shopping, returned home and unpacked/put away groceries *Mood*: 4 *Pleasure*: 3	Napped *Mood*: (asleep) *Pleasure*: (asleep)	Played video game on computer (solitaire) *Mood*: 4 *Pleasure*: 3

Time			
3:00 p.m.	Went to mall with girls *Mood:* 6 *Pleasure:* 6	Watched TV (talk show) *Mood:* 3 *Pleasure:* 2	Watched girls play in backyard *Mood:* 5 *Pleasure:* 4
4:00 p.m.	At mall with girls/shopped *Mood:* 6 *Pleasure:* 7	Watched TV (sports)/ napped off and on *Mood:* 3 *Pleasure:* 2	Baked cookies with help from girls *Mood:* 7 *Pleasure:* 8
5:00 p.m.	Dinner at mall *Mood:* 5 *Pleasure:* 5	Played board game with girls *Mood:* 4 *Pleasure:* 5	Prepared dinner *Mood:* 5 *Pleasure:* 5
6:00 p.m.	Drove home/picked-up dry cleaning *Mood:* 5 *Pleasure:* 4	Prepared dinner/ate dinner *Mood:* 4 *Pleasure:* 4	Ate dinner/walked with girls *Mood:* 6 *Pleasure:* 6
7:00 p.m.	Helped girls with homework/helped girls pick out clothes for tomorrow/packed girls' lunch *Mood:* 5 *Pleasure:* 7	Work on computer/helped girls pick out clothes for tomorrow/packed girls' lunch *Mood:* 4 *Pleasure:* 3	Watched TV with girls/helped girls pick out clothes for tomorrow/packed girls' lunch *Mood:* 5 *Pleasure:* 3
8:00 p.m.	Talked with mother on phone *Mood:* 5 *Pleasure:* 6	Watched TV (news)/sipped wine *Mood:* 3 *Pleasure:* 3	Watched TV (news)/sipped wine *Mood:* 4 *Pleasure:* 3
9:00 p.m.	Watched TV (news)/sipped wine *Mood:* 3 *Pleasure:* 3	Watched TV (news)/sipped wine *Mood:* 3 *Pleasure:* 2	Watched TV (news)/sipped wine *Mood:* 2 *Pleasure:* 2
10:00 p.m.	Prepare for bed/read in bed/sleep *Mood:* 3 *Pleasure:* 3	Prepare for bed/sleep *Mood:* 2 *Pleasure:* 2	Prepare for bed/sleep *Mood:* 3 *Pleasure:* 2

4. *Nightly wine consumption.* She drinks two to three glasses of wine most nights over the course of 2 to 3 hours while watching TV.

5. *Avoidant patterns.* Patterns include frequent TV watching, frequent naps, rumination, and playing video games on the computer to avoid aversive but necessary activities (e.g., paying bills).

Phase 2: Using Problem Solving and Behavioral Experimentation to Identify Activities Associated With Positive Moods

After a week or more of self-monitoring, the client and therapist might work together to identify activities associated with variations in mood. Once activities associated with depressed mood are identified, the therapist might problem solve with the client and come up with one or two alternative activities that could be more enjoyable or associated with positive moods.

When problem solving or coming up with alternative behaviors or activities, the first step is to brainstorm. Brainstorming involves writing down whatever comes to mind as a possible alternative, without any censure, editing, or evaluation. Once this process is complete, the next step is to evaluate whether the activity is likely to be associated with positive moods and if it is possible or desirable for the client to do the activity (e.g., some activities might be difficult for the client to do such as going out for an expensive dinner when he or she is financially strapped). These considerations should result in some narrowing of the list. Before choosing among the remaining options, it might be good for the therapist to consider whether some ideas can be combined or integrated. Additionally, when selecting among alternatives, therapists should pay special attention to depression loops. Interrupting these with a substitute activity might lessen the likelihood of deepening one's depression further while providing the client with an opportunity for experimenting with an alternative coping behavior. After considering these issues, one or two substitute activities might be selected by the therapist and tested by the client during the day(s) and time(s) that the previous activity took place.

Determining whether new behaviors are indeed more effective (e.g., associated with more positive moods and not with depressed moods) involves behavioral experimentation. This process involves trying out a new or substitute behavior in place of the one associated with depressed mood and observing the outcomes associated with this new behavior (see chap. 6 for a detailed description of behavioral experiments). In conducting experiments, the client's objective is to simply observe what occurs as a result of some manipulation. This involves observing what happens to one's mood when doing some other activity. The overall objective is for the client to learn what happens when y is done instead of x and what effect y has on mood or outcome in comparison to *x*'s effect on mood and outcome. This involves the client's adoption of an experimenter's attitude, a sense of objectivity in relation to what one finds, and a willingness for truth to reveal itself rather than the client being overly invested in a particular outcome.

This process does not end with the client's completion of a single behavioral experiment. Rather, experimentation is continuous and ongoing. There is recognition, for example, that changing an activity here or there is not likely to result in a substantial and sustained change in mood. Rather, the goal is to make several contextual changes or shifts in a gradual and systematic fashion and make sustained, if not modest, steps in a valued direction (or in this case, a direction characterized by more favorable moods).

Generating Plans for Testing Ideas From Diane's Activity Monitoring Form

As a result of the self-monitoring process during the first phase of therapy, Diane discovered that watching a 24-hour news channel on TV between 8:00 p.m. and 10:00 p.m. at night while sipping wine is characteristically associated with depressed mood. She also speculated that the wine she has at night results in a less restful sleep and increased tiredness and grogginess the following morning. Perhaps as a result, Diane acknowledged she starts out the day with relatively little energy to do anything.

Diane's therapist suggested that their initial focus might be placed on her evening's activities, as the news watching and wine consumption appear to be not only mood impairing but also a possible depression loop that results in the further lowering of her mood. Diane's therapist subsequently worked up a diagram that illustrated the functional properties of evening TV watching, wine consumption, and rumination to illustrate his point (see Figure 8.1).

In reviewing the diagram with Diane, her therapist observed that these activities generally appeared to help her in a limited way. On the basis of her previous comments, Diane's therapist noted that watching the suffering of others has helped Diane place her own suffering in perspective (i.e., she concluded that her situation is comparatively not that bad), and that this helps her in a limited way by reducing her sense of being overwhelmed by her situation. Because she often worried about her own life while watching the news, Diane initially believed that ruminating helped to solve her problems. In this respect, Diane viewed her worry and rumination as effective coping behavior. Diane's therapist also noted that the wine consumed during TV watching has many immediate reinforcing properties (e.g., stress reduction, mild euphoria). In the aggregate, this pattern of behavior had a number of immediate reinforcing qualities that no doubt contributed to their maintenance over time.

Diane's therapist went on to explore with her the nonimmediate effects of this behavior pattern. When she and her therapist examined her rumination tendencies more closely, Diane concluded that her rumination only in-

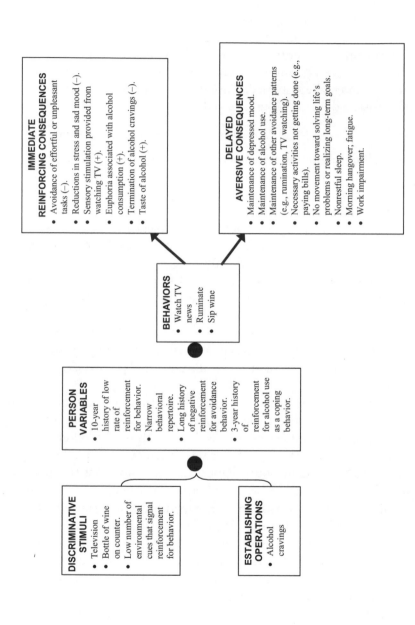

Figure 8.1. Functional analysis of Diane's evening TV watching and wine consumption. Dots between components of the response chain indicate a probability function, whereby a dot represents a probability that the preceding component will influence the following component. Items listed within the *Immediate Reinforcing Consequences* components followed by (+) indicate positive reinforcing consequences whereas items followed by (−) indicate negative reinforcing consequences, both of which maintain or strengthen preceding behavior.

creases her depression and does little in the way of solving her life problems. She also demonstrated understanding that frequent exposure to the suffering of others worsened her mood, as it contributed to her pessimistic and helpless outlook (e.g., "the world is going to hell and there's nothing I can do about it") and reduced the amount of time she had to do other activities that might be mood enhancing. Diane also observed that despite the immediate relieving effects of drinking wine, doing so often made things more difficult for her in the long term (e.g., less restful sleep, slight hangover in the morning, tired the next day).

Diane and her therapist subsequently agreed that this behavior pattern warranted some attention. Together they generated a list of alternative activities that could be substituted for news watching during this time period. These included her hiring a babysitter and going to a movie with a friend or family member, organizing a photo album with the help of her daughters, and calling a friend on the phone that she has not spoken with for a long time. Diane expressed an interest in doing activities that involved other people, as she has felt socially isolated over the past year and she noticed as a result of her entries on the activity monitoring form that her mood is usually more positive when she does activities with others. Her therapist subsequently explored with Diane whom she might go out to a movie with, if she had someone in mind as a possible babysitter, and what movie she might like to see. Diane reported that she would try to arrange this activity for the day after tomorrow, and that tomorrow night she would phone a friend she had not spoken to in awhile rather than watch the news.

On her activity monitoring form, Diane scheduled these activities for the next 3 evenings, and she made a commitment to her therapist to carry these out. She was subsequently instructed by her therapist to record her moods associated with these alternative activities once she had participated in them. She then compared these mood ratings with those that corresponded to times when she watched news during the evening hours to see if these alternative activities had a different effect on her.

Phase 3: Blocking Avoidance Behavior and Facilitating Approach Behavior

The third phase of therapy is directed at substituting avoidance and escape behavioral coping strategies with approach strategies. Avoidance is a common coping strategy. People generally avoid situations or events that are associated with anxious, depressed, or angry emotions. In this respect, avoidance often works, as it produces immediate desirable effects (i.e., the cessation of unpleasant emotions, thoughts, or sensations). Avoidance, however, often precludes the opportunity to actively address or solve life problems related to emotional distress or depression. And although avoidance often results in immediate relief, it is also frequently associated with long-term aversive or unpleasant outcomes. Behavioral activation's focus on counteracting avoidance by facilitating approach behavior places this therapy within the general domain of exposure-based therapies (see chap. 9 of this volume).

One acronym used in behavioral activation to help conceptualize avoidance patterns is TRAP, which refers to the following (Martell et al., 2001):

- A *trigger* is some type of circumstance or event that has an impact on the individual. It may be the start of a series of events, and can be internal or external.
- A *response* is usually an emotional response to the trigger but can also be a thought, a physiological sensation, or an action. Some societal teachings, mores, or values, for example, suggest that negative emotions are "bad" and should be eliminated.
- An *avoidance pattern* is the typical avoidance response to the trigger. This may also be a reaction to the emotional response and the accompanying desire to get rid of the unpleasant feelings. Attempts at getting rid of negative emotions often do not work as intended, however, and often cause problems in their own right.

To understand whether people engage in behavior to avoid certain experiences, we must look to the function of the behavior rather than the form of behavior. Watching TV, for example, may or may not be avoidance behavior. To decide, we must understand what the behavior is doing for the individual (or the purpose that it serves). An examination of the function of avoidance and escape behaviors also aids in the determination as to whether these are adaptive behaviors that are helpful to the individual or maladaptive behaviors that, in the end, are causing more harm than benefit. Does avoidance reduce the likelihood that an individual will actively address an important problem? Do avoidance or escape behaviors prevent the individual from taking steps toward participating in behavioral alternatives associated with positive moods?

Examples of avoidance in relation to depression might include procrastination, rumination, or low-frequency, low-energy behavior (e.g., excessive sleeping, spending hours sitting on the couch). These activities often do little to solve the situation that is being avoided by the client. Complaining might be another avoidance strategy. For many persons, complaints such as "I feel miserable" have been effective in the histories of people who state them. In the past, persons within the social network of complainers may have removed demands or other aversive conditions in response to such complaints. Perhaps because of such histories, frequent complainers are often not particularly interested in advice, solutions, or suggestions that involve active problem solving. If it was that easy, therapists would be well advised to simply provide advice in response to a client's complaints. But it is not, of course, that easy. Rather, complaining is sometimes an act of avoidance, maintained by its own immediate consequences (even if only intermittently experienced), that does little in the way of helping persons solve for themselves the problems associated with their complaints. Although complaining may have short-term reinforcing properties similar to other avoidance coping strategies, it is often associated with the loss of social supports over time (Coyne, 1976).

Rumination is a special example of an avoidance strategy that often has a deleterious effect on mood. In chapter 6, we describe some interventions for reducing rumination, including those associated with the expanded behavioral activation treatment package.

Once a TRAP has been identified, the therapist can use a second acronym that represents a model to help the client get back on TRAC (Martell et al., 2001). A therapeutic goal associated with TRAC is the facilitation of an active approach strategy as a means for promoting effective behavior and for blocking avoidance.

- *T*rigger (same as in TRAP),
- *r*esponse (same as in TRAP), and
- *a*lternative coping involves an active rather than passive or avoidant response, which might include allowing the emotional reaction and other responses to simply be there while continuing to act in accordance with one's objectives, goals, or values (e.g., sometimes people offer reasons for avoidance through statements such as "I would have done that, but I didn't because I felt depressed"; statements like these can be modified so that emotions are no longer reasons for avoidance, such as in "I feel depressed at the moment, and I'm going to do what I planned to do and bring my depressed mood along").

The overall process of identifying and overcoming avoidance coping is summarized by a third acronym, ACTION (Martell et al., 2001).

- Assess behavior and mood. Is current behavior avoidant? How does this behavior serve the client? What emotions does he or she experience when engaging in this behavior?
- Choose alternative behaviors. Does the client activate him- or herself, and engage in behaviors that could reduce depression over time?
- Try the alternative behavior selected.
- Integrate the alternative behavior into a regular routine.
- Observe the outcome of behavior. Does it affect mood in a desirable way, result in effective outcomes, or improve some situation?
- Never give up. Does the client display recognition that trying a new behavior only once is unlikely to lead to significant change? Does he or she acknowledge that overcoming depression and

avoidance takes a lot of hard work and that there will likely be some setbacks along the way? In the face of such setbacks, does the client remain committed to working toward his or her goals?

When changing situations or trying out new behaviors, clients are encouraged to make changes a step at a time rather than all at once. When possible, large activities or event sequences might be broken down into component parts and carried out one component at a time. *Graded task assignments* represent one strategy for taking small yet significant steps toward a goal or overcoming avoidance patterns by approaching avoided activities in small units. In behavioral activation, prior to actually carrying out tasks, the client is encouraged to imagine and mentally rehearse the activity during a therapy session. This mental rehearsal consists of the client overtly describing the activity that he or she will perform, the setting where the activity will take place, and the actual behaviors that the client will carry out during the task. Cleaning the house, for example, can be broken down into smaller components such as first cleaning one identified area of a room. Similarly, the act of approaching something previously avoided, such as high places for someone with acrophobia, can be decomposed into discrete and graded exposure trials.

With the assistance of the therapist, for example, a client might generate a list of avoided areas and arrange these in terms of their associated level of distress. Distress level might be quantified with subjective units of distress (SUDS) ratings, whereby 0 = *no distress or avoidance at all* and 100 = *most distress ever experienced or would not approach under any circumstance.* A first item with the lowest rating for someone with acrophobia might be to climb a three-step stool, and to stand on the top and second steps and remain there until he or she is relatively calm and relaxed (SUDS = 35). A mid-level item might be for a client to look over a second-story balcony until he or she is relatively calm and relaxed (SUDS = 55), and a high-level item might be to go to the observation platform on the top of the highest building in town and remain there until he or she is relatively calm and relaxed (SUDS = 90). Once this list is generated, the client might carry out the activity associated with the lowest SUDS rating and proceed to the next item only when the lower-level item has been carried out with success.

Countering mood-dependent behaviors constitutes another general strategy for blocking avoidance. Individuals who experience significant emotional distress, such as frequent anxious or depressed moods, sometimes adopt the view that if it were not for their depression or anxiety, they would do things that they are currently not doing (e.g., "If I wasn't so depressed, I'd call my buddy from work to see if he'd want to go to the baseball game tomorrow" or "I wanted to go to that party, but my social anxiety stopped me from going"). Among mood-dependent persons, engagement in desired activities, or moving forward in life, is put on hold until emotions change. In countering mood dependence, a therapeutic goal is to go forward and participate in valued activities despite the presence of negative mood. With experience, clients may come to learn that it is possible to behave independently of acute moods and that the very act of behaving in a valued direction is often a catalyst for bringing about mood change.

Another strategy for countering mood-dependent behavior patterns is acting "as if." This strategy involves pursuing a valued course of action "as if" the presumed obstacles for carrying out such an action were absent. A client, for example, might say something like "If I wasn't so socially anxious and if I was more charming I would go to the party tonight." Acting "as if" in this example would involve going to the party and "acting" as if one was somewhat charming and not socially anxious, and to notice the consequences of behaving in this way. By intentionally acting differently when feeling blocked by negative moods or self-doubts, one might learn that goals are obtainable regardless of emotional states and thoughts and that the very act of pursuing valued goals often changes mood and thinking in desirable directions.

Diane's Ongoing Struggles With Avoidance

Perhaps the greatest potential obstacle to Diane's success in therapy is her frequent use of avoidant coping strategies. This idea, in fact, was shared with Diane during the planning phase of therapy. At the time this was discussed, the therapist noted that it was possible that therapy might be challenging at times; that is, difficult topics might be discussed or Diane might find that changing behavior is hard and occasionally frustrating. Her therapist reassured her that they would take small steps toward the realization of her therapeutic goals and that he would work with her to increase the likelihood that lasting benefits are realized from this therapy.

When the issue of avoidance was first discussed, Diane was somewhat unsure if this would emerge as a problem. She did agree, however, to continuously monitor whether avoidance behavior was adversely affecting her progress in therapy, and she agreed to examine this issue with her therapist if he felt that it became a therapy-related issue.

By the 10th therapy session, Diane had made some progress in reducing avoidance. She altered her evening routine whereby she sought out other activities than news watching and drinking wine, with an extra effort given to incorporating others into these activities. Although some progress was made, Diane felt somewhat stuck because most of these alternative activities involved her children. She felt that her next step was to branch out and begin to establish friendships in other areas. She reported, however, that she was unable to branch out because of her feelings of being fatigued. Although these feelings were less pronounced as a result of cutting back on her wine consumption, the experience of fatigue kept her from "having the energy to get out there and meet people."

As Diane and her therapist examined this issue further, it also became apparent that Diane had significant social anxiety and negative thoughts about her self-worth and her suitability as a potential friend to someone. She became insistent that she would never have close friendships and expressed significant hopelessness related to her wish to be integrated into a social network and to date once again.

In response to Diane's insistence and accompanying anger, the therapist challenged her to examine what was happening in this moment during their session. After thinking for a while, Diane suggested that she was in a TRAP and that her reactions were largely avoidance. She recognized that if she were to do something different in relation to her social situation, then she would likely experience social anxiety and self-doubts. She correctly noted that hanging on to her pessimism and expectations of failure helped her avoid the anxiety and doubt associated with doing anything different.

Having previously worked within the TRAP, TRAC, and ACTION frameworks with her therapist, Diane noted that if she were to get on TRAC she would need to do something different that would bring her social anxiety and self-doubts to the forefront. She realized that she would need to allow the emotional reaction and negative thoughts to simply be there while taking active steps to realize her objectives and goals, which in this instance was to become more socially connected to people.

The remainder of the session was spent discussing different steps that Diane could take to become more socially connected. A number of ideas were generated (e.g., become involved in a hobby group, initiate non-work-related activities with coworkers, join a political action committee). One of these activities (i.e., joining a political organization) was subsequently broken down into a sequence of component parts, and Diane made a commitment to follow through with the first two steps prior to their next session. She acknowledged that even though taking these steps might be difficult, any acute discomfort would be less aversive than the prospect of not realizing the long-term social goals she has for herself.

Phase 4: Decreasing Vulnerability to Future Episodes of Depression

The likelihood of a lapse or relapse among formerly depressed clients is high (Hollon, Shelton, & Loosen, 1991). In recognition of this, behavioral activation incorporates elements of relapse prevention into the overall treatment program. One approach for reducing relapse involves therapists encouraging clients to apply the principles of behavioral activation to other areas of their lives, particularly those areas associated with an increased vulnerability to future episodes of depression. This approach promotes skills generalization and increases the likelihood that long-standing problem areas will continue to be addressed by the client once active therapy has ended.

As therapy draws to a close, clients are encouraged to consider what they have learned about themselves over the course of therapy. Clients who have received a course of behavioral activation therapy will generally demonstrate a better understanding of the functional aspects of their behavior. That is, they will be better able to identify triggers that are frequently associated with dysphoric mood as well as observe and acknowledge the effects of their behavior on mood and others in their environment. Clients will also likely have learned that avoidance and escape behaviors often provide immediate relief but result in aversive long-term outcomes and are obstacles in the pursuit of goals and valued activities.

In this latter phase of therapy, therapists emphasize the identification of life circumstances, situations, and issues that increase their clients' vulnerability to future episodes of depression. If there are common triggers for depressed mood, for example, clients might be encouraged to avoid these, if possible. Some important life areas also might be singled out for attention. These might include clients working on relationships with others by purposely engaging in more activities that involve other people. In other cases, clients might take stock of their long-term goals or values and make a deliberate decision to bring day-to-day activities more in line with these. For other clients, this might mean making a significant life change, which would involve changing a major life role or responsibility (husband or wife, one's job) for an alternative (divorcee, a new job). Reducing vulnerability to depressed mood also might involve taking steps to overcome past traumas, move beyond them, and shed the perspective of oneself as "damaged" or a "victim," and instead accept and value oneself. Acting differently is one way for a client to reduce the influence of the past, and the client acting in accordance with long-term goals and objectives increases the likelihood that they will eventually be realized.

Establishing regular routines is also often helpful in preventing relapse, particularly if such routines are regarded as pleasing and consistent with the client's long-term goals. The emphasis on developing regular routines is grounded in research observations that the disruption of routines is often associated with the maintenance of depression (Jacobson et al., 2001). Regular routines provide a regulation function and, provided that they include behaviors that result in positive reinforcement, keep individuals in regular contact with events that maintain behavior.

Diane's Progress in Shifting Contexts to Reduce Likelihood of Future Depression and to Realize Long-Term Goals

Over the course of 22 sessions, Diane made considerable progress in blocking avoidance patterns and accessing reinforcers from her environment. Her mood has steadily improved over the duration of therapy (BDI–II score from last session = 13), and self-report questionnaires indicated improvement in worry (PSWQ = 32) and perceived social support (ISEL = 30).

In reflecting on her progress, Diane indicated that she was much more aware of the relationships that her activities and mood share. She also described the TRAP associated with some coping strategies and avoidance; that is, their tendency to provide immediate relief but negatively influence mood and overall life satisfaction in the long run.

Although Diane has taken several steps to enhance her life through her own actions, she identified two primary areas that she needed to address to reduce her vulnerability to depression further: (a) her fear and avoidance of romantic relationships and (b) her negative views of herself. As Diane and her therapist examined these two issues, it became apparent that her negative self-view was related to her apprehension around the prospect of dating and establishing intimate relations. Her negative thoughts about herself, however, also had more global effects. Diane noticed that whenever she tried something new, these thoughts would often stop her from going forward, and she would revert back to avoidance patterns.

When her therapist challenged her to consider what she had learned from therapy that she can subsequently apply to these outstanding issues, Diane reported that she just needed to continue to do things that are consistent with what she wants to achieve, adding that the successes she has recently had further weakened the negative views that she has of herself. Similarly, she acknowledged that although in some respects it is easier to avoid the possibility of rejection by not dating, she concluded that rejection, if experienced, would hurt for a short period of time, but that not being in a stable and satisfying relationship would likely result in long-term disappointment and further increase her negative self-views and lower her mood. Diane then volunteered that life naturally involves an element of risk and that as a result of therapy, she's discovered that living life is not as threatening as she once viewed it to be.

SUMMARY

When using behavioral activation strategies in the treatment of depression, it is often useful for the therapist to do the following:

- Adopt the view that depression arises from a series of incidents and is not the product of an internal defect or deficit.
- Conduct idiographically based functional analyses of the client's overall activities, with special attention given to circumstances, situations, and events consistently associated with depressed mood.
- Identify harmful behavior patterns that are characteristically associated with depressed mood.

- Institute gradual or small changes in situations associated with depressed mood, and compare resultant outcomes with those typically associated with what the client usually does.
- Block avoidant coping patterns that are associated with the maintenance of depressed mood or incompatible with the realization of important life goals or objectives.
- Assist the client in getting back on track or in taking active steps toward reaching his or her long-term goals and objectives.

9

EXPOSURE-BASED INTERVENTIONS

Problems with emotions are often among a client's primary reasons for seeking therapy. Clients often express difficulties managing anger, a desire for relief from anxious or depressed moods, or a wish to work through emotions associated with the loss of a loved one. One method for helping clients with some of these emotional struggles, particularly those associated with maladaptive avoidance behaviors, is *exposure therapy*.

Within contemporary cognitive behavior therapy (CBT), exposure therapy has been successfully applied to a variety of clinical problems, particularly those in which the emotions of fear and anxiety are central features. Exposure-oriented interventions, for example, have a prominent role in treatments for panic disorder (Barlow & Craske, 1994), social anxiety disorder (Heimberg & Becker, 2002), posttraumatic stress disorder (PTSD; Foa, Keene, & Friedman, 2004), and generalized anxiety disorder (Brown, O'Leary, & Barlow, 2001). Exposure interventions have also been adapted to clinical problems other than fear and anxiety, including anger control problems (Brondolo, DiGiuseppe, & Tafrate, 1997), substance dependence (Conklin & Tiffany, 2002), eating disorders (Toro et al., 2003), and compromised immune system functioning (Ader & Cohen, 1985) as well as an array of painful emotions experienced by persons with complex clinical problems (e.g., borderline personality disorder; Linehan, 1993a).

Given the prominence of exposure therapy among many current evidence-based CBT treatment packages, this chapter provides practical guidance on how to conceptualize and implement exposure interventions in CBT. As such, this chapter addresses the following topics: a brief summary of research findings on exposure therapies, definitions and assumptions of exposure interventions, client problems for which exposure interventions are indicated, mechanisms of change associated with exposure therapies, and methods for applying exposure therapies.

EMPIRICAL BASIS OF EXPOSURE INTERVENTIONS

Exposure-based approaches are among the most powerful behavioral interventions, particularly in the treatment of anxiety. Indeed, for many clinical problems, when complex CBT-based treatment packages are stripped down to their components (e.g., cognitive restructuring, skills training, exposure therapy), the exposure component is often just as efficacious as the entire treatment package. As an example, several studies have compared prolonged exposure (PE) for PTSD with other, more complex treatment packages that include training in coping skills, systematic desensitization, and cognitive interventions (e.g., stress inoculation training; Meichenbaum, 1985). These studies generally have indicated that PE alone is just as effective in treating PTSD as more complex treatments that include cognitive interventions and coping skills (Foa, Rothbaum, Riggs, & Murdock, 1991; Foa et al., 1999; Marks, Lovell, Noshirvani, Livanou, & Thrasher, 1998), although cognitive and exposure interventions may lead to different types of improvements (see Resick & Calhoun, 2001, for a review).

In addition to PTSD, exposure-oriented interventions have demonstrated strong efficacy for panic disorder and social anxiety disorder. Barlow's panic control therapy (PCT; Barlow & Craske, 1994), for instance, includes two forms of exposure therapy—interoceptive exposure and in vivo exposure—and has demonstrated success rates of 80% to 100% in reducing the frequency of panic attacks in individuals with panic disorder (for a review, see Craske & Barlow, 2001). Other exposure-based treatments have been applied to various anxiety disorders and have generally demonstrated noteworthy levels of efficacy and clinical significance (Foa et al., 2004; Heimberg & Becker, 2002).

As we have noted, exposure therapy has also been used effectively in the treatment of other conditions, such as problems with emotions other than anxiety (e.g., anger; Brondolo, DiGiuseppe, & Tafrate, 1997), substance dependence (Conklin & Tiffany, 2002), and eating disorders (Toro et al., 2003). Although it is beyond the scope of this chapter to review the full body of research on exposure therapy, we selectively highlight in the following sections some of the clinical conditions for which exposure therapy has been successfully applied.

DEFINING EXPOSURE THERAPY

Within this section, we provide definitions of exposure interventions as they are currently used in CBT. For ease of explanation, we emphasize throughout this chapter the use of exposure therapy for reducing unwanted and exaggerated emotional responses. In doing so, however, we note that exposure methods have been applied with success to several other problematic conditioned responses (e.g., Ader & Cohen, 1985; Toro et al., 2003).

There is a growing variety of exposure-oriented interventions among contemporary CBT therapies, but there are two key components of each intervention. These components are (a) exposing clients to stimuli that elicit emotional responses in the absence of negative consequences and (b) preventing a behavioral response that is consistent with the emotional response elicited (often avoidance or escape).

Exposure to the Stimulus

Exposure is a term used for several related procedures that reduce unwanted emotional responses by exposing the client to the stimuli that elicit these responses. As such, the first component of exposure therapy involves exposing the client to feared stimuli (e.g., spiders, photos of spiders, or mental images of spiders) or stimuli that elicit other emotional responses (e.g., anger, shame, sadness) until the emotional response extinguishes, habituates, or diminishes in intensity. The therapist and client repeat the exposure over multiple trials until the client's emotional responses no longer occur or are greatly diminished. In this way, exposure essentially is a method for reducing the likelihood and intensity of emotional responses to specific situations.

Prevention of Emotion-Consistent Responses

Another important component of exposure interventions involves asking clients to engage in action tendencies that are inconsistent with the elicited emotional response. Barlow and colleagues (Barlow, 1988; Barlow, Allen, & Choate, 2004) have argued that preventing action tendencies consistent with the emotion (e.g., avoidance or escape, in the case of fear) and helping clients engage in action tendencies that are inconsistent with the emotion (e.g., approaching rather than avoiding) are among the most important aspects of treatments for emotional disorders including depression and anxiety disorders. In an example of a client who is afraid of public speaking, an exposure intervention might involve asking the client to give a speech in front of a small group of people (exposure to the feared stimulus), while helping the client stay in the situation and engage in behaviors that are not consistent with anxiety. Such behaviors might involve making eye contact with the audience, adopting a confident posture, expressing enthusiasm about the topic of the speech, and avoiding behaviors that are consistent with anxiety, such as looking down, fidgeting, or looking away from the audience.

WHEN DO THERAPISTS USE EXPOSURE INTERVENTIONS?

Within this section, we discuss the assumptions underlying exposure interventions and the conditions under which a therapist may choose to use these interventions. Exposure generally is most appropriate with clients who experience unwanted, dysfunctional, or unjustified emotional responses. At first blush, it might seem as if exposure could apply to almost any client. Until relatively recently, however, exposure-based methods almost exclusively targeted anxiety and fear and their related clinical problems and disorders. As mentioned, treatments have begun to apply exposure-oriented skills to a range of different emotional experiences such as anger, shame, and sadness, with research data suggesting that these approaches have merit.

Before using an exposure-based intervention, a solid behavioral assessment is important. When exposure therapy is considered for negative emotional responses, for example, the assessor might attempt to determine whether the emotional experience in question is justified or unjustified and adaptive or maladaptive.

Unjustified Emotional Responses

Unjustified emotional responses are emotional reactions that are not warranted by the situation (Linehan, 1993b). Before embarking on exposure interventions, it is important for the therapist to ensure that the emotional response of the client is unjustified. Consider, for example, the case of a client who is afraid of public speaking. If his or her fear of criticism, heckling, or judgmental comments by the audience is realistic or justified, then exposing the client to public speaking scenarios is likely to strengthen rather than weaken the fear. If the fear is unjustified, however, it is important to expose the client to a public speaking situation in which the anticipated consequences associated with the feared context (e.g., criticism or heckling from the audience) are absent. Otherwise, the presence of these consequences could strengthen the client's anxiety as an emotional response associated with public speaking contexts.

Maladaptive Emotional Responses

Another way to think about emotions has to do with whether they are adaptive or maladaptive. The concept of maladaptive emotions is similar to Foa and Kozak's (1986) conceptualization of "pathological fear." According to Foa and Kozak, pathological fear is excessively intense, associated with problematic responses (e.g., avoidance), and resistant to modification. Within this general framework, we use the term *maladaptive* rather than *pathological* because behavioral approaches tend to focus on whether responding is adaptive or has a useful purpose or function rather than whether it represents pathology of some kind. It is important to note that we are using the term *maladaptive* to describe specific instances in which a client's emotions are intense and associated with problematic action tendencies. Of course, any emotional response or related action could be "adaptive" on some level. Fear and avoidance of public places is "adaptive" in the sense that it helps the individual avoid panic.

Broadened to include emotions other than fear, maladaptive emotions are those that are excessively intense or associated with response tendencies and are rigid, ineffectual, and resistant to change. "Tony," for example, struggled with serious anger management difficulties. One key anger-provoking scenario involved being stuck behind a slow driver in the fast lane on the freeway. Tony reported anger at an intensity of 10 out of 10 whenever he was in such a situation, and he responded by cursing, waving his arms outside his window, displaying rude gestures, and at times, stopping the car and getting out to confront the unsuspecting driver in front of him. Although some degree of anger may be justified in a situation in which a slow driver is preventing someone else from driving from Point A to Point B in a reasonable amount of time, Tony's anger was maladaptive in that it was excessively intense (100% intensity) and accompanied by problematic anger-related behaviors.

Deciding Whether to Use Exposure Interventions

In deciding whether exposure could be an effective intervention, the therapist might consider whether the client's responses are unjustified or maladaptive. The clearest case for exposure is when the emotion is unjustified and maladaptive, and when the client also engages in maladaptive behaviors that help him or her avoid or escape stimuli that elicit the emotional response.

It is important to note that exposure is not advisable when a client has fears that are justified. "Joe," for example, was a 14-year old boy who was afraid of reviewing his homework with his teacher after school. His initial remarks about his fear were rather vague (e.g., "He creeps me out!"), but it turned out that Joe's teacher was physically abusive toward his students. Joe was afraid of getting hit, and his fear was justified. Had the therapist encouraged exposure to the teacher, the consequences could have been disastrous. Similarly, if a client is afraid of cobras or other venomous snakes, life-threatening situations, or engaging in behaviors that are likely to produce feared consequences (e.g., hugging a grizzly bear), exposure is not advisable.

Another consideration is related to the type of emotional response with which the client is struggling. As most of the research on exposure-oriented interventions thus far has focused on fear and anxiety, the most obvious application of exposure is to unjustified and maladaptive fears. As mentioned later, however, some approaches apply exposure-oriented interventions to a variety of emotional experiences other than fear.

As an example of a clear case of unjustified and maladaptive fear, "Maurice" was a client who was intensely afraid of heights. He desperately wanted to eat at the restaurant at the top of the sky tower in the city where he lived but had thus far avoided doing so because of his fear of heights. Whenever he was in a situation in which height-related stimuli were salient (e.g., being in an upper floor of a multilevel building, driving over an overpass, going up glass elevators), he experienced intense fear. His fear levels typically ranged from 65 to 95 out of 100 (where 0 = *no fear at all* and 100 = *the most intense fear possible*). As a result, he avoided overpasses, always parked on the lowest level of multilevel parking garages, and never ate at restaurants that were above ground level. His fear was not justified by the situation, in that he was unlikely to fall to his death in any of these scenarios. The fear was also maladaptive in that it was excessive, associated with considerable distress, and related to behaviors that curtailed his life, such that he avoided some of the very activities that he most enjoyed or wanted to engage in. In this case, treatment involved exposure therapy.

HOW DO EXPOSURE INTERVENTIONS WORK? MECHANISMS OF CHANGE

Several theoretical accounts have been offered to explain how exposure therapy works. There is general consensus within the literature that the primary features of exposure therapies that account for therapeutic change include the act of repeatedly exposing the client to emotion-eliciting stimuli, the prevention of responses that are consistent with the emotional response (e.g., avoidance or escape behaviors), and the nonoccurrence of negative consequences during the exposure process. Less consensus exists, however, on how or why exposure of this kind results in therapeutic change. In the following sections, we discuss some hypothesized mechanisms of change associated with exposure interventions. These include counterconditioning, extinction or habituation of responses, learning new responses, the modification of rules that influence avoidance behavior, and the facilitation of emotional processing.

Counterconditioning

One theoretical account of the change processes involved in exposure therapy is the notion of *counterconditioning*. Counterconditioning involves the substitution of an adaptive alternative response (e.g., relaxation) for a maladaptive response (excessive or unjustified anxiety). This theoretical explanation has been used to account for the effectiveness of Joseph Wolpe's (1958) systematic desensitization approach for eliminating conditioned fears (e.g., Davison, 1968). *Systematic desensitization* involves the presentation of progressively more anxiety-provoking stimuli in imagination while the client is relaxed (the result of participation in progressive muscle relaxation exercises prior to exposure to anxiety-related stimuli). With reference to his theory of reciprocal inhibition, Wolpe suggested that the simultaneous presentation of an anxiety-provoking stimulus and a stimulus that elicits a response that is antagonistic to anxiety would reduce and eventually eliminate fear. From a counterconditioning perspective, systematic desensitization teaches the client to use manifestations of anxiety (e.g., somatic responses) as cues to substitute replacement behaviors (e.g., those associated with relaxation).

Several laboratory-based observations, however, are inconsistent with a counterconditioning explanation of systematic desensitization for reducing fears (Wilson & Davison, 1971). Several applied studies have also indicated that it is not necessary to pair an incompatible response (e.g., relaxation) with exposure to a feared stimulus to reduce anxiety to the feared stimulus (e.g., Cooke, 1968).

Extinction or Habituation

Most accounts of the processes underlying the effects of exposure incorporate both classical and operant conditioning elements. Mowrer's (1947, 1960) two-factor theory, for example, describes classical conditioning as the process by which people develop fears, and operant conditioning as the process that maintains fears. According to this model, an individual develops a specific fear through classical conditioning, whereby previously neutral cues become associated with unconditional stimuli (UCS) that elicit unconditional emotional responses (UCR). Once a bond or associative link has been established between UCS and previously neutral cues, these cues become conditional stimuli (CS). Because CS acquire many of the same stimulus properties as UCS through associative processes, they will often elicit conditional emotional responses (CRs) that are very similar in form to UCRs.

"Roger," for example, climbed a ladder to a high place in a playground when he was young and slipped and fell, resulting in a leg bone fracture. In this case, the impact with the ground after slipping and falling is a UCS. The UCR in this example would be pain, fear, and other unpleasant emotional responses and physiological sensations. Conditioning would occur if the UCS became paired with the CS related to ladders and being in high places, such that the subsequent presentation of the CS alone elicits a variety of unpleasant emotions and physiological sensations. Over time, and through stimulus generalization, a large variety of stimuli related to heights (beyond playground stimuli) may also elicit fear. Roger, for example, might learn through operant conditioning that avoiding high places and ladderlike objects (e.g., step stools, suspended staircases) leads to negative reinforcement as a result of anxiety avoidance or reduction. Eventually, these stimuli become discriminative stimuli (or S^D), signaling that avoidance behavior will lead to negative reinforcement (e.g., cessation for fear).

According to this account, exposure therapy works through the processes of operant and classical extinction. Within Mowrer's (1947, 1960) framework, avoidance of height- and ladder-related stimuli (an operant response) prevents the individual from weakening the association of these CS and the UCS related to falling and impacting the ground. This is because, to weaken these associations, the individual must repeatedly experience the CS (e.g., heights, ladders) in the absence of the UCS (e.g., falling, impact with ground). Avoiding the CS altogether prevents this type of learning from occurring. Exposure shortcuts this process by providing the client with repeated experiences of the height-related stimuli in the absence of danger (i.e., the UCS) and by blocking avoidance behaviors that would prevent this process of classical extinction. Prolonged exposure to height- and ladder-related stimuli in the absence of danger results in the natural extinction of the conditioned fear response (CR). Over several sessions of prolonged exposure, situational cues (e.g., heights, ladders) are associated with a decreasing intensity of the emotional response until the situational cues no longer elicit the maladaptive and unjustified emotional responses.

Exposure therapy, in part, involves classical extinction. From this perspective, exposure therapy results in a reduction in conditioned anxiety or fear because, during exposure, conditional fear stimuli (CS) are not paired with unconditional fear stimuli (UCS), thus weakening or breaking the bond that associates these two stimulus classes (Wilson & Davison, 1971). Furthermore, this weakening of the UCS–CS bond only occurs if avoidance behavior is blocked or inhibited (sometimes referred to as response prevention), and the individual remains in the contact with the CS until the CRs fade or extinguish.

Although exposure therapies developed from the learning models described earlier, researchers have raised some criticisms about traditional classical conditioning or two-factor learning accounts of fear acquisition and maintenance (e.g., Foa & Rothbaum, 1998, pp. 68–70). Criticisms include difficulty distinguishing between UCS and CS in naturalistic environments and rejection of automatic associative processes hypothesized to establish CS–UCS linkages and CS–CR pairings. For these reasons, the concept of "habituation" has occasionally been substituted for "extinction" to signify reductions in anxiety in the presence of anxiety-related cues as a result of exposure (e.g., Jaycox, Foa, & Morral, 1998).

Learning New Responses

Another possible mechanism of action in exposure therapy involves the client learning new responses to the CS that previously elicited the undesired emotional response (e.g., Bouton, 2004). A premise underlying this theory is that exposure therapy does not involve the elimination of prior learning but instead promotes new learning. A consequence of new learning is that CS can assume multiple associations with the UCS and, as a result, CRs will evidence some variability across different contexts.

Consider, for example, a client who is afraid of spiders who undergoes repeated exposure to spider-related stimuli. As a result of exposure therapy, the client may acquire new responses to spiders. Instead of a visceral fear reaction and avoidance of all spider-related phenomena, the client may learn to react with curiosity, mild trepidation, and approach behavior, or at least, lack of avoidance behavior. An intense fear of spiders might continue to be evident, however, in contexts in which considerable fear of spiders was previously experienced (unless these contexts are targeted during exposure and the extinction of fear in the presence of these contextual cues ensues).

This perspective has several practical implications for how both in vivo and imaginal exposure are carried out. Perhaps the most important implication is related to the events that clients are exposed to during therapy sessions. Because there is some evidence of the context specificity of both fear acquisition through conditioning and extinction of fears (Bouton, 2004), it is important for therapists to know the specific context and events that evoke exaggerated fear reactions in the clients' natural environments. Exposure scenarios would, ideally, include as many of these contextual and event features as possible.

Modification of Rules That Influence Avoidance Behavior

An alternative perspective on change processes that is grounded in the rule-governed behavior concept is the notion that exposure therapy results in the discarding of inaccurate rules concerning antecedent–behavior–consequence relations in favor of more accurate rules concerning these relations (see chap. 6 for a discussion of rule-governed behavior). That is, the process of exposure might result in the modification of rules on the basis of experiences that exposure provides. A client with contamination fears, for example, might have held views prior to exposure that suggested, "If I touch dirty things, I will become contaminated and seriously ill" and "If I don't wash, I'll spread contaminants around and make other people ill." As a result of exposure (to dirty objects) and response prevention (blockage of the avoidance response of washing), this client might discover through experience that touching dirty things on the vast majority of occasions does not result in illness. When a client is confronted with evidence as a result of the exposure process and it is inconsistent with previously held rules, he or she may formulate new and more accurate rules (perhaps with assistance from the therapist), such as "If I touch dirty things, the likelihood that I will become ill is very low" and "When I touch objects I regard as contaminated, there is no apparent effect on the health of others around me."

In the case of PTSD, exposure therapy usually involves repeated imaginal reliving of the traumatic event by the client. This process might reduce trauma-related anxiety because it alters the client's thoughts related to the level of danger associated with his or her engagement with the traumatic memory and the experience of trauma-related symptoms (Foa & Jaycox, 1999). When interpreted from the perspective of rule modification, client exposure to traumatic cues in such instances provides the individual with information that is inconsistent with his or her previously held rules concerning trauma-related cues (e.g., memories, PTSD-related symptoms). As a result of the exposure process and the subsequent learning that such cues are not themselves dangerous, the client develops new rules that more accurately describe antecedent–behavior–consequence relations (e.g., "If I think about the trauma, I will likely feel discomfort but will not be harmed or threatened").

Emotional Processing

Foa and Kozak (1986) have outlined a cognitively oriented theory regarding the effects of exposure therapy, called *emotional processing theory* (EPT). According to EPT, fear is represented as a memory structure that involves stimuli (e.g., heights, tall buildings, bridges), responses (e.g., avoidance, freezing, shaking), and cognitive "meaning" elements (e.g., "danger"). Within this framework, this memory structure functions to help people escape danger and therefore includes information indicating that particular stimuli are dangerous. Exposure therapy, according to EPT, must involve the presentation of relevant stimulus elements, the activation of the memory structure, and the incorporation of information that is incompatible with the fear structure. Through the client's habituation of the emotional response in the context that normally elicits fear, the link between the stimulus (e.g., the height-related stimuli) and the avoidance or escape response weakens as the client learns that avoidance and escape are not necessary to reduce fear. Lower fear and arousal allows for the client's incorporation of corrective information indicating that the previously feared stimuli are not dangerous.

Over time, exposure essentially allows for the client's integration of new, non-fear-related memories, and the meaning elements related to the client's fear become divorced from the stimuli that previously elicited them (Foa & Kozak, 1986). Although EPT is somewhat inconsistent with the deemphasis of cognitive "structures" that is apparent in behavioral theory and therapy, EPT has formed the basis of an empirically supported approach to treating fear related to PTSD, called *cognitive processing therapy* (Resick & Schnicke, 1993). In addition, the implications of EPT (i.e., the therapist's need to expose the client to fear-relevant stimuli and prevent avoidance responses) are similar to the implications of other mechanisms of change discussed earlier in this chapter.

APPLYING EXPOSURE INTERVENTIONS

Within this section, we provide information and instructions regarding how to implement exposure interventions in practice. It is important to note that sometimes the key ingredients of exposure may be modified by the therapist to best suit different settings and client populations. Nevertheless, we propose that exposure generally involves most or all of the procedures discussed subsequently and presented in Exhibit 9.1. These procedures include (a) choosing the appropriate type of exposure for the client; (b) orienting the client to exposure; (c) assessing factors that may inform the development of exposure scenarios; (d) selecting an effective format, frequency, and schedule of exposure interventions for the client; and (e) following some key guidelines, such as conducting nonreinforced exposure with the client, preventing the client from developing emotion-consistent behaviors, monitoring the client's emotional responses, continuing exposure until the client's emotional responses diminish, and providing the client with control over the exposure.

Choosing the Appropriate Type of Exposure

After a therapist decides that exposure may be a useful intervention for a particular client, the next step often involves determining what type of exposure to use. There are several different types of exposure interventions. The key task for the therapist is to apply the most effective type of exposure to client in the most effective manner, given the idiosyncrasies of the individual. Several commonly used types of exposure interventions include the following: (a) imaginal exposure, (b) in vivo exposure, (c) informal exposure, (d) interoceptive exposure, (e) opposite action, and (f) cue exposure. Exhibit 9.2 provides a decision-making guide for selecting an appropriate

EXHIBIT 9.1
Essential Steps to Take With Exposure Interventions
for Unwanted Negative Emotions

1. Determine which emotion to target with the client.
2. Determine whether the emotion is justified or adaptive.
3. Decide what type of exposure to implement (see Exhibit 9.2).
4. Orient the client to the exposure intervention.
5. Assess the breadth of stimuli and the intensity of emotional responses to these stimuli (if you have not already done so).
6. Decide between graduated exposure and flooding.
7. Decide how to schedule sessions.
8. Conduct exposure, following key guidelines:
   - Conduct nonreinforced exposure.
   - Prevent emotion-consistent behaviors.
   - Take regular SUDS ratings (e.g., every 5–10 minutes).
   - Facilitate habituation (i.e., do not prematurely remove stimuli to which the client is exposed).
   - Give the client control over exposure.
   - Repeat each session and possibly give exposure homework.

Note. Some of these steps appear in Linehan (1993a) and other treatment manuals that describe exposure interventions.

exposure intervention for particular clinical problems. We also further describe each type of exposure in the following sections.

Imaginal Exposure

Imaginal exposure involves exposing the client to emotionally evocative stimuli in his or her imagination. This type of exposure is often used under a few different conditions: (a) when it is either difficult or impossible to expose the client to relevant stimuli in real life, (b) when the flexibility of the client's (or therapist's) imagination is useful in concocting effective scenarios that trigger emotional responses, or (c) as a precursor for in vivo exposure (discussed subsequently). For instance, imaginal exposure frequently is used in treatments for PTSD, in which the therapist asks the client to imagine a specific traumatic event in considerable detail (including sights, sounds, smells, and tactile sensations). The idea is for the therapist to help the client reduce fear of the *memory* of the traumatic event (Resick & Calhoun, 2001). An individual's fear in response to an actual traumatic event (not just the memory of one), however, would be quite adaptive and justifiable; hence, in vivo exposure to traumatic events makes little sense and would be dangerous. The therapist might start by exposing the client to the trauma memory in his or her imagination, and then progress to in vivo exposure or places and people the client avoids or fears, provided that these fears are maladaptive and unjustified.

"Ann" was a client who experienced intense fear whenever her partner raised his voice. It appeared that this fear was related to a learning history that involved childhood physical abuse. After determining that her current partner was unlikely to engage in physical aggression (he had no history of

EXHIBIT 9.2
Guidelines for Determining What Type of Exposure to Use

Clinical problem	Type of exposure to use	Behaviors to prevent
Fear of particular events, people, places, animals, or objects, often related to PTSD, OCD, specific phobias, social anxiety disorder, among other problems.	**In-vivo exposure** to the feared and avoided events, people, places, animals, or objects, and prevention of the avoidance response.	Avoidance; distraction; escape from the situation, object, person, animal or event.
Fear or other emotional responses to situations that are not readily reproducible in "real life," or fear of recollections of trauma (e.g., as in PTSD).	**Imaginal exposure** to the situation or recollections in the client's imagination.	Avoidance, distraction, imagery that runs contrary to the exposure stimuli.
Client suppressing or avoiding an emotional response in session.	**Informal exposure** to the emotion or topic that is avoided or suppressed.	Any behavior that is consistent with the emotional response, particularly avoidance, distraction, or suppression.
Unjustified emotional responses, including but not limited to, fear or anxiety (e.g., shame, envy, anger, irritation, sadness).	**Opposite action,** which involves exposure to the emotion-eliciting stimuli in combination with acting in a manner opposite to the action urge related to the emotion.	Avoidance, distraction, escape, and any behaviors that are consistent with the action urge(s) associated with the problematic emotion.
Drug or alcohol use or urges to use drugs or alcohol.	**Cue exposure;** sights, smells, or other cues (e.g., paraphernalia) associated with alcohol or drugs.	Avoidance, distraction, escape, and drug or alcohol use; imagining or fantasizing about drug or alcohol use.
Fear and avoidance of specific bodily sensations (i.e., emotion phobia).	**Interoceptive exposure** to specific bodily sensations by engaging in activities that produce those sensations (e.g., spinning for fear of dizziness, exercise for elevated heart rate or sweatiness, staring in a mirror for depersonalization, breathing quickly for hyperventilation).	Avoidance, distraction, or escape from the feared sensation.

Note. PTSD = posttraumatic stress disorder; OCD = obsessive-compulsive disorder.

doing so and was quite averse to any type of physical confrontation), the therapist conducted imaginal exposure by asking Ann to imagine being in a variety of situations in which her partner raised his voice. The imaginal exposure allowed Ann to use her imagination to increase the partner's voice volume, imagine him becoming increasingly agitated, and bring to mind the most fear-provoking scenarios involving her partner. Over time, Ann's fear of these specific behaviors of her partner diminished, and she was subsequently more effective in responding to her partner during conflict situations (because she was no longer inhibited by excess fear).

In Vivo Exposure

In vivo exposure involves exposing the client to emotionally evocative stimuli in real life. In vivo exposure can occur in a variety of settings, including the client's home, the therapist's office, or various places in the client's natural environment. With Maurice, the acrophobic client discussed earlier, in vivo exposure involved the therapist taking him up to high levels of parking garages, dining at the window seat of a fifth-story restaurant, and driving over high bridges and overpasses.

In vivo exposure often is used with clients who have a variety of other disorders. For instance, some clients with obsessive-compulsive disorder are afraid of engaging in activities that expose them to dirt and germs, even though these activities are very unlikely to result in disease. In vivo exposure might involve the therapist asking the client to touch doorknobs, put his or her hands on a well-traveled floor, sit on a public toilet seat, or try other such activities without engaging in compulsive cleaning behavior. In vivo exposure for someone with problematic social anxiety might involve exposing him or her to social performance situations, such as interacting with other people in a group setting, public speaking, going to parties and "mingling" with people, or other such fear-eliciting activities. As mentioned earlier, in-vivo exposure for a person with PTSD might involve exposing the client to cues, situations, places, or people that trigger fear or memories of trauma.

Informal Exposure

Informal exposure involves the therapist exposing the client to stimuli that elicit emotional responses in an ad hoc manner during therapy sessions. Whereas standard in vivo and imaginal exposure interventions are normally conducted formally to a defined set of stimuli in a structured manner, informal exposure is less structured. Informal exposure is used reasonably frequently in DBT when the therapist notices that the client is avoiding or suppressing an emotional response, and such avoidance and suppression is likely to create further suffering or reinforce a longstanding maladaptive pattern of avoidance (Linehan, 1993a).

With informal exposure, the therapist first provides the client with a rationale that explains how informal exposure may be helpful given the client's goals. This is followed by the therapist describing how and under what circumstances informal exposure might be implemented. During subsequent therapy sessions, if the therapist observes the client avoiding discussions of emotionally difficult material, for example, the therapist might clarify whether, in fact, avoidance is occurring. If the client confirms that he or she is avoiding certain topics or emotions, the therapist might encourage the client to describe in detail the experience or recollection that is being avoided and block any avoidance or escape behaviors while he or she is doing so.

"James," for example, often experienced intense shame when the therapist pointed out that he had not completed his therapy homework. He also characteristically averted his eyes and looked downward on such occasions, and all problem solving in the session regarding homework completion would typically come to a halt. Shame is not a justified emotional response to feedback about homework completion. Rather, shame is normally justified when an individual or important group rejects the client following his or her public display of a particular behavior. In this situation, however, the therapist was not going to reject James or terminate his therapy for homework nonadherence. As a result, the therapist oriented James to this problem by saying, "Whenever I bring up your homework, you feel shame. We can't keep moving forward if we keep getting stuck trying to find ways to get your homework done." After orienting, the therapist kept James exposed to the stimulus (i.e., feedback about homework) and blocked all behaviors consistent with shame (i.e., by asking him make eye contact and actively engage in the discussion). Over time, James learned to effectively engage in problem-solving discussions when he had not completed his homework.

Interoceptive Exposure

Interoceptive exposure involves the therapist exposing the client to particular bodily sensations. Most often used in therapy for panic disorder, interoceptive exposure uses exercises that enhance the salience of bodily sensations that are feared by the client. Some clients (e.g., those with panic disorder) are afraid of the experience of dizziness. In this case, interoceptive exposure might involve the client spinning in circles. Other clients are afraid of the experience of a quickly beating heart; hence, exposure might involve the client engaging in brief periods of vigorous exercise.

Interoceptive exposure most often applies when the client has an intense fear of a particular bodily sensation or set of bodily sensations. As noted by Linehan (1993a), however, some clients appear to have a more generalized fear of emotions. Some mental health professionals, for example, have described clients with borderline personality disorder as "emotion phobic," in that they go to great lengths to avoid or escape their emotions. For this type of client, the therapist may elect to conduct full-on exposure to the entire set of emotions, thoughts, and sensations, or may choose to use interoceptive exposure that is focused more specifically on bodily sensations of emotion. One important consideration is that, sometimes, attending to an emotional response and all of its accompanying experiences may be too challenging or overwhelming for a client. In addition, the thoughts that accompany distressing emotions might distract the client from the exposure experience. For these reasons, it is sometimes more effective to have the client focus specifically on bodily sensations of the emotion and to direct his or her attention away from these other experiences.

Opposite Action and Reversing Emotion-Linked Action Tendencies

A more recently developed form of exposure involves acting in a manner that is opposite to the urge that accompanies a particular emotion (Linehan, 1993b). As described by Linehan (1993a) and others (Gross, 1998), emotions often are accompanied by urges to engage in particular actions. For instance, the urge to escape or flee the situation accompanies fear, the urge to yell or fight accompanies anger, and the urge to hide or withdraw accompanies shame.

Opposite action involves exposure to the event that elicited the client's emotion, while acting in a manner that is opposite to the action urge that accompanies the emotion. A socially anxious client, for instance, might be afraid (unjustifiably so) of attending his brother's graduation party. His fear is related to his expectation that he will be humiliated and scorned by other attendees. Opposite action in this instance might involve encouraging the client to attend the party and talk to as many people as possible. Similarly, a person who is afraid of public speaking might be encouraged to actively seek out opportunities to engage in public speaking. Unlike standard exposure procedures, opposite action normally applies to any unjustified emotion (e.g., sadness, shame, anger, envy), not just fear or anxiety. Please see Exhibit 9.3 for the five key steps in conducting opposite action.

It is especially important for therapists to ensure that the client does opposite action thoroughly and with attention to his or her surroundings. For a person who struggles with social anxiety, giving a speech without paying attention to the audience is considered opposite action. For someone who is afraid of germs, touching a faucet in a public bathroom with gloves on is not likely to help him or her learn not to be afraid of germs. In addition, it is important (as in any exposure intervention) for the client to attend to the consequences of his or her actions during opposite action. As with the speech example, if the client does not pay attention to the audience, he or she may never learn that the audience is nonthreatening. Clinicians, therefore, must ensure that clients engage in opposite action in a thorough manner and pay attention to their environments during opposite action.

Cue Exposure

Cue exposure is a behavioral technique that has been applied primarily to therapy for substance use problems, although extensions to other conditions such as bulimia nervosa have been reported (e.g., Toro et al., 2003). When applied to the treatment of substance abuse, cue exposure involves the therapist presenting substance cues to the client (e.g., drug paraphernalia, or sight and smell of preferred beverage). Client consumption of the sub-

EXHIBIT 9.3
Essential Steps for Performing Opposite Action to
Reduce Unwanted Negative Emotions

1. Identify and label the emotional experience (e.g., anxiety, sadness, shame, or anger).
2. Determine whether the emotional experience is justified by the situation, and whether the client wishes to reduce the emotion.
3. Determine the action urge associated with the emotional experience.
4. If the emotional experience is unjustified, figure out what action would be opposite to the action urge.
5. Ask the client to engage in the opposite action thoroughly and repeatedly.

Note. Some of these steps appear in Linehan (1993b).

stance, however, is blocked. Client exposure to drug cues (CS), therefore, is not reinforced, thus weakening the association that the CS has with the UCS (the drug). Cue exposure, then, is regarded by therapists as an extinction-based approach that results in gradual reductions in clients' conditional emotional and physiological responses (e.g., cravings and urges to use) to drug use cues.

Cue exposure has been used by therapists in the treatment of persons with dependence on a variety of substances (e.g., tobacco, alcohol, cocaine, opiates) and has been conducted in inpatient and outpatient settings as well as in virtual environments (Lee et al., 2004). Results from this research suggest that cue exposure itself is generally associated with modest treatment effects, perhaps a consequence of methodological or procedural limitations associated with these studies (Conklin & Tiffany, 2002; Havermans & Jansen, 2003). Until such limitations are satisfactorily addressed or resolved, cue exposure might best be treated as a component of a larger treatment package (e.g., Rohsenow et al., 2001; Sitharthan, Sitharthan, Hough, & Kavanagh, 1997).

Orienting the Client to Exposure

Although exposure interventions are generally effective, they can be quite distressing to the client. For this reason, it is especially important for a therapist to give the client a clear idea of what is involved in exposure therapy and why he or she has been asked to undertake it. The key elements of a clear orientation include the therapist (a) providing information on why exposure is the method of choice and giving some detail about any relevant research, (b) describing how exposure works, and (c) outlining the specific tasks involved in exposure. The following is an example of how a therapist might orient a client to exposure methods for a spider phobia.

> You've said that you really want to work on your fear of spiders. From what we can tell, this is what we call an "unjustified fear." Unjustified fears are fears that are not warranted by the situation. For instance, you

are afraid that the spider is going to jump up and attack you. From what we know about spider behavior, spiders are quite afraid of people and only bite if they are in imminent danger (e.g., they are going to be squished, crushed, or are caught in your clothing).

One way to tackle this fear is with exposure therapy. Exposure therapy has been effective for people with spider fears in several studies. In fact, many clients say that they're no longer afraid of spiders after exposure therapy is over. Exposure works on the basis of the following idea: If you expose yourself to what you are afraid of many times and nothing terrible happens, your fear will eventually go down. You will learn that there's nothing to fear from spiders. Normally, if you are around spiders, you feel fear of 80 out of a scale of 100. With exposure, you spend time in the presence of spiders, looking at spiders, and so forth, and your fear is likely to be quite high when you start. But, the longer you remain in the presence of spiders without escaping, the lower your fear will be as you learn that nothing terrible is happening. The next time you experience exposure to spiders, you might start out with fear of about 60 out 100, and the next time, 50, 40, and so on. So, that's how it works. What do you think?

Assessing Breadth and Intensity

Generally, the second step for therapists conducting exposure-based interventions involves a solid assessment of (a) the breadth of stimuli to which the client responds with the unjustified emotional response and (b) the intensity of the client's emotional response associated with these stimuli. In terms of breadth, it is important for the therapist to know the range of situations in which the client experiences the unjustified emotion. For a socially anxious client, does he only experience fear or anxiety when he might have to give a public presentation, or is he also anxious when he is required to speak up at office meetings, when he is at parties, or when he is flirting or trying to call someone for a date? For a client with fears of contamination, is she only afraid of touching doorknobs, or does she fear public toilets, playgrounds, buses, shaking hands, or other such situations? If the therapist targets one particular situation and misses out on the plethora of other situations associated with fear, anxiety, or another unjustified emotion, the client's emotion may persist in these other situations. Along these lines, Foa and Kozak (1986) noted the importance of the therapist ensuring that all key stimulus elements that elicit fear in the client are captured in the exposure.

In terms of intensity, it is critical for the therapist to know how intense the client's emotional response is to various situational triggers. In most therapy approaches, therapists use a scale called the subjective units of distress scale (SUDS), where 0 = *no distress at all* and 100 = *the most distress possible*. Prior to using exposure, the therapist often asks the client to give SUDS ratings for each situation in which the unjustified emotional response occurs. These situations, in turn, might be hierarchically arranged by the client or therapist in ascending order. The therapist and client organize their exposure sessions according to this hierarchy, often starting with items that do not elicit high SUDS ratings (in the case of graduated exposure). When flooding is used, therapy might be started with the item associated with the highest SUDS rating. Flooding and graduated exposure are further distinguished in the following section.

Deciding Between Graduated Exposure and Flooding

The next step involves the therapist deciding whether to conduct graduated exposure or flooding. *Graduated exposure* involves the therapist or client creating an exposure hierarchy that ranges from items that are relatively low in SUDS to items that are the highest in SUDS. For instance, an exposure hierarchy for Maurice, the acrophobic client described earlier, was as follows: watching television scenes of people rock climbing (SUDS = 20), looking out a second-floor window in a secure building with the window closed (SUDS = 45), driving over a high bridge or overpass (SUDS = 65), walking over a high bridge or overpass (SUDS = 85), and standing at a high level in an open multilevel parking garage and looking down (SUDS = 95). After the therapist and client constructed the exposure hierarchy, the client was exposed to items lower on the hierarchy first and then progressively to items higher and higher on the hierarchy. *Flooding*, in contrast, involves exposing the client to the highest items on the exposure hierarchy first, rather than progressing from low-SUDS items to high-SUDS items.

There are a few considerations for a therapist in deciding between graduated exposure and flooding. First, is the client ready to embark on an intense exposure intervention such as flooding? Some clients are simply too afraid to do this and are unlikely to agree to undergo flooding (e.g., Horne & Matson, 1977). It is important for the therapist to determine whether flooding would be acceptable to the client. Some clients, however, will likely react negatively to the suggestion of any type of exposure (whether flooding or graduated), as they are so afraid of encountering feared stimuli. In this case, we have found it useful to reiterate to the client the rationale for exposure and the expectation that distress may be high at first but will eventually decline, help the client entertain the pros and cons of embarking on the exposure intervention, and give the client the clear message that he or she may terminate the exposure if need be.

A second consideration has to do with the efficacy of flooding versus graduated exposure. Generally, the research indicates that flooding is not detrimental or dangerous to clients (Shipley & Boudewyns, 1980) and that it might have better long-term effects than graduated exposure, especially when the flooding is conducted in a massed format (Feigenbaum, 1988). As a result, flooding may be the more desirable option for clients who are willing to participate in the procedure. A third consideration has to do with the length of sessions. For flooding sessions, the therapist may need to schedule longer sessions to allow the client sufficient time to "come down" from highly fearful or anxious states before leaving the therapy session. If lengthy sessions are not possible, then the therapist might consider a graduated approach.

Deciding How to Schedule Exposure Sessions

Treatment manuals for particular clinical problems outline the typical schedules for exposure used in those treatments; however, there are a few general considerations. In particular, the therapist (and client) must decide whether to conduct exposure in a *massed format* or a *spaced format*. Exposure formats range anywhere from 3 to 4 hours per day over 5 to 6 days per week (massed format) to 30 to 120 minutes during once-per-week sessions (spaced format). Some research has suggested superior short-term effects for massed exposure (Foa, Jameson, & Turner, 1980); however, massed and spaced exposures generally have equivalent effects. Therapists who conduct formal exposure interventions might consider scheduling their sessions for longer than the standard 50-minute "hour." This is because some clients find exposure to be overwhelming and have a difficult time cooling down emotionally in time for the session to end. In addition, as discussed later, it is important to allow enough time for the client's emotional arousal to habituate before terminating the exposure.

Guidelines for Conducting Exposure Interventions

Once the client has been oriented to the exposure, and the therapist and client have collaboratively decided on the format, schedule, and type of exposure, the next step is to conduct exposure. In conducting exposure, there are four important procedural points to remember: (a) conduct nonreinforced exposure, (b) prevent emotion-consistent behaviors, (c) continue exposure until the client's emotional response has habituated, and (d) allow the client some control over the exposure procedure.

Conduct Nonreinforced Exposure

Nonreinforced exposure means that the exposure occurs in the absence of feared consequences, or consequences that would justify or warrant the problematic emotion. For instance, people who are afraid of public speaking often fear that they will be humiliated because of their behavior, demeanor, voice, lack of competence, or appearance. In most cases, humiliation is an unlikely outcome, and as a result, fear of public speaking is often an unjustified fear. If, however, the therapist conducted the client's exposure to public speaking, and the audience humiliated the client, then the fear would be justified and reinforced. The connection between public speaking and humiliation would be strengthened, rather than weakened.

There is also an indication that, at least in the case of exposure therapy for PTSD, clients' emotional engagement with trauma-related stimuli is critically important for treatment success (Jaycox et al., 1998). In setting up exposure interventions, therefore, the therapist must ensure that the client's exposure occurs in a situation (or in imagination) in which the feared consequences (i.e., that would reinforce or justify the emotion) do not occur.

Prevent Emotion-Consistent Responses

Response prevention is an intervention that involves preventing behaviors that are consistent with the client's emotional response or that involve his or her escape or avoidance. If a client who is afraid of public speaking was to sign up for a class presentation, for example, but skipped out on the presentation, he or she would never have the experience that public speaking is relatively safe. The fear of public speaking is essentially kept alive. Similarly, if the client started a speech and then fled the room half way through, he or she would also be keeping the fear of public speaking alive.

In both of these cases, the client is likely to experience fear again when he or she next thinks about or engages in public speaking. For exposure to work, the client has to be exposed to the feared or emotionally evocative situation while the fear or other emotional responses extinguish or diminish in intensity. Over time, the situation becomes associated with an increasingly lower level of fear or emotion. Avoidance or escape behaviors, or behaviors that are consistent with the emotional experience (e.g., yelling for an angry person, or hiding for a person who feels ashamed), must therefore be blocked and prevented.

Monitor Subjective Units of Distress (SUDS) Ratings

In conducting exposure, it is important for the therapist to know if the client's distress level is fluctuating in response to exposure to the stimulus. To do this, therapists repeatedly ask clients for their SUDS ratings during exposure. It is important, however, to remember that giving SUDS ratings can be distracting for clients. The therapist must gather SUDS ratings frequently enough to know how the client is doing, but not frequently enough to distract the client from the exposure. There is no solid rule for how many times to do this within a specified period, but some researchers suggest that the therapist take SUDS ratings every 5 to 10 minutes (e.g., Steketee, 1993).

Continue Exposure Until the Client's Emotional Response Has Habituated

One of the most important goals of exposure therapy is to help the client respond to previously feared or emotionally evocative situations with a lower level of emotional intensity. To accomplish this, the therapist must keep the client exposed to the emotionally evocative stimuli (either in vivo or in imagination) until the client's SUDS ratings have dropped. Normally, the general rule is that exposure must not stop until the client's SUDS ratings are approximately 50% lower than they were prior to the initiation of the exposure session. If a client started with a fear rating of 80 out of 100 in the presence of a spider, the therapist would keep the client exposed to the spider at least until the fear ratings are around 40 out of 100. Additionally, this reduction must be sustained for at least 10 minutes. With some clients, this decrease happens very quickly, but for others, it takes a long time. Some clients might also display a decrease in SUDS ratings for a few minutes but then might report sudden elevations. These are among the reasons to schedule longer-than-usual sessions for exposure.

Give the Client Control Over Exposure

Although avoiding or escaping the feared or emotionally evocative stimulus may hinder exposure, it also is important for the therapist to let the client know that he or she may stop the exposure at any time. We have found it helpful to tell clients during the orientation how important it is to remain exposed to the stimulus and not engage in avoidance, distraction, or escape. At the same time, it is important to give the client an "out."

SUMMARY

- Use exposure interventions when the client's emotional reaction is not justified.
- There are many different types of exposure interventions. Use Exhibit 9.2 as a guide in choosing which type of exposure interventions might work best for specific problems.
- Orient the client to the purpose of exposure and provide information on how it works. Be sure to tell the client that exposure may be distressing at first, but that his or her emotional experiences will decline in intensity over repeated exposure trials.
- Assess the breadth and intensity of any emotional reactions that will be targeted in exposure interventions.
- In deciding between flooding and graduated exposure, consider (a) research findings, (b) client preferences or concerns, and (c) the feasibility of long therapy sessions.
- In scheduling exposures, decide between massed and spaced exposure.
- Conduct nonreinforced exposure by ensuring that events do not occur that would justify or reinforce the client's unwanted emotional response.
- Prevent action tendencies that are consistent with the unwanted emotional response (e.g., escape behaviors in the case of fear).

- Monitor the client's level of distress repeatedly throughout the exposure trial.
- Continue exposure until the client's emotional response has habituated.
- Allow the client to terminate the exposure session if needed.

10

ACCEPTANCE- AND MINDFULNESS-BASED INTERVENTIONS

As reflected throughout this book, behavioral and cognitive interventions traditionally have focused on helping clients change aspects of their behavior, thinking, and environments. Starting in the late 1970s, however, treatment developers began to incorporate a variety of acceptance-oriented practices into cognitive behavior therapy (CBT). As a result, many contemporary forms of CBT include interventions that help clients accept various aspects of themselves, their experiences, the world, and other people. Some of these interventions may have previously been considered outside the purview of behavioral theory and therapy, such as helping clients notice and observe their experience of the here and now or accept their thoughts, emotions, and life experiences. Reflecting this movement in behavior therapy and CBT, several contemporary forms of behavior therapy include "*acceptance*" or "*mindfulness*" in their titles (e.g., acceptance and commitment therapy [ACT], Hayes, Strosahl, & Wilson, 1999; mindfulness-based stress reduction, Kabat-Zinn, 1990; and mindfulness-based cognitive therapy, Segal, Williams, & Teasdale, 2002). Steven Hayes, one of the developers of ACT, has suggested that these types of treatments fit within a qualitatively distinct evolutionary period in behavior therapy that he refers to as the "*third generation*" (Hayes, 2004b). Whether or not this is the case, it is clear that acceptance- and mindfulness-based interventions rapidly are becoming key components of contemporary behavior and cognitive behavior therapy.

Within this chapter, we provide an overview of acceptance and mindfulness interventions as they are used in CBT. We address the following topics: background, brief history, and empirical status of acceptance and mindfulness interventions; when to use acceptance and mindfulness interventions; how acceptance and mindfulness interventions work; specific acceptance and mindfulness interventions and how to apply them; and balancing acceptance and change in therapy.

DEFINING ACCEPTANCE AND MINDFULNESS

Mindfulness interventions, on the one hand, might be considered a subset of acceptance interventions. From this perspective, acceptance is a prerequisite for mindfulness. It would be difficult for a client, for instance, to be mindful of his or her sensations of anxiety without accepting that they are present. In this way, then, mindfulness requires a degree of acceptance.

On the other hand, mindfulness involves clients' being aware of and awake to the experience of the present moment and, in many ways, is necessary for acceptance. When viewed from this perspective, acceptance could be considered a subset of mindfulness interventions, in that one aspect of mindfulness involves the client nonjudgmentally accepting or allowing the current experience to unfold. Nevertheless, acceptance and mindfulness go hand-in-hand and are quite distinct from many of the other interventions that we discuss in this volume.

Defining Acceptance

Merriam-Webster's New Collegiate Dictionary (1985, p. 48) defines the term *accept* as follows, "to receive willingly. . .to be able or designed to take or hold (something applied or added). . .to give admittance or approval to . . . to endure without protest or reaction. . .". At its core, in behavior therapy, acceptance simply involves the client willingly allowing a current experience (e.g., a thought, emotion, bodily sensation, or situation) or past experience (e.g., an aversive event such as trauma or loss in life) to be exactly as it is or was. Acceptance may involve the client actively welcoming particular experiences; acknowledging that certain experiences are occurring or have occurred in the past; or allowing him- or herself, other people, particular events, thoughts, emotions, or experiences to be exactly as they are. As these definitions suggest, acceptance in behavior therapy often involves the therapist completing two tasks:

- helping the client stop the struggle to change ("to receive willingly . . .") particular behaviors, experiences, other people, or environments and
- helping the client "allow" these experiences to occur ("to give admittance or approval to . . .") without restricting his or her life in response to them ("to endure without protest or reaction . . .").

Defining Mindfulness

Mindfulness fits under the rubric of acceptance-based strategies because it involves experiencing reality for what it is, right now, in the present. As Hanh (1976) stated, mindfulness essentially involves "keeping one's consciousness alive to the present reality." In many cases, therapists have filtered mindfulness into behavior therapy by incorporating Zen practice, contemplative prayer, and other spiritual traditions that appear to be at odds with the secular, scientific roots of other behavioral interventions. In behavior therapy, however, treatment developers have distilled aspects of these ancient traditions and practices into specific, operationally defined behaviors and behavioral skills for the client (and, in some cases, for the therapist). In this way, mindfulness in behavior therapy is not a system of thought or a spiritual practice but, rather, another set of tools for the client and therapist. In most applications of mindfulness, therapists emphasize that the client should be paying attention, keeping aware and awake to the experience of the present moment, and in many cases, stepping back and observing the experience of the here and now.

The following is a list of some key components of mindfulness, as described by Linehan (1993b):

- *observing* the experience of the present moment by simply noticing current emotional reactions, bodily sensations, thoughts, or other experiences;
- *describing* the experience of the present moment by describing the facts of the situation or experience without using constructs, labels, judgments, or inferences; and
- *participating* in the present experience by throwing oneself into the activity of the moment with abandon and without self-consciousness.

These components are the standard behaviors of mindfulness, but the client (and therapist) engages in these behaviors in a particular way. For instance, mindful behavior involves the individual openly experiencing the present moment without judging the experience (e.g., as "good" or "bad" or "right" or "wrong"). Mindfulness also involves the person paying attention to one thing at a time and responding to the facts of the current experience in an effective manner (Linehan, 1993b). Others (e.g., Kabat-Zinn, 1990) have emphasized the importance of "beginners mind," or approaching each experience as if it is unique, fresh, and new.

Acceptance and Mindfulness Versus Exposure

As we discuss later, acceptance- and mindfulness-based interventions may work through similar mechanisms as does exposure, but acceptance and mindfulness differ in key ways from exposure interventions. Perhaps most notably, exposure interventions work toward changing the individual's negative emotional responses, whereas acceptance and mindfulness largely do not involve changing the individual's emotions, thoughts, or other internal experiences. In contrast, both acceptance- and mindfulness-based interventions normally work to change the individual's relationship with and reactions to experiences, rather than the experiences themselves. Exposure therapy requires mindfulness to the extent that mindfulness involves the individual's paying attention to current experiences. Indeed, if clients do not attend to relevant aspects of aversive situations or their physiological arousal, exposure is unlikely to work. Exposure therapy also requires the individual's acceptance of current emotional pain in the service of getting rid of it, or at least reducing it, in the long term. In contrast, however, among some acceptance-oriented approaches (e.g., ACT; Hayes, Strosahl, et al., 1999), accepting is a process that the therapist and client continuously strive toward, rather than a means to experience less emotional pain or other unwanted experiences.

Acceptance and Mindfulness Versus Change

On the surface, it appears that acceptance and mindfulness interventions are antithetical to change, or that they represent a marked departure from what therapists have been doing with clients in behavior therapy for decades. We suggest, however, that both mindfulness and acceptance strategies involve change. The target of this change, however, is different than that of traditional CBT. Whereas traditional CBT aims to change the content of thinking, the form of various behaviors, or aspects of the environment, acceptance- and mindfulness-oriented approaches help the client change his or her approach to thoughts, feelings, behaviors, and the environment. Likewise, traditional CBT interventions (as with many of the strategies we discuss in this book) involve a degree of acceptance—namely, the client's acceptance that his or her problems exist as they do in the present. If neither the client nor the therapist accept or acknowledge that problems exist (e.g., they both ignored or avoided thinking about the fact that a client struggles with alcohol dependence), it would be impossible for therapy to change these problems. Therefore, both acceptance and mindfulness interventions and standard behavioral and cognitive interventions involve a degree of both acceptance and change.

BACKGROUND

Acceptance has been a part of psychotherapy for many years. From the early days of Freudian psychoanalysis, theorists posed that one key mechanism of therapeutic change was allowing repressed unconscious conflicts into consciousness (Freud, 1936) or, in essence, accepting and inviting these conflicts into the realm of conscious awareness. Similarly, Gestalt therapies (Wolt & Toman, 2005) have emphasized the importance of openness to and awareness of experiences. In addition, humanistic therapies, such as Rogers' (1995) person-centered therapy, have emphasized the therapist's conveying acceptance of the client. In fact, the therapist's conveying acceptance of the client in one form or another is a feature of most forms of psychotherapy.

In the late 1970s and early 1980s, several treatment developers began to incorporate acceptance- and mindfulness-based practices into behaviorally and cognitive behaviorally oriented treatments. Stemming from his own practice in mindfulness and Zen meditative practices as well as his review of research on the effects of mindful practice on chronic pain and stress, Jon Kabat-Zinn (1990) developed a treatment called mindfulness-based stress reduction (MBSR) and founded a research center aimed at examining the efficacy of MBSR for a variety of clinical problems: the Center for Stress Reduction at the University of Massachusetts.

During the late 1970s, Alan Marlatt and colleagues began to incorporate meditation practices stemming partly from transcendental meditation into the treatment of college students with drinking problems (Marlatt & Marques, 1977; Witkiewitz, Marlatt, & Walker, 2005). Early studies indicated that meditative practices had promise in reducing alcohol consumption (Marlatt, Pagano, Rose, & Marques, 1984). Marlatt and colleagues subsequently refined and built these practices into a comprehensive and widely used approach to preventing drug and alcohol relapse called *relapse prevention* (Marlatt & Donovan, 2005; Marlatt & Gordon, 1985). Marlatt and colleagues are currently developing an iteration of relapse prevention that more heavily emphasizes mindfulness techniques (Witkiewitz et al., 2005).

Around this time, other treatment developers began to see the value of using acceptance- and mindfulness-oriented interventions; however, they took different paths to get to this point. In her work on developing an evidence-based treatment for chronically suicidal women, Marsha Linehan (1993a) discovered that a purely change-oriented version of CBT had serious limitations. Essentially, clients felt pushed too hard to change their thoughts and behaviors and often dropped out of or became noncompliant with treatment. As a result, Linehan incorporated mindfulness practices from her extensive experience with Zen practice and Christian contemplative prayer into her treatment. She also integrated a variety of interventions from other treatments (e.g., client-centered and emotion-focused treatments) geared toward conveying acceptance of the client and promoting client self-acceptance and acceptance of the world and other people into her therapy. Eventually, Linehan (1993a) named this treatment *dialectical behavior therapy* (DBT), and it has since been disseminated widely, demonstrating noteworthy efficacy for treating borderline personality disorder (BPD) and related problems (see C. J. Robins & Chapman, 2004, for a review).

In conjunction with his behaviorally oriented research on human language and cognition, Steven Hayes also began to construct a treatment that was founded on acceptance and mindfulness principles. Hayes proposed that certain aspects of human language and cognition trap people into avoiding and escaping unwanted thoughts, emotions, and other internal experiences and that such experiential avoidance may underlie much of what therapists refer to as "*psychopathology*" (Hayes, Strosahl, et al., 1999; Hayes, Wilson, Gifford, Follette, & Strosahl, 1996). As a result, Hayes, Strosahl, et al. (1999) began to develop a therapy aimed at helping clients learn to accept their experiences while moving forward in life in valued directions. This treatment is referred to as *acceptance and commitment therapy*, and it has been applied with promising success to a variety of clinical problems (Hayes, Luoma, Bond, Masuda, & Lillis, 2005).

Several additional behaviorally or cognitive behaviorally oriented treatments use mindfulness- and acceptance-oriented interventions. *Integrative behavioral couple therapy* (IBCT) developed by Neil Jacobson and Andrew Christensen (1996b), involves interventions geared toward helping partners accept each other's differences. In addition, John Teasdale, Zindel Segal and their colleagues have developed an innovative approach to preventing relapse in depression called *mindfulness-based cognitive therapy* (MBCT), which involves mindfulness as a core therapeutic strategy (Teasdale et al., 2000).

Acceptance- and mindfulness-oriented therapies have demonstrated promising empirical findings. Several studies have demonstrated that MBSR is efficacious in treating a variety of psychological difficulties, most notably chronic pain and anxiety disorders (Baer, 2003; Bishop, 2002; Grossman, Niemann, Schmidt, & Walach, 2004; Kabat-Zinn, Lipworth, Burney, & Sellers, 1986; Kabat-Zinn et al., 1992). To date, researchers have conducted over 20 clinical trials that compared ACT-oriented treatments with active alternative treatments (e.g., cognitive therapy, CBT, workplace stress management, systematic desensitization, and nicotine replacement therapy) and a variety of treatment-as-usual control conditions. Compared with control conditions, ACT-oriented approaches have demonstrated similar or superior efficacy on several relevant outcome measures (see Hayes et al., 2005, for a review). In eight well-controlled randomized clinical trials (e.g., Linehan et al., 2006), DBT has demonstrated superior efficacy reducing parasuicidal behavior and other problems characteristic of individuals with BPD to a variety of active control conditions (for a review, see Robins & Chapman, 2004;

for a discussion of mechanisms of change in DBT, see Lynch, Chapman, Rosenthal, Kuo, & Linehan, 2006).

Compared with the above treatments, the research on MBCT and IBCT is relatively preliminary, but there have been some promising findings. Two large randomized clinical trials have compared MBCT plus treatment as it is usually conducted (TAU) with TAU alone for reducing relapse in previously (but not currently) depressed individuals who had taken antidepressant medications but were now not taking them (Ma & Teasdale, 2004; Teasdale et al., 2000). Findings from both studies indicated that individuals in the MBCT + TAU condition had considerably lower rates of relapse of major depression compared with those individuals in the TAU-only condition; however, this finding only applied to patients who reported three or more previous episodes of depression. For patients who reported only two previous episodes, the MBCT + TAU group actually had higher relapse rates than did the TAU group (Ma & Teasdale, 2004; Teasdale et al., 2000). Ma and Teasdale (2004) suggested that MBCT may work best to help people disengage from the types of depressogenic thinking and rumination that trigger depressive episodes among people who have had several depressive episodes. In contrast, depressogenic thinking and rumination may not be primary triggers for depressive relapse among people who have had two or fewer episodes. Among these individuals, life stressors may play a greater role (Ma & Teasdale, 2004).

IBCT is also associated with promising preliminary findings. In a large clinical trial, Christensen, Atkins, and Berns (2004) randomly assigned chronically distressed couples to either IBCT or traditional behavioral couples therapy (TBCT), which is a well-established and efficacious treatment for couple discord (Jacobson & Margolin, 1979) that does not include acceptance-oriented interventions. Researchers found IBCT and TBCT to be similarly effective in reducing marital discord and dissatisfaction. Although TBCT couples improved more rapidly early in treatment, these improvements tended to plateau later in treatment. In contrast, the IBCT couples demonstrated continual and steady improvements throughout treatment (Christensen et al., 2004).

In summary, the data on the efficacy of acceptance- and mindfulness-oriented therapies are promising and suggest that the use of these interventions in clinical practice may be beneficial in some instances. It is important to keep in mind, however, that acceptance and mindfulness frequently constitute components of larger treatments that also involve other core CBT or behavior therapy interventions. This is particularly the case for DBT and relapse prevention but is also an issue for IBCT, MBCT, and other similar approaches. As such, it is difficult for researchers to ascertain whether acceptance and mindfulness are essential ingredients of these treatments.

WHEN DOES A THERAPIST USE ACCEPTANCE- AND MINDFULNESS-BASED INTERVENTIONS?

One challenge for therapists often involves figuring out when to use change-oriented interventions and when to use acceptance interventions. Generally, we recommend that therapists use these interventions flexibly in response to particular client characteristics and problems and in view of the context of the therapy session. We outline three key principles to consider when deciding whether to use acceptance- and mindfulness- or change-oriented methods: (a) justified versus unjustified reactions, (b) changeability versus unchangeability, and (c) effectiveness versus ineffectiveness. We provide examples of particular domains of acceptance that are especially relevant to these principles and offer practical guidance as to when to use acceptance versus change interventions. In addition, we address the issue of the therapist conveying acceptance of the client.

Justified Versus Unjustified Responses

One general consideration for therapists implementing acceptance and mindfulness interventions has to do with whether the client's experiences or responses are justified or unjustified. This consideration comes directly from Linehan's (1993b) work on emotion-regulation skills in DBT. As discussed in chapter 9 of this volume on exposure interventions, a justified response is one that is warranted by the current situation (e.g., realistic fears), whereas an unjustified response is one that is not warranted by the situation. We suggest that when a client's response is justified, the most effective approach is for the therapist to (a) accept the responses as they occur and (b) help the client change or solve the problem or situation that precipitates these responses. In contrast, when the client's response is unjustified, the most effective approach is for the therapist to either (a) help the client modify his or her response and avoid suggesting that it is a valid response or (b) help the client accept the response but find a way not to act in a manner that is consistent with the response. In the following section, we provide examples of how to apply these principles to emotions and thoughts as well as guidelines for deciding how and when the therapist should convey acceptance of the client.

The Example of Emotions and Thoughts

One potentially fruitful domain for acceptance interventions is emotional responding and thinking. Clients often seek therapy with the goal of changing various aspects of their emotional experiences—namely, the desire to experience less intense or less frequent "negative" emotions or more frequent or intense "positive" emotions. Similarly, clients may present with distress regarding particular thought patterns, such as worrying, negative or judgmental thoughts about themselves or others, ruminative thoughts, and

TABLE 10.1
Considerations in Determining Whether to Use Acceptance- Versus
Change-Oriented Methods

		Justified?	
		Yes	No
Changeable?	Yes	Accept the emotion, thought, or event. Solve the problem or change the event.	Change the emotion or thought. The event does not need to be changed, as the emotion or thought is not justified.
	No	Accept the emotion, thought, and/or event.	Accept the emotion, thought, and/or event.

other distressing thinking patterns. The therapist and client must find an effective way to approach distressing or unwanted emotions and thoughts, with one key decision being whether to implement change- or acceptance-oriented interventions.

Therapists' thinking of thoughts and emotions as justified versus unjustified is pragmatic and has heuristic value in helping clinicians decide whether to use acceptance- or change-oriented interventions (see Table 10.1). If a thought or emotion is justified, for example, then it is warranted by the situation. In this instance, the most effective therapeutic strategy would be to not change the thought or emotion; rather, the most effective strategy would be to accept the thought, emotion, situation, or some combination of these as they occur in the present moment. Subsequently, the therapist and client might work to change the situation, so that the thought or emotion no longer occurs. For example, if a 5' 9" client weighed 280 pounds and had the thought, "I'm overweight, and I would like to be thinner," then this may be a justified thought. The most effective strategy could be for the therapist to help the client accept that she currently is overweight and having distressing thoughts about being overweight. Therapy also might involve assisting her in changing aspects of her behavior to help her lose weight or develop and maintain a healthy lifestyle (perhaps a more useful and achievable goal). The client also may have an emotional response to being overweight, such as shame. In this case, the therapist and client might also consider whether shame is a justified response to being overweight and then work to find ways to use acceptance or change strategies.

If the emotion or thought is unjustified, then therapy might involve a different approach. Unjustified emotions or thoughts do not fit the facts of the situation; hence, solving the problem (e.g., modifying the situation) is unlikely to be helpful given that there is no problem to solve (e.g., the client is not overweight in the first place). If the same 5' 9" client weighed 85 pounds and had the same thought, "I'm overweight, and I would like to be thinner," the therapist would not help her lose weight. In this case, therapy might involve finding ways to change the emotional response or thought (e.g., shame and distressing thoughts about being overweight), possibly through opposite action or other emotion-regulation strategies (see chap. 9) or strategies for modifying rules (see chap. 6). Alternatively, the therapist may help the client accept the fact that although the thoughts or emotions occur, the client does not have to act on them.

Conveying Acceptance of the Client

Conveying acceptance has been part of psychotherapy from its inception, is an important component of behavior therapy and CBT, and often greatly facilitates therapy. As discussed later in this chapter, one primary strategy for conveying acceptance involves the therapist validating the client's experiences. There are many circumstances under which the therapist validating the client's experiences can be extremely helpful (detailed later in this chapter), but one general principle to keep in mind is that it is most effective for the therapist to validate client responses and behaviors that are valid *or* justified, and not to validate responses and behaviors that are invalid or unjustified.

"Sandra" was a client who felt angry whenever her therapist left town, despite the fact that her therapist maintained his availability to her by providing information on how to contact him at his hotel. She felt abandoned and was afraid that she was not capable of coping with her difficulties on her own. She also thought that the therapist's leaving town indicated that he did not care about her, and as a result, she felt angry with the therapist. In conveying acceptance of the client, the therapist's task here was to avoid validating reactions that are not warranted or unjustified and to validate those reactions that were warranted or justified. At the most general level, the therapist conveyed acceptance of the client as a person, and acceptance that she was, indeed, having these reactions to him. More specifically, however, the therapist validated the client's fear about not being capable of coping on her own, given that she had a rather extensive history of considerable difficulty when her therapists left town. The therapist did not, however, validate her emotional reaction of anger directed toward him (beyond acknowledging the fact that the client was angry) or the client's thought that he did not care for her, as these reactions were not valid or justified responses. Instead, the therapist helped the client find a way to change these reactions.

Changeability Versus Unchangeability

Another principle is whether the client's reactions, situation, or problems are changeable or unchangeable. Changeable problems are readily modifiable by the client and therapist working in concert to change aspects of the client's responses or life situation. In contrast, unchangeable problems are not readily changeable, or efforts to change them are likely to produce increased difficulties. We therefore suggest that for unchangeable problems or reactions, acceptance strategies may be the most effective interventions. In the next section we offer some examples of how to apply the concept of changeability to life events that are not changeable.

Many clients seek therapy for issues associated with distressing life events, such as past trauma or abuse, the loss of a loved one through death or changes in relationships, the loss of a job, or other losses or traumas. By definition, these events have occurred and cannot be changed or "undone," no matter how horrifying or distressing they were to the client. Given that one cannot change history, it is often effective to use acceptance-oriented strategies when deciding whether to accept the fact that a particular historical event occurred. "Bobby," for example, lost a leg in a motorcycle accident. For more than a year, he refused to acknowledge the injury. He would not look at himself in the mirror and refused to talk about the incident with others. Although he was undergoing physical therapy at the time, his physical therapist recommended that he enter psychological therapy to work through his reactions associated with the loss of his leg. Ultimately, therapy did not go forward, as Bobby was unwilling to talk about matters related to his injury, or about any other area that pertained to him personally. Bobby's lack of acceptance presented a roadblock to treatment, and he clearly would have benefited from learning to accept that he had, in fact, lost his leg.

Acceptance also is a common component of treatments for grief and bereavement (Humphrey & Zimpfer, 1996) and can be helpful for clients who have lost relationships (not just because of death), jobs, or experienced other significant losses in life that are painful or difficult to accept. Although there has not been extensive research on specific acceptance-based strategies for bereavement or other such losses, we anecdotally have found that therapists having clients allow the sadness and grief to wash over them for a reasonable period of time and then letting go of it and doing whatever is effective in the current situation (e.g., working, cooking, walking, and engaging in ongoing purposeful activities) can be a powerful and effective intervention. In addition, acceptance is a useful and common intervention in clinical work with persons who have experienced trauma or abuse (Walser & Hayes, 1998).

However, it is important for the therapist to assess which aspects of the client's responses or situation might actually be changeable. A woman, for instance, cannot change the fact that she was raped in the past. Through treatment interventions, however, she can reduce or learn to regulate her fear of men and sexual encounters in the present. Although a man who has just been fired cannot change the fact that he was fired, he may be able to change the fact that he is unemployed by searching for new jobs, or change the fact that he is depressed about his unemployment by engaging in behavioral activation (chap. 8). As with the example of the man who lost his leg, however, he is unlikely to make these changes without first accepting his current situation as it is.

Effectiveness Versus Ineffectiveness

Another general principle to consider has to do with the effectiveness or ineffectiveness of responses to emotions, thoughts, situations, or historical events. Effective responses bring a client closer to achieving his or her goals or to acting in a manner that he or she values. Ineffective responses keep a client further from his or her goals or valued behaviors. As indicated in the example of experiential avoidance that follows, when the client's change-oriented responses to experiences or life events are ineffective, the therapist may consider helping the client accept these experiences or events.

As discussed in chapter 2 of this volume, one key area for therapists to assess with clients is the degree to which they engage in experiential avoidance behaviors (Hayes et al., 1996) that engender distress, reduce quality of life, or block goal attainment. Many clinically relevant behaviors may be negatively reinforced by avoidance or escape from unwanted or intolerable thoughts, emotions, bodily sensations, or aversive stimuli or situations. All people engage in experiential avoidance to one degree or another, and avoidance or escape behavior can be effective in some contexts. For a woman whose father just passed away, temporarily distracting herself or pushing away thoughts about her father (examples of escape strategies) might help her get through a challenging day at work; however, chronic avoidance of or escape from such thoughts is unlikely to help her come to terms with her father's death. Indeed, clients engage in a variety of ineffective experiential avoidance behaviors, such as deliberate self-harm (Chapman, Gratz, & Brown, 2006), suicidal behavior (Baumeister, 1990), drug and alcohol use (Witkiewitz, Marlatt, & Walker, 2005), and agoraphobic avoidance (Craske & Barlow, 2001), among many others. In these cases, experiential avoidance is ineffective, and one antidote to this problem could involve the therapist helping the client accept thoughts and emotions regarding her father's passing.

If the client engages in ineffective forms of experiential avoidance, then acceptance-oriented strategies may be the most effective choice. Acceptance is the opposite of avoidance and escape and as such, can be an antidote for maladaptive forms of experiential avoidance.

Balancing Acceptance- and Change-Based Methods

Another important therapist consideration is the relative balance between acceptance- and change-oriented interventions with a particular client. Some clients do well in treatments that almost solely involve changing behavior and problem solving (with some validation and empathy from the therapist), but others require a more even balance of acceptance and change. Linehan (1993a) discussed the tension, or *dialectic*, between acceptance and change in treating clients with BPD. At times, an approach that is purely geared toward changing behavior may be invalidating and not palatable to some clients. Similarly, a therapist applying a purely acceptance-based approach may also be invalidating, in that it does not match the seriousness of the client's problems. For instance, a severely suicidal client with BPD is standing at the edge of a metaphorical cliff, ready to jump. If a therapist moves in solely with change-based methods, it is like forcibly pulling the person away from the cliff and may result in a dangerous tug-of-war. A therapist using only acceptance-based methods is like telling the client, "I can see how much pain you're in, standing there at the edge of the cliff. We need to work to help you accept the pain, and then you won't want to jump." In DBT, the therapist's goal is to find the best balance and synthesis of acceptance- and change-based methods. In treating severely suicidal multiproblem clients, therapists using acceptance in conjunction with change can be quite effective (e.g., "I can see how much pain you're in. And, there's no way that we'll be able to find a way out unless you get away from that cliff. Give me your hand, and we'll work on getting you out of this pain").

MECHANISMS OF CHANGE IN ACCEPTANCE AND MINDFULNESS INTERVENTIONS

There is currently no definitive answer to the question of how acceptance- and mindfulness-based methods work, but several recent developments in theory and research on these approaches have suggested some potential mechanisms of change. As with all of the interventions discussed in this book, it is important to keep these mechanisms of change in mind, as they constitute the answer to the question "Why are we using these interventions?"

Mechanisms of Change Associated With Both Acceptance and Mindfulness Interventions

In many cases, mindfulness is considered a subset of acceptance interventions. As such, our discussion first covers those mechanisms of change that may be similar across both acceptance and mindfulness interventions. These potential mechanisms include (a) increasing the client's repertoire of responses to aversive situations and stimuli and (b) classical and operant extinction.

Increasing the Client's Repertoire of Responses to Aversive Experiences and Situations

Both mindfulness and acceptance involve the therapist assisting clients to stop the struggles they have related to attempts at avoiding or escaping particular experiences. When this is accomplished, the door is open that allows the opportunity for the client to learn alternative and more adaptive responses to these experiences. For instance, an agoraphobic client who is encouraged to accept and notice (i.e., be mindful of) the experience of anxiety when he is outside of his home might develop a broader repertoire of behavioral responses to anxiety. Whereas he initially responded to anxiety with a constriction or narrowing of behavior, including leaving home less often or engaging in fewer activities outside the home, this client may learn that several different types of actions are possible in the presence of anxiety. Such actions may include going to the mall, attending movie theaters, or experiencing other life-enhancing activities outside of home. If the client associates these activities with positive or negative reinforcement, then the client's acceptance may help to bring his or her behavior under the control of these naturally occurring environmental contingencies. By helping the client prevent avoidance and encouraging the client to enter into, accept, attend to, and allow previously avoided experiences to happen, acceptance- and mindfulness-based methods provide the opportunity for the client to increase the flexibility and breadth of his or her behavioral responses to these experiences (Hayes, Strosahl, et al., 1999).

Exposure, Response Prevention, Counterconditioning, and Extinction

In some cases, acceptance and mindfulness are much like exposure and response prevention. The client allows aversive situations, thoughts, or emotional responses to happen and mindfully attends to them (exposure), while stopping him- or herself from engaging in avoidance or escape behaviors. As discussed in chapter 9 of this volume, exposure facilitates the classical extinction or habituation of aversive responses to previously avoided situations, stimuli, or internal experiences (e.g., emotions or thoughts). Similarly, acceptance may actually lead to habituation and eventually weaken the link between the conditioned stimulus (CS) and the unconditioned stimulus (UCS), leading to a lower likelihood that the CS will elicit an emotional response. Response prevention helps extinguish problematic avoidance and escape behaviors by preventing the individual from experiencing negative reinforcement for avoidance or escape (Witkiewitz et al., 2005). In addition, as discussed previously and in chapter 9 (this volume) on exposure, acceptance and exposure may help the client learn alternative, more adaptive responses to previously unwanted situations, thoughts, or feelings.

Mechanisms of Change Associated With Mindfulness Interventions

Within this section, we address some mechanisms of change more specific to mindfulness interventions. These mechanisms include (a) increasing contact with a broad array of stimulus properties, (b) positive and negative reinforcement, and (c) neurobiological changes.

Increasing Contact With a Broader Array of Stimulus Properties

Mindfulness specifically involves attention to and participation in the experience of the present moment (Linehan, 1993a). Whereas acceptance more generally involves welcoming, acknowledging, and allowing particular experiences to occur, including both past (e.g., a history of childhood sexual abuse) and present experiences (e.g., emotional responses to men who resemble the previous abuser), mindfulness more specifically focuses on the current experience. Mindfulness involves the behaviors of attending to, observing, participating in, and not judging the experience of the present moment. As such, mindfulness may essentially crack the moment open like an egg, revealing all of the multifaceted stimulus properties of the current situation.

As discussed in the chapter on exposure therapy, people who avoid events that precipitate unwanted emotional responses actually keep the unwanted emotional responses "alive." In essence, avoidance keeps the stimuli aversive by preventing the individual from weakening his or her aversive responses to these stimuli and learning new, less aversive responses. For example, a person who avoids speaking up in meetings out of fear that she will be criticized may never learn to (a) experience less anxiety and frustration in response to criticism when it occurs or (b) notice the helpful aspects of criticism and respond with curiosity, openness, and a willingness to use criticism constructively. An individual's avoidance of criticism prevents his or her exposure to the array of stimulus functions that comprise criticism, even the helpful ones.

Mindfulness directly counters avoidance and actively involves attending to and observing a variety of stimulus functions related to certain experiences, events, people, places or things. For instance, a client who learns to observe and attend to, rather than escape, large, hairy spiders, gains the opportunity to notice previously unknown aspects of spiders. The spider is not only large and hairy but also quite graceful, quick, agile, skillful at jumping and weaving webs, and sometimes colorful and visually appealing. The multifaceted stimulus functions of the spider may begin to emerge when the client mindfully observes the spider. One of the authors of the volume has had a longstanding fear of spiders and has just recently begun to notice how graceful and interesting they are. Similarly, Jacobson and Christensen (1996b) have applied this idea to work with couples, whereby mindfulness-oriented acceptance interventions increase the individual's contact with the multifaceted stimulus functions of his or her partner's behavior, not just the annoying ones (e.g., the "thoughtful and deliberate" way in which a husband trolls through 25 channels with the remote control before deciding which show to watch).

Positive and Negative Reinforcement

Mindfulness practices are in some ways antithetical to the notion underlying relaxation interventions, which imply that clients are somehow better off if they change their current emotional state from "anxious" to "relaxed." Whereas mindfulness practices often induce a sense of calmness or relaxation, other experiences associated with mindfulness may be of greater value in some instances. Witkiewitz et al. (2005), for example, suggested that an individual's state of "metacognitive awareness" (i.e., observing processes of thinking or feeling as they unfold) and relaxation may positively or negatively reinforce behaviors that involve mindfully attending to the present moment without acting on urges to engage in problematic behaviors such as escape, avoidance, or drug use. In this way, mindfulness may set up conditions whereby adaptive behaviors are reinforced and maintained (e.g., mindful attention, inhibition of acting on urges) and problematic behaviors (avoidance, escape, drug use, or other maladaptive experiential avoidance behaviors) are extinguished.

Biological Mechanisms of Change in Mindfulness

Several studies recently have examined the effects of mindfulness on neurobiological factors. For a brief review, please see Witkiewitz et al. (2005). Several studies have indicated that mindfulness-oriented practices influence neurotransmitter levels and brain activity (Infante, Torres-Avisbal, & Pinel, 2001; Kjaer, Bertelsen, & Piccini, 2002), particularly in the dopaminergic system (Kjaer et al., 2002). Additionally, other researchers have found that meditation is related to the activation of neural structures associated with attention (Lazar, Bush, & Gollub, 2000). These findings suggest that changes in neurological functioning may mediate some of the effects of mindfulness-oriented practices.

APPLYING ACCEPTANCE INTERVENTIONS

There are several different types of acceptance-oriented interventions. The key task for the therapist is to apply the most effective acceptance-based strategy in the most efficient manner, given the idiosyncrasies of the individual client and the context of the session. Here we introduce two broad categories of acceptance-based interventions: (a) acceptance strategies for the client and (b) the therapist conveying acceptance of the client. We describe each category in the following sections.

Acceptance Strategies for the Client

Several acceptance strategies involve the therapist helping the client find ways to accept his or her experiences. Although there are many different ways to do this, we highlight some innovative methods that are developing widespread use in contemporary CBT, including (a) letting go of the struggle for control, (b) defusing language and cognition, (c) willingness, (d) radical acceptance, and (e) acceptance in dyadic interactions.

Letting Go of the Struggle for Control

Perhaps the first and foremost acceptance intervention, and the one that normally constitutes the first step in acceptance, involves the client stopping the struggle to change or modify unwanted or unaccepted experiences. It is often difficult for a client to accept something that he or she is simultaneously working to change or eliminate. The act of escape and avoidance is directly contrary to acceptance. In recognition of this, one acceptance strategy simply involves the therapist encouraging the client to stop controlling, avoiding, or escaping certain thoughts, emotions, or events. This, of course, can be a very difficult idea to sell to a client. "Debra," for example, had a horrific history of childhood trauma—a history that the therapist even had difficulty accepting. Debra went to great lengths to avoid any reminders, cues, hints, suggestions, thoughts, emotions, or other factors related to her traumatic experiences. Avoidant acts severely curtailed her life; for example, she declined to go out at night (the traumatic events typically had occurred in the dark), stayed away from her bedroom (sleeping instead on the floor in the living room), and avoided men completely to the extent that she could (she worked with men but avoided talking to them). It is not surprising that Debra was quite dissatisfied with this truncated existence but was very afraid of making any changes. To this client, the notion of acceptance was frightening.

Before Debra was willing to consider accepting her reactions and her history, she wanted to better understand how acceptance would be helpful. Her therapist suggested that her acceptance and letting go of the struggle would ultimately reduce her suffering. Hayes, Strosahl, et al. (1999) have developed a set of strategies for experientially conveying this rationale, called establishing "*creative hopelessness.*" This strategy assists the client in reaching the conclusion that his or her effort to escape or avoid unwanted experiences has actually resulted in increased suffering. Essentially, this method involves asking the client what he or she has done to cope with emotional pain and then inquiring as to how these strategies have worked. Most commonly, avoidance and escape work quite well in the short term but have a host of negative long-term effects. Clients are often willing to entertain the notion of acceptance once they are aware of the drawbacks of avoidance and escape. In addition, another helpful approach involves the therapist noting that letting go of the struggle to avoid or escape unwanted experiences can lead to an increased sense of freedom. In Debra's case, the therapist started by simply having her stop struggling to suppress or avoid thoughts about the trauma. This intervention involved Debra letting the thoughts come and go without doing anything to change them. Eventually, therapy involved asking her to allow fear and anxiety associated with various situations to occur (e.g., talking to men) and asking her to note change in the experience. As treatment progressed, Debra gradually entered into previously avoided situations, despite her anxiety and fear.

Defusing Language and Cognition

In ACT (Hayes, Strosahl, et al., 1999), the underlying theory associated with this approach is grounded in the view that human language and cognition trap people into behaving in ways that increase their suffering, primarily by promoting and maintaining experiential avoidance. Within this framework, clients tend to engage in rule-governed behavior that restricts their contact with environmental contingencies. A socially anxious client, for example, may avoid public speaking in response to a verbal rule (e.g., "If I speak in front of others, they will chastise me") even though she has never had the direct experience of being chastised during public speaking. One strategy used in ACT to reduce the grip of language and cognition on behavior and promote acceptance involves defusing language and cognition. The following are two examples of specific cognitive defusion interventions:

- *Repeating a troublesome word or phrase.* One such strategy involves the therapist having the client repeat a troublesome word or phrase over and over again, quickly, until the meaning of the word disappears and only auditory stimulus properties of the word remain. The idea is that words are simply arbitrary verbal stimuli that have become connected to the events they describe, they are not, however, events themselves (e.g., the word *wrench* is not itself a wrench, but a word that has come to be associated with a particular tool). A client, for example, who evaluates himself as "worthless" might repeat the word *worthless* or the phrase, "*I'm worthless*" until it becomes meaningless to him.
- *Using paradox to enhance acceptance.* Other strategies used in ACT involve highlighting paradoxes in language, such as making the statement, "Don't do what I am telling you to do." In this case, following the rule involves breaking the rule, and breaking the rule involves following the rule. Ultimately, this strategy aims to create a crack in the wall of language that exists between the client and his or her direct experiences.

Willingness and Willfulness

Willingness is another route toward the client's acceptance of him- or herself that therapists use in both ACT and DBT. In ACT, willingness involves the client being willing to experience painful thoughts, emotions, physical sensations, and other such experiences (Hayes, Strosahl, et al., 1999). Similarly, in DBT, willingness involves the client accepting a situation for what it is, no matter how difficult or unpleasant it is, and acting effectively (Linehan, 1993b) in response to it. In DBT, the opposing concept of willfulness involves the client resisting reality and acting as if things that are true are not actually true, or railing against the reality or facts of the matter.

"Alberto" was a client who became enraged every time he had to wait more than 4 or 5 minutes in a supermarket line. He would intently watch the cashier's every move, inwardly scrutinizing and criticizing him or her for taking too long with the roll of coins, for example, or for chatting with the customers. It was not long before he felt his frustration bubbling up within him into rage, at which point he would make a disparaging comment to the cashier or other customers. Alberto was willful about supermarkets, in that he simply would not accept that he was in line and refused to use effective strategies to cope with the situation. Willingness, in contrast, involves the client accepting that he or she is in a supermarket line and doing what works to calm him- or herself, such as trying a different line, engaging in distracting activities by looking at magazines, finding some polite way of getting the line moving more quickly, or other such helpful strategies.

There are many ways for therapists to weave the concept of willingness into therapy. For instance, the therapist might describe the general concept of willingness to the client, have the client rate his or her degree of willingness to experience particular experiences, and then encourage the client to increase willingness. Provided next is an example of a therapist using willingness with a client who struggles with intractable, chronic lower back pain.

> *Therapist:* There is an important difference between pain and suffering. Pain involves distressing emotional reactions to events, or physical pain or discomfort. Suffering occurs when someone attempts to avoid, escape, ignore, dismiss, or otherwise reject pain. Suffering actually leads to more pain. Sometimes, the antidote to suffering is willingness. Willingness involves allowing pain to happen, and doing what works in your life anyway. How willing are you to experience your lower back pain right now, on a scale from 1 to 10? [1 = *not willing at all*; 10 = 100% *willing*]

> *Client:* Well, not very willing. I hate this pain. It never stops. Maybe like 3 out of 10.

> *Therapist:* OK. How about trying this? Say to yourself "I am willing to experience this pain. It is part of my life. I don't like it, and I am willing to have it and still live my life."

Other willingness-enhancing strategies might involve the following:

- Ask the client to imagine what it would be like to allow herself to accept and experience the pain. What would she do if she were willing to experience the pain?
- Ask the client objectify the pain (e.g., imagine the pain is an object, like a set of keys) and imagine bringing the pain with her when she leaves the house.
- Ask the client, "Are you willing to have this pain and still do what you value in life?" Therapists commonly use the latter two strategies in ACT. (Hayes, Strosahl, et al., 1999)

Radical Acceptance

Another acceptance strategy is called *radical acceptance*. As used in DBT (Linehan, 1993a), radical acceptance essentially involves the therapist helping the client completely accept the experience of the moment for what it is, without struggling to change it or willfully resisting it. There are several ways for therapists to perform radical acceptance. Some of these appear in Linehan's (in press) revised DBT skills training manual:

- Ask the client to simply state the unaccepted experience in a neutral voice over and over again.
- Ask the client to allow thoughts about the unaccepted experience to enter his or her mind without resisting, suppressing, or avoiding them.
- Ask the client to write out all the details of the experience he or she does not want to accept.

"Rebecca" is a married woman who had tremendous difficulty accepting the fact that she was attracted to women. She loved her husband and had no desire to leave him, despite her sexual feelings for women. She felt considerable shame about her attraction to women and struggled against it, to no avail. The more she avoided sexual thoughts about women, the more thoughts she had them, and the more she chastised herself for her attraction to women, the more ashamed and distressed she felt. Her therapist instructed her to practice radical acceptance by saying to herself (when she was alone), "I am sexually attracted to women. I may not want to be, but I am" or "I accept that I am sexually attracted to women." Whenever sexual thoughts about women entered Rebecca's mind, her task was simply to let them come and go, without judgment or attempts to suppress or get rid of them. In addition, her therapist encouraged her to write about her attraction to women. Over time, her attraction to women was less and less distressing to her, and she even confided in her husband about her struggle; he fortunately reacted in a supportive and accepting manner.

Acceptance in Dyadic Interactions

Jacobson and Christensen (1996b) developed an acceptance-oriented treatment for couples called IBCT. In contrast with traditional behavioral approaches to couple therapy (e.g., TBCT; Jacobson & Margolin, 1979), which emphasize changing communication and improving behavioral skills, IBCT primarily involves various methods to help partners accept one another. The following are several of the acceptance-oriented interventions used in IBCT:

- *Empathetic joining* is a technique that involves the therapist asking partners to express the softer side of their emotional experiences when communicating emotions or asking for a change in partner behavior. For instance, a woman who is feeling hurt and angry that her husband plays golf every weekend (and spends little time with her) may amplify her expression of being hurt and deemphasize the anger. Instead of stating, "I'm really angry with you for leaving me every weekend to play golf!" she might say, "I feel sad and I really miss you when you go away golfing all weekend." The idea is that if one partner expresses softer emotions it will elicit empathy and acceptance on the part of the partner.

- *Unified detachment* is another acceptance strategy in IBCT. This strategy involves the therapist asking partners to approach a given relationship problem as an "it" that they are both working collaboratively to solve, rather than a problem that is caused by or situated within one of the partners. Essentially, partners externalize the problem and tackle it together. One partner, for example, might say to another, "We have this problem in our relationship, and it involves having difficulty telling each other what we really want. Let's find a way to attack this problem together so we can be happier." This is in stark contrast to an approach that involves situating the problem within one of the partners: "If you weren't so damn invalidating, I'd be a lot more likely to share my feelings with you."

- *Tolerance building through purposely engaging in undesired behavior* is a set of strategies in IBCT that involves the therapist promoting acceptance by helping the client build tolerance for unwanted partner behavior. One way to do this is for therapist to ask the partners to engage in planned instances of the unwanted behavior as a way of setting up a context in which the undesired behavior occurs without any major negative consequences. Both partners know that it is a "game" rather than a "real" instance of the problem behavior, and in response, they interrupt their typical nonaccepting responses. This type of intervention is much like nonreinforced exposure to the problem behavior. Ultimately, the partner's aversive reactions may habituate over time, and he or she may learn alternative, more effective ways to respond to the partner's undesired behavior. For example, "Bill" and "Ted" are partners who have been together for 10 years. Bill has a family history of alcohol problems (his father frequently drank and was physically abusive), and as a result, he does not drink and has difficulty tolerating it when Ted drinks. Ted, however, came from a family without any alcohol problems, and red wine is one of his great pleasures in life. He generally drinks a glass or two of red wine once or twice per week. The more Bill tries to get Ted to stop drinking, the more Ted feels frustrated and "controlled" by Bill. The therapist might have Bill and Ted agree that Ted will purposely drink red wine at various times over the next 2 weeks. Bill's job would be to simply notice the reactions he has when Ted drinks.

- *Tolerance building through increasing self-care* involves the therapist helping partners get some of their needs met outside of the relationship (called *self-care*). Partners may have particular difficulty accepting each other's quirks and imperfections if they seek their entire interpersonal fulfillment from each other. A man who has no other friends to talk to about stressful events in his life may become quite distressed when his spouse spends a lot of time at work or is occasionally emotionally unavailable. If, however, he broadens his social horizons and seeks out emotional intimacy from friends or family, he may be more accepting of his partner when she is not 100% there for him.

Acceptance Strategies for the Therapist: Conveying Acceptance of the Client

Another way to use acceptance in behavior therapy involves the therapist conveying acceptance of the client. Therapists can convey acceptance of the client in many ways, but perhaps the most primary and commonly used strategy consists of validation.

Validation in CBT

Validation essentially involves the therapist confirming the client's experiences as correct, authentic, or true (Linehan, 1993a) and is used to some extent in almost all behavior and nonbehavior therapies. Validation not only is a helpful way for the therapist to convey acceptance but also can model self-acceptance for the client. Linehan (1993a) has operationalized several different ways for a therapist to convey validation or acceptance of the client:

- *Expressing interest* involves validating by expressing interest in the client, both verbally (e.g., responding to what the client has said, remembering and conveying important information about the client) and nonverbally (leaning forward, nodding, smiling, etc.).
- *Accurately reflecting* involves validating by accurately reflecting the client's behaviors, emotions, thoughts, or other experiences (basic reflective listening). For example, the therapist might ask, "So, you were afraid that you might lose your job after that conflict with your boss. Is that right?"

- *Stating the unsaid (or "mindreading")* involves validating by articulating thoughts, emotions, or experiences that the client has not articulated. Consider, for example, a client who typically feels shame after arguments with her partner, but has not said anything about shame. For this client, the therapist might say, "I'm wondering if you were feeling shame after that fight with your partner."
- *Validating in view of learning history, disease, or pathology* involves validating by communicating that a client's response is valid given his or her learning history, medical problems, characteristics (e.g., a client is very emotional), or psychological difficulties (e.g., depression). For example, "I can see why you feel like staying home and doing nothing, given how much it hurts to walk" (e.g., for a client with chronic back pain).
- *Validating in terms of current circumstances or normative reactions* involves communicating that a client's response is normative, reasonable, wise, or exactly what would be expected given the current circumstances. For example, "You know, I'd be angry, too, if someone sideswiped my car and then just drove off without saying anything."

Validation is a core therapeutic skill. It would be difficult for a therapist to establish a working therapeutic relationship and move a client through effective behavioral interventions in the absence of any acceptance and validation. A client seeing a therapist who does not provide acceptance or validation would be akin to getting counseling for emotional difficulties from Mr. Spock (from the original *Star Trek*) or Mr. Data (from *Star Trek: The Next Generation*). Here are some circumstances, however, under which validation may be particularly needed or helpful:

- at the beginning of therapy, as a way to build rapport and a strong therapeutic relationship and to help the client feel understood and cared for;
- when the client is in extreme emotional or physical pain;
- when the client is not making progress with or is distressed by change-oriented interventions;
- when the client simply needs to be "heard" and understood, at least for now;
- when the client actively invalidates him- or herself, and validation from the therapist may model self-validation for the client; and
- when the therapist does not know what else to do, validation is normally a "safe" intervention. The caveat is that the therapist must search for the valid aspects of the client's responses and avoid validating invalid responses.

An important point to remember about validation is that the therapist can both validate and encourage the client to change (Linehan, 1993a). Validation does not preclude change, and in fact, the therapist might validate the client's responses before helping him or her to change them. A client, for example, who has a history of being abandoned by her parents might perceive abandonment whenever someone is not 100% emotionally or physically available. Her reactions are understandable given her history, and the therapist might choose to validate these reactions (e.g., "I can see why you think I'm abandoning you, given your history of being abandoned by other people"). At the same time, it is not effective for the client to continue thinking that everyone is abandoning her; hence, the therapist might help the client change these reactions. A client who has experienced severe sexual trauma might be afraid to be around men. The therapist may understand where this fear is coming from and validate the client's fear but, at the same time, help the client reduce it—at least when it is not justified. The therapist might even validate the agony of a client's sexual urges and the stress of being in prison for someone who has been arrested for sexually assaulting children, but the therapist would also help the client learn how to reduce or cope with the urges and stop assaulting children.

APPLYING MINDFULNESS-BASED STRATEGIES

Therapists use many different types of mindfulness-based strategies in contemporary behavior and cognitive behavior therapies. Within this section, we briefly review the ways in which different therapeutic approaches use mindfulness strategies. Subsequently, we provide a detailed description of one mindfulness strategy that occurs in virtually all forms of mindfulness-oriented treatments: observing.

Examples of Mindfulness Interventions

Several therapeutic approaches incorporate mindfulness and use a variety of different types of mindfulness-oriented interventions. Within these and other treatments, there is a plethora of different mindfulness strategies for the client and the therapist. Following are some examples of how some contemporary therapeutic approaches use mindfulness:

- In *mindfulness-based stress reduction* (Kabat-Zinn, 1990), therapists often use mindfulness as a strategy to help clients cope with chronic pain or stress. This intervention largely involves the client observing and attending to current physical sensations.

- In ACT (Hayes, Strosahl, et al., 1999), mindfulness is a way for therapists to help clients step back from, observe, and notice the separation between themselves and their experiences.
- In DBT (Linehan, 1993a), therapists encourage clients to observe, describe, and participate in the experience of the current moment while encouraging them to maintain a nonjudgmental stance, focus on one thing at a time ("*one-mindfully*"), and act skillfully and effectively ("*effectiveness*"). In addition, therapists are strongly encouraged to be mindful during therapy sessions and interactions with cotherapists.
- In MBCT (Teasdale et al., 2000), therapists use mindfulness to help previously depressed clients prevent relapses by helping them to observe their current experience and disengage from ruminative, depressogenic thinking.
- In mindfulness-based relapse prevention (Witkiewitz et al., 2005), therapists use mindfulness to help clients resist acting on urges to use drugs by having them simply observe these urges and allowing them come and go.

Observing the Current Experience

Observing is a mindfulness skill therapists use in every behavioral treatment that includes mindfulness interventions. It is the simplest mindfulness intervention, but certainly not the easiest. Observing involves noticing the experience of the present, most commonly by noticing physical sensations, such as sights, sounds, smells, tastes, or tactile sensations, or by noticing thoughts. In most treatments, observing involves the client stepping back and watching the experience of the present moment. In addition, clients generally are encouraged to avoid judging the observed experiences as right or wrong or good or bad and to avoid imposing standards on the observed experience (e.g., not saying that this experience "should" or "must" not be happening).

Another important point about observing is that, although many observing exercises may be relaxing for clients, observing (and mindfulness more generally) is not relaxation. Therapists expressly conduct relaxation exercises with the goal of changing the client's current physical or emotional state from tense, anxious, or simply nonrelaxed to a more relaxed, calm state. Observing does not involve the client changing the current experience; it simply involves one noticing it. That said, many clients (and therapists) find that observing exercises give them a sense of calming the mind. This certainly is a great bonus of observing, but by no means is it the "goal" of observing.

Observing is much like a person being a dispassionate member of the audience for a football game. Observing is not an individual being a fan, or a player, but rather a curious yet neutral spectator. The observer's job is not to jump in and change the way the game is played, avoid watching the game through distracting oneself or paying attention to something else, or escape the game by leaving the stadium altogether. Observing is simply noticing and watching the experience of the present moment without judgment. As such, observing (and mindfulness more generally) is a behavioral act of accepting experiences, thoughts, emotions, life in general, and the universe for what it is, right now, in the present moment.

Many different types of interventions incorporate observing. Generally, these interventions involve the therapist having the client practice observing in session or in his or her natural environment. The following are several different commonly used observing exercises:

- *Observing thinking* involves noticing thoughts as they come and go. One can do this by simply noticing the direct experience of thinking, or by imagining that the thoughts are objects that are passing by (e.g., written on placards marching by in a parade, written on leaves floating down a stream, written on clouds passing by overhead in the sky, sitting on a conveyor belt as it moves along in a factory), or categorizing thoughts as they occur (e.g., as a judgment, a description, an evaluation, a reminiscence).
- *Observing breathing* involves either noticing particular aspects of the sensation of breathing (e.g., the feeling as the air comes in the nose and out the mouth; the feeling of the rise and fall of the stomach or chest), or the entire "gestalt" of the breathing experience.
- *Observing physical sensations* is one of the key strategies in mindfulness-based stress reduction. Therapists teach clients the "body scan" technique, which involves starting at one point on the body and bringing the attention systematically to different parts of the body, one at a time. For instance, a client might start by noticing all of the sensations in his or her foot, and then move up to the calves, thighs, buttocks, and so on, attending only to one body part at a time (Kabat-Zinn, 1990). Observing physical sensations can also involve observing sensations related to emotional experiences, such as the tightness in the chest, quick and heavy heartbeat, sweaty or damp palms associated with anxiety, or the clenching of the muscles, warmth in the cheeks, or other experiences associated with anger.
- *Observing urges* involves the therapist helping the client simply notice urges to do particular things as they come and go. As mentioned, Alan Marlatt (Marlatt & Gordon, 1985) developed this strategy as a way to help clients prevent relapse of alcohol

and drug use, called "*urge surfing*." Urge surfing involves one simply watching an urge come and go, as if it is a wave on the ocean, rising slowly, breaking, and then washing over the beach.

- *Observing sights, sounds, smells, tastes, and tactile sensations* also involves one simply noticing the various experiences of the present moment, either through observing sensations in a particular modality (e.g., sounds only, visual experiences only), or by attending to all of the sensations of the current moment. Most often, however, therapists have clients pick a particular sensory modality and attend to all of the sensations that occur within that modality.

Mindfulness-Based Strategies for the Therapist

Mindfulness can apply to both the therapist and the client. It would be difficult to function effectively in a therapy session if the therapist were not paying attention to what is happening in the present moment. Effective therapy requires the therapist paying close attention to what the client is saying, how the client is saying it, the client's nonverbal and verbal emotional cues, the flow of interactions between the therapist and the client, and the influence of the therapist's responses on the client's behavior (and vice versa). As such, conducting therapy requires the skill of attending to what is happening in the present moment. We have found that beginning therapists often demonstrate a remarkable lack of mindfulness, in that they spend much of their time attending to their own thoughts, feelings, and words as well as planning their next move, and very little time paying attention to the client. When this happens, the interventions that the therapist uses often miss the mark, as the therapist has not chosen them in response to what the client is doing or saying. Indeed, within some therapy approaches (e.g., MBCT; Segal et al., 2002), the therapist is urged to practice mindfulness on a regular basis. As noted by others (Linehan, 1993a), we suggest that therapists using behavioral interventions and mindfulness strategies consider bringing the skill of mindfulness into every interaction with their clients, supervisees, and (if applicable) students.

SUMMARY

- Acceptance involves letting go of the struggle to change unwanted experiences, and willingly and openly allowing such experiences to happen.
- Mindfulness involves attending to the experiences of the present moment.

- When deciding whether to implement acceptance- or mindfulness-oriented interventions, consider whether the client's experiences or struggles are justified or unjustified, changeable or unchangeable, and whether the way in which the client responds to his or her distressing thoughts and emotions is effective or ineffective.
- Consider the relative balance of acceptance- versus change-oriented methods in therapy work, as finding the optimal balance for individual clients can enhance the effectiveness of therapy.
- Acceptance-oriented behaviors largely involve letting go of the struggle to escape, avoid, or control various experiences.
- Therapist-oriented acceptance interventions often involve validating the client's experience in a variety of ways.
- One of the most commonly used mindfulness interventions involves simply observing the direct experience of the current moment without judging it.

11

BRINGING THERAPY TO A CLOSE AND AFTERCARE

Successful psychotherapy . . . should be conceived as making progress toward goals, not necessarily reaching these goals in all of their ramifications. (Weiner, 1975, p. 264)

Therapy is about getting unstuck. It is not about finishing life. (Hayes, Strosahl, & Wilson, 1999, p. 258)

As the quotations suggest, therapy is frequently about helping people break free from unhelpful behavior patterns and assisting them in making their behavior more consistent with personal goals and values. When considered from these perspectives, the conclusion of therapy is not so much an end unto itself but rather a big step—or a big leap—squarely onto a path that has the potential to produce a more satisfying and rewarding life.

In this chapter, we discuss several issues related to ending therapy. Topics within this discussion include determining when it is appropriate to end therapy, the process of ending therapy, and planning for aftercare. Within these areas we also touch on several other topics, such as strategies for reducing the likelihood of relapse, methods for facilitating the client's ongoing generalization of learning that has taken place during therapy, and approaches for establishing a client commitment for ongoing change in directions consistent with personal goals and values.

DECIDING WHEN TO END THERAPY

Weiner (1975) suggested that the length of therapy is likely to be influenced by several factors, including the orientation of the therapist, the depth and intensity of therapy, and the severity and complexity of the client's problem areas. Although cognitive behavior therapies (CBTs) are often time limited, the duration of therapy can range between a few sessions to 1 to 2 years, depending on several factors, including the severity and pervasiveness of the client's problem areas. Although many research studies that evaluated CBT therapies have had fixed durations, therapists in applied settings must consider a number of factors with respect to termination, including whether ending therapy on a particular date would be premature, clinically contraindicated, or likely to result in the client's problematic behaviors reemerging (Barnett & Sanzone, 1997).

Therapy, to be effectively brought to a close, involves a collaborative judgment concerning when the therapist and client have reached an appropriate stopping point and have made a decision as to what procedures to use to consolidate, maintain, and possibly extend treatment gains beyond the acute phase of therapy (Weiner, 1975). Prior to initiating therapy, perhaps during the treatment-planning stage (see chap. 4, this volume), therapists should inform clients of the likely length of therapy, while keeping the door open to a reexamination of this issue as therapy progresses. This way, any misunderstanding concerning the cessation of therapy likely will be reduced.

There are no clear and specific criteria for those deciding when to end therapy; rather, there are often several considerations that vary in relevance across clients. Ideally, by the time therapy closes, the client has made some progress toward the fulfillment of his or her therapy goals and will have acquired and practiced skills that can, in turn, benefit the client when challenging situations arise in the future (Weiner, 1975). Skills acquired during therapy may also help the client develop behavior patterns that are consistent with how he or she would ideally like to be, or are more in harmony with his or her personal goals and values.

Sometimes therapists contemplate adjustments in therapy, or perhaps the termination of therapy, if there is an unexpected lack of treatment response or if the client's condition worsens. According to the American Psychological Association's (APA) "Ethical Principles of Psychologists and Code of Conduct" (2002; hereafter referred to as the APA Ethics Code), psychologists should "terminate therapy when it becomes reasonably clear that the client/patient no longer needs the service, is not likely to benefit, or is being harmed by continued service" (p. 1073).

On other occasions, therapy might end prior to it reaching a natural or optimal conclusion. The client, for example, might unexpectedly indicate a desire to end therapy and may do so with little notice and a sense of urgency. At times, such client-initiated terminations might be in response to life events such as a job change or relocation. On other occasions, however, the client may terminate therapy for unforeseen reasons. When unexpected requests for therapy termination arise, a therapist might explore with the client not only the reasons behind the request but also the associated functional context. Examples of questions for exploring this latter area might include the following:

- Is this something that you recently thought about?
- Is there something happening now that has influenced your thinking about this?
- Do you recall when you first thought about ending therapy?
- Is there something happening in therapy that is related to your decision?
- I'm thinking that up until now therapy hasn't been all that helpful to you. Would you agree?
- I thought that therapy was beginning to help in some ways. Would you agree?
- What are the pros versus cons of ending therapy now?
- How do you think ending therapy now will help you more than continuing with it?
- If we continued with therapy and it helped to resolve some of the problems we've been addressing, would something be lost?

When the client's decision to terminate therapy appears to be somewhat impulsive or in response to some unspecified current situation, it is often useful for the therapist to suggest at least one more meeting, perhaps after a 2- to 3-week break. A brief vacation from therapy might allow enough time for any the acute situation that influenced the client's decision to pass, or provide the client with opportunities to consider and weigh the pros versus cons of therapy termination or alternatives to therapy closure. When a meeting eventually occurs, the therapist might further explore the reasons why the client is proposing a discontinuation of therapy and remind the client about any problem areas that remain. If the therapist believes that the potential harms associated with discontinuation outweigh the benefits, he or she can express this to the client in clear terms. The therapist might also consider a phone call to the client during the therapy break to assess the client's welfare, if it is a potential concern.

Although therapists may take some modest efforts to encourage a client to reexamine his or her decision to end therapy prematurely, it is often not productive for a therapist to repeatedly cajole or plead with a client to continue. When premature termination appears unavoidable, the therapist might elect to end therapy as gracefully as possible. If the client has made a clear decision to terminate therapy and the therapist has helped him or her think this decision through, it can be helpful for the therapist to express encouragement and support in relation to this decision. The therapist also might provide referrals to other mental health care professionals as well as an invitation to return to therapy at a later date, if the client desires to. The therapist might also initiate a follow-up telephone contact to inquire whether the client has sought out additional therapy or offer assistance, if the client needs it (Barnett & Sanzone, 1997).

Sometimes therapists need to prematurely end or suspend therapy, or transfer the client's care to another therapist. This might occur for several reasons, such as job relocation or the conclusion of a training rotation, illness, or pregnancy. The APA Ethics Code (2002) holds that "psychologists make reasonable efforts to provide for orderly and appropriate resolution of responsibility for client/patient care" in such instances, "with paramount consideration given to the welfare of the client/patient" (p. 1073). Penn (1990) also provided some guidelines for negotiating such situations when they occur.

THE PROCESS OF ENDING THERAPY

Ending therapy is not so much an event as it is a multistage process. In this section, we describe some of the processes associated with therapy termination and steps that therapists can take at each stage to increase the likelihood that termination will be a productive transition for the client.

Anticipating Problems That May Arise Around Termination

For some clients, the end of therapy can represent the end of an important relationship (Strupp & Binder, 1984). Therapy termination can be a difficult transition for clients who are overly sensitive or reactive to disruptions in interpersonal relations. For other clients, the end of the therapeutic relationship might have some functional similarity to prior separations or losses and can be an occasion for marked anxiety, fear, hopelessness and sadness. Some clients might exhibit varieties of avoidance behavior (e.g., the development of new problems, the reemergence of behaviors targeted in therapy) that are efforts to cope with or delay the experience of loss (Strupp & Binder, 1984).

Whenever possible, a therapist should try to anticipate a client's adverse reactions associated with therapy termination prior to their occurrence, perhaps as early as the case formulation phase when considering potential obstacles for therapy (see chaps. 3 and 4). Periodically throughout therapy, and as tapering or termination approaches, the therapist might discuss with the client the issue of eventual therapy closure. Discussions around these issues could involve informal problem solving, whereby the therapist and client identify possible future problems and promising solutions. For other clients, examining the meaning associated with separation from the therapist or the loss of therapy could be helpful.

Such an exploration might reveal, for example, the presence of several rules related to loss forged from the client's earlier life experiences that have been generalized to the therapeutic context. If such rules are evident and appear to be inaccurate or biased in relation to this circumstance, the therapist could address them like other rules that incorrectly represent actual antecedent–behavior or behavior–consequence relations (see chap. 6). "Mandy," for example, had a history of rejection from caregivers. When she was distressed or upset, her family members would often ignore or dismiss her, or, when she was older, cut off contact with her altogether (e.g., by telling her to stop calling them). As therapy termination approached, she thought that "If he is ending therapy, it must mean that he does not care about me. If I stop seeing him, I will be left with nobody." In this case, the therapist might discuss these issues with Mandy and perhaps use the strategies highlighted in chapter 6 to target rules or thoughts about termination.

Orienting the Client to the Process of Termination

Just as it is important at the outset of therapy for the therapist to orient the client to what to expect from therapy, it is also helpful to provide the client with some clear expectations regarding termination. Such information might include the following:

- how the therapist and client will work together to ensure that the client will maintain treatment gains following termination;
- whether termination will involve ending therapy abruptly or some kind of tapering schedule;
- the availability of posttermination "booster sessions" (discussed later in this chapter);
- how the client might access services in an emergency, if the therapist has been the primary emergency care provider; and
- how the relationship with the therapist will change following termination.

Providing the client with clear information about termination can help dispel any misconceptions and alleviate some of the concerns that a client might have about termination. "Sandy," for example, was nearing the end of therapy (she had 10 sessions left), and the therapist asked her what she thought would happen after therapy had terminated. Sandy stated, "Well, I'm a little worried about it, but I can still call you from time to time for help if I'm suicidal, right?" The therapist realized that this was the time to talk further with Sandy about therapy termination and clarify that she will not be available to provide Sandy with assistance in the event of a crisis. The therapist and Sandy discussed how the relationship will change once therapy has stopped.

Actually, I'm really glad that you brought this up. When we stop seeing each other for therapy, things will change in several ways, and it is important for you to know how this will happen. For instance, when I am no longer your therapist, I will not be available for phone calls or to help you if you are suicidal or in a crisis. I am happy to be available, however, if you need a referral, if you want to meet to discuss the resumption of therapy, or if you are having trouble figuring out how to get help from someone else. Let's talk a little bit about our plan for termination, so we can make sure that you keep doing well after we stop therapy. . .

Tapering the Frequency of Therapy Sessions

In many situations, the therapist and client will not end therapy abruptly but will instead taper the frequency of sessions. Discussions concerning tapering the acute therapy phase would ideally take place several weeks prior to the implementation of this approach (J. S. Beck, 1995), and perhaps even before therapy is actively initiated. Tapering might involve the therapist increasing the spacing between visits (e.g., from weekly to biweekly to monthly sessions), or scheduling "booster sessions" or follow-up sessions, or some combination of these strategies. These contacts might consist of face-to-face meetings, perhaps for reduced periods of time (e.g., 30 minutes). Alternatively, they might be carried out over the telephone.

J. S. Beck (1995) suggested that both the client and the therapist regard the tapering phase as a type of experiment. Questions that could be tested during the tapering phase include, "Have I gotten anything useful out of therapy?" "Will I be able to handle difficult situations when they come up?" and "Will I be able to tolerate not being in therapy?" The maintaining of therapeutic gains during the tapering process might help the client answer many of these questions for him- or herself. In the event that the client has sustained losses in treatment gains or a significant relapse, the therapist might suspend the tapering and reinstitute regular therapy. If this were to occur, it would be important for the therapist to clarify what association, if any, the thinning of therapy had with the loss of therapy gains. When there is evidence that tapering set the occasion for the worsening of the client's behavior, the therapist might consider whether the client is ready to end therapy, or whether the therapist is inadvertently reinforcing the client's harmful behaviors by offering more frequent therapy contingent on their occurrence.

Relatedly, therapists might perform posttreatment assessments of behavior patterns targeted in therapy immediately following the conclusion of therapy and at spaced intervals thereafter (e.g., 1, 3, 6, and 12 months posttreatment). The main purpose for these assessments is for the therapist to evaluate the maintenance of therapy gains over time and detect instances when targeted behavior patterns recur or regain strength that, if evident, might suggest the need for additional therapy or booster sessions.

Consolidating the Experience of Therapy

As therapy begins to wind down, it is often useful for the therapist to help the client reflect on his or her time in treatment. The therapist might give particular consideration to what has been learned and achieved during therapy, and what aspects of therapy the client can apply to future challenges that are likely to arise.

Evaluating the Outcomes of Therapy

Before concluding the active phase of therapy, it is often useful for the therapist and client to reflect on the outcomes of their work together. The therapist and the client might consider areas from the client's problem list (see chap. 3, this volume) in which progress has been made and additional future attention and work might be directed (Ledley, Marx, & Heimberg, 2005). The therapist might also review with the client graphs of data collected during self-monitoring (e.g., the frequency of target behaviors) or scores on questionnaire measures that were administered repeatedly. The therapist and the client might also talk about the client's previously stated short- and long-term goals for therapy and whether these goals were achieved. Discussions might also center on the extent to which the client is living life in a way that is more consistent with his or her values.

In some cases, therapy might not result in the reduction or elimination of, for example, experiences related to depression, periodic emotional turmoil or distress, unrealistic fears, or other such problems. Even if the client still struggles with these problems, therapy might have helped him or her act in a way that is more consistent with important values. If this is the case, it is important to point out that, in some essential ways, the work that the client did in therapy was helpful.

Clients often attribute progress during therapy to the therapy itself, and often deemphasize their own role in bringing about behavior change. When reviewing areas in which significant gains have been made, it is often useful for therapists to highlight what the client did to help facilitate those changes. Doing so helps the client develop a sense of self-efficacy and mastery and perhaps lessens any anxieties about his or her ability to maintain or build on gains experienced in therapy. In reviewing factual information concerning accomplishments in therapy and the effects of behaving in different ways, the therapist also assists the client in developing new rules related to what he or she can do, and the consequences that behavior can produce.

The therapist might also assess, acknowledge, and validate a client's concerns about backsliding once therapy has concluded. When used therapeutically and strategically, the validation of these concerns might include an acknowledgment that the problem behaviors will likely resurface. The framework for such a discussion might be based on the relapse prevention model, which we describe later in this chapter. When therapy gains have been relatively modest for certain problem areas, the therapist might conceptualize these as future goals that the client might continue to work toward after therapy comes to a close.

Considering What Has Been Learned in Therapy

It is often useful for clients to consider what they have learned about themselves during therapy and comment on any skills that they have found to be useful in responding to or coping with difficult challenges. Clients who have undergone behavioral assessment and interventions will also likely be able to demonstrate a functional understanding of their behavior, as evident by the knowledge of the common antecedents of problematic behaviors or the usual effects that their actions have on situations and those around them. Relatedly, many clients will have an understanding that maladaptive avoidance and escape behaviors provide temporary or immediate relief but often pose additional problems (e.g., obstacles to personal goals or valued activities, aversive delayed outcomes).

It can be helpful for the therapist and the client to come up with a list of some of the important points that the client has learned throughout therapy. Such a list, for example, might include reminders of the relationship between certain behaviors and positive or negative consequences. A client who has struggled with depression and previously avoided activities and people might write down, "Avoiding makes me feel better in the short term, but in the long term, avoidance is my worst enemy." A client who has learned about the effects of her aggressive interpersonal behavior on others might write, "When I yell and push people to do things, they might do what I want, but my relationships suffer. It works much better to use my new assertiveness skills."

Troubleshooting Future Problems That Might Arise

As termination approaches, another useful strategy for the therapist is to troubleshoot, or anticipate and proactively solve problems that might occur following termination. In the previous section, we mentioned that clients will have hopefully learned some important facts about their patterns of behavior during the active phase of therapy. For clients who have acquired such knowledge, it is often useful for the therapist to present future scenarios that represent a challenge and have a good chance of occurring. The therapist might first ask the client to describe his or her typical way of responding to a situation and have him or her comment on the typical consequences associated with such responding, both pro and con. The therapist might subsequently ask the client to reflect on what he or she has learned in therapy and what could be done differently should this situation arise that is both effective and relatively free of aversive outcomes. If the client is able to describe potentially effective alternatives, the therapist might ask him or her about potential obstacles that would make it difficult to behave in this new way. If potential obstacles are identified, the therapist might ask the client about how he or she might work through or around these, and so on. The following are some examples of this strategy:

- "So, you've made lots of progress in terms of reducing your depression and increasing your activity level and social contacts. When we are finished working together, what are you going to do if, say, you wake up one morning and feel too lethargic and sad to do anything?"
- "You have really made some changes. You no longer avoid high places, and even when you are in a high place, you feel a minimal amount of fear. We may not have conquered all of the situations in which you are afraid of heights, though. What will you do if you find yourself sitting in a restaurant on the 6th floor of a building and you start to feel panicky?"
- "You haven't cut yourself for 4 months, and you have coped really well with some incredibly stressful situations, like being fired. I know, however, that going through a breakup is one big trigger for shame and thoughts about self-harm. What would you do to cope if your girlfriend were to break up with you after we are finished with therapy?"

Evaluating the Client's Commitment to Building on Therapeutic Gains

As therapy comes to a close, Hayes, Strosahl, et al. (1999) recommended that the therapist evaluate the client's commitment to continue to move forward in the valued direction that has guided the therapy process. A therapist might ask the client, for example, to provide "a rating on a 1 to 10 scale of how committed you are to moving forward with your planned actions" (Hayes, Strosahl, et al., 1999, p. 258). Provided there is a commitment from the client, the therapist might take time to identify what it means to act in accordance with this valued direction by identifying specific actions or behavior patterns that would be consistent with this commitment. Acting in a manner that is consistent with long-term goals or objectives simultaneously decreases the influence of the past and increases the likelihood that the client will eventually realize his or her goals and objectives.

RELAPSE PREVENTION, THERAPY CONTINUATION, AND MAINTENANCE

High rates of relapse and recurrence of problems targeted for treatment are common for many clinical conditions (Marlatt & Donovan, 2005; Mueller et al., 1999; Simons, Rohde, Kennard, & Robins, 2005; Wilson, 1992). Because of this, many contemporary approaches to therapy include treatment components geared toward reducing the likelihood that problematic behavior patterns will reoccur once successfully reduced or eliminated. These therapy components include the incorporation of (a) relapse prevention intervention strategies into the treatment program, (b) a therapy continuation phase geared toward the prevention of relapse following acute therapy, and (c) a maintenance phase directed at lessening the likelihood of the recurrence of problem areas and behaviors targeted in therapy, or (d) some combination of these approaches.

Relapse Prevention

Relapse prevention is a therapeutic approach based on several different intervention strategies that collectively have as their overarching goal a reduction in the likelihood of relapse following the completion of acute therapy. This is broadly accomplished by the therapist helping the client anticipate and cope with future situations in which he or she might be particularly vulnerable. If one can decrease or eliminate vulnerability factors, and if one can transfer skills learned during therapy and apply them to future challenging situations as they arise, the therapeutic benefits one realized during the acute phase of therapy are more likely to endure (Simons et al., 2005). Although originally developed as part of an intervention package for substance abuse problems, response prevention procedures have been introduced into therapies for a wide variety of clinical concerns (Brunswig, Sbraga, & Harris, 2003).

Central components of relapse prevention include discussions with the client concerning distinctions between a lapse and relapse, and the collaborative development of a plan for preventing or responding to a lapse or relapse (Marlatt & Witkiewitz, 2005). This plan might include extending therapy beyond the acute phase by adding continuation or maintenance phases, both of which are described later in this chapter.

Distinguishing Lapse From Relapse

A *lapse* is a recurrence of a previously ceased behavior or behavior pattern targeted for elimination, whereas a *relapse* is a sustained return to pretreatment levels of a problematic behavior pattern (Marlatt & Witkiewitz, 2005). It is not uncommon for a client who has made substantial changes in the frequency or intensity of a behavior to have a lapse following the termination of the acute phase of therapy. These lapses, in turn, can demoralize the client, a sign that "I'm back where I was before" and "No matter what I do, things just never get better." Feelings of guilt, shame, and hopelessness might also accompany a lapse and, as a result, a lapse often sets the occasion for a full-blown relapse.

Research by Marlatt and others (reviewed in Marlatt & Witkiewitz, 2005) suggests that interpretations of lapses, when they occur, often influence whether clients will progress to a full relapse. Individuals, for example, who interpret a lapse (e.g., an episode of excessive drinking for an otherwise abstinent former alcohol abuser) as a result of internal, global, and uncontrollable factors (e.g., a disease, a personality deficit) are more likely to progress to a relapse compared with others who view a lapse as a result of external, unstable, and controllable factors (e.g., an isolated occurrence in response to a set of unique circumstances, a transitional learning experience). Whereas the former type of individual might regard a lapse as an inevitable outcome and feel hopeless (e.g., "I'll never be anything more than an alcoholic"), individuals like the latter type might instead strive to anticipate similar future circumstances that occasioned the lapse and develop alternative coping strategies for responding to such situations should they again arise.

In working with clients around these issues, the therapist conveys the message that lapses can be anticipated and regarded as natural part of the behavior change process. Clients are encouraged to exercise a level of acceptance when a lapse has occurred and view a lapse as an opportunity for new learning and for adjusting coping responses. The therapist might, for example, use a metaphor to illustrate some of these points.

> Therapy and learning new things in life are a lot like taking a road trip. So far, in therapy, you have driven quite a long way. You have stopped using drugs, gotten a job, and are in a relationship with a woman whom you love. You have driven away from 'Hell' and are now many miles closer to where you want to be. It is always possible, though, that you might decide to exit the freeway that you are on. You might see a sign that says, 'heroin—this way.' Let's say that you take the exit and use heroin. This is a lapse, not a relapse. It's a lapse, because you have already made many gains in treatment, and you slipped up and took the wrong exit. You can always get back to the freeway that you were on. You just need to stop using heroin and find a good map. If this happens, see it as a learning opportunity. It's your chance to learn how to get back on track when you fall off track. And we all fall off track from time to time. A relapse is more like deciding to turn around completely and drive all the way back to 'Hell' again.

Anticipating High-Risk Situations

Relapse prevention interventions include the identification of *high-risk situations* or psychosocial factors associated with possible relapse, such as specific triggers historically linked to problematic behavior (e.g., interpersonal situations in which there is pressure to drink, certain places where the problematic behavior often occurred, negative emotions, physiological states such as sleep deprivation), or associated lifestyle factors (e.g., high rates of stressful life events, low rates of participation in pleasurable activities). Psychosocial and lifestyle factors associated with the recurrence of depressed mood, for example, include family environments characterized by high expressed emotion, frequent family conflicts and discord, unpleasant or stressful life events, and cognitive factors such as attributional style and dysfunctional attitudes (Lewinsohn & Gotlib, 1995; Simons et al., 2005).

In the chain of behaviors that eventuate into a full-blown relapse, an *abstinence violation effect* (Curry, Marlatt, & Gordon, 1987) often occurs somewhere near the beginning. Abstinence violation involves a breach of a self-imposed rule or standard that specifies how things should be. When applied to problematic or harmful behaviors that have been eliminated, these rules or standards might involve prohibitions against any future recurrence of the targeted behaviors. The abstinence violation effect occurs when a lapse sets the occasion for a full-blown relapse. In this case, the client who struggles with binge eating might think, "I've had one piece of chocolate cake, so I've blown it. I might as well eat the whole cake, because it doesn't really matter anymore. I'm back to being a binge eater again!" A person who has struggled with depression might stay in bed all day and then think, "Well, I've messed up this behavioral activation stuff, so I might as well just stay in bed for the rest of the week!" Some individuals regard recurrences such as these as serious violations of abstinence and evidence of a return to pretreatment levels of functioning. As a result, a wholesale loss in self-regulation (a relapse) sometimes occurs in response to a mild self-regulation loss (a lapse). In relapse prevention, therapists anticipate possible lapses such as these, reframe them as a natural part of the behavior change process, and view them as an opportunity to test out relapse prevention plans.

Developing New Behavior Patterns

In addition to identifying such high-risk situations, the therapist might also evaluate the range of the client's coping skills and resources that can be used in such situations should they occur. Where indicated, the therapist may use additional skills training (e.g., drink-refusal skills, stress-management techniques, and inactive-coping strategies such as noticing and observing but not otherwise responding to an urge to drink), cognitive interventions (e.g., directed at enhancing self-efficacy, reducing positive outcome expectations associated with substance use) and psychoeducation might aid the client in responding differently in high-risk situations and reduce the likelihood of future relapse (Marlatt & Witkiewitz, 2005).

Establishing Sustained Patterns of Behavior

Once the client has identified, anticipated, and learned coping responses for high-risk situations, the therapist emphasizes relapse prevention steps that the client can take to achieve *lifestyle balance* (Marlatt & Gordon, 1985). A lifestyle is imbalanced, for example, if the ratio of external demands, or "shoulds," outweighs participation in enjoyable activities, or "wants." Imbalance tends to be associated with stress that, in turn, is often an establishing operation for lapses or relapses. Conversely, balance is typically associated with lower levels of stress and hence critically important for the maintenance of treatment gains and for reducing the likelihood of future relapse (Marlatt & Witkiewitz, 2005). Achieving balance might also involve the client avoiding high-risk situations as well as making concerted efforts to engage in valued or pleasurable activities or improving social networks.

The therapist might also develop *relapse road maps* in collaboration with the client (Marlatt & Witkiewitz, 2005). In this case, the client and therapist consider possible outcomes associated with various ways of responding in high-risk situations, and map these out in such a way that they can serve as guides to help clients navigate difficult situations that might arise in the future. Such road maps would show where the client would be headed if he or she were to take certain courses of action. If, for example, the client just suffered a breakup with a partner, and noticed the exit to his drug dealer's house up ahead, the relapse road map might involve the therapist showing the client how taking this exit might propel him down the road to using drugs.

Regular routines, particularly those that promote well-being and are consistent with life goals, can serve a regulating function and, consequently, lessen the likelihood of relapse. The maintenance of routines is often a protective factor against the recurrence of mood disturbance or problematic behavior patterns (e.g., Jacobson, Martell, & Dimidjian, 2001). Similarly, if routines result in beneficial outcomes that are pleasing and rewarding, or maintained by positive (rather than negative) reinforcement, they also keep persons in contact with influences that will maintain their behavior over time.

One strategy for developing and sustaining routines is *social rhythm metric self-monitoring* (Monk, Kupfer, Frank, & Ritenour, 1991). This self-monitoring approach is used to keep track of habits that if disrupted, could result in an increased vulnerability to returning to old and harmful behavior patterns. Areas that might be monitored with this method include eating and sleeping habits, exercise, mood patterns, and engagement in social activities. Goals of such monitoring include (a) reducing certain establishing operations that might occasion problematic behavior (e.g., sleep deprivation, oversleeping, erratic sleeping habits, skipping meals, unhealthy snacking on junk foods), (b) increasing engagement in social activities, and (c) linking mood and behavior variations in adherence to or deviations from routines. If regular routines are disrupted, for example, a client who self-monitors these areas is in an excellent position to evaluate effects that such disruptions cause. Similarly, daily monitoring of these areas might reveal that engagement in regular routines contributes to stability in mood and behavior patterns. Daily social rhythmic monitoring increases the likelihood that a person will spot progressions that signal change, for the worse or better, thus creating opportunities for reestablishing routines before further deterioration occurs.

Address Any Ambivalence Concerning Permanent Behavior Change

Therapists can also facilitate a *sustained motivation for change* by talking with clients about any remaining ambivalence about making permanent changes in their behavior (Marlatt & Witkiewitz, 2005). This might involve a discussion of the pros versus cons of continuing with such change, or on whether continued engagement in the harmful behavior is consistent with or in opposition to the client's values or life objectives. This process also involves taking active steps to reduce the harm associated with problematic behaviors, particularly during a lapse episode.

The Continuation Phase

The *continuation phase*, as described here, refers to an extension of the acute therapy phase with the explicit goal of preventing relapse. An example of the goals and structure of a continuation phase of therapy is nicely illustrated in the Treatment for Adolescents With Depression Study (TADS; Rohde, Feeny, & Robins, 2005; Simons et al., 2005). Stage I of this three-stage treatment approach consists of 12 weeks of acute CBT therapy. Stages II and III are primarily focused on continuation and maintenance, respectively. The 6-week continuation phase is tailored according to the client's needs and progress, with the primary goals being the consolidation, generalization, and integration of skills into the client's daily life. The number of sessions a client receives during this 6-week period, either two or four, is influenced by how well the client responded to the acute phase, with those who demonstrated only a partial response receiving more therapy sessions (nonresponders to the acute phase in this study were referred for an alternative therapy; Simons et al., 2005).

During the continuation phase, therapy work includes distinguishing between lapses and relapses, anticipating challenging situations that could arise, and identifying and using skills or coping strategies for such situations. An additional goal of this stage is to transfer skills from the therapist to the client, or to assist the client in becoming his or her own therapist.

Teaching the Client to Be His or Her Own Therapist

A central component in CBT therapies is skills building. Therapists typically teach clients skills that are relevant for responding to problem areas. They also often teach clients skills for responding to problems more generally. As CBT comes to a close, therapists will often promote the generalization of skills application and usage to future scenarios that might arise. In so doing, therapists teach the clients to be their own therapist (J. S. Beck, 1995; Ledley et al., 2005).

Therapists can use several different strategies to facilitate the use of skills following the conclusion of the active phase of therapy. These might include role playing likely future scenarios (Ledley et al., 2005) or perspective-taking exercises, whereby the client is asked to describe what the therapist might suggest as approaches for responding to a specific challenging situation.

Generalization of Skills Usage

Another feature of the continuation phase is the promotion of *generalization* in skills usage. Behavioral interventions based on operant or Pavlovian learning principles, when effective, do not destroy past learning but instead promote new learning (Bouton, 2000). New learning that occurs during the course of therapy is likely to transfer to situations or contexts most similar to those emphasized in therapy. The likelihood that this new learning, however, will transfer to contexts not explicitly targeted is comparatively small (Bouton, 2000). Lapses and relapse, then, might be particularly common given that new learning is often context dependent, and that harmful behaviors that have persisted for some time have likely occurred and been reinforced in a multitude of contexts not explicitly targeted in therapy.

One way to enhance this transfer of learning is for therapists to provide clients with reminders of therapy and therapeutic strategies that they can bring into new situations that might represent a particular risk for lapse or relapse. Such reminders might include reminder or coping cards that promote the retrieval of skills or strategies learned in therapy, periodic telephone calls from the therapist, or materials that summarize the skills learned over the course of therapy (Bouton, 2000). One may develop coping cards, for example, that list high-risk situations or triggers (e.g., certain environments, emotions, thoughts, cravings) and coping responses that can be used in those situations (J. S. Beck, 1995). These cards can be carried in the client's wallet or purse, and he or she can take them out and review them whenever high-risk situations are anticipated or present. Such cards also act as a reminder of therapy, with these reminders thus available in situations in which therapy may not have explicitly occurred.

A goal of this phase of therapy, then, is to anticipate or allow some exposure to signals associated with problem behavior (e.g., sensibly incorporate occasional desserts into one's eating habits in the case of someone who received therapy for binge eating, watch a sad movie for someone who has made good progress in overcoming a depressive episode). This could consist of controlled exposure to relapse cues (or controlled lapses). In the case of cigarette smoking, for example, relapse-prevention strategies might seek to weaken or extinguish the connection between smoking a few cigarettes and smoking many of them (Bouton, 2000). Alternatively, therapists might encourage clients to avoid certain contexts that represent high-risk situations for lapse or relapse. This approach, known as cue elimination, involves the removal of cues that signal the availability of reward for engagement in harmful behavior. A goal of cue elimination is to remove as many of these cues as possible. In some extreme circumstances, such as might be the case with a client with a long-standing and severe substance abuse problem, cue elimination might involve physically relocating to another city or town in and effort to eliminate the variety of cues that have become associated with drug use and drug intoxication (Cunningham, 1998).

Maintenance Phase

The *maintenance phase*, as discussed here, is primarily directed at reducing the recurrence of problem areas or behaviors targeted in therapy. In TADS (Rohde et al., 2005; Simons et al., 2005), for example, the maintenance phase (i.e., Stage III) consisted of three sessions stretched out in regular intervals over 18 weeks, with the overall focus on relapse prevention. Within this stage, the therapist does not teach the client new skills. Rather, emphasis is placed on the use and generalization of skills the client already learned.

The maintenance phase concept, then, is similar to the idea of booster sessions. In traditional CBT, therapists use booster sessions to facilitate the use of coping skills as difficulties emerge, thus providing opportunities for clients to solidify or consolidate previous learning. Booster sessions are frequently problem focused. The goal of these sessions is to challenge the client to reflect on what he or she has learned in therapy and evaluate if there is anything previously used that can be applied to current circumstances. In this respect, booster sessions constitute a preventive measure for reducing or eliminating the potential for additional harm.

Identifying Signs That Suggest a Return to Therapy

During the preparation for termination, the therapist and client might clarify signs that would indicate that it might be useful to return to therapy, whether it is with the same therapist or with someone else. It can be useful for the therapist and the client to come up with a plan to implement if certain problems return. This plan might include the client contacting the therapist to reenter therapy, even for a relatively brief period, until reemergence of the problem area subsides. The plan might also include accessing other mental health resources, speaking with a primary care physician, or other such activities that would connect the client to the type of help that he or she might need.

Signs that indicate the need for help will vary according to the client and the problem areas addressed during his or her therapy. For any former client, however, the emergence of self-harm urges, suicidal ideation, ideation or urges to harm others, or an inability to care for oneself in several basic life areas are signs to return to therapy or seek immediate help. For other clients, signs might be more specific to the problem areas targeted in treatment. An individual who pursued a course of therapy for alcohol-related problems, for example, should consider returning to therapy if the sustained patterns of binge drinking reemerge. For a client who received therapy for bulimia, the sustained recurrence of binge-eating episodes would be a sign to return to therapy. Similarly, for a client who received CBT interventions for bipolar disorder in addition to pharmacotherapy, sudden changes in sleep patterns, mood, and activity levels suggest the emergence of a manic episode, which should be addressed as soon as possible. When such signs are evident, the therapist might schedule booster sessions, particularly if the client believes that he or she is not responding effectively to emerging problem areas.

SUMMARY

Prior to ending the acute phase of therapy, it is often useful for therapists to do the following:

- Consider the amount of progress made in therapy and whether termination is indicated, while taking into account any agreements reached with the client concerning the duration and course of therapy.
- Explore the client's perceptions as to whether he or she is approaching a suitable stopping point, or a point at which therapy might be tapered before being brought to full closure.
- Anticipate any problems that may arise around therapy tapering or termination, and discuss these periodically with the client, particularly prior to reducing or ending therapy.
- Address any client concerns about backsliding as therapy contacts become less frequent or cease.
- Thoroughly examine any client requests for premature termination, not only the reasons the client offers but also the functional context surrounding the request.
- Review with the client his or her progress toward the realization of therapy-related goals, and highlight the client's role in bringing about behavior change.
- Encourage the client to discuss what he or she has learned during therapy, including specific skills associated with effective responding.
- Anticipate lapses as part of the normal behavior-change process, and collaboratively develop plans with the client for responding to high-risk situations should they arise.
- Work with the client to develop regular routines, lifestyle balance, and environments that will reinforce and maintain therapeutic gains.

- Consider the use of booster sessions periodically in the months following the completion of the acute or continuation phases of therapy as a means for reducing the recurrence of problematic behavior patterns.
- Develop a list with the client of signs that, if present, suggest a need to contact the therapist and explore whether a return to therapy is indicated.

REFERENCES

Achenbach, T. M. (1991). *Manual for the Child Behavior Checklist: 4–18 and 1991 profile.* Burlington: University of Vermont.

Adams, A. N., Adams, M. A., & Miltenberger, R. G. (2003). Habit reversal. In W. O'Donohue, J. E. Fisher, & S. C. Hayes (Eds.), *Cognitive behavior therapy: Applying empirically supported techniques in your practice* (pp. 189–195). Hoboken, NJ: Wiley.

Addis, M. E., & Carpenter, K. M. (2000). The treatment rationale in cognitive behavioral therapy: Psychological mechanisms and clinical guidelines. *Cognitive and Behavioral Practice, 7,* 147–156.

Addis, M. E., & Martell, C. R. (2004). *Overcoming depression one step at a time: The new behavioral activation approach to getting your life back.* Oakland, CA: New Harbinger.

Ader, R., & Cohen, N. (1985). CNS immune system interactions: Conditioning phenomena. *Behavioral and Brain Sciences, 8,* 379–426.

Alarcon, R. D., Foulks, E. F., & Vakkur, M. (1998). *Personality disorders and culture.* New York: Wiley.

Alessi, G. (1992). Models of proximate and ultimate causation. *American Psychologist, 47,* 1359–1370.

American Psychiatric Association. (1980). *Diagnostic and statistical manual of mental disorders* (3rd ed.). Washington, DC: Author.

American Psychiatric Association. (2000). *Diagnostic and statistical manual of mental disorders* (4th ed., text rev.). Washington, DC: Author.

American Psychological Association. (2002). Ethical principles of psychologists and code of conduct. *American Psychologist, 57,* 1060–1073.

Anderson, C. M., Hawkins, R. P., Freeman, K. A., & Scotti, J. R. (2000). Private events: Do they belong in a science of human behavior? *Behavior Analyst, 23,* 1–10.

Ayllon, T. (1963). Intensive treatment of psychotic behaviour by stimulus satiation and food reinforcement. *Behaviour Research and Therapy, 1,* 53–61.

Ayllon, T., & Michael, J. (1959). The psychiatric nurse as a behavioral engineer. *Journal of the Experimental Analysis of Behavior, 2,* 323–334.

Baer, R. A. (2003). Mindfulness training as a clinical intervention: A conceptual and empirical review. *Clinical Psychology: Science and Practice, 10,* 125–143.

Bandura, A. (1977). *Social learning theory.* Englewood Cliffs, NJ: Prentice-Hall.

Bandura, A. (1986). *Social foundations of thought and action: A social cognitive theory.* Englewood Cliffs, NJ: Prentice-Hall.

Barkley, R. A. (1997). Behavioral inhibition, sustained attention, and executive functions: Constructing a unifying theory of ADHD. *Psychological Bulletin, 121,* 65–94.

Barlow, D. H. (1988). *Anxiety and its disorders: The nature and treatment of anxiety and panic* (2nd ed.). New York: Guilford Press.

Barlow, D. H., Allen, L. B., & Choate, M. L. (2004). Toward a unified treatment for emotional disorders. *Behavior Therapy, 35,* 205–230.

Barlow, D. H., & Craske, M. G. (1994). *Mastery of your anxiety and panic—II.* San Antonio, TX: Graywind/Psychological Corporation.

Barlow, D. H., & Craske, M. G. (2000). *Mastery of your anxiety and panic: Client workbook for anxiety and panic (MAP–3).* San Antonio, TX: Graywind/Psychological Corporation.

Barlow, D. H., Esler, J. L., & Vitali, A. E. (1998). Psychosocial treatments for panic disorders, phobias, and generalized anxiety disorder. In P. E. Nathan & J. M. Gorman (Eds.), *A guide to treatments that work* (pp. 288–318). New York: Oxford University Press.

Barnes-Holmes, D., O'Hora, D., Roche, B., Hayes, S. C., Bissett, R. T., & Lyddy, F. (2001). Understanding and verbal regulation. In S. C. Hayes, D. Barnes-Holmes, & B. Roche (Eds.), *Relational frame theory: A post-Skinnerian account of human language and cognition* (pp. 103–117). New York: Kluwer Academic/Plenum Publishers.

Barnett, J. E., & Sanzone, M. (1997). Termination: Ethical and legal issues. *The Clinical Psychologist, 50 (1),* 9–13.

Baron, R. A. (1970). Attraction toward the model and model's competence as determinants of adult imitative behavior. *Journal of Personality and Social Psychology, 14,* 345–351.

Baum, W. M. (1994). *Understanding behaviorism: Science, behavior, culture.* New York: HarperCollins.

Baumeister, R. F. (1990). Suicide as escape from self. *Psychological Review, 97,* 90–113.

Bechdolf, A., Knost, B., & Kuntermann, C. (2004). A randomized comparison of group cognitive-behavioral therapy and group psychoeducation in patients with schizophrenia. *Acta Psychiatrica Scandinavica, 110,* 21–28.

Beck, A. T. (1963). Thinking and depression: Idiosyncratic content and cognitive distortions. *Archives of General Psychiatry, 9,* 324–333.

Beck, A. T. (1976). *Cognitive therapy and the emotional disorders.* New York: International Universities Press.

Beck, A. T., Freeman, A., & Associates. (1990). *Cognitive therapy for personality disorders.* New York: Guilford Press.

Beck, A. T., Rush, A. J., Shaw, B. F., & Emery, G. (1979). *Cognitive therapy of depression.* New York: Guilford Press.

Beck, A. T., Steer, R. A., & Brown, G. K. (1996). *Beck Depression Inventory—II manual.* San Antonio, TX: Psychological Corporation.

Beck, J. S. (1995). *Cognitive therapy: Basics and beyond.* New York: Guilford Press.

Beck, J. S. (2005). *Cognitive therapy for challenging problems: What to do when the basics don't work.* New York: Guilford Press.

Becker, R. E., Heimberg, R. G., & Bellack, A. S. (1987). *Social skills training treatment for depression*. Elmsford, NY: Pergamon Press.

Bednar, R. L., & Peterson, S. R. (1995). *Self-esteem: Paradoxes and innovations in clinical theory and practice* (2nd ed.). Washington, DC: American Psychological Association.

Bellack, A. S., Mueser, K. T., Gingevich, S., & Agrista, J. (1997). *Social skills training for schizophrenia: A step-by-step guide*. New York: Guilford Press.

Bennett-Levy, J. (2003). Mechanisms of change in cognitive therapy: The case of automatic thought records and behavioural experiments. *Behavioural and Cognitive Psychotherapy, 31*, 261–277.

Bennett-Levy, J., Butler, G., Fennell, M., Hackmann, A., Mueller, M., & Westbrook, D. (Eds.). (2004). *Oxford guide to behavioural experiments in cognitive therapy*. Oxford, England: Oxford University Press.

Bennett-Levy, J., Westbrook, D., Fennell, M., Cooper, M., Rouf, K., & Hackmann, A. (2004). Behavioural experiments: Historical and cultural underpinnings. In J. Bennett-Levy, G. Butler, M. Fennell, A. Hackmann, M. Mueller, & D. Westbrook (Eds.), *Oxford guide to behavioural experiments in cognitive therapy* (pp. 1–20). Oxford, England: Oxford University Press.

Benton, M. K., & Schroeder, H. E. (1990). Social skills training with schizophrenics: A meta-analytic evaluation. *Journal of Consulting and Clinical Psychology, 58*, 741–747

Biglan, A. (2003). Selection by consequences: One unifying principle for a transdisciplinary science of prevention. *Prevention Science, 4*, 213–232.

Biglan, A., & Hayes, S. C. (1996). Should the behavioral sciences become more pragmatic? The case for functional contextualism in research on human behavior. *Applied and Preventive Psychology, 5*, 47–57.

Bijou, S. W., & Baer, D. M. (1966). Operant methods in child behavior and development. In W. K. Honig (Ed.), *Operant behavior: Areas of research and application* (pp. 718–789). New York: Appleton-Century-Crofts.

Bishop, S. R. (2002). What do we really know about mindfulness-based stress reduction? *Psychosomatic Medicine, 64*, 71–83.

Borkovec, T. D. (1994). The nature, functions, and origins of worry. In G. Davey & F. Tallis (Eds.), *Worrying: Perspectives on theory, assessment, and treatment* (pp. 5–33). New York: Wiley.

Borkovec, T. D., Weerts, T. C., & Bernstein, D. A. (1977). Assessment of anxiety. In A. R. Ciminero, K. S. Calhoun, & H. E. Adams (Eds.), *Handbook of behavioral assessment* (pp. 367–428). New York: Wiley.

Bouton, M. E. (2000). A learning theory perspective on lapse, relapse, and the maintenance of behavior change. *Health Psychology, 19*(Suppl.), 57–63.

Bouton, M. E. (2004). Context and behavioral processes in extinction. *Learning & Memory, 11*, 485–494.

Bowers, A. H. (2003). Satiation therapy. In W. O'Donohue, J. E. Fisher, & S. C. Hayes (Eds.), *Cognitive behavior therapy: Applying empirically supported techniques in your practice* (pp. 349–353). Hoboken, NJ: Wiley.

Boyce, T. E., & Roman, H. R. (2003). Contingency management interventions. In W. O'Donohue, J. E. Fisher, & S. C. Hayes (Eds.), *Cognitive behavior therapy: Applying empirically supported techniques in your practice* (pp. 109–113). Hoboken, NJ: Wiley.

Brondolo, E., DiGiuseppe, R., & Tafrate, R. C. (1997). Exposure-based treatment for anger problems: Focus on the feeling. *Cognitive and Behavioral Practice, 4*, 75–98.

Brown, T. A., O'Leary, T. A., & Barlow, D. H. (2001). Generalized anxiety disorder. In D. H. Barlow (Ed.), *Clinical handbook of psychological disorders* (3rd ed., pp. 154–208). New York: Guilford Press.

Brummett, B. H., Babyak, M. A., Siegler, I. C., Vitaliano, P. P., Ballard, E. L., Gwyther, L. P., et al. (2006). Associations among perceptions of social support, negative affect, and quality of sleep in caregivers and noncaregivers. *Health Psychology, 25*, 220–225.

Brunswig, K. A., Sbraga, T. P., & Harris, C. D. (2003). Relapse prevention. In W. O'Donohue, J. E. Fisher, & S. C. Hayes (Eds.), *Cognitive behavior therapy: Applying empirically supported techniques in your practice* (pp. 321–329). Hoboken, NJ: Wiley.

Bryant, M. J., Simons, A. D., & Thase, M. E. (1999). Therapist skill and patient variables in homework compliance: Controlling an uncontrolled variable in cognitive therapy outcome research. *Cognitive Therapy and Research, 23*, 381–399.

Burke, B. L., Arkowitz, H., & Menchola, M. (2003). The efficacy of motivational interviewing: A meta-analysis of controlled clinical trials. *Journal of Consulting and Clinical Psychology, 71*, 843–861.

Burns, D. D. (1980). *Feeling good: The new mood therapy*. New York: Signet.

Burns, D. D., & Spangler, D. (2000). Does psychotherapy homework lead to changes in depression in cognitive behavioral therapy? Or does clinical improvement lead to homework compliance? *Journal of Consulting and Clinical Psychology, 68*, 46–46.

Butzlaff, R. L., & Hooley, J. M. (1998). Expressed emotion and psychiatric relapse: A meta-analysis. *Archives of General Psychiatry, 55*, 547–552.

Catania, A. C. (1984). *Learning* (2nd ed.). Englewood Cliffs, NJ: Prentice-Hall.

Catania, A. C. (1994). The natural and artificial selection of verbal behavior. In S. C. Hayes, L. J. Hayes, M. Sato, & K. Ono (Eds.), *Behavioral analysis of language and cognition: The fourth international institute on verbal relations* (pp. 31–49). Reno, NV: Context Press.

Chambless, D. L. Baker, M. J., Baucom, D. H., Beutler, L. E., Calhoun, K. S., Crits-Christoph, P., et al. (1998). Update on empirically validated treatments II. *The Clinical Psychologist, 51*, 3–18.

Chambless, D. L., Sanderson, W. C., Shoham, V., Bennett Johnson, S., Pope, K. S., Crits-Cristoph, P., et al. (1996). An update on empirically validated therapies. *The Clinical Psychologist, 49*, 5–18.

Chapman, A. L., Gratz, K. L., & Brown, M. (2006). Solving the puzzle of deliberate self-harm: The experiential avoidance model. *Behaviour Research and Therapy*, 44, 371–394.

Chiles, J. A., & Strosahl, K. D. (1995). *The suicidal patient: Principles of assessment, treatment, and case management.* Washington, DC: American Psychiatric Press.

Christensen, A., Atkins, D. C., & Berns, S. (2004). Traditional versus integrative behavioral couple therapy for significantly and chronically distressed married couples. *Journal of Consulting and Clinical Psychology*, 72, 176–191.

Ciminero, A. R., Calhoun, K. S., & Adams, H. E. (Eds.). (1977). *Handbook of behavioral assessment.* New York: Wiley.

Ciminero, A. R., Calhoun, K. S., & Adams, H. E. (Eds.). (1986). *Handbook of behavioral assessment* (2nd ed). New York: Wiley.

Cohen, S., Mermelstein, R., Kamarck, T., & Hoberman, H. (1985). Measuring the functional components of social support. In I. G. Sarason & B. R. Sarason (Eds.), *Social support: Theory, research and application* (pp. 73–94). Newbury Park, CA: Sage.

Cohen, S., & Wills, T. A. (1985). Stress, social support, and the buffering hypothesis. *Psychological Bulletin*, 98, 310–357.

Conklin, C. A., & Tiffany, S. T. (2002). Applying extinction research and theory to cue-exposure addiction treatments. *Addiction*, 97, 155–167.

Conners, C. K. (1997). *Conners' Rating Scales—Revised: Technical manual.* New York: Multi-Health Systems.

Cooke, G. (1968). Evaluation of the efficacy of the components of reciprocal inhibition psychotherapy. *Journal of Abnormal Psychology*, 73, 464–467.

Coyne, J. C. (1976). Toward an interactional description of depression. *Psychiatry*, 39, 28–40.

Craske, M. G., & Barlow, D. H. (2001). Panic disorder and agoraphobia. In D. H. Barlow (Ed.), *Clinical handbook of psychological disorders* (3rd ed., pp. 1–59). New York: Guilford Press.

Cuijpers, P., van Straten, A., & Warmerdam, L. (2007). Behavioral activation treatments of depression: A meta-analysis. *Clinical Psychology Review*, 27, 318–326.

Cunningham, C. L. (1998). Drug conditioning and drug-seeking behavior. In W. O'Donohue (Ed.), *Learning and behavior therapy* (pp. 518–544). Boston: Allyn & Bacon.

Curry, S., Marlatt, G. A., & Gordon, J. R. (1987). Abstinence violation effect: Validation of an attributional construct with smoking cessation. *Journal of Consulting and Clinical Psychology*, 55, 145–149.

David, D., & Szentagotai, A. (2006). Cognitions in cognitive-behavioral psychotherapies: Towards an integrative model. *Clinical Psychology Review*, 26, 284–298.

Davis, M., Eshelman, E. R., & McKay, M. (2000). *The relaxation and stress reduction workbook* (5th ed.). Oakland, CA: New Harbinger.

Davis, T. E., III, & Ollendick, T. H. (2005). Empirically supported treatments for specific phobia in children: Do efficacious treatments address the components of a phobic response? *Clinical Psychology: Research and Practice, 12,* 144–160.

Davison, G. C. (1968). Systematic-desensitization as a counter-conditioning process. *Journal of Abnormal Psychology, 73,* 91–99.

Derogatis, L. R. (1992). *Brief Symptom Inventory (BSI).* Minneapolis, MN: National Computer Systems.

Dimeff, L. A., Rizvi, S. L., Brown, M. Z., & Linehan, M. M. (2000). Dialectical behavior therapy for substance abuse: A pilot application to methamphetamine-dependent women with borderline personality disorder. *Cognitive and Behavioral Practice, 7,* 457–468.

Dimidjian, S., Hollon, S. D., Dobson, K. S., Schmaling, K. B., Kohlenberg, R. J., Addis, M. E., et al. (2006). Randomized trial of behavioral activation, cognitive therapy, and antidepressant medication in the acute treatment of adults with major depression. *Journal of Consulting and Clinical Psychology, 74,* 658–670.

Dobson, K. S. (Ed.). (2001). *Handbook of cognitive-behavioral therapies* (2nd ed.). New York: Guilford Press.

Dobson, K. S., & Dozois, D. J. A. (2001). Historical and philosophical bases of the cognitive behavioral therapies. In K. S. Dobson (Ed.), *Handbook of cognitive-behavioral therapies* (2nd ed., pp. 3–39). New York: Guilford Press.

Dobson, K. S., & Khatri, N. (2000). Cognitive therapy: Looking backward, looking forward. *Journal of Clinical Psychology, 56,* 907–923.

Dougher, M. J., & Hayes, S. C. (2000). Clinical behavior analysis. In M. J. Dougher (Ed.), *Clinical behavior analysis* (pp. 11–25). Reno, NV: Context Press.

Dow, M. G. (1994). Social inadequacy and social skill. In L. W. Craighead, W. E. Craighead, A. E. Kazdin, & M. J. Mahoney (Eds.), *Cognitive and behavioral interventions: An empirical approach to mental health problems* (pp. 123–140). Boston: Allyn & Bacon.

D'Zurilla, T. J., & Nezu, A. M. (2001). Problem solving therapies. In K. S. Dobson (Ed.), *Handbook of cognitive-behavioral therapies* (2nd ed., pp. 211–245). New York: Guilford Press.

Earls, C. M., & Castonguay, L. G. (1989). The evaluation of olfactory aversion for a bisexual pedophile with a single-case multiple baseline design. *Behavior Therapy, 20,* 137–146.

Eells, T. D. (1997). Psychotherapy case formulation: History and current status. In T. D. Eells (Ed.), *Handbook of psychotherapy case formulation* (pp. 1–25). New York: Guilford Press.

Eifert, G. H., Schulte, D., Zvolensky, M. J., Lejuez, C. W., & Lau, A. W. (1997). Manualized behavior therapy: Merits and challenges. *Behavior Therapy, 28,* 499–509.

Ellis, A. (1957). Rational psychotherapy and individual psychology. *Journal of Individual Differences, 13,* 38–44.

Ellis, A. (1962). *Reason and emotion in psychotherapy.* New York: Lyle Stuart.

Endicott, J., & Spitzer, R. L. (1978). A diagnostic interview: The Schedule for Affective Disorders and Schizophrenia. *Archives of General Psychiatry, 35*, 837–844.

Etkin, A., Pittinger, C., Polan, J., & Kandel, E. R. (2005). Toward a neurobiology of psychotherapy: Basic science and clinical applications. *Journal of Neuropsychiatry and Clinical Neurosciences, 17*, 145–158.

Eysenck, H. J. (1959). Learning theory and behaviour therapy. *Journal of Mental Science, 105*, 61–75.

Eysenck, H. J. (Ed.). (1960). *Behavior therapy and the neuroses.* New York: Pergamon Press.

Eysenck, H. J. (1983). A biometrical–genetic analysis of impulsive and sensation seeking behavior. In M. Zuckerman (Ed.), *Biological bases of sensation seeking, impulsivity, and anxiety* (pp. 1–27). Hillsdale, NJ: Erlbaum.

Farmer, R. F. (2000). Issues in the assessment and conceptualization of personality disorders. *Clinical Psychology Review, 20*, 823–851.

Farmer, R. F. (2005). Temperament, reward and punishment sensitivity, and clinical disorders: Implications for behavioral case formulation and therapy. *International Journal of Behavioral Consultation and Therapy, 1*, 56–76.

Farmer, R. F., & Chapman, A. L. (2002). Evaluation of *DSM–IV* personality disorder criteria as assessed by the Structured Clinical Interview for *DSM–IV* Personality Disorders. *Comprehensive Psychiatry, 43*, 285–300.

Farmer, R. F., & Latner, J. L. (2007). Eating disorders. In P. Sturmey (Ed.), *Functional analysis in clinical treatment* (pp. 379–402). Boston: Academic Press.

Farmer, R. F., Nash, H. M., & Dance, D. (2004). Mood patterns and variations associated with personality disorder pathology. *Comprehensive Psychiatry, 45*, 289–303.

Farmer, R. F., & Nelson-Gray, R. O. (1995). Anxiety, impulsivity, and the anxious-fearful and erratic-dramatic personality disorders. *Journal of Research in Personality, 29*, 189–207.

Farmer, R. F., & Nelson-Gray, R. O. (2005). *Personality-guided behavior therapy.* Washington, DC: American Psychological Association.

Farmer, R. F., & Rucklidge, J. J. (2006). An evaluation of the response modulation hypothesis in relation to attention-deficit/hyperactivity disorder. *Journal of Abnormal Child Psychology, 34*, 545–557.

Feigenbaum, W. (1988). Long-term efficacy of ungraded versus graded massed exposure in agoraphobics. In I. Hand & H. Wittchen (Eds.), *Panic and phobias: Treatments and variables affecting course and outcome* (pp. 149–158). Berlin, Germany: Springer-Verlag.

Fenigstein, A. (1996). Paranoia. In C. G. Costello (Ed.), *Personality characteristics of the personality disordered* (pp. 242–275). New York: Wiley.

Ferguson, K. E. (2003). Shaping. In W. O'Donohue, J. E. Fisher, & S. C. Hayes (Eds.), *Cognitive behavior therapy: Applying empirically supported techniques in your practice* (pp. 374–383). Hoboken, NJ: Wiley.

Ferster, C. B. (1973). A functional analysis of depression. *American Psychologist, 28,* 857–870.

Feske, U., & Chambless, D. L. (1995). Cognitive behavioral versus exposure only treatments for social phobia: A meta-analysis. *Behavior Therapy, 26,* 695–720.

Fiester A. R., & Rudestam, K. E. (1975). A multivariate analysis of the early dropout process. *Journal of Consulting and Clinical Psychology, 43,* 528–535.

First, M. B., Gibbon, M., Spitzer, R. L., Williams, J. B. W., & Benjamin, L. S. (1997a). *User's guide for the Structured Clinical Interview for DSM–IV Axis II Personality Disorders (SCID–II).* Washington, DC: American Psychiatric Press.

First, M. B., Spitzer, R. L., Gibbon, M., & Williams, J. B. W. (1997b). *Structured Clinical Interview for DSM–IV Axis I Disorders (SCID–I), Clinician Version.* Arlington, VA: American Psychiatric Press.

Foa, E. B., Dancu, C., Hembree, E., Jaycox, L., Meadows, E. A., & Street, G. P. (1999). A comparison of exposure therapy, stress inoculation training, and their combination for reducing posttraumatic stress disorder in female assault victims. *Journal of Consulting and Clinical Psychology, 67,* 194–200.

Foa, E. B., Hembree, E. A., Cahill, S. P., Rauch, S. A. M., Riggs, D. S., Feeny, N. C., et al. (2005). Randomized trial of prolonged exposure for posttraumatic stress disorder with and without cognitive restructuring: Outcome at academic and community clinics. *Journal of Consulting and Clinical Psychology, 73,* 953–964.

Foa, E. B., Jameson, J. S., & Turner, R. M. (1980). Massed vs. spaced exposure sessions in the treatment of agoraphobia. *Behaviour Research and Therapy, 18,* 333–338.

Foa, E. B., & Jaycox, L. (1999). Cognitive-behavioral theory and treatment of posttraumatic stress disorder. In D. Spiegel (Ed.), *Efficacy and cost effectiveness of psychotherapy* (pp. 23–61). Washington, DC: American Psychiatric Press.

Foa, E. B., Keene, T. M., & Friedman, M. J. (Eds.). (2004). *Effective treatments for PTSD: Practice guidelines from the international society for traumatic stress studies.* New York: Guilford Press.

Foa, E. B. & Kozak, M. J. (1986). Emotional processing of fear: Exposure to corrective information. *Psychological Bulletin, 99,* 20–35.

Foa, E. B., Riggs, D. S., Dancu, C. V., & Rothbaum, B. O. (1993). Reliability and validity of a brief instrument for assessing post-traumatic stress disorder. *Journal of Traumatic Stress, 6,* 459–474.

Foa, E. B., & Rothbaum, B. O. (1998). *Treating the trauma of rape: Cognitive-behavior therapy for PTSD.* New York: Guilford Press.

Foa, E. B., Rothbaum, B. O., Riggs, D. S., & Murdock, T. B. (1991). Treatment of posttraumatic stress disorder in rape victims: A comparison between cognitive-behavioral procedures and counseling. *Journal of Consulting and Clinical Psychology, 59,* 715–725.

Follette, W. C., & Callaghan, G. M. (1995). Do as I do, not as I say: A behavior-analytic approach to supervision. *Professional Psychology: Research and Practice, 26,* 413–421.

Follette, W. C., & Hayes, S. C. (2000). Contemporary behavior therapy. In C. R. Snyder & R. E. Ingram (Eds.), *Handbook of psychological change: Psychotherapy process and practices for the 21st century* (pp. 381–408). New York: Wiley.

Follette, W. C., Naugle, A. E., Linnerooth, P. J. N. (2000). Functional alternatives to traditional assessment and diagnosis. In M. J. Dougher (Ed.), *Clinical behavior analysis* (pp. 99–125). Reno, NV: Context Press.

Forsyth, J. P., & Eifert, G. H. (1998). Phobic anxiety and panic: An integrative behavioral account of their origin and treatment. In J. J. Plaud & G. H. Eifert (Eds.), *From behavior theory to behavior therapy* (pp. 38–67). Boston: Allyn & Bacon.

Fowles, D. C. (2001). Biological variables in psychopathology: A psychobiological perspective. In P. B. Sutker & H. E. Adams (Eds.), *Comprehensive handbook of psychopathology* (3rd ed., pp. 85–104). New York: Kluwer Academic/Plenum Publishers.

Franklin, M. E., & Foa, E. B. (1998). Cognitive-behavioral treatments for obsessive-compulsive disorder. In P. E. Nathan & J. M. Gorman (Eds.), *A guide to treatments that work* (pp. 339–357). New York: Oxford University Press.

Fresco, D. M., Mennin, D. S., Heimberg, R. G., & Turk, C. L. (2003). Using the Penn State Worry Questionnaire to identify individuals with generalized anxiety disorder: A receiver operating characteristic analysis. *Journal of Behavior Therapy and Experimental Psychiatry, 34,* 283–291.

Freud, S. (1936). *The ego and mechanisms of defense.* New York: International Universities Press.

Friman, P. C., & Finney, J. W. (2003). Time-out (and time-in). In W. O'Donohue, J. E. Fisher, & S. C. Hayes (Eds.), *Cognitive behavior therapy: Applying empirically supported techniques in your practice* (pp. 429–435). Hoboken, NJ: Wiley.

Froyd, J. E., Lambert, M. J., & Froyd, J. D. (1996). A review of practices of psychotherapy outcome measurement. *Journal of Mental Health, 5,* 11–15.

Garner, D. M. (1997). Psychoeducational principles in treatment. In D. M. Garner & P. E. Garfinkel (Eds.), *Handbook of treatment for eating disorders* (2nd ed., pp. 145–177). New York: Guilford Press.

Ghezzi, P. M., Wilson, G. R., Tarbox, R. S. F., & MacAleese, K. R. (2003). Token economy. In W. O'Donohue, J. E. Fisher, & S. C. Hayes (Eds.), *Cognitive behavior therapy: Applying empirically supported techniques in your practice* (pp. 436–441). Hoboken, NJ: Wiley.

Goldfried, M. R., & Davison, G. C. (1976). *Clinical behavior therapy.* New York: Holt, Rinehart & Winston.

Goldfried, M. R., & Kent, R. N. (1972). Traditional versus behavioral assessment: A comparison of methodological and theoretical assumptions. *Psychological Bulletin, 77,* 409–420.

Goldfried, M. R., & Sprafkin, J. N. (1976). Behavioral personality assessment. In J. T. Spence, R. C., Carson, & J. W. Thibaut (Eds.), *Behavioral approaches to therapy* (pp. 295–321). Morristown, NJ: General Learning Press.

Goldiamond, I. (1974). Toward a constructional approach to social problems: Ethical and constitutional issues raised by applied behavioral analysis. *Behaviorism*, 2, 1–85.

Gortner, E., Gollan, J., Dobson, K. S., & Jacobson, N. S. (1997). Cognitive-behavioral treatment of depression: Relapse prevention. *Journal of Consulting and Clinical Psychology*, 66, 377–384.

Gottlieb, G. (1998). Normally occurring environmental and behavioral influences on gene activity: From central dogma to probabilistic epigenesis. *Psychological Review*, 105, 792–802.

Greenberger, D., & Padesky, C. A. (1995). *Mind over mood: Change how you feel by changing the way you think.* New York: Guilford Press.

Gross, J. J. (1998). The emerging field of emotion regulation: An integrative review. *Review of General Psychology*, 2, 271–299.

Grossman, P. L., Niemann, L., Schmidt, S., & Walach, H. (2004). Mindfulness-based stress reduction and health benefits: A meta-analysis. *Journal of Psychosomatic Research*, 57, 35–43.

Hanh, T. N. (1976). *The miracle of mindfulness: An introduction to the practice of meditation.* Boston: Beacon Press.

Hannan, S. E., & Tolin, D. F. (2005). Mindfulness- and acceptance-based behavior therapy for obsessive compulsive disorder. In S. M. Orsillo & L. Roemer (Eds.), *Acceptance and mindfulness-based approaches to anxiety: Conceptualization and treatment* (pp. 271–299). New York: Springer.

Havermans, R. C., & Jansen, A. T. M. (2003). Increasing the efficacy of cue exposure treatment in preventing relapse of addictive behavior. *Addictive Behaviors*, 28, 989–994.

Hawkins, R. P. (1986). Selection of target behaviors. In R. O. Nelson & S. C. Hayes (Eds.), *Conceptual foundations of behavioral assessment* (pp. 331–385). New York: Guilford Press.

Hayes, S. C. (2004a). Acceptance and commitment therapy and the new behavior therapies. In S. C. Hayes, V. M. Follette, & M. M. Linehan (Eds.), *Mindfulness and acceptance: Expanding the cognitive-behavioral tradition* (pp. 1–29). New York: Guilford Press.

Hayes, S. C. (2004b). Acceptance and commitment therapy, relational frame theory, and the third wave of behavioral and cognitive therapies. *Behavior Therapy*, 35, 639–665.

Hayes, S. C., Barlow, D. H., & Nelson-Gray, R. O. (1999). *The scientist-practitioner: Research and accountability in the age of managed care* (2nd ed.). Boston: Allyn & Bacon.

Hayes, S. C., Barnes-Holmes, D., & Roche, B. (Eds.). (2001). *Relational frame theory: A post-Skinnerian account of human language and cognition.* New York: Kluwer Academic/Plenum Publishers.

Hayes, S. C., Brownstein, A. J., Zettle, R. D., Rosenfarb, I. S., & Korn, Z. (1986). Rule-governed behavior and sensitivity to changing consequences of responding. *Journal of the Experimental Analysis of Behavior*, 45, 237–256.

Hayes, S. C., Follette, V. M., Linehan, M. M. (Eds.). (2004). *Mindfulness and acceptance: Expanding the cognitive-behavioral tradition*. New York: Guilford Press.

Hayes, S. C., & Follette, W. C. (1992). Can functional analysis provide a substitute for syndromal classification? *Behavioral Assessment, 14*, 345–365.

Hayes, S. C., Hayes, L. J., Reese, H. W., & Sarbin, T. R. (Eds.). (1993). *Varieties of scientific contextualism*. Reno, NV: Context Press.

Hayes, S. C., Luoma, J. B., Bond, F. W., Masuda, A., & Lillis, J. (2005). Acceptance and commitment therapy: Model, processes, and outcomes. *Behaviour Research and Therapy, 44*, 1–25.

Hayes, S. C., Nelson, R. O., & Jarrett, R. B. (1986). Evaluating the quality of behavioral assessment. In R. O. Nelson & S. C. Hayes (Eds.), *Conceptual foundations of behavioral assessment* (pp. 463–503). New York: Guilford Press.

Hayes, S. C., & Smith, S. (2005). *Get out of your mind and into your life: The new acceptance and commitment therapy*. Oakland, CA: New Harbinger.

Hayes, S. C., & Strosahl, K. D. (Eds.). (2004). *A practical guide to acceptance and commitment therapy*. New York: Springer Publishing Company.

Hayes, S. C., Strosahl, K. D., Bunting, K., Twohig, M., & Wilson, K. G. (2004). What is acceptance and commitment therapy? In S. C. Hayes & K. D. Strosahl (Eds.), *A practical guide to acceptance and commitment therapy* (pp. 3–29). New York: Springer Publishing Company.

Hayes, S. C., Strosahl, K. D., & Wilson, K. G. (1999). *Acceptance and commitment therapy: An experiential approach to behavior change*. New York: Guilford Press.

Hayes, S. C., Wilson, K. G., Gifford, E. V., Follette, V. M., & Strosahl, K. D. (1996). Experiential avoidance and behavioral disorders: A functional dimensional approach to diagnosis and treatment. *Journal of Consulting and Clinical Psychology, 64*, 1152–1168.

Haynes, S. N. (1986). The design of intervention programs. In R. O. Nelson & S. C. Hayes (Eds.), *Conceptual foundations of behavioral assessment* (pp. 386–429). New York: Guilford Press.

Haynes, S. N., Kaholokula, J. K., & Nelson, K. (1999). The idiographic application of nomothetic, empirically based treatments. *Clinical Psychology: Science and Practice, 6*, 456–461.

Haynes, S. N., & O'Brien, W. H. (1990). Functional analysis in behavior therapy. *Clinical Psychology Review, 10*, 649–668.

Heatherton, T. E., & Baumeister, R. F. (1991). Binge eating as escape from self-awareness. *Psychological Bulletin, 110*, 86–108.

Heim, C., & Nemeroff, C. B. (1999). The impact of early adverse experiences on brain systems involved in the pathophysiology of anxiety and affective disorders. *Biological Psychiatry, 46*, 1509–1522.

Heimberg, R. G., & Becker, R. E. (2002). *Cognitive-behavioral group therapy for social phobia: Basic mechanisms and clinical strategies*. New York: Guilford Press.

Heinssen, R. K., Levendusky, P. G., & Hunter, R. H. (1995). Client as colleague: Therapeutic contracting with the seriously mentally ill. *American Psychologist, 50*, 522–532.

Helzer, J. E., Robins, L. N., Taylor, J. R., Carey, K., Miller, R. H., Combs-Orme, T., et al. (1985). The extent of long-term moderate drinking among alcoholics discharged from medical and psychiatric treatment facilities. *New England Journal of Medicine, 312*, 1678–1682.

Hennin, A., Otto, M. W., & Reilly-Harrington, N. A. (2001). Introducing flexibility in manualized treatments: Application of recommended strategies to the cognitive-behavioral treatment of bipolar disorder. *Cognitive and Behavioral Practice, 8*, 317–328.

Herrnstein, R. J. (1961). Relative and absolute strength of response as a function of frequency of reinforcement. *Journal of the Experimental Analysis of Behavior, 4*, 267–272.

Higgins, S., Budney, A. J., & Sigmon, S. C. (2001). Cocaine dependence. In D. H. Barlow (Ed.), *Clinical handbook of psychological disorders* (3rd ed., pp. 434–469). New York: Guilford Press.

Higgins, S. T., Delaney, D. D., Budney, A. J., Bickel, W. K., Hughes, J. R., Foerg, F., et al. (1991). A behavioral approach to achieving initial cocaine abstinence. *American Journal of Psychiatry, 148*, 1218–1224.

Hollon, S. D., Shelton, R. C., & Loosen, P. T. (1991). Cognitive therapy and pharmacotherapy for depression. *Journal of Consulting and Clinical Psychology, 59*, 88–99.

Hopko, D. R., Lejuez, C. W., & Hopko, S. D. (2004). Behavioral activation as an intervention for coexistent depressive anxiety symptoms. *Clinical Case Studies, 3*, 37–48.

Hopko, D. R., Lejuez, C. W., LePage, J. P., Hopko, S. D., & McNeil, D. W. (2003). A brief behavioral activation treatment for depression: A randomized pilot trial within an inpatient psychiatric hospital. *Behavior Modification, 27*, 458–469.

Hopko, D. R., Lejuez, C. W., Ruggiero, K. J., & Eifert, G. H. (2003). Contemporary behavioral activation treatments for depression: Procedures, principles, and progress. *Clinical Psychology Review, 23*, 699–717.

Hopko, D. R., Sanchez, L., Hopko, S. D., Dvir, S., & Lejuez, C. W. (2003). Behavioral activation and the prevention of suicidal behaviors in patients with borderline personality disorder. *Journal of Personality Disorders, 17*, 460–478.

Horne, A. M., & Matson, J. L. (1977). A comparison of modeling, desensitization, flooding, study skills, and control groups for reducing test anxiety. *Behavior Therapy, 8*, 1–8.

Houmanfar, R., Maglieri, K. A., & Roman, H. R. (2003). Behavioral contracting. In W. O'Donohue, J. E. Fisher, & S. C. Hayes (Eds.), *Cognitive behavior therapy: Applying empirically supported techniques in your practice* (pp. 40–45). Hoboken, NJ: Wiley.

Hull, D. L., Langman, R. E., & Glenn, S. S. (2001). A general account of selection: Biology, immunology, and behavior. *Behavioral and Brain Sciences, 24*, 511–573.

Humphrey, G. M., & Zimpfer, D. G. (1996). *Counselling for grief and bereavement.* London: Sage.

Iguchi, M. Y., Belding, M. A., Morral, A. R., Lamb, R. J., & Husband, S. D. (1997). Reinforcing operants other than abstinence in drug abuse treatment: An effective alternative for reducing drug use. *Journal of Consulting and Clinical Psychology, 65,* 421–428.

Ilardi, S. S., & Craighead, W. E. (1994). The role of non-specific factors in cognitive-behavior therapy for depression. *Clinical Psychology: Science & Practice, 1,* 138–156.

Infante, J. R., Torres-Avisbal, M., & Pinel, P. (2001). Catecholamine levels in practitioners of the transcendental meditation technique. *Physiology & Behavior, 72,* 141–146.

Iwata, B. A., Pace, G. M., Dorsey, M. F., Zarcone, J. R., Vollmer, T. R., Smith, R. G., et al. (1994). The functions of self-injurious behavior: An experimental–epidemiological analysis. *Journal of Applied Behavior Analysis, 27,* 215–240.

Jacob, R. G., & Rapport, M. D. (1984). Panic disorder: Medical and psychological parameters. In S. M. Turner (Ed.), *Behavioral theories and treatment of anxiety* (pp. 187–237). New York: Plenum Press.

Jacobson, N. S., & Christensen, A. (1996a). *Acceptance and change in couple therapy: A therapist's guide to transforming relationships.* New York: Norton.

Jacobson, N. S., & Christensen, A. (1996b). *Integrative couple therapy.* New York: Norton.

Jacobson, N. S., Dobson, K. S., Truax, P. A., Addis, M. E., Koerner, K., Gollan, J. K., et al. (1996). A component analysis of cognitive-behavioral treatment for depression. *Journal of Consulting and Clinical Psychology, 64,* 295–304.

Jacobson, N. S., & Margolin, G. (1979). *Marital therapy: Strategies based on social learning and behavioral exchange principles.* New York: Brunner/Mazel.

Jacobson, N. S., Martell, C. R., & Dimidjian, S. (2001). Behavioral activation treatment for depression: Returning to contextual roots. *Clinical Psychology: Science & Practice, 8,* 255–270.

Jaycox, L. H., Foa, E. B., & Morral, A. R. (1998). Influence of emotional engagement and habituation on exposure therapy for PTSD. *Journal of Consulting and Clinical Psychology, 66,* 185–192.

Johansen, E. B., Aase, H., Meyer, A., & Sagvolden, T. (2002). Attention-deficit/hyperactivity disorder (ADHD) behaviour explained by dysfunctional reinforcement and extinction processes. *Behavioural Brain Research, 130,* 37–45.

Johnson, W. G., Schlundt, D. G., Barclay, D. R., Carr-Nangle, R. E., & Engler, L. B. (1995). A naturalistic functional analysis of binge eating. *Behavior Therapy, 26,* 101–118.

Johnston, P., Hudson, S. M., & Marshall, W. L. (1992). The effects of masturbatory reconditioning with nonfamilial child molesters. *Behaviour Research and Therapy, 30,* 559–561.

Jones, M. C. (1924a). The elimination of children's fears. *Journal of Experimental Psychology, 7,* 382–390.

Jones, M. C. (1924b). A laboratory study of fear: The case of Peter. *Pedagogical Seminary, 31*, 308–315.

Kabat-Zinn, J. (1990). *Full catastrophe living: Using the wisdom of your body and mind to face stress, pain, and illness*. New York: Dell.

Kabat-Zinn, J., Lipworth, L., Burney, R., & Sellers, W. (1986). Four-year follow-up of a meditation-based program for the self-regulation of chronic pain: Treatment outcomes and compliance. *Clinical Journal of Pain, 2*, 159–173.

Kabat-Zinn, J., Massion, A. O., Kristeller, J., Peterson, L. G., Fletcher, K., Pbert, L., et al. (1992). Effectiveness of a meditation-based stress reduction program in the treatment of anxiety disorders. *American Journal of Psychiatry, 149*, 936–943.

Kallman, W. M., Hersen, M., & O'Toole, D. H. (1975). The use of social reinforcement in a case of conversion reaction. *Behavior Therapy, 6*, 411–413.

Kaminer, Y., Burleson, J. A., & Goldberger, R. (2002). Cognitive-behavioral coping skills and psychoeducation therapies for adolescent substance abuse. *Journal of Nervous and Mental Disease, 190*, 737–745.

Kandel, E. R. (1998). A new intellectual framework for psychiatry. *American Journal of Psychiatry, 155*, 457–469.

Kanfer, F. H., & Busemeyer, J. R. (1982). The use of problem solving and decision making in behavior therapy. *Clinical Psychology Review, 2*, 239–266.

Kanfer, F. H., & Saslow, G. (1969). Behavioral diagnosis. In C. M. Franks (Ed.), *Behavior therapy: Appraisal and status* (pp. 417–444). New York: McGraw-Hill.

Kazantzis, N., Deane, F. P., & Ronan, K. R. (2000). Homework assignments in cognitive and behavioral therapy: A meta-analysis. *Clinical Psychology: Science & Practice, 7*, 189–202.

Kazdin, A. E. (1978). *History of behavior modification: Experimental foundations of contemporary research*. Baltimore: University Park Press.

Kazdin, A. E. (1984). *Behavior modification in applied settings* (3rd ed.). Homewood, IL: Dorsey Press.

Kazdin, A. E. (2001). *Behavior modification in applied settings* (6th ed.). Homewood, IL: Dorsey Press.

Kazdin, A. E., & Krouse, R. (1983). The impact of variations in treatment rationales on expectancies for therapeutic change. *Behavior Therapy, 14*, 73–99.

Kearney, A. J. (2006). A primer of covert sensitization. *Cognitive and Behavioral Practice, 13*, 167–175.

Kelly, G. (1955). *The psychology of personal constructs*. New York: Norton.

Kernberg, O. F., Selzer, M. A., Koenigsberg, H. W., Carr, A. C., & Appelbaum, A. H. (1989). *Psychodynamic psychotherapy of borderline patients*. New York: Basic Books.

Kessler, R., McGonagle, K., Zhao, S., Nelson, C., Hughes, M., Eshelman, S., et al. (1994). Lifetime and 12-month prevalence of *DSM–III–R* psychiatric disorders in the United States. *Archives of General Psychiatry, 51*, 8–19.

Kjaer, T. W., Bertelsen, C., & Piccini, P. (2002). Increased dopamine tone during meditation-induced change of consciousness. *Cognitive Brain Research, 13,* 255–259.

Koerner, K., & Linehan, M. M. (1997). Case formulation in dialectical behavior therapy for borderline personality disorder. In T. D. Eells, *Handbook of psychotherapy case formulation* (pp. 340–367). New York: Guilford Press.

Kohlenberg, R. J., & Tsai, M. (1991). *Functional analytic psychotherapy: Creative intense and curative therapeutic relationships.* New York: Plenum Press.

Korotitsch, W. J., & Nelson-Gray, R. O. (1999). An overview of self-monitoring research in assessment and treatment. *Psychological Assessment, 11,* 415–425.

Kozma, A., & Stones, M. J. (1983). Predictors of happiness. *Journal of Gerontology, 38,* 626–628.

Krasner, L., & Ullmann, L. P. (1965). *Research in behavior modification—New developments and implications.* New York: Holt, Rinehart & Winston.

Laraway, S., Snycerski, S., Michael, J., & Poling, A. (2003). Motivating operations and terms to describe them: Some further refinements. *Journal of Applied Behavior Analysis, 36,* 407–414.

Latner, J. D., & Wilson, G. T. (2000). Cognitive-behavioral therapy and nutritional counseling in the treatment of bulimia nervosa and binge eating. *Eating Behaviors, 1,* 3–21.

Laws, D. R., Meyer, J., & Holman, M. L. (1978). Reduction of sadistic sexual arousal by olfactory aversion: A case study. *Behaviour Research and Therapy, 16,* 281–285.

Lazar, S. W., Bush, G., & Gollub, R. L. (2000). Functional brain mapping of the relaxation response and meditation. *Neuroreport, 11,* 1581–1585.

Lazarus, A. A. (1958). New methods of psychotherapy: A case study. *South African Medical Journal, 32,* 660–663.

Leahy, R. L. (2003). *Cognitive therapy techniques: A practitioner's guide.* New York: Guilford Press.

Ledley, D. R., Marx, B. P., & Heimberg, R. G. (2005). *Making cognitive-behavioral therapy work: Clinical process for new practitioners.* New York: Guilford Press.

Lee, J., Lim, Y., Graham, S. J., Kim, G., Wiederhold, B. K., Wiederhold, M. D., et al. (2004). Nicotine craving and cue exposure therapy by using virtual environments. *CyberPsychology & Behavior, 7,* 705–713.

Lejuez, C. W., Hopko, D. R., & Hopko, S. D. (2001). A brief behavioral activation treatment for depression: Treatment manual. *Behavior Modification, 25,* 255–286.

Lejuez, C. W., Hopko, D. R., & Hopko, S. D. (2002). *The brief behavioral activation treatment for depression (BATD): A comprehensive patient guide.* Boston: Pearson Custom Publishing.

Lewinsohn, P. M. (1974). A behavioral approach to depression. In R. M. Friedman & M. M. Katz (Eds.), *The psychology of depression: Contemporary theory and research* (pp. 157–185). New York: Wiley.

Lewinsohn, P. M., Antonuccio, D. O., Steinmetz-Breckenridge, J., & Teri, L. (1984). *The coping with depression course*. Eugene, OR: Castalia.

Lewinsohn, P. M., Biglan, A., & Zeiss, A. S. (1976). Behavioral treatment of depression. In P. O. Davidson (Ed.), *The behavioral management of anxiety, depression, and pain* (pp. 91–146). New York: Brunner/Mazel.

Lewinsohn, P. M., & Gotlib, I. H. (1995). Behavioral theory and treatment of depression. In E. E. Beckham & W. R. Leber (Eds.), *Handbook of depression* (2nd ed., pp. 352–375). New York: Guilford Press.

Lewinsohn, P. M., & Libet, J. (1972). Pleasant events, activity schedules, and depression. *Journal of Abnormal Psychology, 79*, 291–295.

Lindenboim, N., Chapman, A. L., & Linehan, M. M. (2006). Homework use in dialectical behavior therapy for borderline personality disorder. In N. Kazantzis & L. L'Abate (Eds.), *Handbook of homework assignments in psychotherapy: Research, practice, and prevention* (pp. 227–245). New York: Springer Publishing Company.

Lindsley, O. R., Skinner, B. F., & Solomon, H. C. (1953). *Studies on behavior therapy: Status report 1*. Waltham, MA: Metropolitan State Hospital.

Linehan, M. M. (1993a). *Cognitive-behavioral treatment of borderline personality disorder*. New York: Guilford Press.

Linehan, M. M. (1993b). *Skills training manual for treating borderline personality disorder*. New York: Guilford Press.

Linehan, M. M. (in press). *Skills training manual for disordered emotion regulation*. New York: Guilford Press.

Linehan, M. M., Comtois, K. A., Murray, A. M., Brown, M. Z., Gallop, R. J., Heard, H. L., et al. (2006). Two-year randomized controlled trial and follow-up of dialectical behavior therapy vs. therapy by experts for suicidal behaviors and borderline personality disorder. *Archives of General Psychiatry, 63*, 757–766.

Linehan, M. M., Dimeff, L. A., Reynolds, S. K., Comtois, K. A., Welch, S. S., Heagerty, P., et al. (2002). Dialectical behavior therapy versus comprehensive validation therapy plus 12-step for the treatment of opioid dependent women meeting criteria for borderline personality disorder. *Drug and Alcohol Dependence, 67*, 13–26.

Livesley, W. J. (2001). A framework for an integrated approach to treatment. In W. J. Livesley (Ed.), *Handbook of personality disorders: Theory, research, and treatment* (pp. 570–600). New York: Guilford Press.

Logue, A. W. (1998). Self-control. In W. O'Donohue (Ed.), *Learning and behavior therapy* (pp. 252–273). Boston: Allyn & Bacon.

Longmore, R. J., & Worrell, M. (2007). Do we need to challenge thoughts in cognitive behavior therapy? *Clinical Psychology Review, 27*, 173–187.

Loro, A. D., & Orleans, C. S. (1981). Binge-eating in obesity: Preliminary findings and guidelines for behavioral analysis and treatment. *Addictive Behaviors, 6*, 151–166.

Lovaas, O. I., Freitag, G., Gold, V. J., & Kassorla, I. C. (1965). Experimental studies in childhood schizophrenia. I. Analysis of self-destructive behavior. *Journal of Experimental Child Psychology, 2,* 67–84.

Lynch, T. R., Chapman, A. L., Rosenthal, M. Z., Kuo, J. K., & Linehan, M. M. (2006). Mechanisms of change in dialectical behavior therapy: Theoretical and empirical observations. *Journal of Clinical Psychology, 62,* 459–480.

Ma, S. H., & Teasdale, J. D. (2004). Mindfulness-based cognitive therapy for depression: Replication and exploration of differential relapse prevention effects. *Journal of Consulting and Clinical Psychology, 72,* 31–40.

MacPhillamy, D. J., & Lewinsohn, P. M. (1974). Depression as a function of levels of desired and obtained pleasure. *Journal of Abnormal Psychology, 83,* 651–657.

Magaro, P. A. (1980). *Cognition in schizophrenia and paranoia: The integration of cognitive processes.* Hillsdale, NJ: Erlbaum.

Mahoney, M. J. (1974). *Cognition and behavior modification.* Cambridge, MA: Ballinger.

Mahoney, M. J. (1991). *Human change processes: The scientific foundations of psychotherapy.* New York: Basic Books.

Malott, R. W. (1989). The achievement of evasive goals: Control by rules describing contingencies that are not direct acting. In S. C. Hayes (Ed.), *Rule-governed behavior: Cognition, contingencies, and instructional control* (pp. 269–322). New York: Plenum.

Malott, R. W., Malott, M. E., & Trojan, E. A. (2000). *Elementary principles of behavior* (4th ed.). Upper Saddle River, NJ: Prentice-Hall.

Markovitz, P. (2001). Pharmacotherapy. In W. J. Livesley (Ed.), *Handbook of personality disorders: Theory, research, and treatment* (pp. 475–493). New York: Guilford Press.

Marks, I., Lovell, K., Noshirvani, H., Livanou, M., & Thrasher, S. (1998). Treatment of post-traumatic stress disorder by exposure and/or cognitive restructuring: A controlled study. *Archives of General Psychiatry, 55,* 317–325.

Marlatt, G. A., & Donovan, D. M. (Eds.). (2005). *Relapse prevention: Maintenance strategies in the treatment of addictive behaviors* (2nd ed.). New York: Guilford Press.

Marlatt, G. A., & Gordon, J. R. (Eds.). (1985). *Relapse prevention: Maintenance strategies in the treatment of addictive behaviors.* New York: Guilford Press.

Marlatt, G. A., & Marques, J. K. (1977). Meditation, self-control, and alcohol use. In R. B. Stuart (Ed.), *Behavioral self-management: Strategies, techniques and outcomes* (pp. 117–153). New York: Brunner/Mazel.

Marlatt, G. A., Pagano, R., Rose, D., & Marques, J. (1984). Effect of meditation and relaxation training upon alcohol use in male social drinkers. In D. Shapiro & R. Walsh (Eds.), *The science of meditation: Theory, research, and experience* (pp. 105–120). New York: Aldine Publishing.

Marlatt, G. A., & Witkiewitz, K. (2005). Relapse prevention for alcohol and drug problems. In G. A. Marlatt & D. M. Donovan (Eds.), *Relapse prevention: Main-*

tenance strategies in the treatment of addictive behaviors (pp. 1–44). New York: Guilford Press.

Marshall, W. L. (1979). Satiation therapy: A procedure for reducing deviant sexual arousal. *Journal of Applied Behavior Analysis, 12,* 377–389.

Martell, C. R., Addis, M. E., & Jacobson, N. S. (2001). *Depression in context: Strategies for guided action.* New York: Norton.

McCrady, B. S. (2001). Alcohol use disorders. In D. H. Barlow (Ed.), *Clinical handbook of psychological disorders* (3rd ed., pp. 376–433). New York: Guilford Press.

McCullagh, P. (1987). Model similarity effects on motor performance. *Journal of Sport Psychology, 9,* 249–260.

McKnight, D. L., Nelson, R. O., Hayes, S. C., & Jarrett, R. B. (1984). Importance of treating individually assessed response classes in the amelioration of depression. *Behavior Therapy, 15,* 315–335.

McLeod, J. D., Kessler, R. C., & Landis, K. R. (1992). Speed of recovery from major depressive episodes in a community sample of married men and women. *Journal of Abnormal Psychology, 101,* 277–286.

McManus, F., & Waller, G. (1995). A functional analysis of binge eating. *Clinical Psychology Review, 15,* 845–863.

Meichenbaum, D. H. (1977). *Cognitive-behavior modification: An integrative approach.* New York: Plenum Press.

Meichenbaum, D. H. (1985). *Stress inoculation training.* New York: Pergamon Press.

Meichenbaum, D. H., & Goodman, J. (1971). Training impulsive children to talk to themselves: A means of developing self-control. *Journal of Abnormal Psychology, 77,* 115–126.

Merckelbach, H., Arntz, A., & deJong, P. (1991). Conditioning experiences in spider phobics. *Behaviour Research and Therapy, 29,* 333–335.

Merriam-Webster's New Collegiate Dictionary (9th ed.). (1985). Springfield, MA: Merriam-Webster.

Meyer, T. J., Miller, M. L., Metzger, R. L., & Borkovec, T. D. (1990). Development and validation of the Penn State Worry Questionnaire. *Behaviour Research and Therapy, 28,* 487–495.

Michael, J. (1982). Distinguishing between the discriminative and motivational functions of stimuli. *Journal of the Experimental Analysis of Behavior, 37,* 149–158.

Michael, J. (2000). Implications and refinements of the establishing operation concept. *Journal of Applied Behavior Analysis, 33,* 401–410.

Miklowitz, D. J. (2001). Bipolar disorder. In D. H. Barlow (Ed.), *Clinical handbook of psychological disorders* (3rd ed., pp. 523–561). New York: Guilford Press.

Miller, W. R., & Rollnick, S. (1991). *Motivational interviewing: Preparing people to change addictive behavior.* New York: Guilford Press.

Miller, W. R., Zweben, A., DiClemente, C. C., & Rychtarik, R. G. (1995). *Motivational enhancement therapy manual: A clinical research guide for therapists treating individuals with alcohol abuse and dependence.* Rockville, MD: U.S. Department of Health and Human Services.

Miltenberger, R. G. (2004). *Behavior modification: Principles and procedures* (3rd ed.). Belmont, CA: Wadsworth/Thomson.

Miltenberger, R. G. (2005). The role of automatic negative reinforcement in clinical problems. *International Journal of Behavioral Consultation and Therapy, 1,* 1–11.

Mischel, W., & Grusec, J. (1966). Determinants of the rehearsal transmission of the neutral and aversive behaviors. *Journal of Personality and Social Psychology, 3,* 197–205.

Mitchell, J. E., Mussell, M. P., Peterson, C. B., Crow, S., Wonderlich, S. A., Crosby, R. D., et al. (1999). The hedonics of binge eating in women with bulimia nervosa and binge eating disorder. *International Journal of Eating Disorders, 26,* 165–170.

Mitchell, W. S., & Stoffelmayr, B. E. (1973). Application of the Premack principle to the behavioral control of extremely inactive schizophrenics. *Journal of Applied Behavior Analysis, 6,* 419–423.

Monk, T. H., Kupfer, D. J., Frank, E., & Ritenour, A. M. (1991). The social rhythm metric (SRM): Measuring daily social rhythms over 12 weeks. *Psychiatry Research, 36,* 196–207.

Monti, P. M., Abrams, D. B., Binkoff, J. A., Zwick, W. R., Liepman, M. R., Nirenberg, T. D., et al. (1990). Communication skills training, communication skills training with family and cognitive behavioral mood management training for alcoholics. *Journal of Studies on Alcohol, 51,* 263–270.

Morganstern, K. P., & Tevlin, H. E. (1981). Behavioral interviewing. In M. Hersen & A. S. Bellack (Eds.), *Behavioral assessment: A practical handbook* (2nd ed., pp. 71–100). New York: Pergamon Press.

Morin, S. F., & Rothblum, E. D. (1991). Removing the stigma: Fifteen years of progress. *American Psychologist, 46,* 947–949.

Morrison, J. (1995). *The first interview: Revised for DSM–IV.* New York: Guilford Press.

Mowrer, O. H. (1947). On the dual nature of learning: A re-interpretation of "conditioning" and "problem-solving". *Harvard Educational Review, 17,* 102–148.

Mowrer, O. H. (1960). *Learning theory and behavior.* New York: Wiley.

Mowrer, O. H., & Mowrer, W. M. (1938). Enuresis—a method for its study and treatment. *American Journal of Orthopsychiatry, 8,* 436–439.

Mueller, T. I., Leon, A. C., Keller, M. B., Soloman, D. A., Endicott, J., Coryell, W., et al. (1999). Recurrence after recovery from major depressive disorder during 15 years of observational follow-up. *American Journal of Psychiatry, 156,* 1000–1006.

Mueser, K. T., Levine, S., & Bellack, A. S. (1990). Social skills training for acute psychiatric inpatients. *Hospital & Community Psychiatry, 41,* 1249–1251.

Muraven, M., Tice, D. M., & Baumeister, R. F. (1998). Self-control as a limited resource: Regulatory depletion patterns. *Journal of Personality and Social Psychology, 74,* 774–789.

Naugle, A. E., & Follette, W. C. (1998). A functional analysis of trauma symptoms. In V. M. Follette, J. I. Ruzek, & F. R. Abueg (Eds.), *Cognitive-behavioral therapies for trauma* (pp. 48–73). New York: Guilford Press.

Naugle, A. E., & O'Donohue, W. (1998). The future of behavior therapy: Some applied implications of contemporary learning research. In W. O'Donohue (Ed.), *Learning and behavior therapy* (pp. 545–557). Boston: Allyn & Bacon.

Nelson, R. O. (1977). Assessment and therapeutic functions of self-monitoring. In M. Hersen, R. Eisler, & P. Miller (Eds.), *Progress in behavior modification: Vol. 5* (pp. 236–308). New York: Academic Press.

Nelson, R. O., & Barlow, D. H. (1981). Behavioral assessment: Basic strategies and initial procedures. In D. H. Barlow (Ed.), *Behavioral assessment of adult disorders* (pp. 13–43). New York: Guilford Press.

Nelson, R. O., & Hayes, S. C. (Eds.). (1986a). *Conceptual foundations of behavioral assessment*. New York: Guilford Press.

Nelson, R. O., & Hayes, S. C. (1986b). Nature of behavioral assessment. In R. O. Nelson & S. C. Hayes (Eds.), *Conceptual foundations of behavioral assessment* (pp. 3–41). New York: Guilford Press.

Nelson, R. O., Hayes, S. C., Jarrett, R. B., Sigmon, S. T., & McKnight, D. L. (1987). Effectiveness of matched, mismatched, and package treatments for depression. *Psychological Reports, 61*, 816–818.

Nelson-Gray, R. O., & Farmer, R. F. (1999). Behavioral assessment of personality disorders. *Behaviour Research and Therapy, 37*, 347–368.

Nelson-Gray, R. O., & Paulson, J. F. (2003). Behavioral assessment and the DSM system. In M. Hersen (Series Ed.), S. N. Haynes, & E. M. Heiby (Vol. Eds.), *Comprehensive handbook of psychological assessment: Vol. 3. Behavioral assessment* (pp. 470–486). New York: Wiley.

Nezu, A. M. (1989). A problem solving formulation of depression: A literature review and proposal for a pluralistic model. *Clinical Psychology Review, 7*, 121–144.

Nezu, A. M., & Perri, M. G. (1989). Social problem solving therapy for unipolar depression. An initial dismantling investigation. *Journal of Consulting and Clinical Psychology, 57*, 408–413.

Nisbett, R. E., & Wilson, T. D. (1977). Telling more than we can know: Verbal reports on mental processes. *Psychological Review, 84*, 231–259.

Novaco, R. W. (1975). *Anger control: The development and evaluation of an experimental treatment*. Lexington, MA: Heath.

Novaco, R. W. (1995). Clinical problems of anger and its assessment and regulation through a stress coping skills approach: Clinical techniques and applications. In W. T. O'Donohue & L. Krasner (Eds.), *Handbook of psychological skills training: Clinical techniques and applications* (pp. 320–338). Needham Heights, MA: Allyn & Bacon.

O'Donohue, W. (1998). Conditioning and third-generation behavior therapy. In W. O'Donohue (Ed.), *Learning and behavior therapy* (pp. 1–14). Boston: Allyn & Bacon.

O'Donohue, W. T., & Krasner, L. (1995). *Handbook of psychological skills training: Clinical techniques and applications*. Boston: Allyn & Bacon.

O'Leary, K. D., & Wilson, G. T. (1987). *Behavior therapy: Application and outcome* (2nd ed.). Englewood Cliffs, NJ: Prentice-Hall.

Otto, M. W., Reilly-Harrington, N. A., Kogan, J. N., & Winett, C. A. (2003). Treatment contracting in cognitive-behavior therapy. *Cognitive and Behavioral Practice, 10,* 199–203.

Overholser, J. C. (2003). Cognitive-behavioral treatment of depression: A three-stage model to guide treatment planning. *Cognitive and Behavioral Practice, 10,* 231–239.

Paradise, L. V., Conway, B. S., & Zweig, J. (1986). Effects of expert and referent influence, physical attractiveness, and gender on perceptions of counselor attributes. *Journal of Counseling Psychology, 33,* 16–22.

Patterson, C. M., & Newman, J. P. (1993). Reflectivity and learning from aversive events: Towards a psychological mechanism for the syndromes of disinhibition. *Psychological Review, 100,* 716–736.

Pavlov, I. P. (1927). *Conditioned reflexes* (G. V. Anrep, Trans). London: Oxford University Press.

Penn, L. S. (1990). When the therapist must leave: Forced termination of psychodynamic therapy. *Professional Psychology: Research and Practice, 21,* 379–384.

Persons, J. B. (1989). *Cognitive therapy in practice: A case formulation approach.* New York: Norton.

Persons, J. B., Roberts, N. A., Zalecki, C. A., & Breechwald, W. A. G. (2006). Naturalistic outcome of case formulation-driven cognitive-behavior therapy for anxious depressed outpatients. *Behaviour Research and Therapy, 44,* 1041–1051.

Persons, J. B., & Tompkins, M. A. (1997). Cognitive-behavioral case formulation. In T. D. Eells (Ed.), *Handbook of psychotherapy case formulation* (pp. 314–339). New York: Guilford Press.

Peterson, D. R. (1968). *The clinical study of social behavior.* Englewood Cliffs, NJ: Prentice-Hall.

Petry, N. M., Petrakis, I., Trevisan, L., Wiredu, G., Boutros, N. N., Martin, B., et al. (2001). Contingency management interventions: From research to practice. *American Journal of Psychiatry, 158,* 694–702.

Phillips, L., & Zigler, E. (1961). Social competence: The action thought parameter and vicariousness in normal and pathological behaviors. *Journal of Abnormal and Social Psychology, 63,* 137–146.

Pike, K. M. (1998). Long-term course of anorexia nervosa: Response, relapse, remission, and recovery. *Clinical Psychology Review, 18,* 447–475.

Poling, A., & Gaynor, S. T. (2003). Stimulus control. In W. O'Donohue, J. E. Fisher, & S. C. Hayes (Eds.), *Cognitive behavior therapy: Applying empirically supported techniques in your practice* (pp. 396–401). Hoboken, NJ: Wiley.

Pratt, S., & Mueser, K. T. (2002). Social skills training for schizophrenia. In S. G. Hoffman & M. C. Tompson (Eds.), *Treating chronic and severe mental disorders* (pp. 18–52). New York: Guilford Press.

Premack, D. (1959). Toward empirical behavioral laws: I. Positive reinforcement. *Psychological Review, 66*, 219–233.

Rachlin, H. (1976). *Introduction to modern behaviorism* (2nd ed.). San Francisco: Freeman.

Rakos, R. F. (1991). *Assertive behavior: Theory, research, and training.* Florence, KY: Taylor & Francis/Routledge.

Rehm, L. (1979). A comparison of self-control and assertion skills treatments of depression. *Behavior Therapy, 10*, 429–442.

Resick, P. A., & Calhoun, K. S. (2001). Posttraumatic stress disorder. In D. H. Barlow (Ed.), *Clinical handbook of psychological disorders: A step-by-step treatment manual* (3rd ed., pp. 60–113). New York: Guilford Press.

Resick, P. A., & Schnicke, M. K. (1993). *Cognitive processing therapy for rape victims: A treatment manual.* Newbury Park, CA: Sage.

Rhee, S. H., Feigon, S. A., Bar, J. L., Hadeishi, Y., & Waldman, I. D. (2001). Behavior genetic approaches to the study of psychopathology. In P. B. Sutker & H. E. Adams (Eds.), *Comprehensive handbook of psychopathology* (3rd ed., pp. 53–84). New York: Kluwer Academic/Plenum Publishers.

Robins, C. J., & Chapman, A. L. (2004). Dialectical behavior therapy: Current status, recent developments, and future directions. *Journal of Personality Disorders, 18*, 73–79.

Robins, C. J., Schmidt, H., III., & Linehan, M. M. (2004). Dialectical behavior therapy: Synthesizing radical acceptance with skillful means. In S. C. Hayes, V. M. Follette, & M. M. Linehan (Eds.), *Mindfulness and acceptance: Expanding the cognitive-behavioral tradition* (pp. 30–44). New York: Guilford Press.

Robins, L. N., Helzer, J. E., Croughan, J., & Ratcliffe, K. S. (1981). National Institute of Mental Health Diagnostic Interview Schedule: Its history, characteristics, and validity. *Archives of General Psychiatry, 38*, 381–389.

Rogers, C. R. (1995). *Client-centered therapy: Its current practice, implications, and theory.* Philadelphia: Trans-Atlantic Publications.

Rohde, P., Feeny, N. C., & Robins, M. (2005). Characteristics and components of the TADS CBT approach. *Cognitive and Behavioral Practice, 12*, 186–197.

Rohsenow, D. J., Monti, P. M., Rubonis, A. V., Gulliver, S. B., Colby, S. M., Binkoff, J. A., et al. (2001). Cue exposure with coping skills training and communication skills training for alcohol dependence: 6- and 12-month outcomes. *Addiction, 96*, 1161–1174.

Rouf, K., Fennell, M., Westbrook, D., Cooper, M., & Bennett-Levy, J. (2004). Devising effective behavioural experiments. In J. Bennett-Levy, G. Butler, M. Fennell, A. Hackmann, M. Mueller, & D. Westbrook (Eds.), *Oxford guide to behavioural experiments in cognitive therapy* (pp. 21–58). Oxford, England: Oxford University Press.

Sacco, W. P., & Beck, A. T. (1995). Cognitive theory and therapy. In E. E. Beckham & W. R. Leber (Eds.), *Handbook of depression* (2nd ed., pp. 329–351). New York: Guilford Press.

Salter, A. (1949). *Conditioned reflex therapy.* New York: Creative Age Press.

Schlinger, H. D. (1993). Separating discriminative and function-altering effects of verbal stimuli. *Behavior Analyst, 16,* 9–23.

Schunk, D. H., & Hanson, A. R. (1985). Peer models: Influence on children's self-efficacy and achievement. *Journal of Educational Psychology, 77,* 313–322.

Segal, Z. V., Williams, J. M. G., & Teasdale, J. D. (2002). *Mindfulness-based cognitive therapy for depression: A new approach to preventing relapse.* New York: Guilford Press.

Shipley, R. H., & Boudewyns, P. A. (1980). Flooding and implosive therapy: Are they harmful? *Behavior Therapy, 11,* 503–508.

Sitharthan, T., Sitharthan, G., Hough, M. J., & Kavanagh, D. J. (1997). Cue exposure in moderation drinking: A comparison with cognitive–behavior therapy. *Journal of Consulting and Clinical Psychology, 65,* 878–882.

Simons, A. D., Rohde, P., Kennard, B. D., & Robins, M. (2005). Relapse and recurrence prevention in the Treatment of Adolescents With Depression Study. *Cognitive and Behavioral Practice, 12,* 240–251.

Skinner, B. F. (1938). *The behavior of organisms: An experimental analysis.* New York: Appleton-Century-Crofts.

Skinner, B. F. (1969). *Contingencies of reinforcement: A theoretical analysis.* New York: Appleton-Century-Crofts.

Skinner, B. F. (1971). *Beyond freedom and dignity.* New York: Knopf.

Skinner, B. F. (1981, July 31). Selection by consequences. *Science, 213,* 501–504.

Skinner, B. F. (1989). *Recent issues in the analysis of behavior.* Columbus, OH: Merrill.

Sobell, L. C., & Sobell, M. B. (2003). Using motivational interviewing techniques to talk with clients about their alcohol use. *Cognitive and Behavioral Practice, 10,* 214–221.

Spanier, G. B. (1976). Measuring dyadic adjustment: New scales for assessing quality of marriage and similar dyads. *Journal of Marriage and Family Therapy, 38,* 15–28.

Spiegler, M. D. (1983). *Contemporary behavioral therapy.* Palo Alto, CA: Mayfield Publishing.

Spiegler, M. D., & Guevremont, D. C. (2003). *Contemporary behavior therapy* (4th ed.). Belmont, CA: Wadsworth/Thomson Learning.

Spielberger, C. D., Gorsuch, R. L., Lushene, R., Vagg, P. R., & Jacobs, G. A. (1983). *Manual for the State–Trait Anxiety Inventory (Form Y).* Palo Alto, CA: Consulting Psychologists Press.

Steketee, G. S. (1993). *Treatment of obsessive-compulsive disorder.* New York: Guilford Press.

Street, L. L., & Barlow, D. H. (1994). Anxiety disorders. In L. W. Craighead, W. E. Craighead, A. E. Kazdin, & M. J. Mahoney (Eds.), *Cognitive and behavioral interventions: An empirical approach to mental health problems* (pp. 71–87). Boston: Allyn & Bacon.

Strupp, H. H., & Binder, J. L. (1984). *Psychotherapy in a new key: A guide to time limited dynamic therapy*. New York: Basic Books.

Sturmey, P. (1996). *Functional analysis in clinical psychology*. New York: Wiley.

Sundberg, N. D., Taplin, J. R., & Tyler, L. E. (1983). *Introduction to clinical psychology: Perspectives, issues, and contributions to human service*. Englewood Cliffs, NJ: Prentice-Hall.

Sundberg, N. D., Winebarger, A. A., & Taplin, J. R. (2002). *Clinical psychology: Evolving theory, practice, and research* (4th ed.). Upper Saddle River, NJ: Prentice-Hall.

Tabakoff, B., & Hoffman, P. L. (1988). A neurobiological theory of alcoholism. In C. D. Chaudron & D. A. Wilkinson (Eds.), *Theories on alcoholism* (pp. 29–72). Toronto, Ontario, Canada: Addition Research Foundation.

Tarrier, N., & Calam, R. (2002). New developments in cognitive–behavioural case formulation. Epidemiological, systemic, and social context: An integrative approach. *Behavioural and Cognitive Psychotherapy, 30*, 311–328.

Teasdale, J. D., Segal, Z. V., Williams, J. M. G., Ridgeway, V. A., Soulsby, J. M., & Lau, M. A. (2000). Prevention of relapse/recurrence in major depression by mindfulness-based cognitive therapy. *Journal of Consulting and Clinical Psychology, 68*, 615–623.

Thase, M., Simmons, A., McGeary, J., Cahalane, J., Hughes, C., Harden, T., et al. (1992). Relapse after cognitive behavioral therapy of depression: Potential implications for longer courses of treatment. *American Journal of Psychiatry, 149*, 1046–1052.

Thorndike, E. L. (1898). Animal intelligence. *Psychological Review Monograph Supplement, 2*(4, Whole No. 8).

Tice, D. M., Bratslavsky, E., & Baumeister, R. F. (2001). Emotional distress regulation takes precedence over impulse control: If you feel bad, do it! *Journal of Personality and Social Psychology, 80*, 53–67.

Todd, J. T., & Morris, E. K. (1983). Misconception and miseducation: Presentations of racial behaviorism in psychology textbooks. *Behavior Analyst, 6*, 153–160.

Toro, J., Cervera, M., Feliu, M. H., Garriga, N., Jou, M., Martinez, E., et al. (2003). Cue exposure in the treatment of resistant bulimia nervosa. *International Journal of Eating Disorders, 34*, 227–234.

Turkat, I. D. (1986). The behavioral interview. In A. R. Ciminero, K. S. Calhoun, & H. E. Adams (Eds.), *Handbook of behavioral assessment* (2nd ed., pp. 109–149). New York: Wiley.

Twohig, M. P., Masuda, A., Varra, A. A., & Hayes, S. C. (2005). Acceptance and commitment therapy as a treatment for anxiety disorders. In S. M. Orsillo & L. Roemer (Eds.), *Acceptance and mindfulness-based approaches to anxiety: Conceptualization and treatment* (pp. 101–129). New York: Springer Publishing Company.

Ullmann, L. P., & Krasner, L. (Eds.). (1965). *Case studies in behavior modification*. New York: Holt, Rinehart & Winston.

Upper, D., & Cautela, J. R. (Eds.). (1979). *Covert conditioning.* New York: Pergamon Press.

Van Brunt, D. L. (2000). Modular cognitive-behavioral therapy: Dismantling validated treatment programs into self-standing treatment plan objectives. *Cognitive and Behavioral Practice, 7,* 156–165.

van den Hout, M., Arntz, A., & Hoekstra, R. (1994). Exposure reduced agoraphobia but not panic, and cognitive therapy reduced panic but not agoraphobia. *Behaviour Research and Therapy, 32,* 447–451.

Vitousek, K., Watson, S., & Wilson, G. T. (1998). Enhancing motivation for change in treatment-resistant eating disorders. *Clinical Psychology Review, 18,* 391–420.

Vohs, K. D., & Baumeister, R. F. (2004). Understanding self-regulation: An introduction. In R. F. Baumeister & K. D. Vohs (Eds.), *Handbook of self-regulation: Research, theory, and applications* (pp. 1–9). New York: Guilford Press.

Vollmer, T. R., & Wright, C. S. (2003). Noncontingent reinforcement as a treatment for problem behavior. In W. O'Donohue, J. E. Fisher, & S. C. Hayes (Eds.), *Cognitive behavior therapy: Applying empirically supported techniques in your practice* (pp. 266–272). Hoboken, NJ: Wiley.

Wallace, M. D., & Robles, A. C. (2003). Differential reinforcement of other behavior and differential reinforcement of alternative behavior. In W. O'Donohue, J. E. Fisher, & S. C. Hayes (Eds.), *Cognitive behavior therapy: Applying empirically supported techniques in your practice* (pp. 136–143). Hoboken, NJ: Wiley.

Walser, R. D., & Hayes, S. C. (1998). Acceptance and trauma survivors: Applied issues and problems. In V. M. Follette, J. I. Ruzek, & F. R. Abueg (Eds.), *Cognitive-behavioral therapies for trauma* (pp. 256–277). New York: Guilford Press.

Weiner, I. B. (1975). *Principles of psychotherapy.* New York: Wiley.

Wilson, G. T., & Davison, G. C. (1971). Process of fear reduction in systematic desensitization: Animal studies. *Psychological Bulletin, 76,* 1–14.

Wilson, P. H. (Ed.). (1992). *Principles and practice of relapse prevention.* New York: Guilford Press.

Witkiewitz, K., Marlatt, G. A., & Walker, D. (2005). Mindfulness-based relapse prevention for alcohol and substance use disorders. *Journal of Cognitive Psychotherapy, 19,* 211–228.

Wolpe, J. (1958). *Psychotherapy by reciprocal inhibition.* Stanford, CA: Stanford University Press.

Wolpe, J., & Lazarus, A. A. (1966). *Behavior therapy techniques.* New York: Pergamon Press.

Wolpe, J., & Turkat, I. D. (1985). Behavioral formulation of clinical cases. In I. D. Turkat (Ed.), *Behavioral case formulation* (pp. 5–36). New York: Pergamon Press.

Wolt, A. L., & Toman, S. N. (2005). *Gestalt therapy: History, theory, and practice.* Thousand Oaks, CA: Sage.

Wulfert, E., Greenway, D. E., & Dougher, M. J. (1996). A logical functional analysis of reinforcement-based disorders: Alcoholism and pedophilia. *Journal of Consulting and Clinical Psychology, 64,* 1140–1151.

Young, J. E. (1994). *Cognitive therapy for personality disorders: A schema-focused approach* (Rev. ed.). Sarasota, FL: Professional Resource Press.

Young, J. E., Weinberger, A. D., & Beck, A. T. (2001). Cognitive therapy for depression. In D. H. Barlow (Ed.), *Clinical handbook of psychological disorders* (3rd ed., pp. 264–308). New York: Guilford Press.

Zanarini, M. C., Williams, A. A., Lewis, R. E., Reich, R. B., Vera, S. C., Marin, M. F., et al. (1997). Reported pathological childhood experiences associated with the development of borderline personality disorder. *American Journal of Psychiatry, 154,* 1101–1106.

Zettle, R. D., & Hayes, S. C. (1982). Rule-governed behavior: A potential theoretical framework for cognitive-behavioral therapy. In P. C. Kendall (Ed.), *Advances in cognitive-behavioral research and therapy* (pp. 73–118). New York: Academic Press.

Zimbardo, P. G., & Gerrig, R. J. (1996). *Psychology and life* (14th ed.). New York: HarperCollins.

Zimmerman, B. J., & Koussa, R. (1979). Social influences on children's toy preferences: Effects of model rewardingness and affect. *Contemporary Educational Psychology, 4,* 55–66.

AUTHOR INDEX

Choate, M. L., 229
Christensen, A., 18, 256–257, 265, 270
Ciminero, A. R., 16, 48
Cohen, N., 227, 229
Cohen, S., 32, 210
Conklin, C. A., 227–228, 243
Conners, C. K., 28
Conway, B. S., 195
Cooke, G., 233
Cooper, M., 147
Coyne, J. C., 219
Craighead, W. E., 90, 205
Craske, M. G., 13, 54, 179, 186, 227–228, 262
Croughan, J., 28
Cuijpers, P., 203
Cunningham, C. L., 81, 112, 294
Curry, S., 290

Dance, D., 91
Dancu, C. V., 28
David, D., 3
Davis, M., 162–163
Davis, T. E., 12
Davison, G. C., 124–125, 233–234
Deane, F. P., 85
deJong, P., 14
Derogatis, L. R., 56
DiClemente, C. C., 165
DiGiuseppe, R., 227–228
Dimeff, L. A., 112
Dimidjian, S., 12, 164, 203–204, 206–207, 291
Dobson, K. S., 3–4, 12–13, 17, 206
Donovan, D. M., 255, 287
Dougher, M. J., 11, 22
Dow, M. G., 184
Dozois, D. J. A., 13, 17
Dvir, S., 203
D'Zurilla, T. J., 205

Earls, C. M., 133
Eells, T. D., 25, 53
Eifert, G. H., 18, 77, 126, 151
Ellis, Albert, 16
Emery, G., 4, 54, 145
Endicott, J., 27
Engler, L. B., 41
Eshelman, E. R., 162
Esler, J. L., 12
Etkin, A., 59
Eysenck, H. J., 16

Farmer, R. F., 4–5, 7, 9, 11, 13, 27, 39, 43–44, 46, 60, 63, 65–66, 69, 78–79, 81, 91, 153
Feeny, N. C., 292
Feigenbaum, W., 245
Feigon, S. A., 44
Fenigstein, A., 158
Fennell, M., 147
Ferguson, K. E., 124–125
Ferster, C. B., 42, 204
Feske, U., 12
Fiester, A. R., 24
Finney, J. W., 133
First, M. B., 28, 56
Foa, E. B., 12–13, 28, 75, 179, 227–228, 231, 235–237, 244, 246
Follette, V. M., 18, 46, 79, 256
Follette, W. C., 8, 21, 27, 46, 57–58, 61, 78, 115, 153, 158, 183, 201
Forsyth, J. P., 18, 151
Foulks, E. F., 6
Fowles, D. C., 41, 66
Frank, E., 291
Franklin, M. E., 13
Freeman, A., 3
Freeman, K. A., 40, 152
Freitag, G., 16
Fresco, D. M., 210
Freud, S., 255
Friedman, M. J., 227
Friman, P. C., 133
Froyd, J. D., 28
Froyd, J. E., 28

Garner, D. M., 34, 43
Gaynor, S. T., 116
Gerrig, R. J., 6
Ghezzi, P. M., 137–138
Gibbon, M., 28, 56
Gifford, E. V., 46, 79, 256
Gingevich, S., 179
Glenn, S. S., 7
Gold, V. J., 16
Goldberger, R., 180
Goldfried, M. R., 16, 37, 43, 58, 124–125
Goldiamond, I., 73
Gollan, J., 12, 206
Gollub, R. L., 266
Goodman, J., 195
Gordon, J. R., 112, 255, 276, 290
Gorsuch, R. L., 102
Gortner, E., 12, 206

Lamb, R. J., 128
Lambert, M. J., 28
Landis, K. R., 32
Langman, R. E., 7
Laraway, S., 39
Latner, J. D., 43
Latner, J. L., 39, 63
Lau, A. W., 77
Laws, D. R., 133
Lazar, S. W., 266
Lazarus, A. A., 16, 101
Leahy, J. E., 4
Ledley, D. R., 285, 292–293
Lee, J., 243
Lejuez, C. W., 77, 126, 203, 206
LePage, J. P., 206
Levendusky, P. G., 136
Levine, S., 178
Lewinsohn, P. M., 32, 42, 54, 101, 125, 203–205, 290
Libet, J., 204
Lillis, J., 256
Lindenboim, N., 198
Lindsley, O. R., 16
Linehan, M. M., 18, 24, 30–31, 34–35, 44, 48, 74–75, 77–78, 82–83, 110, 112, 115–116, 121, 126, 134, 166, 179, 183, 188–189, 198–199, 228, 230, 240–242, 253, 255–258, 262, 264, 268, 270, 272, 274–275, 277
Linnerooth, P. J. N., 8, 21, 78, 115
Lipworth, L., 256
Livanou, M., 228
Livesley, W. J., 24
Longmore, R. J., 12, 141
Loosen, P. T., 222
Loro, A. D., 41
Lovaas, O. I., 16
Lovell, K., 228
Luoma, J. B., 256
Lushene, R., 102
Lynch, T. R., 257

Ma, S. H., 257
MacAleese, K. R., 137
MacPhillamy, D. J., 101, 204
Magaro, P. A., 158
Maglieri, K. A., 136
Mahoney, M. J., 4, 17
Malott, M. E., 40, 106, 152
Malott, R. W., 40, 106, 118, 131, 152–153, 166

Margolin, G., 179, 257, 270
Markovitz, P., 5
Marks, I., 228
Marlatt, G. A., 112, 255, 262, 276, 287–292
Marques, J., 255
Marshall, W. L., 117
Martell, C. R., 5–6, 18, 30, 54, 58–59, 81, 142–145, 150–151, 162–164, 166, 203–204, 206–208, 218–219, 291
Marx, B. P., 285
Masuda, A., 161, 256
Matson, J. L., 245
McCrady, B. S., 112, 199
McCullagh, P., 195
McKay, M., 162
McKnight, D. L., 55
McLeod, J. D., 32
McManus, F., 41
McNeil, D. W., 206
Meichenbaum, D. H., 17, 179, 195, 228
Menchola, M., 165
Mennin, D. S., 210
Merckelbach, H., 14
Mermelstein, R., 210
Merriam-Webster's New Collegiate Dictionary, 252
Metzger, R. L., 210
Meyer, A., 153
Meyer, J., 133
Meyer, T. J., 210
Michael, J., 16, 39
Miklowitz, D. J., 48
Miller, M. L., 210
Miller, W. R., 86–87, 165
Miltenberger, R. G., 39, 118, 124–125, 131, 135–137, 143, 166
Mischel, W., 195
Mitchell, J. E., 41
Mitchell, W. S., 127
Monk, T. H., 291
Monti, P. M., 179
Morganstern, K. P., 24, 27, 36
Morin, S. F., 6
Morral, A. R., 128, 235
Morris, E. K., 6
Morrison, J., 24, 26, 31, 33, 56
Mowrer, O. H., 15, 233–234
Mowrer, W. M., 15
Mueller, T. I., 287
Mueser, K. T., 124, 178–179
Muraven, M., 192
Murdock, T. B., 228

SUBJECT INDEX

Behavioral consequences, 7, 9, 40–43, 95, 108
    modifying, 118–134
    reinforcing, 143
Behavioral context, 8–9, 18, 21. *See also* contextual factors
Behavioral contingency, 106
Behavioral contracting, 118, 135–136, 166
Behavioral deficits, 29, 57, 183–184
Behavioral excesses, 29, 41, 57
Behavioral experiments, 81, 145–151, 157
    in behavioral activation for depression, 214–217
    within CBT, 146–147
    illustration, 166–174
    mechanisms of change, 150–151
    procedures, 147–150
Behavioral inertia, 81
Behavioral interventions in CBT, 5–13
    common features, 10–12
    effectiveness, 12–13
Behavioral interview, 36
Behavioral marital therapy (BMT), 179
Behavioral rehearsal, 124–125
Behavioral repertoire, 29, 81, 109, 185
    and acceptance interventions, 263–264
    in behavioral assessments, 8–9
    as therapeutic goal, 73–74
Behavior change, and learning theories, 15
Behaviorism, use of term, 6
Behavior modification, use of term, 6, 16
Behavior theory, 4
Behavior therapy, 6, 13–17
Behaviour Research and Therapy (journal), 16
Bennett-Levy, J., 146, 150
Bereavement, and acceptance, 261
Berns, S., 257
Between-session activities, 85–86
Binge eating, 41
Biological factors, 66, 266
Biological therapies, 8
Body scan technique, 276
Booster sessions, 294
Borderline personality disorder (BPD), 44, 262–263
Borkovec, T. D., 144
Brainstorming, 214
Breadth assessment, in exposure therapy, 244–245
Breathing skills, 186, 276
"Broken record" strategy, 183
Burning bridges, 112

Burns, D. D., 157

Calhoun, K. S., 48
Capabilities, 180–181
Capacities, 180–181
Carpenter, K. M., 83–84
Case consultation meetings, 83
Case formulation, 25, 53, 60
    and client communication, 68–70
    developing, 58–68
    illustration, 91–102
    in modular approach, 79–80
    validity, 60–61
Castonguay, L. G., 133
Catastrophizing, 156
Cautela, J. R., 133
Chaining, and skills acquisition, 191
Chain of behaviors, demonstrating, 194–195
Change, and acceptance/mindfulness, 254, 262–263
Changeability, and acceptance interventions, 260–261
Change mechanisms, 12
    in acceptance/mindfulness interventions, 263–266
    for behavioral experiments, 150–151
    for exposure therapy, 232–237
    in skills training, 185–186
Chapman, A. L., 198
Checklist assessments, 28–29
Child Behavior Checklist, 28
Chiles, J. A., 117
Christensen, A., 256–257, 265, 270
Ciminero, A. R., 48
Classical (respondent) conditioning, 13–14, 107, 230, 233
Client. *See also* multiproblem clients; therapeutic context; therapist–client collaboration; therapist–client relationship
    and acceptance therapy, 266–272
    and case formulation, 60–61
    and control over exposure, 248
    and decision to terminate therapy, 280–282
    as own therapist, 292–293
Client characteristics, in treatment planning, 72
Client orientation
    for contingency management, 110
    and exposure therapy, 243–244
    for skills training, 189–191

for termination of therapy, 283–284
client–therapist relationship. *See* therapist–client relationship
Closing, of initial interview, 50
Coaching, in skills training, 200–201
Cognitive–behavioral, use of term, 3
Cognitive behavior therapy (CBT), 3–4, 72, 205–206
    and acceptance/mindfulness practices, 251–252, 254
    and behavioral experiments, 146–147
    emergence, 16–17
    and exposure therapy, 227–228
    new generation, 17–19
    and thinking behavior, 142–144
Cognitive change, and behavioral experiments, 150–151
Cognitive distortions, 155–157
Cognitive model, 3–5, 65
Cognitive modeling, 195
Cognitive-participant modeling, 195
Cognitive processing therapy, 237
Cognitive restructuring, 17
Cognitive revolution, 17
Cognitive therapies, 8, 17, 142–143, 146, 205
Commitment for action, 86–89, 118, 287
Commonalities, among problem areas, 63
Communication strategies
    for acceptance of client, 260
    in case formulation, 68–70
    for discussion of treatment plan, 83–86
    in skills training, 193
Competence, defined, 182
Competing response training, 137
Complaining, as avoidance strategy, 218–219
Component behaviors, demonstrating, 194
Conditional homework, in skills training, 199–200
Conditional response (CR), 14, 233–235
Conditional stimulus (CS), 14, 107, 143, 230, 233–235
Conditioned emotional responses, 14
Conners' Rating Scales, 28
Construct labels, avoidance of, 23
Context, defined, 58–59. *See also* behavioral context; therapeutic context
Contextual change, as risk factor for depression, 206–207
Contextual factors, 109, 184
Contextual flow, 8
Contextualism, 8

Contingency contracting. *See* behavioral contracting
Contingency management, 105–111, 162
    key assumptions, 108–109
    steps for, 109–111
Continuation phase, 292–294
Continuing exposure, 247–248
Continuous schedule, 119
Conveying information, as teaching strategy, 192
Coping behaviors, evaluating, 29–31
Coping cards, 293
Coping modeling, 196
Coping skills, 87
Coping with depression course, 204
Core processes, in problem behaviors, 79
Cost–benefit analysis, of problem behaviors, 78
Counterconditioning, 233, 264
Countering mood dependent behaviors, 220–221
Covert behavior, 6–7
Covert self-instruction, 195
Covert sensitization, 131–133
Creative hopelessness, 267
Cue elimination, 112, 293–294
Cue exposure, 237, 242–243
Cultural selection, 15
Culture, as context for behavior, 5–6
Current life situation
    as determinant of behavior, 59, 63–65, 95
    evaluating, 34–35

Darwinian evolutionary theory, 7–8, 15
Davison, G. C., 125
Decentering, 150
Defusing language and cognition, 268
Delay of gratification, 135
Density, in coaching, 200–201
Depression
    and behavioral activation, 203–224
    and RCPR, 42
Depression loops, 209, 214
Depressive disorders, and behavioral interventions, 12
Desired behaviors, reinforcing, 125–127
Diagnostic approach, in case formulation, 67
Diagnostic assessments, 27–28
Diagnostic labels, appropriate use of, 69–70
Diagram, in case formulation, 69
Dialectical behavior therapy (DBT), 18, 74–76, 83, 112, 121, 134, 166, 240, 256,

Ferster, C., 204
Flexibility, and skills training, 183
Flexible approach, 11
Flooding, 245–246
Foa, E. B., 231, 236, 244
Follette, W. C., 79, 115
Format
    for exposure therapy, 246
    for skills training, 188–190
Fowles, D. C., 41
Framework
    for case formulation, 60–68
    for treatment, 99
Freedom, personal, 74
Free speech period, 26
Functional analysis of behavior, 37–46
    and development of hypotheses, 63–64
    illustration, 44–46
    in selection of interventions, 77–79
    validity, 63
Functional analytic psychotherapy (FAP),
    18, 49, 121
Functional domain, in case formulation, 60
Functional impairment, evaluating, 31–36
Functionalism, 7–8
Functional properties, of thinking patterns,
    141
Functional response class, 46, 78–79
Funneling process, in initial assessment, 54–
    57

Generalization of skills usage, 293–294
Genetic influences, 44, 66
Gestalt therapies, 255
Ghezzi, P. M., 138
Goals, and values, 160–161
Goal setting, 161–163
Goals of therapy. *See* therapeutic goals
Goldfried, M. R., 125
Goodman, J., 195
Graded task assignments, 220
Graduated exposure, 245–246
Group therapy, and skills training, 188–189

Habit behaviors, 136–137
Habit reversal procedures, 136–137
Habituation, 233–235
Hanh, T. N., 253
Hayes, S. C., 48, 90, 161, 163, 251, 256, 267,
    287
Haynes, S. N., 78, 91
Health/medical status, evaluating, 34

Heinssen, R. K., 136
Herrnstein, R. J., 126
Higgins, S. T., 123
High-risk situations, identifying, 289–290
Holman, M. L., 133
Homework, 85–86, 198–200
Homosexuality, 6
Houmanfar, R., 136
Hudson, S. M., 117
Humanistic therapies, 255
Hypothesis-testing approach, in behavioral
    experiments, 146–147
Hypothesized origins, in case formulations,
    66–67

Imaginal exposure, 237–240
Immediate gratification, 135
Impairment, use of term, 31–32
Impulsivity, 135
Individual, and environment, 58–59
Individualized Fear and Avoidance Hierar-
    chy, 101
Individual therapy, 83, 188–189
Informal exposure, 237, 240–241
Integrative behavioral couple therapy
    (IBCT), 18, 256–257, 270–272
Intensity assessment, in exposure therapy,
    244–245
Interoceptive exposure, 237, 241–242
Interpersonal-effectiveness skills, 179
Interpersonal Support Evaluation List
    (ISEL), 210
Interpresonal therapies, 8
Interventions. *See also specific types of inter-
    ventions*
    for altering faulty rules, 154–160
    characteristics, 72
    effectiveness, 61
    selecting, 76–82, 99
Intervention strategies, values-based, 164–
    165
In vivo experiments, 147
In vivo exposure, 237, 240

Jacobson, N. S., 204–205, 208, 256, 265, 270
Johnston, P., 117
Jones, M. C., 15, 178

Kabat-Zinn, J., 255
Kazdin, A. E., 125
Kearney, A. J., 133
Kelly, G., 16

Otto, M. W., 88
Outcome expectations, 64
Outcomes of therapy, evaluating, 285–286
Overgeneralization, 155–156
Oversatiation therapy, 116–117
Overt behavior, 6, 10
Overt self-instruction, 195

Panic control therapy (PCT), 179, 228
Panic disorder, 228, 241
Paranoid thinking, 158
Pathological fear, 231
Pavlov, I., 13–14
Penn, L. S., 282
Penn State Worry Questionnaire (PSWQ), 210
Perfectionistic thinking, 157–158
Performance, distinguished from skill, 182
Personal functioning, evaluating, 32. *See also* functional analysis
Personalization, 155
Person-centered approach, 22, 55, 255
Persons, J. B., 61–62, 73, 89, 91
Person variables, 43–44, 66, 95
Perspective-taking exercises, 293
Petry, N. M., 123
Phillips, L., 178
Phylogenetic selection, 15
Physical sensations, observing, 276
Physiological sensations
  in behavioral assessments, 10
Pleasant Events Schedule, 101, 204
Positive punishment, 42, 131–133
Positive reinforcement, 40–41, 80–81. *See also* response-contingent positive reinforcement (RCPR)
Posttraumatic stress disorder (PTSD), 115, 228, 236–238, 247
Posttraumatic stress responses, as target, 75
Practice, in skills training, 197–200
Praise, 120–121, 123
Precipitants, 63, 95
Predictive ability, of case formulation, 60
Premacking, 126–127
Present focus, 11–12
Presenting problem, 26–27
Primary assumptions (personal rules, core beliefs), 65
Principle-driven approaches, 77
Problem and learning focus, 12
Problem list, 61–63
Problems

changeable vs. unchangeable, 260–261
cost–benefit analysis, 78
future, 286–287
persistence, 44
prioritizing, 74–76
in treatment planning, 73
Problem solving, 30, 144, 214–217
Professional journals, 16
Progress, reinforcing, 121–124
Protocol-driven approach, 54, 77
Psychiatric diagnoses, 22, 67
Psychoanalysis, Freudian, 255
Psychodynamic models, 5
Psychodynamic therapies, 8
Psychoeducation, and skills training, 180
Psychopathology, 256
Punishing consequences, 143
Punishment, 41–42, 108, 110

Quality of life, evaluating, 34–35
Quality-of-life interfering behaviors, as target, 75
Questionnaire assessments, 28–29, 55–56

Radical acceptance, 270
Random support call, 117
Rapport, establishing, 24–25
Rating scale assessments, 28–29
Rationale, for skills training, 189–190
Reciprocal determinism, 17
Reciprocal inhibition, 16, 233
Recordkeeping, in token system, 138
Referral, 27, 82
Reinforcement, 29, 108, 110, 119–120, 138. *See also* negative reinforcement; positive reinforcement; shaping
  in contingency management, 119–124
  differential, 127–131
  and mindfulness, 265–266
  and skills training, 185–186, 191, 196–197
Reinforcers, 120, 125–126
Relapse, likelihood of, 90
Relapse prevention, 222–224, 255, 275, 285–286, 288–292
Relapse road map, 291
Relaxation, and mindfulness, 275
Response-contingent positive reinforcement (RCPR), 42, 204
Responses, 218–219. *See also* emotional responses
  to assessment measures, 27–29

Values-based intervention strategies, 164–165
Variable ratio schedule, 119–120
Verbal report, client's, 123

Wallace, M. D., 131
Watson, J. B., 178
Weinberger, A. D., 142
Weiner, I. B., 279
Willfulness, 268–269

Willingness, 268–269
Witkiewitz, K., 266
Wolpe, J., 16, 233
Working hypothesis, in case formulation, 67
Worry, 144–145

Young, J. E., 142

Zigler, E., 178

ABOUT THE AUTHORS

Richard F. Farmer, PhD, is currently a researcher at Oregon Research Institute in Eugene. After completing a clinical internship at Duke University Medical Center in Durham, North Carolina, and earning a doctorate degree in clinical psychology from the University of North Carolina at Greensboro, he served as an associate professor of psychology at Idaho State University in Pocatello and as a senior lecturer in psychology at the University of Canterbury in Christchurch, New Zealand. Dr. Farmer's main areas of interest include behavior therapy, behavioral and personality assessment, depression, personality disorders, impulsivity, eating disorders, and experiential avoidance.

Alexander L. Chapman, PhD, is currently an assistant professor in psychology at Simon Fraser University in Burnaby, British Columbia, Canada. Dr. Chapman received his doctorate degree in clinical psychology from Idaho State University in Pocatello in 2003, after completing his clinical internship at Duke University Medical Center in Durham, North Carolina. He then completed a postdoctoral fellowship with Marsha Linehan at the University of Washington in Seattle. His research focuses on borderline personality disorder, dialectical behavior therapy, emotion regulation, self-harm, and impulsivity, and he has published numerous articles and book chapters on these topics. Dr. Chapman is also cofounder of the Dialectical Behaviour Therapy Centre of Vancouver in British Columbia, Canada.